THE SPIRIT OF LAWS

To Professor Paul Spurlin
with sincere appreciation
for the inspiration
provided by his work
and by his generosity.

David W. Carithers
11/15/77

Charles Louis de Secondat, Baron de la Brède et de Montesquieu (1689-1755).

THE SPIRIT OF LAWS

by *Montesquieu*

A Compendium of the First English Edition

EDITED, WITH AN INTRODUCTION, NOTES,
AND APPENDIXES, BY
David Wallace Carrithers

together with An English Translation of
AN ESSAY ON CAUSES AFFECTING MINDS
AND CHARACTERS (1736–1743)

UNIVERSITY OF CALIFORNIA PRESS
Berkeley · Los Angeles · London

University of California Press
Berkeley and Los Angeles, California

University of California Press, Ltd.
London, England

ISBN 0-520-02566-0
Library of Congress Catalog Card Number: 73-85783
Printed in the United States of America

1 2 3 4 5 6 7 8 9 0

To the memory of Leo Gershoy

Contents

Introduction

🍂 *The Spirit of Laws*

Part One

Part Five

Part Six

An Essay on Causes Affecting Minds and Characters

Part One

Part Two

xi

❧ *Appendices*

Preface

In 1760 a youthful John Adams noted in his diary that he had begun to read *The Spirit of Laws* and planned to compile comprehensive marginal notes to insure his proper attention to the work. Roughly a decade and a half later, Thomas Jefferson, who was to succeed Adams to the Presidency, devoted no less than twenty-eight pages of his *Commonplace Book* to extracts from this same work, and in 1792, in an essay on "Spirit of Governments," James Madison compared Montesquieu's role in the science of government to that of Francis Bacon in natural philosophy. According to Madison, Montesquieu "had lifted the veil from the venerable errors which enslaved opinion and pointed the way to those luminous truths of which he had but a glimpse himself."[1] The interest these future chief executives displayed in Montesquieu was by no means atypical. The two leather-bound volumes of Thomas Nugent's translation of *The Spirit of Laws*, not to speak of various French editions of Montesquieu's works, found their way into the libraries of many eighteenth-century Americans, and Montesquieu was widely quoted as a contemporary political sage whose wisdom rivaled that of the ancients.

If Montesquieu was practically required reading for eighteenth-century statesmen and political philosophers on both sides of the Atlantic, he still merits thoughtful consideration today. The precise forms of states have changed, but the problem of forestalling tyranny remains, and freedom has rarely found so

---

[1] See Paul M. Spurlin, *Montesquieu in America, 1760–1801* (New York: Octagon Books, 1969; orig. ed., 1940), pp. 88, 153–157, 241.

eloquent a spokesman. Unfortunately, however, the modern reader is likely to find a work that ran to over a thousand pages in its two-volume first edition a bit overwhelming. In fact, it is generally agreed that the contours of Montesquieu's work at times eluded him and that he sometimes lost his way. He was not always sufficiently discriminating concerning what data should be excluded from his finished work and what information should remain, and the resulting problem, as Ernst Cassirer once remarked, is that "Montesquieu's delight in particulars is so great that at times his illustrative anecdotes overshadow the main lines of his thought and threaten to make them unrecognizable."[2] Even d'Alembert, Montesquieu's least reserved contemporary panegyrist, admitted that *The Spirit of Laws* demands a "diligent and studious reading,"[3] and Montesquieu himself recognized that his main ideas were sometimes obscured by historical asides and rhetorical flourishes. Roughly a year following publication of *The Spirit of Laws* Montesquieu remarked in one of his *Pensées*: "What good would it do me to have made reflections during the course of twenty years, if I had neglected to make the first one of all: that life is short? I haven't even time to abridge what I have done."[4]

Presented herein, therefore, is what an eighteenth-century editor might well have entitled: *Montesquieu Epitomized: a Carefully Selected and Useful Compendium of his Spirit of Laws, together with his Essay on Causes, the latter now first translated for his English and American audience.* No compendium can or should take the place of the original for those undertaking detailed research, but it

[2] *The Philosophy of the Enlightenment*, trans. by Fritz C. A. Koelln and James P. Pettegrove (Boston: Beacon Press, 1955), p. 210.

[3] "Éloge de Monsieur Le Président de Montesquieu, mis à la tête du cinquième volume de L'Encyclopédie" [1755], in Nagel, I, p. xvi.

[4] *Pensée* 204 (1706. III, f. 42): 1749.

is hoped that this edition will place Montesquieu's ideas before a wider audience than he has lately enjoyed. The principle guiding the "economizing" of Montesquieu has been the preservation of the most significant Books of *The Spirit of Laws* nearly uncut and the pruning of others of some of the dense underbrush of historical example with which he so loved to embellish an argument. Historical asides instrumental to the main argument have been retained. It has seemed wise to preserve the grand sweep of the thirty-one-book structure of the original since, as C. H. McIlwain once observed in an edition of the political writings of James I, "the student needs to know not alone *what* the masters thought, but also *how* they thought." Each Book of *The Spirit of Laws* is preceded by a brief Analysis of its contents, and paragraph numbers have been added both to aid discussion of the work and to provide a ready means for ascertaining where the text has been abridged.[5]

The division of the work into six Parts according to Montesquieu's original plan of organization has been reintroduced. In this division, Book IX was the first in the second Part of the work, Part Three began with Book XIV, Part Four with Book XX, Part Five with Book XXIV, and Part Six with Book XXVIII. Jacob Vernet, who handled many of the details of the original publication in 1748, failed to detect a printer's oversight in which only the sixth and final Part was designated as such in the printing, and at the last moment he convinced Montesquieu that it would be easier to alter this one page by means of a cancel than to use five cancels to indicate Parts One to Five in the text where they had been left out.[6] Montesquieu was persuaded to abandon his plan of

[5] These paragraph numbers appear in brackets in the text and notes.

[6] See "Vernet to Montesquieu," July-August 1748, in Nagel, III, pp. 1121–1122, and "Vernet to Montesquieu," September 4, 1748, in Nagel, III, p. 1130.

organization, and although it was followed in the edition of 1750, it was set aside again in the posthumous edition of 1757.

One of the most interesting aspects of contemporary reaction to *The Spirit of Laws* was the intense hostility Montesquieu's work aroused in ecclesiastical circles. Hence the notes to *The Spirit of Laws* texts summarize ecclesiastical objections to the work as well as Montesquieu's replies to his Jansenist and Jesuit critics in his *Defense of the Spirit of Laws* (1750) and his *Responses and Explanations Given to the Faculty of Theology of the University of Paris* (1752–54). Important textual changes made for the edition of 1757 (see Note on the Text) are also indicated in the notes, and the reader's attention is called to selected passages that had a substantially different tone or meaning in the manuscript copy of *L'Esprit des lois* now owned by the Bibliothèque Nationale.

Following *The Spirit of Laws* and the notes the reader will find this editor's English translation of the *Essai sur les causes qui peuvent affecter les esprits et les caractères* (1736–1743). The importance of this posthumously published manuscript is discussed in the Introduction (see pp. 26, 36–37, 44–51), and portions of Book XIV of *The Spirit of Laws* that were originally part of this *Essai* are designated as such in the notes. Appendix I presents a tabulation of passages of *The Spirit of Laws* censured by Montesquieu's Jansenist critic, the Abbé de La Roche, and by the Jesuit Faculty of Theology of the University of Paris. Appendix II provides full bibliographical citations of the works of travel literature to which Montesquieu referred in his own notes to the volume, and Appendix III contains information concerning the sole surviving manuscript copy of *L'Esprit des lois* now owned by the Bibliothèque Nationale. Appendix IV prints the clarification of the meaning of political *virtue* added to the posthumous edition of 1757.

Several individuals have rendered valuable assistance during the course of this project. C. P. Courtney reviewed a prospectus for the volume and offered useful advice concerning the natural law-positivism question in *The Spirit of Laws*. Paul Spurlin read a draft of the Introduction and made a number of helpful suggestions, one of them leading to a sharper distinction between Montesquieu's theories of separate powers and of mixed government. Thomas S. Hall supplied information on medical terminology of the eighteenth century and responded to a number of queries concerning fine points of seventeenth- and eighteenth-century physiological theory. Communications from Lester G. King and Lelland J. Rather were similarly helpful in the early stages of my research on Montesquieu's medical ideas. I am particularly grateful to Aram Vartanian for valuable suggestions with respect to the translation of the *Essai sur les causes* and to Charles-Jacques Beyer for much encouragement and counsel, including the identification of the "Materials" segment of the *Essai sur les causes* as fragments of the *De la différence des génies* (1717).

The major portion of the research was conducted at the Bibliothèque Nationale, the Bibliothèque municipale de Bordeaux, the British Library, and the Wellcome Institute for the History of Medicine, and I am grateful for the hospitality and assistance I invariably received. I particularly wish to thank the staff of the Salle de travail du département des manuscrits of the Bibliothèque Nationale for graciously making the manuscript copy of *L'Esprit des lois* available to me during the summer of 1974. The University of Chattanooga Foundation and the Faculty Research Grants Committee of the University of Tennessee at Chattanooga sponsored much of my research in Paris, Bordeaux, and London, and defrayed the costs of typing the manuscript. Mr. Alain L. Hénon, Associate Editor of the University of California Press, has encouraged me from the early stages of this project through to its completion and has rendered much useful advice, for which I am very grateful.

Note on the Text

The text of this edition is Thomas Nugent's translation (London: Nourse, 1750) of the first French edition (Geneva: Barillot, 1748). In order to preserve the flavor of the eighteenth-century translation, the original spelling and punctuation have been preserved, except in the case of some proper names and place names. The capitalization of words within chapter titles has been standardized, and what were clearly printer's errors have been corrected. In addition, the placement of some of Montesquieu's footnotes has been altered so that the reader is not interrupted mid-phrase or mid-sentence.

Montesquieu was indeed fortunate to procure such an able translator as Thomas Nugent. At the time he undertook his work on Montesquieu, Nugent had already completed English translations of Dubos's *Réflexions critiques sur la poésie et la peinture* (1719) and Burlamaqui's *Principes du droit naturel* (1748), and later in his career, after completing his translation of *The Spirit of Laws*, Nugent went on to produce English editions of Voltaire's *Essai sur les moeurs* (1756), Rousseau's *Émile* (1762), and works by Hénault and Grosley. Furthermore, as late as 1916 Thomas Nugent's *Pocket-Dictionary of the French and English Languages* (1767) was still being revised and reprinted.

Montesquieu's satisfaction with Nugent's efforts on his behalf is evident in a letter dated October 18, 1750. "I cannot help myself, sir," Montesquieu wrote to Nugent, "from giving you my thanks. I gave them to you already, because you translated for me; I give them to you now because you translated so well. Your translation has no other fault than that of the original; and I must remain indebted to you for disguising them so well. It seems you wished to convey my style as well, and you created this resemblance *qualem decet esse sororum.*[1] No doubt part of Nugent's success was his obvious appreciation for the subject matter of *The Spirit of Laws*. In the dedication to the 1766 edition of his translation he compared Montesquieu's importance to that of Cicero and remarked that "whoever finds a pleasure in perusing *The Spirit of Laws* must be deemed to have greatly improved in the study of politics and jurisprudence."

The chief criticism one need make of Thomas Nugent is that in the years after 1750 he did not revise his text to keep abreast of the changes Montesquieu made in the original edition of 1748. The most important of these textual alterations resulted from ecclesiastical attacks on his work (see Appendix I), and it was in the 1757, posthumous edition of *The Spirit of Laws*, supervised by François Richer, that some of the contemplated changes were made. The legacy of Nugent's oversight in failing to revise his translation to keep pace with Montesquieu's revisions of the original has been considerable textual ambiguity in previous English-language editions of *The Spirit of Laws*. No English-language edition has faithfully presented the text of the 1757 edition. An 1823 London edition of Nugent's translation bore on its title page the immodest advertisement "A New Edition Carefully Revised and Compared with the Best Paris Edition," but even a cursory examination reveals that many changes made in the 1757 edition were not reflected in the English text. The Bohn's Standard Library edition, edited in two volumes by J. V. Prichard (London: G. Bell, 1878), similarly ignored changes made in the 1757 edition, as did, more

---

[1] "Montesquieu to Nugent," in Nagel, III, p. 1333.

recently, the well-known Hafner edition of 1949, with an Introduction by Franz Neumann, in which no attempt was made to
establish the text either of the original edition of 1748 or that of
the posthumous edition of 1757.[2] Given the textual confusion
within existing English editions of *The Spirit of Laws*, it has
seemed advisable to utilize the text of the original edition for this
compendium. This will enable the reader to first approach the text
as originally conceived by Montesquieu and then, by means of the
notes, to assess the changes Montesquieu made in response to his
critics.

[2] An important new chapter on slavery, for example, was not incorporated,
and numerous other, substantive changes made for the 1757 edition are similarly
absent from the work. (See Book XV, note 12, for an English translation of the
chapter on slavery previously absent from English editions of *The Spirit of
Laws*.)

Chronological Table of Major Events in Montesquieu's Life

Early Years (1689–1721)

1689   Birth of Charles-Louis de Secondat at La Brède.

1696   Death of Montesquieu's mother, Marie Françoise de Pesnel, whose dowry had included the Château de La Brède.

1700–1705   Montesquieu receives his formal education at the Collège de Juilly, an Oratorian institution near Paris.

1705–1708   Montesquieu studies law in Bordeaux, where he receives a bachelor of law degree from the University of Bordeaux (July 29, 1708), is licensed to practice law (August 12, 1708), and is received as an advocate in the Parlement of Bordeaux (August 14, 1708).

1708   Having learned he will one day inherit from his childless uncle the name Montesquieu and the position *président à mortier* of the Parlement of Guyenne, Charles-Louis de Secondat begins to use the title "Seigneur de Montesquieu, Baron de La Brède."

1709–1713   Montesquieu resides in Paris, where he continues his legal studies, composes an essay maintaining that pagans do not merit eternal damnation (1711), and begins the notebook *Le Spicilège*, first published in 1944.

1713   Death of Montesquieu's father, Jacques de Secondat, who had pursued a military career. Montesquieu returns to Bordeaux.

1714   Becomes a counsellor in the Parlement of Bordeaux.

1715   Marries Jeanne de Lartigue, a Protestant. Composes *Memoir concerning the State's Debts* (Nagel, III, pp. 23–31), a plan for reducing France's national debt.

1716   Birth of Jean-Baptiste de Secondat, only son of Montesquieu (February 10). Montesquieu is elected to the newly founded Academy of Bordeaux (April 3). At the death of his uncle, he becomes *président à mortier* of the Parlement of Guyenne (July 13). Composes an *Essay concerning Roman Politics in Religion* (Nagel III, pp. 37–50). Endows a prize for anatomy at the Academy of Bordeaux.

1717   Birth of Marie-Catherine de Secondat, elder daughter of Montesquieu. Drafts the *Discourse on Cicero* (Nagel, III, pp. 15–21). Begins work on *Persian Letters*.

1718–1720   Elected Director of the Academy of Bordeaux. Composes summaries of works submitted on the causes of echo (Nagel, III, pp. 69–75), the functioning of the kidneys (Nagel, III, pp. 77–83), and the cause of heaviness and transparency of matter (Nagel, III, pp. 89–93; 95–97).

1719   Continuing to be interested in science, Montes-
        quieu publishes, in the *Journal des Savants*, a re-
        quest for information to further his projected *Physi-
        cal History of the Earth, both Ancient and Modern.*

1721   Publication of *Persian Letters* in Amsterdam. Mon-
        tesquieu reads to the Academy of Bordeaux his *Ob-
        servations on Natural History* (Nagel, III, pp. 99–
        118), the results of the previous two years of his
        scientific labors.

Paris (1721–1728)

1721   In the wake of the success of the *Persian Letters*,
        Montesquieu begins to divide his time between
        Paris and the Southwest.

1724   Publication of *The Temple of Cnidus* (Nagel, I, pp.
        571–603C).

1725   Reads part of the *Treatise on Duties* to the Academy
        of Bordeaux. Composes the *Discourse on the Motives
        inclining us towards Science* (Nagel, III, pp. 221–
        227).

1726   40,000 livres in debt, Montesquieu sells his par-
        lementary office (July 7). Elected to second term as
        Director of Academy of Bordeaux.

1727   Birth of Marie-Josephe-Denise de Secondat,
        younger daughter of Montesquieu. Composes *Con-
        siderations on the Wealth of Spain*, begun in 1726
        (Nagel, III, pp. 137–155). Reads his *Dialogue of*

Sulla and Eucrates (1724) [Nagel, I, pp. 533–563 C[1]] to the Club de L'Entresol.

1728   Montesquieu is received into the French Academy (elected December, 1727).

Voyages (1728–1731)

1728   Montesquieu leaves Paris on what will become nearly a four-year absence from La Brède and his family. Visits Vienna, Hungary, Venice, Padua, Milan, Turin, Genoa, Pisa, and Florence.

1729   Visits Sienna, Rome, Naples, Bologna, Munich, Augsburg, Frankfort, Mainz, Bonn, Cologne, Düsseldorf, Munster, Osnabrück, Hanover, Utrecht. Arrives Amsterdam October 15. Arrives London, November 3.

1730–1731   Resides in England until May 1731. Becomes a member of the Royal Society of London and a Freemason.

The Epoch of *The Spirit of Laws* (1731–1748)

1731–1733   Montesquieu returns to Bordeaux via Paris (May–June), where he continues work on the history of Rome he had begun in England. He also composes *Lysimachus* (Nagel, I, pp. 497–503B), *Reports on Mines* (i.e., in Hungary and Hartz) [Nagel, III,

---

[1] Nagel, vol. I, reprints the whole of the three-volume, 1758 edition of Montesquieu's *OEuvres*, and it therefore encompasses three sets of pagination. Hence the designations A, B, and C to distinguish the three segments.

pp. 435–467], *Reflections on Universal Monarchy in Europe* (portions of which were later transcribed nearly verbatim into *The Spirit of Laws*) [Nagel, III, 361–382], *Reflections on the Character of Some Princes and on Some Events in Their Lives* (Nagel, III, pp. 537–551), and *Reflections on the Sobriety of the Inhabitants of Rome compared with the Intemperance of the Ancient Romans* (Nagel, III, 357–360).

1734 Publishes his history of Rome (*Considerations on the Causes of the Greatness of the Romans and on their Decline*). Commits himself to what eventually becomes *The Spirit of Laws*. Displays renewed interest in science.

1735 Elected to third term as Director of Academy of Bordeaux.

1736–1743 Composes the *Essay on Causes Affecting Minds and Characters* (Nagel, III, 397–430; English trans. in this volume).

1738 Composes *History of France*, portions of which are in *Pensées* 595 (1302. II, f. 141): 1738–1739, and 596 (1306. II, f. 173): 1738–1739.

1739–1740 Composes *History of Louis XI* (not published; manuscript not extant).

1746 Elected, with support of Maupertuis, to the Berlin Academy of Science.

1748 Second sale of office in Parlement of Guyenne (August); publication in Geneva of *The Spirit of Laws*. Elected to fourth term as Director of Academy of Bordeaux.

Last Years (1749–1755)

1749   Mild censure of *The Spirit of Laws* in Jesuit periodical, *Mémoires de Trévoux* (April). Vigorous attack by Abbé de La Roche in the Jansenist periodical, the *Nouvelles Ecclésiastiques* (October 9 and 16).

1750   Publication of Montesquieu's lengthy rebuttal of the Abbé de La Roche: the *Defense of the Spirit of Laws* (February). Reply to *Defense* by Abbé de La Roche in *Nouvelles Ecclésiastiques* (April 24, May 1). Faculty of Theology of University of Paris drafts but does not publish a thirteen-point censure of *The Spirit of Laws* (September).

1751   *The Spirit of Laws* placed on Papal Index (November 29).

1752   Faculty of Theology of the University of Paris drafts but does not publish a seventeen-point censure of *The Spirit of Laws*.

1752–1754   Montesquieu drafts a response to the objections of the Paris Faculty of Theology: the *Responses and Explanations given to the Faculty of Theology of the University of Paris concerning the 17 Propositions they have extracted from the book entitled The Spirit of Laws* (Nagel, III, pp. 649–674; first published, Barckhausen, 1904.)

1753–1755   Montesquieu composes for Diderot's *Encyclopédie* an *Essay on Taste*. Turns down invitation to write the article on "Despotism."

1755   Stricken by fever on January 29, Montesquieu dies in Paris (February 10).

Posthumous Events

1757   Publication of posthumous edition of *The Spirit of Laws* incorporating important revisions Montesquieu left in manuscript form.

1770   Death of Jeanne de Lartigue, widow of Montesquieu.

1796   Publication of five-volume Plasson edition of *Œuvres de Montesquieu.*

1889   Bicentennial of Montesquieu's birth. His descendants arrange for the publication of the major unpublished manuscripts in cooperation with the Société des Bibliophiles de Guyenne: *Deux Opuscules* (1891); *Mélanges inédits* (1892); *Pensées et fragments inédits*, 2 vols. (1889–1901); *Voyages*, 2 vols. (1894–1896); *Correspondence*, 2 vols. (1914).

1939   Sale of important Montesquieu manuscripts; Bibliothèque Nationale purchases the manuscript of *The Spirit of Laws* and the manuscript of *Collectio Juris* for 401,000 francs. *Pensées* and much of the *Correspondence* purchased by Bibliothèque municipale de Bordeaux.

1944   Publication of *Le Spicilège*, edited by André Masson.

1950   Château de La Brède declared a French historical monument. Discovery at La Brède by Professor Shackleton of manuscript copy of catalogue of Montesquieu's library and of *Geographica*, tom. II.

1950–1955   Publication, by Nagel in Paris, of three-volume

edition of Montesquieu's *Œuvres*. Vol. II, pp. 1–667, provides first complete publication of *Pensées* in the chronological order of the original manuscript.

1950–1961   Publication by Société Les Belles Lettres in Paris of four-volume critical edition of *De L'Esprit des Loix*, edited with extensive notes, including manuscript variants, by Jean Brèthe de La Gressaye.

1961   Publication of Professor Shackleton's *Montesquieu. A Critical Biography* (Oxford, 1961).

Abbreviations

Barckhausen (1904)   Henri Barckhausen, *L'Esprit des lois et les archives de La Brède* (Bordeaux, 1904).

Catalogue   *Catalogue de la Bibliothèque de Montesquieu*, publié par Louis Desgraves (Genève, 1954).

Considérations   *Considérations sur les causes de la grandeur des Romains et de leur Décadence* (1734).

Derathé   *De L'Esprit des Lois*, Introduction, chronologie, bibliographie, relevé de variantes et notes par Robert Derathé, 2 vols. (Paris: Garnier frères, 1973).

Défense   *Défense de L'Esprit des lois* (Genève: Barillot et fils, 1750).

Essay on Causes   *Essai sur les causes qui peuvent affecter les esprits et les caractères* (1736–1743). The manuscript was divided into two parts by Barckhausen when first published in *Mélanges inédits de Montesquieu* (Bordeaux, 1892). As cited in the Introduction, references are given to the relevant Part and bracketed paragraph number. The translation in this volume introduces bracketed subheadings into the body of the text.

G   *De L'Esprit des Loix*, texte établi et présenté par Jean Brèthe de La Gressaye, 4 vols. (Paris: Société Les Belles Lettres, 1950–1961). When cited in the notes, references are given to the relevant volume and page number.

Grosley   Pierre-Jean Grosley, author of a letter assessing *The Spirit of Laws* that Montesquieu answered at some length on April 8, 1750 (see Nagel, III, pp. 1293–1297).

Haller, *First Lines*   Albrecht von Haller, *Primae linae physiologiae in usum praelectionum academicarum* (Göttingen, 1747). All references to this work are by paragraph number to the following English translation: *First Lines of Physiology* (Edinburgh: Bell and Bradfute, 1801).

Institutiones medicae   Herman Boerhaave, *Institutiones medicae in usus annuae exercitationis domesticos digestae ab H. Boerhaave* (Leyden, 1708). The 1713 edition of this work was annotated by Albrecht von Haller and published as the *Praelectiones academicae in proprias institutiones rei medicae* (Göttingen-Amsterdam, 1739–1742), English translation:

Academical Lectures on the Theory of Physic. Being a Translation of his [H. Boerhaave's] *Institutes and Explanatory Comment*, 6 vols. (London: W. Innys, 1742–1746).

References to Boerhaave's text of the *Institutes* are by volume and paragraph number of this 6 vol. English translation (e.g., Boerhaave, *Institutiones medicae*, II[273]). References to Haller's annotations follow the full citation of Boerhaave's work (e.g., Boerhaave, *Institutiones medicae*, II [273], Haller, note 1).

Mélanges   *Mélanges inédits de Montesquieu* (Bordeaux, 1892).

M.   Montesquieu.

MS.   Manuscript copy of *The Spirit of Laws* purchased by the Bibliothèque Nationale in 1939 (see Appendix III). The MS. is now bound in five volumes and is referred to in the notes by volume and folio number (e.g., MS. I, f. 60).

Nagel   *Œuvres complètes de Montesquieu*, publiées sous la direction de M. André Masson, 3 vols. (Paris: Les Éditions Nagel, 1950).

Nouv. Ecclés.   *Les Nouvelles Ecclésiastiques, ou mémoires pour servir à l'histoire de la con-*

stitution Unigenitus, a Jansenist weekly published in Paris and Utrecht after the condemnation of the Jansenists in 1713 in the Bull *Unigenitus*. The Abbé de La Roche, editor of this journal, attacked *The Spirit of Laws* in an article published in two parts in October 1749.

References to this article in the notes to this volume include the date as well as the page number (e.g., *Nouv. Ecclés.* Oct. 9, 1749: 164b). All notes summarizing criticisms contained in the *Nouv. Ecclés.* are marked with an asterisk, and a tabulation of passages censured by the Abbé de La Roche is given in Appendix I.

Pensées   *Mes Pensées* (1727–1754), a series of three notebooks kept by Montesquieu and now owned by the Bibliothèque municipale de Bordeaux. The complete text of the *Pensées* was first published, in the rearranged, topical order given them by Henri Barckhausen, as *Pensées et fragments inédits*, 2 vols. (Bordeaux, 1899–1901). They were reprinted in this same order in the Pléiade edition of Montesquieu's works and were only first printed in chronological order in the second volume of the Nagel edition.

Reference to the *Pensées* in the notes to this volume are cited as follows: *Pensée* 1965 (1665. III, f. 13v.): 1749. The first number refers to the rearranged order as printed in the Pléiade edition and the second to the chronological order as printed in the Nagel edition. The Roman numeral gives the relevant volume number of the three-volume manuscript now in Bordeaux.

The dating of the Pensées is that provided by Jean Jacques Granpre Molière in his *La Théorie de la Constitution Anglaise chez Montesquieu* (Leyden: Presse Universitaire de Leyde, 1972), pp. 349–351.

Pléiade *Œuvres complètes de Montesquieu*, texte présenté et annoté par Roger Caillois, 2 vols. (Paris: Bibliothèque de la Pléiade, 1949).

Réponses et Explications *Réponses et Explications données à la Faculté de théologie de L'Université de Paris sur les dix-sept propositions qu'elle a extraites du livre intitulé L'Esprit des Lois, et qu'elle a censurées* (1752–1754). First printed in Barckhausen (1904), the manuscript of this point by point reply by Montesquieu to the censure of his work by the Sorbonne

in August, 1752, is now lost. Notes
referring to censures of *The Spirit of
Laws* by the Sorbonne are marked with
an asterisk. A list of those passages
censured by the Sorbonne is provided in Appendix I.

INTRODUCTION

THE LIFE AND TIMES OF MONTESQUIEU

Early Years

On the eighteenth of January, 1689, in the very month in which
the English Bill of Rights was signed, Charles-Louis de Secondat,
later known as Baron de Montesquieu, was born at the Château de
La Brède, a fifteenth-century castle situated near Bordeaux in the
wine-growing regions of southwestern France.[1] The appearance at
the Château of a beggar from the nearby village of La Brède
coincided with Montesquieu's birth and conveniently secured for
him a humble godfather so that he might ever be cognizant of his
obligations to the poor. Nor was this Montesquieu's sole contact
with the rude and unlettered during his early years. Sent out to
nurse among peasants at the mill of La Brède during his first three
years, he learned to speak the patois, a rustic Gascon accent, which
he never lost and which he is said to have exaggerated somewhat in
later life, perhaps to show a degree of disdain for the glitter and
affected polish of eighteenth-century Paris.

As a child, Montesquieu spent his first eleven years at home and

---

[1] The definitive biographical account of Montesquieu is Robert Shackleton's magiste-
rial *Montesquieu. A Critical Biography* (Oxford: Oxford University Press, 1961) from
which a number of biographical details have been drawn for this first section of the
Introduction. Also useful for the early period of Montesquieu's life is Pierre Barrière's
Un grand provincial: Charles Louis Secondat baron de La Brède et de Montesquieu (Bordeaux, 1946).

in the village of La Brède, and it was not until the year 1700, four years after the death of his mother, that he was sent with two cousins to the Collège de Juilly, an Oratorian institution near Paris which stressed the Classics and offered instruction in modern and in scientific subjects as well. At this institution Montesquieu displayed both industry and talent, and it was here that his consuming passion for *les choses Romaines* was aroused, as evidenced by a notebook at La Brède in a child's hand containing questions and answers on elementary facts of Roman history. Having completed his studies at Juilly in 1705, and aware that he would one day inherit from his childless uncle the office of *président à mortier* of the Bordeaux parlement, Montesquieu undertook legal studies at the University of Bordeaux. Three years later he received a license in law and was accepted as an advocate in the Parelement of Bordeaux.

From 1709 until 1713 Montesquieu resided in Paris, continuing his study of law and other subjects and familiarizing himself with Parisian society as well. One of the most important influences during these early years in Paris was the friendship of an Oratorian priest, Nicolas Desmolets, who may have taught Montesquieu at Juilly and was a onetime acquaintance of Montesquieu's father. It was Desmolets who lent the young Montesquieu the commonplace book which became the *Spicilège*, an intellectual repository of a miscellaneous nature in which Montesquieu housed thoughts on a variety of scientific and historical matters.[2] Also of interest is Montesquieu's composition in 1711 of an essay in which he maintained that pre-Christian pagans do not merit eternal damnation.

[2] The *Spicilège* was discovered among the Montesquieu papers at La Brède in 1939 and catalogued as MS. 1867 in the Bibliothèque municipale de Bordeaux. It was first published in 1944 by André Masson: *Montesquieu. Un carnet inédit: Le Spicilège* (Paris, 1944), and constitutes, along with the *Pensées*, one of the most important sources for studying the evolution of Montesquieu's ideas.

Such questions of religious belief and practice proved to be one of his lifelong fascinations.

Life in the Provinces

Montesquieu's Parisian stay was terminated by the death of his father in November 1713. At the age of twenty-four he returned to La Brède and Bordeaux, where, in February 1714, he was accepted as *conseiller* in the Parlement of Bordeaux, and where, in April 1715, he married Jeanne de Lartigue, a French Protestant, who bore him three children: Jean-Baptiste (1716), Marie-Catherine (1717), and Denise (1727). This marriage is usually described as one of convenience. Whatever virtues Mme de Montesquieu may have had, other than her capacity for managing the family estates and vineyards during the long absences of her husband, Montesquieu himself seems to have been aware of very few. In fact, in a letter of March 1725, to a Madame de Grave, whose company seems to have been more to his liking, Montesquieu wrote sarcastically of his wife: "There is a woman here that I like very much because she doesn't answer me when I speak to her and because she has already bestowed upon me five or six insults on account, she says, of her poor disposition."[3] However far short of his expectations Montesquieu's domestic life may have fallen, he seems to have done his duty by his family. "With my children I have lived as with my friends," he once wrote in the *Pensées*.[4] There is evidence, however, the Montesquieu never allowed familial obligations to compromise his work. "I liked my family enough to do what was expected in essential matters," he wrote, "but I escaped the petty details."[5]

[3] "Montesquieu to Madame de Grave," in Nagel, III, p. 779.
[4] *Pensée* 4 (213. I, p. 220): 1727–28.
[5] *Ibid.*

Approximately a year after his marriage in 1715 Montesquieu inherited his uncle's parlementary post. Although not very attached to his official duties as a *président à mortier*, he does seem to have derived pleasure from his status in society as a member of the *noblesse de robe*. "Although my name is neither good nor bad," he wrote in the *Pensées*, "having scarcely 350 years of proven nobility, yet I am very attached to it, and I would not be the man to make substitutions."[6] Montesquieu's lineage was a distinguished one, partaking of both the minor *noblesse d'épée* and the *noblesse de robe*. The Secondat family had obtained the lordship of the tiny village of Montesquieu in southwest France in 1561, and Henry IV had made it a barony in 1606. It was Montesquieu's grandfather, Jean-Baptiste-Gaston de Secondat, who had used his wife's dowry to buy the office that eventually passed to Montesquieu himself in 1716. Jacques de Secondat, Montesquieu's own father, had chosen a military career and in 1686 had found a wife whose considerable wealth brought the now famous château at La Brède into the Secondat family.

Scientific Interests

In 1716, the same year he became a *président à mortier* of the Bordeaux Parlement, Montesquieu affiliated himself with the local Académie de Bordeaux, a body of literary and scientific orientation that provided him periodic escape from the tedium of his official functions. He served four times as president, funded a prize for anatomical research, and composed summaries of papers submitted to the Académie by various scientists on such diverse subjects as the causes of echo, the functioning of the kidneys, and the weight and transparency of solid bodies.[7] Furthermore, in

---

[6] *Ibid.*

[7] These summaries are printed in Nagel, III, pp. 69–86 and 89–98, and in Pléiade, I, pp. 10–20 and 23–28.

1719 he advertised in the *Mercure* and the *Journal des savants*[8] for information from all over the world for a projected *Histoire de la terre ancienne et moderne*, which, had he completed it, would have made him a precursor of Buffon. So enthusiastic was he concerning this project in natural history that he offered to pay the postage for any contributions submitted.

During the first year of his membership Montesquieu presented two nonscientific papers, one analyzing Roman statecraft in religion[9] and the other proposing a method for reducing France's national debt.[10] Soon thereafter he embarked upon scientific experimentation. By all accounts, 1718 was something of an *annus mirabilis*. During that year he subjected to the microscope such diverse subject matter as ducks, geese, frogs, insects, mistletoe, and moss. The tone of the report of 1721,[11] in which he conveyed the results of his experimentation, is buoyant throughout and at times jubilant. We learn, for example, that he beheld "avec plaisir" various internal structures within two different frogs, and that he believed he had found a valve in the frog's trachea explaining its horse croak. Furthermore, he reports that on May 29, 1718, he made several observations concerning the nature and germination of mistletoe and moss and that on December 9 and 10, 1718, he arrived at comparative judgments on the length of time a duck and a goose can continue to live while submerged in water. Equally interesting are passages in Montesquieu's report hinting that as of 1721 he envisioned somewhat protracted scien-

[8] Reprinted in Nagel, III, pp. 87–88, and in Pléiade, I, pp. 21–22.

[9] *Dissertation sur la politique des Romains dans la religion* (1716) in Nagel, III, pp. 37–50, and in Pléiade, I, pp. 81–92.

[10] *Mémoire sur les dettes de L'État* (1716) in Nagel, III, pp. 23–31, and in Pléiade, I, pp. 66–71.

[11] *Essai d'observations sur l'histoire naturelle* (1719–1721), in Nagel, III, pp. 99–118, and in Pléiade, I, pp. 29–43.

tific labors for himself. After detailing his attempts, for instance, to compare the temperature of blood in a goose and in a chicken by means of *des grands thermomètres communs*, he assures his audience that he stands waiting for a supply of *petits thermomètres* with which he will be able to continue his experimentation *"avec plus de succès."* In addition, he observes toward the end of the manuscript that he hopes to find time in the future to examine what makes certain plants nourishing and others not. He allows himself the preliminary observation that there does not seem to be a direct correlation between the food value of a plant and the richness of the soil in which it is grown.

Early Reputation and Writings

During the early years of association with the Parlement and with the Académie de Bordeaux, Montesquieu was also busy with the composition of his *Persian Letters* (1721). Begun in 1717, these witty letters took Paris by storm. Purportedly written by two Persian visitors to France, Usbek and Rica, the volume satirizes French society, religion, and politics. Furthermore, correspondence between Usbek and Rica and their fellow Persians back home satisfied the eighteenth-century craving for knowledge of the East by providing glimpses of polygamous life in the seraglios of Turkey. The germ of many an idea developed more fully in *The Spirit of Laws* is found in these *Persian Letters*, and Montesquieu's conviction of the relative nature of *les choses humaines* also appears in full force. In addition, the satirical criticism of French politics and religion so typical of philosophe wit is much evident, as is Montesquieu's interest in comparing national personality types and his keen delight in things foreign and exotic. Finally, one also encounters in this early work two important series of letters, one

revealing Montesquieu's lifelong conviction that self-imposed virtue is superior to coercion by government,[12] and the other analyzing what he took to be Europe's declining population.[13] Following
the literary triumph of his *Persian Letters* Montesquieu began to
spend more time in Paris. He was often seen at the Entresol Club,
in the salons of Mme de Lambert, Mme Geoffrin, and Mme de
Tencin, and in the entourage of the Duc de Bourbon, second in
command to the Regent, the Duc d'Orléans. Under the influence
of polite Parisian society, Montesquieu tried his hand at several
highly stylized literary pieces, such as the mildly pornographic
Temple of Cnidus (1725), a tale of love designed to give pleasure
rather than enlighten the intellect.

In spite of his increasing fascination with Parisian society, the
decade of the 1720s was not without serious literary effort for
Montesquieu. In 1725 he completed the important *Treatise on
Duties*, a work inspired by Cicero and Pufendorf. Now lost, save
for some fragments preserved in the *Pensées* and some passages
incorporated in Book I, chapter 1, of *The Spirit of Laws*, this
treatise utilized natural-law absolutes to combat Hobbes's emphasis
on man-made, positive law as the sole and legitimate criterion of
justice. During the same year, he finished a brief work, *Of Politics*,[14] which reveals his interest in the role of determinism in
human affairs. Furthermore, the decade of the 1720s also marked
the completion of a manuscript in which Montesquieu speculated
on the motives underlying work in the sciences,[15] and of a treatise

---

[12] *Persian Letters* XI–XIV.

[13] *Persian Letters* CXII–CXXII. See also *Spirit of Laws*, Book XXIII.

[14] *De la politique* (1725) in Nagel, III, pp. 165–174, and in Pléiade, I, pp. 112–119.

[15] *Discours sur les motifs qui doivent nous encourager aux sciences* (1725) in Nagel, III, pp. 222–227, and in Pléiade, I, pp. 53–57.

on the wealth of Spain,[16] later incorporated in Book XXI of *The Spirit of Laws*.

Travels in Europe

Montesquieu found little satisfaction in the duties associated with his parlementary office. Although undoubtedly prepared, educationally, for this post, he was not disposed by temperament to spend his life as an official within one of the twelve Parlements of France. He was more attracted to the larger picture of the "spirit" of the laws than to the daily transactions of a judicial court. His mind pursued the universal over the specific, the problems of humanity over those of the individual, broad philosophical questions over narrow detail. The life of a *magistrat bordelais* clearly did not appeal to him. He grew restless and bored. The following oft-quoted *Pensée* conveys his positive distaste for his inherited position: "As for my profession as president," Montesquieu writes, "I was very sincere. I understood the questions in themselves rather well; but as for the procedure, I didn't understand a bit of it. Yet I applied myself to it, and what disgusted me the most was that I saw in idiots that very talent that escaped me, so to speak."[17] Also revealing of Montesquieu's lack of enthusiasm for his parlementary duties is his suggestion in 1723 that *présidents à mortier* not be compelled to attend afternoon sessions of the parlement.[18]

Given this distaste for his parlementary activities, it is little wonder that, in debt and desirous of freedom, Montesquieu sold

[16] *Considérations sur les richesses de l'Espagne* (1726–27) in Nagel, III, 140–155, and in Pléiade, II, pp. 9–18.

[17] *Pensée* 4 (213. I, p. 220): 1727–28.

[18] Cited by Shackleton, p. 18, from C.-B.-F. Boscheron des Portes, *Histoire du Parlement de Bordeaux*, 2 vols. (Bordeaux, 1878), II, pp. 247–248.

his office in 1726 with the provision that it would revert back to the Secondat family at the buyer's death.[19] The sale was completed in July 1726, and by the beginning of the new year Montesquieu had left La Brède for Paris for what proved to be a four-year absence involving, before he returned home, an extended Continental and English tour. The importance of Montesquieu's travels to his intellectual development ought not to be underestimated. Like Darwin a century later on the H.M.S. *Beagle*, he found new inspiration for his life's work: the comparative study of laws and institutions, East and West, past and present.

It was in April 1728, in the company of Waldegrave, nephew to the Duke of Berwick, that Montesquieu crossed over from France into the Holy Roman Empire to make his way first to Vienna and then to Hungary, Venice, Milan, Turin, Genoa, Pisa, Florence, Rome, and Naples. His Italian experiences developed his taste for the fine arts, and he was moved by the works of Raphael in particular. He was also able to observe the Republic of Venice firsthand, and this opportunity is known to have tempered somewhat his enthusiasm for republics, so evident in the *Persian Letters*. In 1729, Montesquieu left Italy and traveled north through southern Germany, the Rhineland, and Holland, finally arriving on October 23, 1729, in England on the private yacht of Chesterfield. Once in England he rapidly penetrated both Court and scientific circles, and, through the friendship of Martin Folkes, he was elected a member of the Royal Society. Furthermore, as the friend of Chesterfield, Montesquieu became acquainted with such important figures as David Hume, Robert Wallace, Pierre Coste (the translator of Newton, Locke, and

---

[19] The original buyer died in 1747, and the office was resold in that year. At the time of the first sale in 1726 Montesquieu owed a Bordeaux banker 31,000 livres and had other unpaid debts amounting to 15,500 livres. See Shackleton, pp. 81–84, 206–208.

Shaftesbury), and John Conduitt (inheritor of Newton's papers and husband of Newton's niece). D'Alembert may have exaggerated in suggesting that England was to Montesquieu during his tour "what the isle of Crete had formerly been to Lycurgus,"[20] but there is no doubt that he was fascinated by the workings of the English parliamentary system. He attended parliamentary debates, read Bolingbroke's *Craftsman*, began work on his history of Rome, and perhaps nurtured those thoughts eventually incorporated in his famous sketch of the English constitution in Book XI, chapter 6, of *The Spirit of Laws*.[21]

Roman History

In August of 1731, after an absence from La Brède of more than four years, Montesquieu returned home via Paris to the southwest of France. Once arrived, he set out on his serious labors. The playful mood of *The Temple of Cnidus* was for a time left behind, and the arduous work leading to *The Spirit of Laws* was begun. The first fruit of what were to be Montesquieu's lengthy and heroic efforts to unlock the secrets of *les choses humaines* was his *Considerations on the Causes of the Grandeur of the Romans and of Their Decline* (1734). While this work did not enjoy anything like the reception of his earlier *Persian Letters*, it did much to inspire Gibbon, and it made an important contribution to the historian's art. Montesquieu provided a highly selective causal analysis of factors leading first to Roman aggrandizement and political health in the period of the Republic and then to decline in the period of the Empire. Rome had been great, Montesquieu argued, so long as

---

[20] *Éloge de M. de Montesquieu*, in Nagel, I, p. xvi.

[21] See Jean Jacques Granpre Molière, *Le Théorie de la constitution anglaise chez Montesquieu* (Leyde: Presse Universitaire, 1972), pp. 78–111, for the view that Montesquieu's famous analysis of the English constitution dates from 1736.

her territorial conquests had not undermined the unified spirit of selfless devotion to the commonweal that had characterized her political life in the period of the early Republic. Originally, Rome had been a tight-knit collectivity supported by the political virtue Montesquieu later idealized in his portrait of democratic governments in Book II, chapter 4, of his *Spirit of Laws*. But once the rights of Roman citizenship were extended to all the peoples of the Italian peninsula, and once Roman soldiers began to consider themselves allegiant not to the state but to their immediate commander, the original spirit supporting Roman liberty and greatness was dissipated.[22] Nor was this psychological transformation accompanying growth in size alone responsible for Roman demise, according to Montesquieu. The Romans declined in part because they failed to change their laws once greatness had been achieved. The same laws, he suggested, that make for initial greatness do not automatically insure political longevity.[23]

L'Esprit des lois

It was late in 1734, at the age of forty-five, with the preparatory work of his causal analysis of Roman decline behind him, that Montesquieu committed himself to the composition of what became *The Spirit of Laws*.[24] Few would deny the magnificence of his achievement. The sheer length of the treatise, not to mention the profundity of its contents, bespeaks an extraordinary degree of effort. The edition of 1757 ran to over a thousand pages, and owing to seriously failing eyesight, Montesquieu had to dictate much of the work to secretaries. The five volumes of the manu-

---

[22] *Considérations*, chap. IX, in Nagel, I, C, pp. 411–414, and in Pléiade, II, pp. 116–119.

[23] *Ibid.*, in Nagel, I, C, pp. 415–416; Pléiade, II, pp. 119–120.

[24] See Shackleton, p. 228.

script copy of the *Laws*, now owned by the Bibliothèque Nationale, movingly convey the enormity of the undertaking. Reading page after page of the manuscript, some in the sprawling hand that resulted from Montesquieu's visual difficulties, one cannot help wondering what kept Montesquieu going during the long years of composition. What muses sustained his arduous labors? It was partly a desire to instruct mankind that spurred Montesquieu on. The didactic aims of *The Spirit of Laws* are sometimes lost sight of amid what some see as the objective flavor the work possesses as a whole, and yet Montesquieu clearly conceived the work as more than an exercise in pure thought, useful only to scholars. His own Preface suggests utilitarian ambitions: "It is not a matter of indifference that the minds of the people be enlightened. The prejudices of magistrates have arisen from national prejudice." Nor is it just the people who need enlightening: "Could I but succeed so as to persuade those who command to increase their knowledge in what they ought to prescribe . . . , I should think myself the most happy of mortals."[25]

As much as he hoped *The Spirit of Laws* might instruct both rulers and subjects alike, Montesquieu must nevertheless have drawn sustenance from more than the thought of practical application alone. He was surely sustained by purely scholarly interests as well. Like his fellow Gascon, Montaigne, he was a man in love with books. These were his permanent company. Judging the pleasures of study to be far more permanent than the sensual plea-

---

[25] An even more striking example of the pedagogical intent of Montesquieu is provided by *Pensée* 200 (1864. III, f. 111): 1749: "This work would not be useless for the education of young princes and would perhaps be worth more to them than vague exhortations to govern well, to be great princes, and to make their subjects happy; which is the same thing as if one asked a man who didn't know Euclid's first propositions to solve complex geometry problems."

sures much sought after in one's youth, he once remarked as
follows, in a little-noticed paper on motives encouraging research
in the sciences: "Our love of study is almost our sole eternal
passion. All the others leave us progressively as this miserable
machine which gives them to us approaches ruin." In one's old
age, he continued, one comes to "feel that our soul is our principal
part; and as if the chain tying it to the senses were broken."[26] In
these statements we catch a glimpse of the man who remarked in
an autobiographical *Pensée* that he had never experienced any
displeasure that an hour's reading could not dispel.[27] Whatever
excesses may have marked Montesquieu's generally moderate life
must have been mainly excesses of industry. Whereas most religions offer their devotees blissful ease and idleness, Montesquieu
would think this a perfect description of hell.[28]

The labor of Montesquieu's *Spirit of Laws* was not completed
without considerable pain having been extracted. His eyes were a
major problem. "If I were not mad," he wrote to his friend Barbot
in 1742, "I would not write a line. But what devastates me is
envisioning the lofty things I could do if I had eyes."[29] Near
completion of his work a half decade later, his exhaustion was
nearly total. "I am overwhelmed with fatigue," he wrote to Cerati
in 1747. "I count on resting for the remainder of my days."[30] No
doubt there were moments of exhilaration when his labors seemed

---

[26] "Discours sur les motifs qui doivent nous encourager aux sciences" (1725), in
Nagel, III, p. 224, and in Pléiade, I, pp. 55.

[27] *Pensée* 4 (213. I, p. 220): 1727–28.

[28] *Pensée* 2128 (1085. II, f. 67v.): 1736–1737.

[29] "Montesquieu to Barbot," February 2, 1742, in Nagel, III, p. 1015. Montesquieu's visual difficulties, eventually culminating in blindness, are discussed in J. M.
Eylaud, "Montesquieu et ses yeux," *Journal de medécine de Bordeaux*, 1956.

[30] "Montesquieu to Cerati," March 31, 1747, in Nagel, III, p. 1083.

to him nearly finished. After writing to Barbot in 1741 that he was working eight hours a day on his treatise and considered any time spent elsewhere wasted, he remarked in a moment of such optimism, "I dare tell you that I do not believe people will waste their time on account of the abundance of material."[31] But these moments of exhilaration seem to have been outweighed by moments of doubt and fatigue. Montesquieu was no vain and self-satisfied author. The manuscript of *The Spirit of Laws* now housed in the Bibliothèque Nationale reveals that much of the work had been completed by 1743, but still he struggled on to give his work precisely the detail, shape, and polish he desired. Nor was he free from fears that his work would be ill received. "This work is the fruit of the reflections of a lifetime," he wrote, in the third volume of the *Pensées*, "and it is possible that from this immense labor, a labor accomplished with the best intentions, a labor undertaken for the benefit of all, I will gain only sorrow and will be rewarded by ignorance and envy."[32]

Montesquieu surely knew that his *Spirit of Laws* would be his final major contribution, and yet he displayed the sort of humility so attractive in a great author. Few of the *Pensées* are as moving as that in which Montesquieu reveals, not the misguided zeal of an author foolishly unaware of the flaws of his work, but rather the full awareness that no work is ever fully finished and no work is ever quite what the author hoped it would become. "I had conceived the idea of giving greater breadth and depth to certain areas of this work," he wrote. "I have become incapable of it. My reading has weakened my eyes, and it seems to me that the light which remains to me is but the dawn of the day when my eyes will close forever. I have almost reached the moment when I must begin and

---

[31] "Montesquieu to Barbot," December 20, 1741, in Nagel, III, pp. 1011–1012.
[32] *Pensée* 201 (1868. III, f. 112v.): 1749.

end, the moment which unveils and conceals all, the moment mixed with bitterness and joy, the moment when I shall lose everything including my weakness. . . . In the deplorable state in which I find myself, it has not been possible for me to give this work the final finish, and I would have burned it a thousand times, if I had not thought it noble to make oneself useful to men up until one's very last sighs."[33]

Finally, *The Spirit of Laws* was ready. It appeared in the year 1748 and rapidly became one of the most popular books of the age. Montesquieu was not soon to enjoy peace of mind, however. His fear that he would be rewarded for his work by ignorance and envy proved warranted. Both Jansenists and Jesuits objected to what they considered his temporizing treatment of suicide, usury, divorce, polygamy, and slavery, and they claimed he meant to imply an absence of morality in monarchies such as France by making honor — not virtue — the principle of such governments. Furthermore, Montesquieu had dared to call Bayle a great man, and to make matters worse, he had quoted Plato — a pagan — as a supreme authority in matters of religion.[34] Montesquieu fought back with pique and spirit, and some have thought his writing powers reached their zenith in his *Defense of the Spirit of Laws* (1750)[35] and in his *Responses and Explanations Given to the Faculty of Theology of the University of Paris* (1752–1754).[36] There was no stopping the onslaught of ecclesiastical displeasure, however, and in spite of efforts on his behalf the work was Indexed in

[33] *Pensée* 206 (1805. III, f. 80v.): 1749.

[34] *The Spirit of Laws*, XXIV, 6 [2]; XXV, 7 [1].

[35] Originally published Geneva, 1750. Reprinted in Nagel, I, B, pp. 433–496, and in Pléiade, II, pp. 1121–1166.

[36] First published in Henri Barckhausen, *Montesquieu, L'Esprit des lois, et les archives de La Brède* (Bordeaux, 1904), pp. 93–117. Reprinted in Nagel, III, pp. 649–674, and in Pléiade, II, pp. 1172–1195.

November 1751. Montesquieu was only to survive this act by four years. On February 10, 1755, he died in Paris, and France lost one of the great first-generation philosophes who, along with Voltaire, had done so much to formulate dominant Enlightenment ideals.

THE METHODOLOGY OF *THE SPIRIT OF LAWS*

Quest for Order

No man's ideas exist in a vacuum wholly set apart from the intellectual climate of his day. Therefore the recollection that the seventeenth century had been the epoch of Galileo, Descartes, and Newton will be helpful in assessing the methodological revolution inherent in Montesquieu's works. The chief legacy of the age of seventeenth-century science had been the conviction of the order of nature in all its parts. Far from being subject to random and unfathomable variations, the physical universe was discovered to be a well-ordered machine, all of whose motions display mathematical uniformity. Nor was order thought to be restricted to the heavens. All the various plant and animal species on earth were believed to have resulted, not from the blind evolutionary necessity of the Darwinian principle of natural selection, but rather from the original designing intelligence of an Omniscient Architect, who bestowed on all species, in one act of special creation, precisely those characteristics necessary for survival.

The seventeenth-century conviction of order in nature suggested to some the possibility of a similar order in the social and political realm, and Montesquieu was one of those who took up this challenge. He would discern order where others had seen only chaos. He would seek general laws where others had rested content with inexplicable diversity. Men are not wholly conducted by "the ca-

price of fancy," he became convinced, in spite of the undeniable
diversity of laws and manners. This is surely what Paul Hazard
had in mind when he remarked: "Montesquieu's greatness lay in
his resolve to regain those lofty peaks whence he could look down
and discern order and disorder, and all his life was one long
upward climb towards those commanding heights."[37] And it was
what Montesquieu's own contemporary Charles Bonnet had in
mind when, after reading *The Spirit of Laws*, he wrote to Montesquieu: "Newton discovered the laws of the material world. You,
Monsieur, have discovered the laws of the intelligent world."[38]

One need not delve far into *The Spirit of Laws* to encounter
Montesquieu's conviction of an underlying order in the social
world paralleling that of nature. It is inherent in his very definition of laws as "the necessary relations deriving from the nature of
things. In this sense all beings have their laws, the material world
its laws, the intelligences superior to man their laws, the beasts
their laws, man his laws" (Book I, chap. 1, par. [1]).[39] In
short, there are laws for everything. Nothing is left to chance. The
laws by which God chose to create the universe are those same laws
by which he now governs it, that is, those laws brought to light by
Galilean-Newtonian science. Hence Montesquieu rejected the
Democritean-Epicurean world-view that had been resurrected by
Hobbes. The chance motion of atoms in space without any guiding principle directing their movements could not, in his view,
have produced beings as complex as man. "There is then, a primi-

---

[37] Paul Hazard, *European Thought in the Eighteenth Century. From Montesquieu to
Lessing*, trans. by J. Lewis May (Cleveland: Meridian Books, 1963; orig. ed. Paris,
1946), p. 153.

[38] "Charles Bonnet to Montesquieu," November 14, 1753, in Nagel, III, p. 1478.

[39] All references to *The Spirit of Laws* will hereafter be given within the text rather
than in a footnote.

tive reason; and laws are the relations subsisting between it and different beings, and the relations of these to one another" (I, 1 [3]). Man has his laws, as do all other created beings. There are some laws, in fact, written into the very fibres of man's being. These laws of nature, equivalent in Montesquieu's definition to physiological-psychological descriptions of human nature prior to the formation of societies, are five in number: (1) cognizance of a Creator ("first in importance, though not in order"), (2) innate timidity resulting in peaceful behavior toward one's fellow men (*contra* Hobbes), (3) the need for nourishment, (4) mutual attraction between the sexes, and (5) a desire to live together in societies (I, 2 [2–8]).

If, as a result of possessing free will and the corresponding capacity for error, man obeys his laws less unfailingly than other beings, God has accordingly provided laws of religion and morality to recall man to his duty (I, 1 [14]). If, as a result of the natural conflicts ensuing from life in society, man soon violates the second of the laws of nature (I, 3 [1]), there is a remedy. International law among nations and political law within nations can be so fashioned that men do as little harm to one another as possible (I, 3 [3–5]). Properly formed, with this admirable goal in mind, public and political law need not be a disordered mass of rules contravening "primitive reason." Rather it will be possible to affirm that "law in general is human reason, inasmuch as it governs all the inhabitants of the earth: the political and civil laws of each nation ought to be only the particular cases in which human reason is applied" (I, 3[11]).

Convinced that order rather than chaos characterizes the world of man as well as the realm of nature, Montesquieu sought to demonstrate that social phenomena are more subject to causal analysis than had been perceived. Nearly all social phenomena, he became convinced, are rationally explicable if one probes for causes with sufficient care. The interest in causation in Montesquieu's history of Rome proved no idle venture. It became a central concern of his life's work. Montesquieu became convinced that diverse mores, religions, governments, and laws need not only baffle and amuse. The penetrating gaze of the social scientist can see beyond the seemingly accidental record of events to the root causes of social phenomena. What seems arbitrary can be made to yield its natural causes. The social world, like that of nature, can be forced to yield the secrets of its structure. Polygamy, for example, may seem wholly arbitrary and irreducible to an overall pattern until one recognizes its origins in a greater number of females than males, or in a climate conducive to the easy support of several wives (XVI, 3 [4]). Similarly, slavery may seem solely the reflection of the avarice and insensitivity of slave owners until one recognizes that an exceptionally hot climate may render slavery a possible means of inducing men to labor (XV, 7). The discovery of what Montesquieu termed the natural causes of polygamy and slavery surely did not justify those practices, but it did render them subject to a form of causal investigation distinct from the plain and simple denunciation Montesquieu's Jesuit and Jansenist critics would have preferred.

Montesquieu's methodological goals make him, in a manner of speaking, both the Isaac Newton and the Francis Bacon of social science. He would seek the laws of social phenomena as Newton had sought the laws of universal gravitational attraction, and he would apply to the social world Bacon's strictures concerning the need to vex, tamper with, and violate Nature in order to force her to divulge her secrets. An important message of Montesquieu's work is that, given proper methods and diligence, nearly all social and political phenomena are rationally explicable. It is only when we neglect to approach a given society on its own terms that we fail to unlock its secrets. And since what might appear irrational in one society, or in one century, might seem the height of reason in another, the task of the careful student of societies is to reconstruct the context in which a given practice can be seen to derive from natural causes. "When a law appears strange," Montesquieu wrote in his *Pensées*, "and one cannot see that the Legislator had an interest in making it in such a manner . . . , one must assume that it is more rational than it appears and that it is based upon sufficient reason."[40] One must admit the danger of "overexplaining," of attributing reason to social and political *faits* where none exists — and Montesquieu has been accused of preceding Hegel in the conviction that the real is rational and the rational real; but within proper limits, the conviction of the rational explicability of human phenomena must be judged a crucial turning point in the emergence of modern social science.

Montesquieu's concern with causation is readily apparent in his conviction that those positive laws men make for themselves ought to display a rational connection to the existing nature of things, whether in supplementing the effects of the underlying environment when they are benign, or in opposing them when they are harmful. Far from being arbitrary creations having no logical relationship to their surroundings, laws should bear a tangible relation to the total political, social, economic, religious, and geophysical environment of the society giving rise to them. The content of a legal system should owe as much to the underlying conditions, both physical and social, as to the freely-creating intelligence of the legislator. In fact, the legislator's function ought to be that of taking the pulse of his society in order to discover which

[40] *Pensée* 410 (1934. III, f. 153): 1749.

laws will insure health and stability. Less an innovating architect than a skilled physician observing existing symptoms, the legislator should act on the basis of a careful diagnosis of existing ills and potential remedies. And in making his diagnosis he need pay attention to such things as the nature and principle of the established government, the extremes of climate and the quality of the soil in a given region, the overall size of the polity with which he is dealing, the occupations of the inhabitants of the country, the degree of liberty the constitution will bear, and the religion that is practiced (I, 3 [14]). All these diverse factors must be taken into account. They constitute, in fact, "the spirit of laws."

The Concept of the General Spirit

In *The Spirit of Laws* Montesquieu was wrestling with two related methodological problems. While clearly searching for the "spirit" of the laws, that is, for the complex relations laws bear to the environments from which they arise, he was also exploring the possibility that all of the various factors influencing the "spirit" of any given legal system also take on a character or tone permeating the whole life-style and outlook of that society. He called this character or tone — it is in essence the overall psychological disposition of a society — the *génie d'une nation* (genius or spirit of a nation), the *caractère commun* (common character), the *âme universelle* (universal soul), the *caractère d'esprit* (mental disposition), the *esprit général* (general spirit), or the *caractère général* (general character). The terminology varied from work to work as the idea gradually took shape in Montesquieu's writings, but by the time the concept was incorporated in Book XIX of his *Laws*, "general spirit" was the favored phrase.

Expressed simply, the general spirit of a nation is the national character resulting from the impact over centuries of time of such basic influences upon a people's behavior as climate, religion, laws, maxims of government, precedents, morals, and customs (XIX, 4). Since these influences vary from society to society, every people will be characterized by an overall mental outlook uniquely its own. The French, for example, are, according to Montesquieu, social, openhearted, cheerful, cultured, sprightly, sometimes imprudent, often indiscreet, and possessed of courage, generosity, frankness, and honor (XIX, 5). The English are, by way of contrast, haughty, bashful, impolite, independent, passionate, and fiercely attached to liberty (XIX, 27). The people of India are judged proud and lazy (XIX, 9), and the Chinese emerge from Montesquieu's analysis of their general spirit as greedy, dishonest, industrious, and respectful of their elders (XIX, 19, 20).

Montesquieu's earliest formulation of the idea of the *esprit général* was in a paper dating from 1717 entitled *De la différence des génies*. Since only fragments of this essay are extant, however, the early discussion of the concept in *Of Politics* (1725) takes on added importance. In this youthful and spirited essay, Montesquieu toyed with the idea that once a general spirit is formed, it exerts a near deterministic influence. "It alone governs, and all that sovereigns, magistrates, and the people can do . . . always relates to it; it dominates even to total destruction." [41] Montesquieu's example was the "taste for fanaticism and rapture" that he believed dominated English society as a result of Henry VIII's freeing "formerly repressed minds" by liberating England from papal jurisdiction. Henry Tudor's successors, Edward, Mary, and Elizabeth, found that "a trace of the former tone" of obedience to constituted authority remained, but James I, in the seventeenth century, discovered that "no more than a ghost of royalty" still

---

[41] *De la politique*, in Nagel, III, pp. 168–169, and in Pléiade, I, p. 114.

existed. Hence all the problems that he and his son Charles I faced with their various parliaments were in reality the result of the influence of the general spirit to which Henry VIII's actions largely contributed.[42] However questionable the interpretation of history embodied in these thoughts, its fascination is undeniable. The determinist, or fatalist, inclination clearly evident in *Of Politics* was later mostly abandoned by Montesquieu, though there are still tones of it in the following brief description of the *esprit général* in the *Considerations on the Causes of the Greatness of the Romans and Their Decline* (1734): "There is in each nation a general spirit upon which power itself is founded: when this power shocks this spirit, it suffocates itself, and it necessarily comes to a halt."[43]

In the years during which he was shaping the ideas that eventually entered *The Spirit of Laws*, Montesquieu experimented with several different explanations for how the component elements of the *esprit général* interact. In a *Pensée* dating from 1730–1731 he expressed concern with the destabilizing consequences of any alteration of the gradually developed and fragile equilibrium constituting the general spirit. "States are governed by five different things," he wrote. "By religion, by general maxims of government, by specialized laws, by customs and by manners. These things all have a mutual relation one to another. If you change one, the others lag behind for a time, and this introduces a sort of disharmony everywhere."[44] Whereas this conservative line of thought did not explicitly influence the formulation of the concept

---

[42] *Ibid.*, in Nagel, III, p. 169, and in Pléiade, I, p. 115.

[43] *Considérations*, chap. IX, in Nagel, I, C, p. 519, and in Pléiade, II, p. 203.

[44] *Pensée* 645 (542. I, f. 432v.): 1730–31. See also *Pensées* 1903 (854. I, f. 543): 1735–36, and 318 (1903. III, f. 136): 1749, for other brief formulations of the concept of the general spirit.

of national character in *The Spirit of Laws*, there is ample evidence that Montesquieu continued to be inclined in the direction of opposing major change as destructive of an historically-conditioned balance of social forces. (See below, pp. 30–31.)

In the *Essay on Causes Affecting Minds and Characters* (1736–1743) Montesquieu's thinking on the interrelation of component elements of the *esprit général* took an important turn. In this work he subdivided the contributing elements of national character into two broad categories, *causes physiques* and *causes morales*. The first half of the *Essay* deals with the manner in which such physical causes as climate, food, and even the air one breathes influence human pyschology and behavior, whereas the whole second part examines such nonphysical and nonphysiological influences on human behavior as education, the people with whom one associates, customs, beliefs, and religion. Montesquieu was convinced that "there is, in every people a general character that more or less leaves its stamp on the character of each individual. It is produced in two ways: by physical causes depending on climate . . . and by moral causes, which are the combined result of laws, religion, customs, and manners, and that sort of emanation of the general way of thinking and of the mannerisms and foolishness of the court and the capital that spreads far afield."[45] Given the intriguing possibilities for analyzing societies inherent in Montesquieu's insight into two basic types of influence on societal characteristics, one might wish that he had extended the idea in his *Spirit of Laws* — and to a degree he did. Although somewhat lost amid the structural idiosyncrasies of the lengthy treatise, the notion of physical as opposed to moral causes in not entirely submerged. Books XIV–XVIII constitute a distinct sec-

[45] *Essay on Causes*, Part Two [31].

tion treating *causes physiques*, and Books II–XIII, as well as XXIV–XXV, are devoted to *causes morales*.

The idea of the *esprit général*, suggested in *Of Politics*, alluded to briefly in the history of Rome, developed further in the *Essay on Causes*, and tucked away as well in the manuscript folios of the *Pensées*, was finally announced to the public with what amounts to surprisingly little fanfare in Book XIX of *The Spirit of Laws*, entitled "Of Laws in Relation to the Principles Which Form the General Spirit, the Morals, and Customs of a Nation." It is the fourth chapter that contains the idea that had so long intrigued Montesquieu:

Men are influenced by various causes, by the climate, the religion, the laws, the maxims of government; by precedents, morals and customs, from whence is formed a general spirit that takes its rise from these.

In proportion, as in every nation any one of these causes acts with more force, the others in the same degree become weak. Nature and the climate rule almost alone over the savages; customs govern the Chinese; the laws tyrannize in Japan; morals had formerly all their influence at Sparta; maxims of government, and the ancient simplicity of manners, once prevailed at Rome.

Clearly evident in this passage is Montesquieu's continued interest in how the component elements of the *esprit général* relate to one another. He has concluded that one element tends to become dominant over the others. Where one component is strong, the others recede. Modern sociologists would call this a "functionalist" approach to society, and its importance is paramount. Émile Durkheim even went so far as to suggest that it was precisely this realization of the interrelatedness of social phenomena that brought social science into being.[46] Montesquieu's function-

[46] Émile Durkheim, *Montesquieu and Rosseau. Forerunners of Sociology*, trans. by Ralph Manheim (Ann Arbor: University of Michigan Press, 1960), pp. 56–57.

alist orientation led him to a holistic rather than an atomistic approach to societies. He was interested in the overall tone or mental disposition of a given people rather than in a compartmentalized dissection of society focusing upon individual elements but neglecting the cumulative result. Rather than treating the customs, institutions, laws, forms of government, and beliefs of a given people as separate components isolated one from the other, Montesquieu regarded them as contributing parts of an integrated totality whose nature is expressed in the concept of the *esprit général*.

This aspect of Montesquieu's method is apparent in his treatment of the Chinese in Book XIX of *The Spirit of Laws*. In China, Montesquieu contends, religion, laws, manners, and customs are all confounded into one cohesive philosophy whose rites are learned in one's youth and practiced throughout the remainder of one's life. The result is that the Chinese character is remarkably impervious to forces of change. In fact, Montesquieu aroused the wrath of the Paris University Faculty of Theology by suggesting that even Christian missionaries should expect to make little headway when confronted by such a stable compound of ingrained custom, religion, and law (XIX, 18 [1–3]).

Other than clearly maintaining that moral causes are by no means overwhelmed by physical causes (see below, pp. 48–51), Montesquieu made no systematic attempt, either in *The Spirit of Laws* or elsewhere in his writings, to explain which of the component elements of the *esprit général* is likely to dominate the others. And in fact this will depend on the circumstances surrounding a given society. Montesquieu did establish the general rule, however, that physical causes are likely to display more force in primitive than in advanced societies (XIX, 4 [2]), and he did imply, if indirectly, that maxims of government often have a particularly

powerful influence. It is true that he did not single out "maxims of
government" for special attention in Book XIX, chapter 4, but
there exists, in Book I, chapter 3, a passage suggesting that among
all the diverse factors cumulatively creating the "spirit" of any
legal system, the nature and principle of government are particularly significant. Once these are clearly comprehended, "the laws
will soon appear to flow thence as from their source" (I, 3 [17]).
We may assume, then, that since laws are a component element of
the general spirit and are in turn very considerably influenced by
the nature and principle of government, Montesquieu meant to
award "maxims of government" a prominent role in the shaping of
national character.

Whatever the incompleteness in Montesquieu's treatment of
esprit général, the importance of the concept is undeniable. In
Montesquieu we find the realization so important slightly later in
Herder, namely, the conviction of the uniqueness of diverse
peoples. If Montesquieu never arrived at such a Teutonic concept
as the *Volkgeist*, he did speak of a less mystical expression of
national character, the *génie d'une nation*, or the *esprit général*. This
general spirit is the cumulative result of the interaction of all the
diverse *causes physiques* and *causes morales* at work within any given
society, and no two nations will possess anywhere near the same
general spirit. All nations are a unique blend of idiosyncratic
elements. This recognition of the unique quality of all sociocul-
tural units led Montesquieu to display far less ethnocentrism than
many of his contemporaries. While proud of being a Frenchman
and a European, he was not incapable of recognizing the utility and
even the merit of strange customs in the contexts of their own
particular life-situations. He sensed that what might be thought
irrational in one country might be deemed the height of reason in

another. This was one of the central messages of the *Persian Letters*, and it was a conviction informing *The Spirit of Laws* as well.

Conservatism-Liberalism

Montesquieu's fascination with the interdependence of the various components of a society caused him to neglect the overall problem of historical development embodying evolutionary change. Only in his history of Rome and in his historical discussion of French feudal law in Books **XXVIII**, **XXX**, and **XXXI** did he evince a sustained interest in historical progression. In general, he neglected a chronological approach in favor of a functionalist orientation wherein the scientific observer dissects a society at a given moment in time to examine how the component elements are adjusted one to another. The evolutionary approach was given a tremendous boost by Darwinism in the mid-nineteenth century, but Montesquieu lived in the world of Linnaeus and Buffon, not Darwin. He sought, not patterns of unilinear progression towards a millennial end, but rather the unraveling of a thread interconnecting phenomena that might at first sight not seem to be interdependent. He toyed with the idea that a rough sort of equilibrium is maintained. Where one component of the general spirit is particularly strong, the others recede in importance accordingly (XIX, 4 [2]).

Believing that societies resemble stable compounds whose equilibrium results from the adjustment and interaction of component elements of the *esprit général*, Montesquieu distrusted all-encompassing political change. If within a given society all the contributing elements are adjusted one to another and to the given nature of things, then "laissez-faire" is the safest policy for the legislator (XIX, 5). Far from approaching societies with axe in hand, the legislator ought to display a degree of caution such as was later recommended by Burke, who not surprisingly referred to Montesquieu as "the greatest genius which has enlightened this age."[47]

Various *Pensées* reveal Montesquieu's distrust of radical change. In one brief fragment he contrasts politics with mathematics and suggests that, whereas in arithmetic the subtraction of one figure produces a calculable effect, "it is not at all the same with politics where one can never predict the result of the change that one makes."[48] And since the result of political change is uncertain, he asserts in another *Pensée*, "the grievance is often preferable to the correction, or at least a good which is established is always preferable to something better which is not."[49] Even more basic to Montesquieu's conservatism than the sentiments quoted above was his conviction that the very spirit of change can be dangerous. Its mood is catching, and one change may well develop a taste for further changes, thereby upsetting the historically conditioned balance of forces contributing to the prevailing general spirit.[50]

Montesquieu's functionalist orientation, as well, no doubt, as his aristocratic status in a hierarchical society, obviously fed the conservative side of his temperament. There was, however, a contrasting side to his personality. As Arthur Lovejoy once remarked, there is almost no great thinker whose thought does not embody unresolved contradictions, and this is clearly the case with Montesquieu. Alongside his conservatism there existed idealism

---

[47] *Abridgment of English History* (1757), *Works* (Bohn's British Classics), Vol. VI, p. 297, quoted by C. P. Courtney, *Montesquieu and Burke* (Oxford: Basil Blackwell, 1963).

[48] *Pensée* 1918 (941. II, f. 19): 1735–36.

[49] *Pensée* 1920 (1436. II, f. 207): 1740–42.

[50] *Pensée* 1916 (184. I, f. 175): 1727–28.

and liberalism nurtured by the tradition of natural law.[51] Montesquieu was by no means willing to see the positive laws men make
for themselves become self-contained absolutes defining
standards of justice and morality. There is, he was convinced, a
higher law to which positive laws should conform. There exist
timeless principles of justice and morality written into the very
nature of things. Hence, if in the normal course of events radical
political engineering is to be shunned, action is nonetheless called
for when absolutes of justice and morality do not receive their just
due. In short, we can say of Montesquieu what Ernest Barker once
remarked of Aristotle: things as they are appeal to him only when
they are what they ought to be. If he saw fit to analyze the *raisons
naturelles* of despotism, or slavery, or polygamy, this analysis is
not equivalent to unthinking approbation. The role of the political
philosopher as Montesquieu conceived it is not merely to describe
what exists. His comment to that effect in the Preface to *The Spirit
of Laws* is not an accurate description of either the tone or the
content of his work. If Montesquieu may have found the role of
critic less comfortable than did Voltaire, who seemed born for that
niche, Montesquieu was a reformer nonetheless, and in his *chef-
d'oeuvre* there is a lengthy list of abuses upon which he heaps
scorn. Montesquieu did not entirely neglect what "ought to be," as
Rousseau charged in the sixth book of *Émile*. Slavery, despotism,
fanaticism, the Inquisition, cruel punishments, burdensome

[51] For recent studies emphasizing Montesquieu's debt to the tradition of natural law,
see C. P. Courtney, "Montesquieu," in *French Literature and its Background*, ed. J.
Cruickshank. Vol. III. *The Eighteenth Century* (New York: Oxford University Press,
1968), pp. 30–43; Jean Ehrard, *L'Idée de nature en France dans la première moitié du
XVIIIe siècle*, 2 vols. (Paris; 1963), II, 497–503 and *passim*; Paul H. Meyer, "Politics
and Morals in the Thought of Montesquieu," in *Studies on Voltaire and the Eighteenth
Century*, Vol. LVI (1967), pp. 845–891; and Mark H. Waddicor, *Montesquieu and the
Philosophy of Natural Law* (The Hague: Martinus Nijhoff, 1970).

taxes, excessive armaments, the system of tax-farming, courtiers making their way by influence rather than ability — all these ills are clearly opposed, if with a quiet dignity and calm reserve.

The Spirit of Laws is, then, among other things a breviary of liberal and humanitarian politics, a catechism of enlightened reform. Montesquieu's relativistic appreciation for diversity (see below, pp. 34—40) by no means obliterated the influence of Grotius and Pufendorf and other theorists of natural law. In the opening chapter of his treatise Montesquieu invoked the timeless absolutes of law and justice in order to combat the legacy of Hobbes, who had cut law away from its natural-law moorings and made the definition of political right and wrong hinge upon the decrees of the ruler of a Leviathan state. That justice exists independently of natural law, Montesquieu was firmly convinced. "Before laws were made," he wrote, "there were relations of possible justice. To say that there is nothing just or unjust but what is commanded or forbidden by positive laws, is the same as saying that before the describing of a circle all the radii were not equal. We must therefore acknowledge relations of justice antecedent to the positive law by which they are established" (I, 1 [8, 9]). In Montesquieu's writings the objective and descriptive world of an emerging social science methodology had not yet fully displaced the hierarchical universe of clearly defined rights and wrongs. He stood astride two worlds, one moralistic and the other positivistic. He made, as Raymond Aron has pointed out, an original attempt to combine the two. Montesquieu remained substantially a philosophe — however eager some have been to push him ahead into the nineteenth century. To recognize that some parts of Montesquieu's work were distinctly sociological in their conviction of the rational explicability of social phenomena and their determination to solve the riddle of diverse customs and laws is not to ignore the more traditional natural-law orientation pervading his whole treatise. One can find passages in *The Spirit of Laws* where Montesquieu seems for a time to forget all save the relative and to cease to judge and condemn; but ultimately, he returns to the natural-law absolutes as the touchstone of political right. Well might Montesquieu have remarked, in fact, in a *Pensée* written after the publication of his work: "I thank Mr. Grotius and Mr. Pufendorf for having accomplished a large part of what this work required of me, with a height of genius which I could never have attained."[52] If by his own admission, the bent of his mind was not to retrace what everyone already knew,[53] it must not be thought that the familiar absolutes of natural-law theory ceased to function as the vital moralistic backdrop against which he investigated diverse customs and mores, East and West, past and present. Justice is not always listened to amid the tumult of the passions, but it remains ever present as an ideal to be striven for by legislators, rulers, and citizens alike.

Relativism

As basic to Montesquieu's outlook as his natural-law orientation, his conviction of the order and rational explicability of *faits sociaux*, and his functionalist approach to societies was his sensitivity to the necessary diversity of various societies. Few Frenchmen of the eighteenth century were so affected by the onslaught of travel literature describing distant and exotic lands as was Montesquieu. If among his favorite sources were Chardin's *Voyages en Perse et aux Indes orientales* (1687), Du Halde's *Description . . . de l'Empire de la Chine . . .* (1735), and Ricaut's *Histoire de l'État Présent de l'Empire Ottoman* (1670), he also cited

52 *Pensée* 191 (1863. III, f. 111): 1749.
53 *Pensée* 192 (1866. III, f. 112): 1749.

such works as Bernier's *Voyages, contenant la description des États du Grand Mogul* (1709–1710), Flacourt's *Histoire de la grande isle de Madagascar* (1658), Gage's *Survey of the West Indies* (1648), Labat's *Nouveau voyage aux isles de l'Amérique* (1722), La Loubère's *Du Royaume de Siam* (1691), and Perry's *The State of Russia under the Present Czar* (1716), to name only a very few. Montesquieu's library at La Brède became a means of reaching the world beyond Europe, and his extensive reading taught him, as it had taught Montaigne two centuries before, the lesson of relativity. A European shakes with his right hand, a Turk with his left, Montaigne had remarked, and it was Montesquieu who largely developed the revolutionary political and social implications of this realization. The whole design of the *Persian Letters* stems from the basic conviction of relativism. Turkish visitors to France express shock, surprise, and dismay at customs Frenchmen would never think of questioning. What seems natural to a Frenchman, a Turk is shown to abhor — and vice versa of course.

Symptomatic of Montesquieu's relativistic outlook was his statement in his *Notes on England*: "When I travel to a country, I do not investigate whether there are good laws, but whether those that exist are executed, for there are good laws everywhere."[54] And quite similar in tone is the following passage, also from the period of Montesquieu's travels between 1728 and 1731: "It seems to me that no nation's customs and practices, *when not contrary to morality*, can be judged superior to those of others. For by what rule would one judge? They do not have a common measure except that each nation makes an example of its own and by them judges all the others."[55] This insight, brilliantly set forth in the *Persian*

---

[54] *Notes sur L'Angleterre*, in Nagel, III, p. 287, and in Pléiade, I, p. 879.

[55] *Voyages en Italie, en Allemagne, et en Hollande* (1728–29), in Nagel, II, 1199, and in Pléiade, I, 767. Italics not in original.

Letters, was clearly strengthened by Montesquieu's voyages in Europe and England, and it received its fullest expression in Montesquieu's treatise on laws.

Relativism was hardly new in European thought by the eighteenth century. In many respects, Montesquieu's outlook was the heritage of the revival of classical Greek skepticism in the mid-sixteenth century. Skeptics from Montaigne to Bayle had suggested that there exists no unchanging criterion for establishing moral and political absolutes by which to judge all men. Accordingly, the real significance of Montesquieu's relativism derives, not from its absolute novelty, but rather from its scope.

Montesquieu's conviction of relativism was twofold. On the one hand, he appreciated, very possibly with the help of Sextus Empiricus and certainly with the aid of Bayle and Montaigne,[56] the relative and subjective nature of individual perception. He sensed that no two men see things exactly alike, and he developed that notion at considerable length in Part Two of his *Essay on Causes Affecting Minds and Characters* (1736–1743). Owing to differences in physiological make-up, education, experiences, and modes of perception engendered by one's occupation, few men, Montesquieu suggested, will have the same reactions even to the same objects and the same ideas. Our idiosyncratic experiences and outlooks, he argued, lead us to see as if through tinted glasses that distort external objects by coloring them with our own predispositions and attitudes towards life. "A man who has imagination and another who has not," Montesquieu wrote in the *Essay on Causes*, "see things as differently as two fictional heroes, one of

[56] Montesquieu owned a 1659 Latin edition of Sextus Empiricus that contained both the *Pyrrhonian Hypotyposes* and the *Adversus Mathematicos*, two editions (1595 and 1727) of Montaigne's *Essais*, and three works by Bayle.

whom is captivated by what he sees and the other not."[57] So different are the physiological mechanisms of each individual that "one person will be convinced by rhetoric and another only by plain logic. One person will be struck by mere words and another only by evidence. One person will never see a proposition without also visualizing various objections and will be uncertain. Another will see the proposition better than the objections to it and will believe all. . . . One person will have an active mind, while another will merely take things in like a purse yielding nothing but the money placed therein. Ideas that will only brush against the brain of one man will pierce that of another . . . even to the point of engendering madness."[58]

It is not alone differences in individual perception, however, that make relativism a proper means of approaching the diversity of human societies. Montesquieu's relativistic outlook also derived from his conviction that the circumstances affecting the development of societies are so diverse that no two societies can conceivably profit from the same customs, religion, government, or laws. Bluntly put, there exist no universally valid prescriptions. A central message of *The Spirit of Laws* is that a legal system contributing to overall health in one society may prove detrimental in the context of another. Hence Montesquieu's uncompromising statement that laws "should be adapted in such a manner to the people for whom they are made, as to render it very unlikely for those of one nation to be proper for another" (I, 3 [12]). Laws, Montesquieu became convinced, should be judged not only in accordance with absolute standards but also in terms of the needs of the particular society in which they are applied. And if laws are

[57] *Essay on Causes*, Part Two [22].
[58] *Ibid*. [23].

relative to the precise nature of things in any given polity, then wide differences in political and social practices are not only to be tolerated but are to be anticipated. Take an economic condition such as luxury, for example. Whereas luxury was forthrightly condemned by most of the philosophes regardless of context, Montesquieu's attitude was more complex. He regarded luxury as inappropriate in democratic states whose stability is dependent upon frugality and equality; but luxury can be positively beneficial in monarchical states where there are to be gradations of classes — not equality — and where the wealth of the privileged few trickles down to the poor through charity (VII, 2 [4]). In short, if a formula is desired, it cannot be absolute. Luxury is permissible where equality is not the goal and where the food yield of the land compares favorably with population size. Under contrasting conditions, luxury ought to be shunned. And luxury is just one example among countless other political, social, and economic phenomena that must be assessed, not exclusively from the vantage point of absolute standards, but from a relativistic viewpoint as well. Insofar as the nature of things varies from society to society, so too will the institutions and social practices of those societies, within the limits, that is, prescribed by natural law.

Montesquieu's appreciation of the relativity of diverse customs and mores also influenced his outlook on religion. Religions, he became convinced, will necessarily be at least partially relative to the environment in which they are practiced. Montesquieu was very conscious of the amazing variety of religious systems adhered to in various parts of the world. "God is like that monarch who has several nations under his empire," he remarked in the *Pensées*. "They all come to pay him tribute, and each speaks its own language to him."[59] If, as he claimed in Book XXIV, Montesquieu regarded Christianity as superior to other faiths (1[5]), he nevertheless became skeptical of attempts to export the Christian or any other faith beyond the region in which it had taken natural root. He could no more conceive of any one set of dogma and ceremonies being suited for all men and all environmental conditions than he could imagine one form of government being automatically suited to all men. Consider the harm that would derive from transplanting Hinduism to European soil. Blessed with the Ganges river, Hindus experience no difficulties in offering prayers to God in a running stream, but such a doctrine would clearly be irrational and even destructive in an area where there is little water or where the water is contaminated (XXIV, 26 [2]).[60] Similarly, the Hindu belief in the transmigration of souls is well adapted to India. There are few cattle in India, and the doctrine of metempsychosis serves to prohibit the slaughter of cows (XXIV, 24). But such a doctrine would hardly suit a region whose economy is dependent upon the slaughter of cattle for food. In the eyes of the Church, Montesquieu was treading heretical ground. The doctrine of the relativity of religious customs clearly conflicted with the messianic impulse of Western Catholicism, and Book XXIV was one of the most heavily censored of the whole treatise. Its approach to religion was too radical for the watchdogs of orthodoxy, and Montesquieu spent much precious time during his final years trying to explain his position to his ecclesiastical critics. Ultimately, however, there was no reconciling Montesquieu's method with the old formulas of revealed religion. The objections

---

[59] *Pensée* 2117 (1454. II, f. 213v.): 1742.

[60] See also "Dossier de L'Esprit des Lois," in Nagel, III, p. 595, and in Pléiade, II, p. 1003.

Jansenists and Jesuits raised to Montesquieu's work were a micro-cosm of a battle being waged all across Europe throughout the eighteenth century, a battle between revealed truths and natural truths, between biblical truths literally interpreted and new modes of explanation that shattered orthodoxy.

Rationalism-Empiricism

Considerable difference of opinion exists concerning the relative influence of empirical and rationalist methods on the composition of *The Spirit of Laws*. The view that Montesquieu was essentially collecting and organizing empirical data was succinctly stated by Auguste Comte in his "Plan des Travaux Scientifiques Nécessaires pour Réorganiser la Société" (May 1822), printed as an appendix to the fourth volume of his *Système de politique positive*. . . . 4 vols. (Paris, 1851–1854). According to Comte, Montesquieu made the first direct effort to treat politics as a science of facts rather than dogmas. Far more than his contemporaries, he prac-ticed an objective and empirical method, arranging all the political facts at his disposal under a certain number of heads in order to bring to light the laws of their concatenation. Thus Montesquieu began the process whereby social phenomena would one day be placed on a positivistic footing. Comte admitted that Montes-quieu's method was not purely positivistic and empirical — some aspects of the metaphysical remained — but compared with his contemporaries, the degree of Montesquieu's positivism marked an important advance. And Comte's view is by no means devoid of modern adherents. Simone Goyard-Fabre has vigorously restated it in her *La Philosophie du droit de Montesquieu* (Paris: Klincksieck, 1973), wherein she affirms that Montesquieu allowed the facts to speak for themselves, believing, like Galileo and Newton, that intelligibility is immanent in the phenomena. Other recent adhe-

rents of the empirical, positivistic view find the analogy of the
naturalist useful. For John Hermann Randall, Montesquieu represents the Buffon or the Linnaeus of social science, patiently
classifying societies in order to arrive at general principles through
inductive, empirical methods.[61] And Werner Stark has also
stressed Montesquieu's love of facts rather than speculation.
Whatever traces remain of a rationalist Cartesian outlook in *The
Spirit of Laws*, these are in Stark's view "few and far between,
accidental rather than essential." The overall character of the work
is decidedly Baconian.[62]

While there is a degree of truth in the empirical view, particularly if one is comparing Montesquieu with the more polemical
writers of his day, the extent of Montesquieu's empiricism is too
often exaggerated. If Montesquieu was more concerned with facts
than many of his contemporaries, the age of the positivistic
monograph still lay a century off. If he made use of large amounts
of material culled from his reading, travels, and conversation, he
nevertheless picked and chose his facts with all due care. And the
comment is his Preface that he had drawn his principles not from
his prejudices but from the nature of things is misleading. His
actions belie his words. As has already been suggested in the
discussion of natural law (see above, pp. 32–34), Montesquieu
was far from content simply to describe what exists without advancing value judgments concerning political good and evil. He
did not simply allow facts to speak for themselves but rather
introduced those facts that helped him to prove the points he
wished to make. His method was comparable to that of the artisan

[61] *The Career of Philosophy*. Volume I. *From the Middle Ages to the Enlightenment*
(New York: Columbia University Press, 1962), p. 947.

[62] *Montesquieu. Pioneer of the Sociology of Knowledge* (Toronto: University of Toronto
Press, 1960), p. 1.

who constructs a complex mosaic along the lines of his own design.

However much empirical data Montesquieu managed to squeeze into his work, there is an unmistakably Cartesian flavor to the manner in which he reached important conclusions. He first constructed models of three ideal-types of government and then, throughout much of the treatise, described how each of these three governments of his own definition ought to act if equilibrium is to be maintained. He described not so much how particular governments actually act as how republics, monarchies, and despotisms — as he defines them — should act if the nature and principle of each type is to be preserved.

Students of Montesquieu's discussion of despotism have been particularly sensitive to the rationalist component of his method. In his "Montesquieu et le monde Musulman, d'après L'Esprit des Lois,"[63] Paul Vernière spoke of Montesquieu's method as "believing itself experimental when it is only deductive" and suggested that *The Spirit of Laws* is both classical and Cartesian. Montesquieu's logic, Vernière remarked, "consists in integrating in a grill facts chosen not without the exclusion and neglect of those which do not suit his thesis." Muriel Dodds had earlier reached the same conclusion in her *Les récits de voyages. Sources de L'Esprit des Lois* (Paris, 1929). According to Miss Dodds, "Montesquieu is Cartesian to the inner depths of his spirit. He first formulated his theories, and then searched history for examples that convey proof of his reasoning. The examples drawn from the travel literature did not influence his opinion. They fortified it."[64] Françoise

[63] Pp. 175–190 in *Actes du Congrès Montesquieu réuni à Bordeaux du 23 au 26 mai 1955 pour commémorer le deuxième centenaire de la mort de Montesquieu* (Bordeaux: Delmas, 1956)

[64] P. 169.

Weil, another student of Montesquieu's theory of despotism, has assessed Montesquieu's method as displaying "a certain off-handedness with regard to texts, inventing rarely, but choosing the elements that agree with a theory established in advance."[65] And Joseph Dedieu once termed Montesquieu's rationalism a *"vice de méthode"* and claimed that in *The Spirit of Laws* "the facts are not represented such as they are in and of themselves but are tinted with the color they have taken in passing through the imagination of the author."[66]

Nor did the degree of rationalism in *The Spirit of Laws* go unnoticed among Montesquieu's contemporaries. In writing a course of lectures in 1789, David Williams, the English dissenting minister, friend of Franklin, translator of Voltaire, and discerning critic of Montesquieu's ideas, remarked that "Montesquieu assumes principles and truths, searches the universe for circumstances to corroborate them; warmly interests the heart in their favor; and points and directs his language, with a delicate and irresistible hand."[67] Nor did Voltaire fail to touch upon the issue of excessive rationalism in Montesquieu's methodology. "I cannot comprehend," he wrote, "how supposed rules can be established which are continually contradicted by experience. It must be acknowledged that nearly the whole book is founded on assumptions that the least care demolishes."[68]

Perhaps one's final judgment of Montesquieu's use of facts must

---

[65] "Montesquieu et le Despotisme," pp. 191–215, in *Actes*, p. 193.

[66] *Montesquieu* (Paris, 1913), pp. 97, 99.

[67] *Lectures on Political Principles; The Subjects of Eighteen Books, in Montesquieu's Spirit of Laws: Read to Students under the Author's Direction* [Vol. IV of *Lectures on Education*] (London: John Bell. 1789), p. 2.

[68] Article "Lois (Esprit des)" in *Dictionnaire Philosophique*, Vol. IV, in *Œuvres complètes de Voltaire*, ed. by Louis Moland, 52 vols. (Paris: Garnier frères, 1877–1885), Vol. XX, p. 10.

be a comparative one. If *The Spirit of Laws* does not conform to nineteenth- and twentieth-century standards of empirical research, it is fairer to judge Montesquieu according to the standards of his own age. If he blended rationalism and empiricism, this is perhaps to be anticipated, given his role as a transitional figure between an age of polemics and an age of positivism. Montesquieu stands at the beginning of a rich tradition of empirical research in the social sciences. His footnotes reveal the extent to which he sought to rely upon the available sources for understanding a given contemporary or historical problem. If he sometimes transformed his data to conform to his needs and at times left out information tending to contradict the general laws he discerned, he did make historical data and contemporary travel books the laboratory in which he reached his conclusions. Far more than such a work as Rousseau's *Social Contract* (1762), *The Spirit of Laws* concerns itself with the real and the existent, leaving the realm of utopia to more fantastical thinkers.

Climate

Aside from Montesquieu's exposition of the principles of the English constitution, no aspect of his thought has proven so controversial as his treatment of the influence of climate on human behavior. Books XIV–XVII of *The Spirit of Laws* typify, in fact, a law of literature wherein a thinker's most controversial speculations are indelibly annexed to his name and reputation — and are quite often misunderstood — whereas other, less sensational, but equally important ideas too soon cease to be influential or even widely noted. In the context of *The Spirit of Laws* Montesquieu often seems to advance generalizations concerning climate based on little careful study. A careful reading of the *Essay on Causes Affecting Minds and Characters* (1736–1743), however, reveals that he gave considerable thought to the physiological theory on which Books XIV–XVII are based. If analysis of this posthumously published manuscript by no means redeems Montesquieu's ideas from the modern scientific standpoint, it does render them more comprehensible and serves to caution one against regarding Montesquieu as a dilettante advancing ideas little supported by painstaking thought.

Fundamental to the physiological theory presented in Part One of the *Essay on Causes* — and much current in the scientific literature of the day — was the conviction that the body is composed of two basic materials: solid parts and the fluids those solids contain. Various fibres were thought to compose all the solid parts of the body from bones, to cartilage, to ligaments, to muscles, to the various liquid-carrying vessels of the body — that is, arteries, veins, lymphatics, lacteals, and glands. Depending on the particular size, moisture, and flexibility of the various fibres making up the nerves and the blood-carrying vessels of the body, and depending on the volume of fluids those vessels contain, the individual would enjoy a state of mental alertness or sluggishness and a state of health or sickness. Such ideas were spelled out with particular clarity in the *Institutiones medicae* (1708) of Hermann Boerhaave, a Dutch professor of medicine, botany, and chemistry, and in the works of John Arbuthnot, an English doctor, writer, and collaborator of Pope and Swift.[69] But fibre theory was clearly

---

[69] Montesquieu owned Boerhaave's *Institutiones medicae* in a Latin edition of 1735 (*Catalogue*, 1050), and there was also a two-volume French translation by La Mettrie published in Paris in 1739–1740. Arbuthnot's *An Essay concerning the Nature of Aliments and the Choice of Them, According to the Different Constitutions of Human Bodies* (1731) was available in French translation in 1741, and his *An Essay concerning the Effects of Air on Human Bodies* (1733) was issued in a French translation in 1742. The similarities between Arbuthnot and Montesquieu were first pointed out by Joseph Dedieu in his *Montesquieu et la tradition politique Anglaise de L'Esprit des Lois* (Paris, 1909), pp. 212–225. The similarities between Boerhaave and Montesquieu deserve study.

central to most of the physiological theory of the day. Diderot, for example, contributed an article entitled "fibre" to volume six of the *Encyclopedia*. "In general," he began, "one understands by the fibres of the bodies of animals, and consequently of the bodies of humans, the most simple filaments that enter into the composition and structure of the solid parts of which they are formed." And Diderot went on to point out that fibre theory was known to the ancients, if imperfectly, and that *distractilité, elasticité, vibratilité*, and *irritabilité* are the four basic caracteristics of the body's fibres.[70]

In terms of an individual's mental life, the fibres of the brain and nerves were thought most important, and in the *Essay on Causes* Montesquieu concentrated his attention on these. Following an assumption as ancient as Hippocrates and elaborated in some detail in Galenic physiology of the second century A.D., Montesquieu believed that the nervous system consists of hollow nerve tubules conveying nerve juice, or animal spirits, throughout the body. The distinction between motor and sensory nerves was not established prior to the work of Charles Bell and François Magendie in the early nineteenth century, and Montesquieu considered the nerve juice flowing through a given portion of the nerve network both the medium by which sense impressions impinging on the body from the external world are conveyed to the brain, and the medium by which the brain sends messages to the muscles resulting in locomotion. It was the first of these two functions, that involving perception, that most interested Montesquieu. He believed that the condition of the fibres of the nerve tubes necessarily conditions the effectiveness of the nerve fluid and hence largely determines the acuity of an individual's perceptions.

[70] *Encyclopédie, ou Dictionnaire raisonné des sciences, des arts et des métiers*, 1751–1772. Vol. VI (1756), p. 662b.

The soul, says Montesquieu, is like a spider in its web in that its fate is dependent upon the arrangement, structure, and condition of the nerve tubes branching out from the brain to all parts of the body.[71] The condition of the brain fibres themselves was thought to be equally important, and Montesquieu cautioned against damaging these fibres. Opium ought to be avoided, for example, since it so stretches the brain's fibres that they cease to be sensitive. And alcohol was deemed to make the brain fibres similarly sluggish.[72]

Very important to the theory of climate as presented in Book XIV of *The Spirit of Laws* are the fibres composing the arteries and veins. People are vigorous in cold climates because cold air contracts the fibres of their cardiovascular systems, causing the blood to flow with greater velocity. And cold air also contracts the fibres of the nerve endings close to the surface of the skin, causing reduced sensibility to both pleasure and pain. As empirical proof of this fact, Montesquieu reported freezing the tongue of a sheep and actually observing with a microscope the papillae in a contracted position (XIV, 2 [5–7]).

The physiological basis of the theory of climate had been present in the manuscript of the *Essay on Causes*. What was new in *The Spirit of Laws* were the deductions drawn from that theory. In Book XV Montesquieu speculated that slavery might be less contrary to *la raison naturelle* in hot climates than in cold since the indolence brought on by extremes of high temperature might make it difficult to find people willing to work (XV, 7). And in Book XVI he contended that polygamy, while indefensible in and of itself, might be less irrational in hot climates than in cold, since nature matures women early in hot climates but little assists them

[71] *Essay on Causes*, Part One [37].
[72] *Ibid.*, [45–46].

in maintaining their charms (XVI, 1). In Book XVII Montesquieu speculated that cold climates engender the energy necessary for the maintenance of freedom, whereas the indolence produced by hot climates assists the despot in ruling by force rather than law (XVII, 2).

One of the most difficult problems in interpreting Montesquieu's climatological theory is judging the exact degree to which he believed that climate influences mankind. He has sometimes been portrayed as a climatological determinist bent on demonstrating the stranglehold of climate on human development. Even such a discerning critic of ideas as R. G. Collingwood was prone to this point of view. In his *The Idea of History* he remarked that "Montesquieu conceived human life as a reflection of geographical and climatic conditions not otherwise than the life of plants" and that in Montesquieu's thought "institutions appear not as free inventions of human reason in the course of its development, but as the necessary effects of natural causes."[73] This judgment is extreme. There is a considerable difference between exploring possible connections between climate and various sociopolitical phenomena and claiming that relationships are *necessary* connections completely beyond the control of the human beings involved. There is no question that Montesquieu exaggerated both the impact of diverse climates on the body's physiology and the societal consequences of those physiological influences. He did not maintain, however, that some societies are *necessarily* propelled by the influence of hot climates down the path to slavery and despotism, whereas others are certain to achieve freedom because of climatological advantages. The demonstration by Montesquieu of a possible connection is not equivalent to his maintaining that the

---

[73] (Oxford: At the Clarendon Press, 1946), p. 79.

connection *has to exist*. If climate exerts a great influence on man, that influence is not unalterable. At the same time that Montesquieu emphasized the influence of climate on human beings, he consistently counseled means by which that influence can be counteracted. In Book XIV, for example, he was much concerned to suggest ways to encourage husbandry in hot climates where people possess little energy. The Chinese emperor is praised for ceremoniously beginning the plowing each year and for offering prizes to the most productive farmer. And the reason for these carefully calculated ploys against the force of climate is clearly stated: "The more the physical causes incline mankind to inaction, the more the moral causes should estrange them from it" (XIV, 5 [3]).

Book XV is similarly instructive in terms of Montesquieu's consistent interest in how the physical cause of climate can be counteracted by human ingenuity. True, Montesquieu advances the thesis that there may be a natural reason for slavery in hot climates, but his final judgment is that there is no climate so hot as to render slavery necessary, given intelligent use of "commodious machines" to augment human strength and a system of just rewards to encourage paid labour (XV, 8 [3]). And there is no evidence in Book XVI that Montesquieu believed that hot climates *necessarily* produce polygamy. There may exist *raisons naturelles* for polygamy in hot climates beyond any existing in colder areas, but this belief is by no means equivalent to a determinist view. And in Book XVII Montesquieu established no *necessary* connection between cold climates and freedom and between hot climates and despotism. Possibility — or even probability — is not equivalent to necessity. Much closer to the mark than Collingwood in assessing Montesquieu's climatological theory was Ernst Cassirer, who remarked that "Montesquieu rejects a simple derivation from the purely physical factors and he subordinates the material to the spiritual causes. . . . Bad legislators submit to unfavorable climatic conditions; good legislators recognize these disadvantages and counteract them by spiritual and moral force. . . . Man is not simply subject to the necessity of nature; he can and should shape his own destiny as a free agent, and bring about his destined and proper future." [74]

Examination of Part Two of the *Essay on Causes* yields further evidence against the determinist charge. The whole of Part Two of this *Essay* examines moral causes, and Montesquieu asserts that these "moral causes shape the general character of a nation and determine the quality of its mind more than do physical causes." [75] Various proofs are advanced. One argument is that although southern peoples are originally blessed with finer minds than northern peoples, the effects of despotic governments are so debilitating that the action of nature is reversed. "Nature is so greatly betrayed that the people whom she created with better minds have less sense, and those to whom she gave less sense have better minds." [76] The chief antidote to diverse *causes physiques*, and the key element in shaping the mind, is education. Without education the fibres of the brain receive little exercise and the mind will be dull. [77] Other *causes morales* of great influence in shaping the mind, according to Montesquieu, are the company one keeps, the books one reads, the traveling one undertakes, and the profession one follows. [78] All these *causes morales* mold the mind along a distinctive path. Far from believing the character of one's mind derives solely from the influence of such *causes physiques* as the tempera-

[74] *The Philosophy of the Enlightenment*, trans. by Fritz C. A. Koelln and James P. Pettegrove (Boston: Beacon Press, 1955), p. 214.

[75] *Essay on Causes*, Part Two [38].

[76] *Ibid*. [42].

[77] *Ibid*. [4].

[78] *Ibid*. [44–48; 52–56].

ture and humidity of the air where one resides, the nature of the food one consumes, and the amount of rest one receives — all these acting directly upon the fibres of the nervous system — Montesquieu believed that "we create for ourselves the type of mind that pleases us." Our occupation in life greatly shapes our mental outlook. "Engravers see figures on the walls which are not there, because their brains have received the impressions of figures they have carved. . . . Those who have accustomed their minds to see numerical or geometrical relationships see and find relationships everywhere, and measure and calculate everything."[79] A teacher may be obstinate because he is supposed never to err. A clergyman may be vain because the people with whom he has contact rely so completely on his aid. A scholar may be prone to long speeches because he has many ideas arduously achieved and is eager to share them.[80] These *déformations professionnelles* determine more the character of the mind than do the various *causes physiques* at work on man. Hence Montesquieu by no means attributed to climate a stranglehold on human psychology and development. If there are some passages in *The Spirit of Laws* where his love of colorful rhetoric might seem to imply this, both Part Two of the *Essay on Causes* and the bulk of the texts on climate in his *chef d'oeuvre* lead to a different conclusion.

Religion

Most subjects Montesquieu treated in *The Spirit of Laws* were transformed by his touch, and religion was no exception. His perspective was that of the political writer rather than the theologian, and he consciously neglected the question of the truth or falsehood of various religious dogmas in order to concentrate on

[79] *Ibid.* [52].
[80] *Ibid.* [56].

the question of utility. His utilitarian declaration of independence from orthodoxy reads in part as follows: "I shall examine the several religions of the world, in relation only to the good they produce in civil society, whether I speak of that which has its root in heaven, or those which spring from the earth" (XXIV, 1 [2]). "The most true and holy doctrines may be attended with the very worst consequences, when they are not connected with the principles of society; and on the contrary, doctrines the most false may be attended with excellent consequences, when contrived so as to be connected with these principles" (XXIV, 19 [1]). The welfare of society, then — not the reaffirmation of Christian truths — was to be Montesquieu's chief concern. Religion was to have no sacrosanct status beyond the reach of the probing scalpel of the sociologist. The ecclesiastical detractors of Montesquieu's treatise on laws would have preferred pieties, and they were presented instead with analysis.

The clear danger posed to orthodoxy by Montesquieu's secular approach in Book XXIV of *The Spirit of Laws* was that a new idol of utility threatened to replace the traditional God of Christian apologetics. The truth or falsity of a religious doctrine was deemed less important than its ramifications on the society in which it is practiced. Montesquieu praised, for instance, the religion of the inhabitants of Pegu in Burma. It is not likely, he reports, that their simple, straightforward religion has been revealed by God, and it may even contain false doctrines, but, more important, it serves to restrict murder, stealing, and uncleanliness (XXIV, 8 [2]). And what finer goals, Montesquieu wonders, can a religion embody? Likewise, the religion practiced by the ancient Essenes merits Montesquieu's approval, since the Essenes vowed to be just, kind, faithful, and truthful as well as to avoid unlawful gain (XXIV, 9). Islam, on the other hand, whatever its doctrinal validity — we have said Montesquieu avoided this issue — fails to humanize those who practice it, and it therefore merits no praise (XXIV, 4). And also worthy of contempt is the religion of the people of Formosa who, by Montesquieu's account, believe that hell exists only to punish those who have not gone naked during a certain season, or have not worn silk, or have hunted oysters, or consulted the song of the birds (XXIV, 14 [7]).

Judged particularly destructive by Montesquieu are religions that misconstrue the doctrine of the immortality of the soul and cause individuals to murder themselves, thinking they will thereby join departed loved ones (XXIV, 19 [3]). And also falling under Montesquieu's utilitarian gaze is the doctrine of predestination, a doctrine sometimes productive of ill consequences for society at large. Believing that salvation is predestined by a deity rather than earned as a result of praiseworthy conduct on this earth, some men have been tempted to become transgressors of earthly laws (XXIV, 14 [3]).

Chief among Montesquieu's utilitarian concerns was that a religion should inculcate proper morality among its practitioners. "Dogma is disputed, and morals are not practiced at all," Montesquieu lamented in the *Pensées*, and "this is because it is difficult to practice morals and very easy to dispute dogma." [81] So convinced, however, was Montesquieu of the potential moralizing and humanizing benefits of religion that he vigorously opposed Bayle's contention that it is better to have no religion at all than a bad one. Even an idolatrous religion, Montesquieu contends, is preferable to atheism, since even a false religion is the best guarantee of the probity of men (XXIV, 2 [3]). And Montesquieu is particularly impressed with the moderating influence of religion on heads of

[81] *Pensée* 2112 (481. I, p. 402): 1730–31.

state. "A prince who loves and fears religion," he writes, "is a lion, who stoops to the hand that strokes, or to the voice that appeases him. . . . He who has no religion at all is that terrible animal who perceives his liberty only when he tears in pieces and when he devours" (XXIV, 2 [2]).

In addition to stressing the benefits of proper morality, Montesquieu also envisioned the question of religious utility in terms of the economic necessity all peoples face of feeding themselves. However otherworldly its eventual goal, religion must not compromise life here and now. "Penances ought to be joined with the idea of labor, not with that of idleness" (XXIV, 12), he writes, and he is equally convinced that a religion ought not to establish too many religious holidays that might interfere with labor and commerce, particularly in the Protestant north where livelihood is wrested from nature only with considerable labor (XXIV, 23 [4]). Furthermore, religion ought not to impose overly contemplative ideals. Men who spend the whole day praying do not make productive husbandmen. A whole nation of contemplative clerics would surely starve. Such convictions led Montesquieu to question the wisdom of the five daily prayers of Islam as well as the practice of monasticism in Western Catholicism (XXIV, 11; XIV, 7).

In Book XXV, chapter 1, of *The Spirit of Laws*, Montesquieu advances interesting insights on the subject of the psychology of religion. Absent for the most part is the famous wit with which, in the *Persian Letters*, he had slashed through accepted religious beliefs and ceremonials — *The Spirit of Laws* was, after all, a wholly serious enterprise — but there was sufficient novelty to irritate the orthodox. The chief objection was that Montesquieu tended to reduce the popularity of religions to certain, readily explicable aspects of their psychological appeal. "The different religions of the world," he wrote, "do not give to those who profess them equal motives of attachment." Their appeal depends upon whether they agree with "the turn of thought and perceptions of mankind" (XXV, 2 [1]). Montesquieu began his psychology of religion by weighing the relative attractiveness of pagan religions possessing numerous deities against that of a monotheistic religion such as Christianity, with an elevated, spiritual Deity. Whereas the polytheistic religions appeal to the senses, the monotheistic religions appeal more to the intellect. Some men take pride, Montesquieu suggests, in being able to conceptualize an abstract God, and these men will accordingly find a monotheistic religion to their liking. Furthermore, a monotheistic religion, such as Catholicism, that also compensates the senses with images of saints or bits of relics, can further augment its appeal.

Also greatly contributing to the attractiveness of any given religion, according to Montesquieu, is the restriction of promised rewards to the followers of that religion alone. Such a doctrinal stipulation provides a feeling of exclusiveness that people find very comforting. They come to feel themselves truly chosen. A doctrine of both rewards and punishments also increases the psychological attractiveness of a religion, according to Montesquieu. Striving to reach Heaven while seeking to avoid Hell constitutes precisely the sort of tangible goal people find most appealing. A call to morality is also an inducement to religion. Men may not be addicted to morality as a matter of actual conduct, but the command to be moral is one all men crave to hear. Stage a moral drama and you will attract a wide audience. Portray base values, and you will surely displease. Men also derive pleasure from the habitual practice of certain religious ceremonies that soothe by their very perfunctoriness. Finally, religion, according to Montesquieu, is not without aspects of the publicly staged spectacle. Surround its practice with pomp and riches, and followers will likely be attracted (XV, 2 [2–9]).

There was clearly much in Books XXIV and XXV of *The Spirit of Laws* to arouse the wrath of the orthodox. Montesquieu's ecclesiastical critics saw only subterfuge in his contention that since he was not a divine, but a political writer, he could "advance things which are not otherwise true, than as they correspond with a worldly manner of thinking, not as considered in their relation to truths of a more sublime nature" (XXIV, 1 [3]). He was not to be allowed such freedom. The sociological and psychological approach to religion evident in Books XXIV and XXV was judged offensive, and so too was Montesquieu's adoption of an evolutionary perspective toward religion in Book II, chapter 2. Here Montesquieu had suggested, as David Hume was to affirm slightly later in his *Natural History of Religion* (1757), that the capacity to conceptualize a monotheistic God was a gradual achievement rather than a capacity innate in all men since birth. Primitive man's initial ideas, Montesquieu suggested, would be practical, not abstract, and would not include belief in a Deity. Montesquieu would give religion, then, an earthly rather than a divine history. The qualifying statement that the belief in a Deity, although not first in order among natural laws, was first in importance did little to take away the sting of his general remarks, and *The Spirit of Laws* was placed on the Papal Index in November 1751.

FORMS OF GOVERNMENT

Introductory

Montesquieu's eighteenth-century image was that of a political philosopher classifying forms of government. His analysis of re-

publics, monarchies, and despotisms, and of the English combination of democracy, aristocracy, and monarchy insured a large and
enthusiastic readership for his work. The English were flattered by
his eulogy of their constitution, the Americans were captivated by
the wisdom of separating executive, legislative, and judicial
power, and the nobility in France were much taken by the glowing
constitutional role Montesquieu had awarded them as the *corps
intermédiaires* stabilizing the realm. To Montesquieu's contemporaries *The Spirit of Laws* possessed the appeal of a compendium
of political knowledge, a comprehensive encyclopedia of politics.
No reader can fail to be struck by the variety of polities with which
Montesquieu was conversant. He makes use of political data as
divergent as the Athens of Solon, the Rome of Sulla, the Carthage
of Hannibal, the Sparta of Lycurgus, the Peru of Atahualpa, the
Mexico of Montezuma, the Spain of Ferdinand and Isabella, the
France of Richelieu, the England of Cromwell, the Russia of
Peter the Great, and the Pennsylvania of William Penn. Some
among his contemporaries simply concluded that Montesquieu had
written the best available contemporary treatise on politics and
forms of government. Horace Walpole remarked that *The Spirit of
Laws* was "the best book that ever was written,"[82] and even
Thomas Jefferson, who came to distrust Montesquieu's praise for
monarchical government and for the nobility, once wrote that
whereas in economics Adam Smith is generally recommended, in
politics and government Montesquieu's treatise enjoys a similar
status.[83]

---

[82] H. Walpole to H. Mann, January 10, 1750, in *Letters of Horace Walpole* (Oxford,
1903–1905), II, p. 419, quoted by Shackleton, p. 357.

[83] "Jefferson to Randolph," New York, May 30, 1790, in *The Writings of Thomas
Jefferson* (Memorial ed.), VIII, 31. Quoted by Paul M. Spurlin, *Montesquieu in
America, 1760–1801* (Baton Rouge: Louisiana State University Press, 1940), p. 96.

Montesquieu identified three basic forms of government: republics, monarchies, and despotisms. (The republican form he further subdivided into democracies and aristocracies, but since he regarded aristocracy as an imperfect form of democracy, this analysis will concentrate on the latter.) Democratic governments rest on three chief supports: political virtue, equality, and frugality. Political virtue induces citizens to place public needs above private interests, a rough sort of equality is maintained, and consumption is held to frugal levels so that greed does not undermine loyalty to the state. In monarchical states, stability derives from the existence of honor, inequality, and luxury. Those of exalted rank and station strive to uphold their distinctions and prerogatives, inequality is unchallenged, and consumption is maintained at conspicuous levels. Finally, in despotic states, there is, as in democracies, a rough sort of equality, but it is only an equality of subjection. The despot is all, and the people are nothing. Despotic power is unchecked, Montesquieu reports, save by tenets of religion.

Montesquieu's three forms of government need be thought of as ideal-types. There was enough data to swamp a mere mechanical compiler, and Montesquieu sought to impose order by seeking the quintessence of each form. The result is that none of his models directly corresponds to any one particular government, whether historical or contemporary. There are elements of empirical description in all three, but each one remains Montesquieu's own theoretical creation. His vision of democracy, for example, is uniquely his own, juxtaposing democratic practices lifted from quite distinct settings (mainly Athens, Rome, and Sparta). And even Montesquieu's discussion of monarchical government, which is modeled primarily on firsthand knowledge of France, contains a dose of wishful thinking concerning the powers and prerogatives of the nobility. We might say that Montesquieu describes France, not precisely as she was in his day, but as he would like her to have been, and this means that the model is not, strictly speaking, empirical. When turning to Montesquieu's portrait of despotism, we need reach the same conclusion. The distance separating him from the Orient could only be partially overcome by books, and as a result his portrait does not correspond to empirical reality. Similarly, Montesquieu's depiction of the English constitution, however influential in its theoretical appeal, is somewhat deficient from the vantage point of precise empirical detail.

Montesquieu's analysis of forms of government was far removed from a mere synthesis of the observations of other political philosophers. He abandoned the threefold Aristotelian schematization based largely on number (kingship, aristocracy, polity, with corresponding debased forms, tyranny, oligarchy, and democracy) and replaced it with a classification based on differences in the structure of societies and in the collective psychology activating each government. The difference between monarchies and despotisms, he makes clear, relates not to the number of those who rule — in each case one individual holds the reins of power — but rather to the type of human passions that set the government in motion and to the nature of the political and social relationships characterizing each society. In monarchies there exist distinct classes, whereas in despotisms all save the despot are on one, equally debased level. And there are other significant points of contrast between Montesquieu and earlier political writers. Whereas Aristotle had distinguished a perfect and a corrupt form of each of his three types of government, Montesquieu broadly distinguished between moderate and immoderate governments. Both republics and monarchies are moderate and therefore worthy of praise, whereas despotisms are immoderate and deserve only censure. And most important of all, Montesquieu recognized that political institutions are in and of themselves lifeless and hollow. They are only as workable as the commitment shown to them. Hence he went a step beyond traditional discussions of governmental institutions to theorize that in each form of government there is a supporting principle activating the "spring" of government and forestalling decline from within. In republics, Montesquieu suggested, this inner dynamic, this *ressort psychologique*, is virtue. In monarchies it is honor. In despotisms it is fear.

Democracy

Like such theorists as Machiavelli, Harrington, and Sidney, Montesquieu was captivated by classical models of republicanism. Ancient Athens, Rome, and Sparta were his chief inspiration, and for documentation he relied upon Plato, Aristotle, Plutarch, Livy, Dionysius Halicarnassus, Xenophon, and Strabo. From these and other writers he distilled what he considered the best features of democracy. Other data he was content to ignore, such as, for example, the existence of slavery in the classical republics and the prevalence of factions in democracies — a point he had emphasized in the *Pensées*. Nor did he pay much attention to chronology, since he was not writing a history of ancient democracy, but rather extracting an ideal of democracy from ancient data. He analyzed all of the diverse data, decided what ideally epitomizes democracy, and introduced, to illustrate his points, material drawn from quite disparate historical settings. This method drew upon empirical data but resulted in a rationalist model uniquely Montesquieu's own.

The principle, or life-force, of democratic governments, according to Montesquieu, is virtue — not Christian, moral virtue, but political virtue: love of country, love of equality, self-sacrificing patriotism, in short, a wholehearted, public-spirited

devotion to the commonweal, implying a coalescence of private
and public interest nearly as close as that later envisioned by Rousseau in *The Social Contract* (1762) (III, 3; IV, 5; V, 2). Montesquieu conceives no conflict between the interests of the individual
citizen and the democratic government he serves. The individual
citizen is to love and serve his government instinctively, always
placing its interests first, and the citizen is in turn to be served by
his government. To insure that private individuals readily perceive
the public good, the republic is to be kept small (VIII, 16), and
since inequality and luxury undermine patriotism, strict inheritance laws are to guard against anyone's amassing excessive wealth
(VII, 2). Furthermore, the parcels of land are to be kept small in
order to encourage frugality (V, 6 [1]; XVIII, 1). In addition, it
will be a happy coincidence if the soil is not so excessively fertile as
to enable farmers to enjoy a life of luxury and ease (XVIII, 4).
Interestingly enough, commerce need not be forbidden. Montesquieu anticipated Weber's belief that the spirit of commerce can be
thrift, and he therefore concluded that commerce need not necessarily destroy the spirit of frugality and equality (V, 6 [3–6]).

Montesquieu's discussion of the institutional framework of
democratic government is unfortunately rather incomplete. One
must piece together relevant information from a presentation that
lacks full explanations.[84] One can gather, however, that there is to
be a senate elected by lot and that this senate is to direct foreign
policy, submit laws for ratification by a popular assembly, and, in
times of crisis or emergency, possess the power to rule for a time
by legislative decree. There is also to be a popular assembly, but it

---

[84] David Lowenthal includes a useful summary in pp. 260–263 of his "Montesquieu
and the Classics: Republican Government in *The Spirit of the Laws*," in *Ancients and
Moderns. Essays on the Tradition of Political Philosophy in Honor of Leo Strauss*, ed. by
Joseph Cropsey (New York: Basic Books, 1964), pp. 258–284.

is difficult to determine what Montesquieu believed its exact functions should be. The precise nature of the magistracies or executive
officers of the democratic state is similarly unspecified, although
we do learn that civil magistracies attended with great expense
should be elected rather than chosen by lot. The magistracies are to
be restricted to the wealthiest classes, since their influence is less
likely to be bought. Finally, there are to be judges, but the sole
function specifically attributed to them is that of assessing the
conduct of magistrates elected by lot (II, 2 [5, 16, 21, 23]).

The *Pensées* reveal that Montesquieu's enthusiasm for democracy was tempered by his realization that this form of government
is prone to factions as destructive to liberty as any wrathful prince.
Caught between two warring factions, no man can remain neutral.
"The moderate man is hated by both sides."[85] Hence he who
chooses no side is sure to have enemies, and he is guaranteed of no
friends. Support for one side or the other is equally dangerous,
however, since even the dominant faction must have its martyrs.
There is, in short, no refuge from the destructive effects of faction. And the republic fares no better than the citizen: "When
there are factions in a republic, the weakest party is no more
overpowered than is the strongest; it is the Republic that is overwhelmed."[86]

This fear on Montesquieu's part that the popular element may
render democracy tumultuous, produce factions, and disrupt liberty led him to stress the necessity to obey the magistrate who
represents the force of law. Hence in Montesquieu's view, freedom in democracies is by no means equivalent to license. The
magistrate's authority is judged to be as crucial to stability within
the state as is the father's authority within the family. Since

[85] *Pensée* 1802 (32. I, f. 35): 1728.
[86] *Pensée* 1816 (371. I, f. 358): 1729.

anarchy is contrary to natural law, the power of the magistrate
must be judged at least consistent with, if not actually sanctioned
by, natural law.[87] Hence Montesquieu praises the idea of "a perfect subordination between the citizens and the magistrate" and
cites with pleasure Xenophon's allusion to the Spartans running
when the magistrate calls, in contrast with the rich Athenian who
would not like to be thought dependent on the magistrate (V, 7
[12]).

Montesquieu thought the authority of the magistrate would
likely be ignored unless proper emphasis was placed, both at home
and at school, on the preservation of ancient customs, the subordination of young to old, the need for parental authority, and the
benefits of moral conduct. Hence his depiction of democracy as an
ideal-type places more emphasis on "private" virtue than is often
recognized. If he made "political" virtue, or patriotism, the "principle" of republican government, he also stressed the importance
of virtue in the traditional moral sense. If he protested to his
ecclesiastical critics in the *Defense of the Spirit of Laws* (1750) that
he had not meant to attribute more morality to democracies than to
monarchies, since he had attributed "political" not private virtue to
democracies, he did nevertheless portray democracy in moral
dress. He did not speak in terms of Christian ideals of morality in
the service to some higher ideal, but he emphasized morality
nonetheless as good in and of itself, both for the individual and for
the democratic state the moral citizen serves. Accordingly, the
existence of censors in democracies is forthrightly advocated (V, 19
[15]), and women in particular are counseled to retain their virtue
for the good of the republic. And particularly praiseworthy in
Montesquieu's view is a custom of the Samnites granting to that
young man who had displayed the best qualities and the most

[87] *Pensée* 1848 (883. II, f. 6): 1734–35.

service to his country the first choice of a wife from among an assembly of the young girls of the whole nation (VII, 16).

The modern reader will not likely regard Montesquieu's portrait of democracy as particularly liberal. It is based on ancient not modern models, and it fails to enthrone the standards of equality we have come to expect as heirs of the French Revolution and of nineteenth-century liberals. The existence of classes based on degrees of wealth is accepted (II, 2 [14, 16]), and it is apparent that Montesquieu expects the best born and the best educated to guide the rudest and the least tutored. For offices not decided by lot, the suffrage is to be public rather than by secret ballot so that the higher classes can guide the lower (II, 2 [25]). And not all citizens are to be eligible for the highest public office. In fact, Montesquieu praises Solon's restriction of eligibility for the magistracies of Athens to the highest three of the four classes he established (II, 2 [16]), and he misses few opportunities to point out the inadequacies of the masses. "The public business," he writes, "must be carried on with a certain motion, neither too quick nor too slow. But the motion of the people is always either too remiss or too violent. Sometimes with a hundred thousand arms they overturn all before them; and sometimes with a hundred thousand feet they creep like insects" (II, 2 [13]).

Some will perceive in these and similar sentiments only the legitimate bias of a man influenced by his own exalted status in French society, whereas others will blame Montesquieu for feeding reactionary currents by supporting the privileged classes, thereby impeding the healthy rise of the bourgeoisie. This is surely not the proper forum for this debate, but criticism of Montesquieu should perhaps be tempered by his own remark that "to apply the idea of a present time to distant ages is the most fruitful source of error" (XXX, 14). Many theorists and statesmen in Montesquieu's day shared his bias against what they considered the unruly, anarchic populace — unschooled, rural, and crude. "Direct" democracy as Montesquieu portrayed it in *The Spirit of Laws* represented no serious option in the eighteenth century. James Madison, for example, carefully distinguished between a system of representatives insuring that the capable govern — he termed this "republicanism" — and "democracy" as the ancients practiced it and as Montesquieu described it, a word that conveyed a pejorative sense of instability and even anarchy resulting from granting the people too great a role.[88] Even the supreme democrat among the philosophes, Jean-Jacques Rousseau, remarked that "there is no government so liable to civil war and internecine strife as is democracy or popular government," and in Book III of *The Social Contract* (1762) he advocated "elective aristocracy" over pure democracy, remarking that "it is the best and most natural arrangement for the wisest to govern the multitude."[89] There are, of course, passages more flattering to the humblest citizens, and Rousseau does eventually oppose representatives as usurping the functions of the people, but his reservations concerning the political capacity of the common people do help to place Montesquieu's own discussion of direct democracy in their proper historical context. In short, it would be unfair to expect Montesquieu to have written like John Stuart Mill in an age when the transforming prospects of universal education and widespread equality were little imagined.

[88] See for example the well-known *Federalist Paper* No. 10, in which Madison discusses how republics curb the factions to which pure democracies are prone.

[89] *The Social Contract*, trans. by Maurice Cranston (Baltimore: Penguin Books 1968), Book III, chaps. 4–5, pp. 113, 115.

Monarchy

Montesquieu identifies monarchy as the second ideal-type of government, and here his portrait is based largely on eighteenth-century France. The Estates-General goes unmentioned, seemingly a forgotten organ of the body politic — it had not been convened since 1614 — but the remainder of the discussion, and particularly the allusion to the parlements under the rubric "depositaries of laws," corresponds roughly to France. The altruism attributed by Montesquieu to the nobility, however, renders his portrait rather more a blueprint for an ideal France than an objective description of her actual condition.

The most striking aspect of Montesquieu's portrait of monarchy is his identification of monarchical stability with nobiliary and ecclesiastical privilege. At a time when physiocratic reformers were recommending the modernization of the French government through the overthrow of feudal rights, Montesquieu was providing the first two estates of France with a carefully reasoned apologia of their function as vital *corps intermédiaires* precluding the extremes of both absolutism and democracy. Just as the House of Lords played a critical balancing role in England's mixed government, so too, in Montesquieu's view, did the nobility and the Church, along with the privileged corporations and the chartered municipalities, function in pure monarchies as a *rang intermédiaire* stabilizing the realm. The preservation of the nobility is judged just as crucial to monarchy as Charles I had judged bishops indispensable to Stuart rule in England. Hence Montesquieu's well-known conclusion: *"point de monarque, point de noblesse; point de noblesse, point de monarque"* (II, 4 [2]).

Montesquieu believed that the preservation of the prerogatives of the nobility assures both common liberty and a check on the monarch, and he argued his case persuasively. He understood the principle of monarchy to be honor. Pride in one's rank (III, 7), the desire to perform actions "shining," "great," and "extraordinary" (IV, 2), consideration of the whole world as one's censor (V, 19), the ambition to distinguish oneself in the eyes of one's compatriots (IV, 2) — these are the psychological traits leading the nobility to exercise its prerogatives and thereby prevent the concentration of excessive power in the hands of the king. There is more to honor, however, according to Montesquieu's definition, than glorification of one's own position in society to fulfill an ingrained psychological need. Willingness to support the Crown in all save dishonorable actions, and a readiness to serve one's monarch in a military capacity, are also involved (IV, 2). Only those "who watch day and night over the welfare of the empire" are deserving of honor (XIII, 20 [3]), writes Montesquieu. Wealth alone confers no honor. Albert Sorel communicated a sense of the altruistic aspect of honor as Montesquieu portrayed it in defining honor as "love of the monarch and of privilege — a love that causes men to serve the monarch, and by their service to restrain him."[90]

The *mentalité monarchique* undoubtedly makes lesser demands on the citizen than does the *mentalité republicaine*. Whereas the political virtue of democracies requires "self-renunciation, which is ever arduous and painful" (IV, 5 [1]), the monarchical state runs smoothly upon the baser human passions of self-esteem and regard for one's own interests. In reading Montesquieu on monarchy, in fact, one is reminded of Adam Smith's theory of en-

[90] Albert Sorel, *Montesquieu*, trans. by Melville B. Anderson and Edward Playfair Anderson (Port Washington, N.Y.: Kennikat Press, Inc., 1969, orig. ed. 1888), p. 118.

lightened self-interest whereby each individual's desire to seek his own profit automatically furthers the common good. "Each individual advances the public good," Montesquieu remarks, "while he only thinks of promoting his own interest" (III, 7 [3–4]). "Hence in well-regulated monarchies, they are almost all good subjects, and very few good men; for to be a good man, a good intention is necessary" (III, 6 [2]). Hence the honor of monarchies is false honor. It is honor directed primarily to one's own good. But it serves its purpose nonetheless. Thus, "in the nicest machines, art has reduced the number of movements, springs, and wheels" (III, 5 [1]).

Montesquieu's depiction of the ideal-type of monarchy cannot be judged void of all polemical intent. Eighteenth-century France was divided into two ideological camps, each girding its loins with historical data to prove it had correctly solved the riddle of France's feudal past, and Montesquieu's uncompromising defense of the nobility made him an influential proponent of the political ideology known as the *thèse nobiliaire*. Adhering roughly to a path already hewn by Comte de Boulainvilliers, in his *Histoire de l'ancien gouvernement de la France* (1727), Montesquieu attempted to establish, through painstaking research — he said this portion of his labors turned his hair white — Germanic rather than Roman origins for the French monarchy (XXVIII, XXX, XXXI). The Frankish institution of monarchy, he wrote, from which the present French state was directly descended, had been a limited kingship with the nobility welcomed as active partners of the Crown. Hence the *thèse nobiliaire* conclusion that there had been no legal precedent for the absolutism of Louis XIV and his successors. Proponents of the *thèse royale* disagreed. They maintained that the nobility had illegally usurped powers from a Crown originally based on the Roman concept of *imperium*. It was time, they argued, to end the state of siege by a feudal nobility on a Crown so beleaguered it could barely act.[91]

According to Montesquieu, the crucial element in the monarchical constitution were the *dépots des lois* corresponding to the Parlements of France. He did not refer to the Parlements by name, but his support for their role in the French monarchy is transparent in his statement in Book II that "it is not enough to have intermediate powers in a monarchy. There must be also a depositary of the laws. This depositary can only be the political bodies that announce the laws when they are made and recall them when they are forgotten" (II, 4 [10]). Montesquieu's cautious approval of the right of the Parlements to register the Crown's edicts before they become law, barely visible in the phrase "announce the laws when they are made," contained a wealth of meaning to his French compatriots, and his work became the Bible of the *parlementaires*. Louis XIV had curbed the much debated right of remonstrance, but the Duc of Orléans, regent of Louis XV, had reinstated it in 1715 in return for parlementary support in altering a provision in Louis XIV's will. The result was that throughout the eighteenth century France experienced an aristocratic resurgence that brought Crown and robe nobility into frequent conflict. In the *Persian Letters* Montesquieu had expressed his satisfaction with the action of Orléans;[92] he remained a firm advocate of parlementary privilege throughout his life.

In point of historical fact, proponents of the *thèse royale* — including Voltaire — had the better of the historical argument, and one can argue that by supporting the claims of feudal privilege, Montesquieu contributed to the intransigence of the

---

[91] The authoritative statement of the *thèse royale* was the Abbé Dubos's *Histoire critique de l'établissement de la monarchie Française* (1734).

[92] *Persian Letter* XCII.

Parlements during the crucial years of Louis XVI's reign (1774–1793) when financial reforms, had they not been blocked by the Parlement of Paris, might conceivably have averted the deadlock leading to the call of the Estates-General and the rapid series of events that soon engulfed France in revolution. It would be erroneous, however, to characterize Montesquieu as a mere apologist for his own class, although Mathiez and Althusser have repeated a charge Voltaire made in the eighteenth century.[93] It was logical for Montesquieu to have drawn his model from France, and given the humiliation and even emasculation of the French nobility and the Parlements under Louis XIV, he undoubtedly regarded defense of the nobility as a liberal doctrine intended to save France from a return to despotism. Furthermore, Montesquieu was no doubt sincere in his belief that a balanced monarchical constitution requires a strong nobiliary component, and although normally no defender of ecclesiastical privilege, he welcomed a strong Church in monarchical government as part of the *corps intermédiaires* averting tyranny. In short, Montesquieu arrived at his uncompromising defense of the role of the Parlements as *dépôts des lois* through constitutional conviction as much as through personal ambition or family pride — in spite of his family's possession of a parlementary post. The chief factor distinguishing monarchy from despotism is the existence of fundamental laws binding sovereign and subjects alike. And the need to safeguard these fundamental laws rationalizes the role of the nobility of the robe.

Not being inclined by nature to utopian flights of the imagina-

[93] Albert Mathiez, "La place de Montesquieu dans l'histoire des doctrines politiques du XVIIIe siècle," in *Annales Historiques de la Révolution Française*, VII (1930), pp. 97–112. Louis Althusser, *Montesquieu. La politique et l'histoire* (Paris: Presses Universitaires de France, 1959). For Voltaire, see for example, p. 512 of the dialogue *L'A, B.C.* in *Philosophical Dictionary*, trans. by Peter Gay (New York: Harcourt, Brace & World, Inc., 1962).

tion, Montesquieu was prone to make the best of things taken as they are. And given "the nature of things" in France of his day, the *thèse nobiliaire* was certainly no less misguided than the equally uncompromising *thèse royale*. Proponents of the royal thesis rested their hopes for freedom on the benign supposition that they might be blessed with a king at once obedient to fundamental laws and clement toward his subjects. Given the experience of the reign of Louis XIV, it is perhaps understandable that Montesquieu preferred to rest his hopes for a moderate government on the existence of privileged groups whose sense of honor renders them a suitable counterweight to the Crown's power. Furthermore, Montesquieu clearly regarded the prospects for liberty as just as favorable in a monarchical state with a pronounced aristocratic component as in popular states where the people rule. He expressed the point epigrammatically in one of his *Pensées*: "Liberty is no farther removed from the throne than from a senate."[94]

Both Montesquieu and proponents of the *thèse royale* can be faulted in having possessed so little regard for the political capacities and fundamental rights of the third estate, who were soon to gain the upper hand. If the ancient democracies were based on a substantial degree of slave labor that freed the citizens for public duties, the ideal monarchical state of Montesquieu's description presupposed the subservience of the third estate. One may assume Montesquieu's advocacy of the fair treatment of all in dealings with the criminal law (see Book VI), but monarchical politics are clearly to be the preserve only of the Crown and privileged classes. One seeks in vain in Montesquieu's discussion of monarchy for any expressed concern at the paltry political role of commoners and middle-class men. He specifically warns against the transferral to commoners of any rights enjoyed by the

[94] *Pensée* 631 (884. II, f. 6): 1734–35.

privileged (V, 9 [7]), and he rests his hopes for stability on the balance of power between Crown and intermediate bodies, chief of which are the *noblesse* and the Church (II, 4 [1–8]). Absent from monarchy as he defines it is one of the crucial sides of the triangle stabilizing England's "mixed constitution." There is no call for an assembly of the people, whether on the model of the Estates-General such as France formerly convoked, or a bicameral legislature along the lines of the English Parliament. Hence, from the vantage point of modern times, his portrait of monarchy cannot help seeming excessively weighted toward the prerogatives of a class that was soon to be displaced by an emerging capitalist bourgeoisie.

Despotism

Evident throughout Montesquieu's political writings is a profound distrust of unchecked political power. The cycle of Troglodyte history presented in *Persian Letters* X–XIV constitutes a clear warning that self-government and self-restraint are far preferable to the yielding of power even to a philosopher-king, and Montesquieu's treatment of Caesar in the *Considerations on the Greatness of the Romans and Their Decline* serves the same end. Furthermore, it is surely his dread of the abuse of political power that moves Montesquieu to characterize Caesar as the villain of the late republican period, as a devious and power-hungry general who destroyed senatorial power and deserved the assassination that proved his eventual fate.[95] No better a reception in Montesquieu's writings has Richelieu, the architect of French absolutism, who emerges as a man "bewitched with the love of despotic power" (V, 10 [2]).

Montesquieu's passionate denunciation of despotic government,

---

[95] *Considérations*, chap. XI, in Nagel, I, C, pp. 419–431, and in Pléiade, II, pp. 123–132.

steeped in the conviction that a constitution without intermediary powers between king and populace fails to provide the power-checking-power formula that forestalls tyranny, stood as a warning of the fate that awaits all governments that fail to moderate political power. Montesquieu considered the threat of despotism in monarchies omnipresent. Monarchical power may, like a river, drop out of sight and run underground for a time, but there always exists the threat that it will rise above ground to sweep away everything in its path.[96] Without conscious effort, despotism will prevail. It is the most natural form of government, since it is founded on the basest sort of passions. "To form a moderate government, it is necessary to combine the several powers; to rule, temper, and set them in motion; to give as it were, ballast to one, in order to enable it to resist another. This is a masterpiece of legislation, rarely produced by hazard, and seldom attained by prudence" (V, 14 [30]). Thus it is not surprising that the English system of moderating power captured Montesquieu's attention.

Montesquieu's portrait of despotism only roughly corresponds to the Asian and Middle Eastern kingdoms he thought he was describing, and the exaggerated contours of his portrait no doubt account for its rhetorical appeal. In despotic governments as Montesquieu portrays them, all power is centered in one source. There is no healthy distribution of power among competing bodies such as the English constitution displayed. Sovereignty remains substantially undivided, and, as Émile Durkheim remarked, this gives despotism "the aspect of a monster, in which only the head is alive, having absorbed all the energies of the organism."[97] What is left of the body politic after the despot's appetite for power has

---

[96] *Persian Letter* CXXXVI.
[97] Émile Durkheim, *Montesquieu and Rousseau* (Ann Arbor, 1960), p. 31.

been satiated cowers in fear that is so widespread as to constitute the very principle of government.

The absence of a complex legal system safeguarding liberty is the chief distinguishing feature of despotism. Since the liberty of the subject is directly proportional to the complexity of laws safeguarding it, there can be no freedom in despotisms. One man decrees and all the rest obey. There exist no rights to be defended and no fundamental laws to be upheld. There are no presentations of grievances and there is no liberty. In Turkey, writes Montesquieu, "the pasha, after a quick hearing, orders which party he pleases to be bastinadoed, and then sends them about their business" (VI, 2 [3]). A despot will always seek to rule without laws, Montesquieu observed, and he believed that both Caesar and Cromwell demonstrated this fact. Although a comprehensive legal system may be frustrating in its complexity, it is far better to support the plodding legal processes than to have none at all.

The absence of complex social and class gradations is another aspect of despotic government. In despotisms there are no noblemen constituting *pouvoirs intermédiaires* that preclude excessive power in the head of government. There exist no subtle gradations of classes, each one checking the others. All save the despot constitute one class. All are equal, having been flattened at the bottom of the social and political ladder by the oppressive weight of despotic power. Without any privileged classes to check its sway, despotic power is unchecked and ruthless. There are no narrow channels through which power must flow; the despot's reach is unlimited, his touch is deadly. Void of the noisy conflict that marks a healthy polity where power is checked by power, despotisms are characterized by the silence of the cowed, by an airy tranquillity resembling the silence of cities the enemy is about to occupy.[98]

[98] *Pensée* 1822 (809. I, p. 517): 1735–36.

Equally tragic is the debasement of human nature that inevitably transpires in a despotism. Neither goodness nor excellence is fostered since neither is rewarded. "Despotic government obstructs the talents of the subjects and of great men as the power of men obstructs the talents of women."[99] Despotisms are "nations that live in slavery, where men are like beasts, whose lot is only obedience and insinct."[100] "When we want to break a horse, we take care not to let him change his master, his lesson, or his pace. Thus an impression is made on his brain by two or three motions, and no more" (VI, 14 [2]). With such words as these does Montesquieu depict the lot of those so unfortunate as to reside in a despotic government. Despotism, he believed, "is productive of the most dreadful calamities to human nature," and were that debased form of government to find its way into Europe "human nature would be exposed . . . even in this beautiful part of the world, to the insults with which she has been abused in the other three" (II, 4 [6]).

The English Constitution

Daily confronted with the excesses of Bourbon absolutism, French political philosophers were naturally concerned with the problem of controlling political power. If the reign of Louis XV was slightly less oppressive than that of Louis XIV, who had emasculated *noblesse d'épée* and *noblesse de robe* alike, eighteenth-century France was no liberal state with guaranteed rights and freedoms for all. Across the Channel, however, the English had created a more liberal state. The combined impact of two seventeenth-century revolutions had established a constitutional monarchy enthroning a degree of political liberty unknown to Frenchmen. Throughout

[99] *Pensée* 1820 (596. I, f. 446v.): 1730–31.
[100] *Pensée* 1825 (466. I, f. 395): 1730–31.

the seventeenth and eighteenth centuries the English Parliament was making constitutional headway while the French Estates-General remained unconvened, a forgotten organ of the body politic finally revived only in 1788 when compromise was nearly a dead letter and substantial change widely desired. In short, if the English government of the eighteenth century hardly wins the praise of modern twentieth-century democrats, and if it took two electorate-expanding reform bills, in 1832 and 1867, and two acts of Parliament, in 1911 and 1947, reducing the House of Lords, to bring real "democracy" to Britain, the English system was nevertheless a cut above the top-heavy French absolutism that came crashing down in the Revolution of 1789.

It is ironic that it should have fallen to a Frenchman to explain the British constitution to British subjects, and yet this is precisely the case. So authoritative was Montesquieu's analysis considered that it was amplified by William Blackstone in his *Commentaries on the Laws of England*, 4 vols. (1765–1769), adopted by De Lolme in his *Constitution de L'Angleterre* (1771) and twice reprinted in translation as a separate volume in 1750 and 1781.[101] So closely identified with Montesquieu's contemporary fame was his portrait of English government that some among his countrymen judged him guilty of a lack of patriotism in lavishing such attention upon the British. Montesquieu never recommended the English system for export, and he clearly believed the French monarchy capable of arriving at liberty (XI, 7), but he could not help admiring the British solution to the vexing problem of moderating power.

[101] *Two Chapters of a Celebrated French Work, intitled, De l'esprit des loix, translated into English. One, treating of the Constitution of England; another of the Character and Manners which result from this Constitution* (Edinburgh: Hamilton & Balfour, 1750). *A View of the English Constitution. By . . . Baron de Montesquieu. Being a Translation* [by F. Masères] *of the Sixth Chapter of the Eleventh Book of his . . . L'Esprit des Loix.* (London, 1781.)

Like Voltaire, whose visit to England slightly preceded his own, Montesquieu enjoyed firsthand knowledge of British society. Arriving on the yacht of Lord Chesterfield in November 1729, he remained in England for eighteen months. Interestingly enough, his first impressions, as recorded in his "Notes on England," convey little of the complimentary tone that characterizes Book XI, chapter 6, of *The Spirit of Laws*. He found little beauty in London, save the parks, was horrified by the ill-repair of English streets, and found her citizens cold and unapproachable. As for British politics, he regretted that a pervasive desire for riches had offset any interest in honor or virtue, lamented that corruption was widespread, and quipped that every vote was for sale given the proper price. He accordingly concluded that the English do not deserve their liberty, so ready are they to sell it to the king.[102]

When it came to composing his memorable portrait of British government, however, set forth in Book XI, chapter 6, of *The Spirit of Laws*, such negative judgments gave way to the shining truth that the English had achieved freedom while others remained yet in bondage. English freedom, Montesquieu concluded, rested upon two chief supports: the substantial "separation" of executive, legislative, and judicial power, and the "mixture" of monarchy, aristocracy, and democracy in Crown, Lords, and Commons. The theory of the mixed constitution was a commonplace by the eighteenth century — Polybius had given it a classic formulation in the sixth book of his history of Rome — but Montesquieu did much to create the theory of separate powers, though seeds of it can be found both in Locke's *Second Treatise* and in various numbers of Bolingbroke's *Craftsman*.

It was with forthright advocacy of the theory of separation that

[102] *Notes sur L'Angleterre*, in Nagel, III, 283–288, and in Pléiade, I, pp. 875–878; 880.

Montesquieu began his analysis of English government. "When the legislative and executive powers are united in the same person, or in the same body of magistrates," he wrote, "there can be no liberty" (XI, 6 [4]). "Again, there is no liberty, if the power of judging be not separated from the legislative and executive powers" (XI, 6 [5]). And finally, "Miserable indeed would be the case, were the same man, or the same body . . . to exercise those three powers, that of enacting laws, that of executing the public resolutions, and that of judging the crimes or differences of individuals" (XI, 6 [6]). It becomes evident, however, that these passages convey a political ideal rather than a political necessity, for Montesquieu asserts that where executive and legislative power are joined, one can still have a moderate government — *so long as* the judiciary power is at least separate (XI, 6 [7]). Thus was he able to keep such European monarchies as his own native France within the syllabus of defensible kingdoms.

Montesquieu's chief interest in Book XI, chapter 6, of *The Spirit of Laws* is not actually the separation of powers but rather England's "mixed" constitution involving the complex interrelationships between Crown, Lords, and Commons. The transition from the rather brief discussion of "separating" powers to his fuller analysis of England's mixed constitution is the assertion that, compared with King and Parliament, the judiciary power is "in some measure next to nothing" (*en quelque facon nulle*) (XI, 6 [31]). Montesquieu's ideas concerning judicial power within the English system encompassed only the jury system involved in criminal and civil cases of law. He was not thinking in terms of a coequal branch of government such as the United States Supreme Court has become, and he therefore concentrated mainly on how England combined elements of monarchy, aristocracy, and democracy in her executive and legislative institutions.

According to the theory of England's mixed constitution as presented by Montesquieu, the democratic and aristocratic elements of the state, that is, Commons and Lords, mutually temper one another as dual participants in a bicameral Parliament. These two legislative bodies are in turn checked by the Crown's right of veto (XI, 6 [55]). And the Crown is in turn checked by the legislature's right to impeach the Crown's ministers — but not the king himself — and by their right to investigate how the laws they have enacted are being carried out. All three components of the constitution, democratic, aristocratic, and monarchical, are to work together in the enactment of successful legislation. They must "move in concert" (XI, 6 [56]). Were one of the three to act entirely on its own and cease to be checked by the other two, the crucial triangle circumscribing liberty would be broken. Montesquieu perceived the virtue of England's mixed constitution, then, in the balance between the king, the aristocrats, and the populace, which enabled England to avoid the vices peculiar to monarchy, aristocracy, and democracy as individual forms of government.

The idea of the mixed constitution as employed by Montesquieu was a mechanical model well suited to a Newtonian age. The images are those of attraction and repulsion. Any tendency for one component of the mixed constitution to attract all power to itself must be counteracted by a carefully structured equipoise of competing powers. Crown, Lords, and Commons at times impinge upon one another in the legislative process, but they are for the most part to gravitate in their own orbits. The lines of force between the three must not be fundamentally altered, or else the political universe will collapse into one power-heavy center. Equilibrium, constant force, the maintenance of distance — these are the mechanical metaphors that Montesquieu's treatment of the English constitution brings to mind.

Recent scholarly treatment of Montesquieu's theory of the English constitution has stressed that he did not actually advocate the "separation" of powers;[103] and it is true that he did not recommend the rigid and absolute form of separation sometimes attributed to him. He used the actual word *separation* only once (XI, 6 [5]), and he elaborated a number of instances wherein executive, legislative, and judicial power overlap. The Crown's power of veto substantially involves it in the legislative branch, and Parliament's right to investigate the manner in which laws are executed and to impeach the king's ministers causes it to overlap the executive power. Furthermore, the House of Lords functions as a court of law in hearing impeachments, trying one of their own members accused of a crime, or moderating a sentence handed down by a lower court (XI, 6 [49–50]). Nevertheless, Montesquieu surely meant to imply that, compared with a despotic government where all power is wielded by one person, the English government embodied a substantial and clearly recognizable separation of powers. If the powers of King, Parliament, and Bench intermingle, these bodies are nevertheless separate entities possessing identifiable rights and powers as well as distinct personnel. In marked contrast was the situation in France under Louis XIV, where the Crown combined executive and legislative power, leaving the parlements to struggle for a share of legislative power through their much contested right of registering all edicts before they became law. (See p. 69 above.)

Montesquieu did perceive, then, within British government a separation, or distribution, of powers among different bodies sufficiently marked to deserve serious comment. James Madison

---

[103] See, for example, two articles by Charles Eisenmann, "L'Esprit des lois et la séparation des pouvoirs," in *Mélanges R. Carré de Malberg* (Paris, 1933), pp. 163–192, and "La pensée constitutionnelle de Montesquieu," in *Recueil Sirey du bicentenaire de l'Esprit des Lois* (Paris: Recueil Sirey, 1952), pp. 133–160.

well discerned Montesquieu's meaning in remarking that "Montesquieu did not mean that these departments [executive, legislative, and judicial] ought to have no partial agency in or no control over, the acts of each other." He meant only that "where the *whole* power of one department is exercised by the same hands which possess the *whole* power of another department, the fundamental principles of a free constitution are subverted."[104]

The question of whether the English government of the eighteenth century actually displayed even the degree of separation of powers as Montesquieu discerned is a different matter. The deficiency of his analysis, as Bagehot pointed out in his study of the English constitution a century and a quarter later,[105] was that the emergence of cabinet government contradicted even such a moderate degree of separation as Montesquieu envisioned. Under the "inner" cabinet system gradually emerging during the period of Walpole's Whig ascendancy (1721–1742), the head of the majority party in the House of Commons was relied upon by the king to steer affairs in a direction coinciding with the Crown's will. Close contact between the first, or "prime" minister, meant there was less separation between executive and legislative branches than even Montesquieu's account would suggest. In Montesquieu's defense, however, it ought to be admitted that it was far less clear in the eighteenth century than a hundred years later that the gradually evolving cabinet constituted, in Bagehot's words, "a *hyphen* which joins, a *buckle* which fastens, the legislative part of the state to the executive part of the state."[106]

The absence of the cabinet system from Montesquieu's portrait

---

[104] *Federalist Paper* No. 47.

[105] *The English Constitution*. Reprinted from the "Fortnightly Review" (London: Chapman and Hall, 1867).

[106] *Ibid.*, p. 15.

does, nevertheless, render his analysis of English government no more strictly empirical than his discussions of republics, monarchies, and despotisms in Books II through VIII of *The Spirit of Laws*. In both cases, Montesquieu embellished the facts at his disposal, or simply left some out. He was, after all, no slavish copier of minutiae, but rather an independent theorist in his own right. If he made no allusion to cabinet government and preferred to relegate the English party system to Book XIX, chapter 27, he nonetheless fulfilled a useful service in establishing the separation of executive, legislative, and judicial power as a proper goal, broadly conceived, and in characterizing England's "mixed constitution" as a praiseworthy attempt at making power check power to preserve liberty. Furthermore, the theory of separate powers, moderately interpreted, as it was by Montesquieu himself, is not the invalid theorem of politics that some recent commentators have claimed it to be. It is only when the doctrine is interpreted in so rigid a fashion as to bear no similarity to Montesquieu's formulation that it becomes an unworkable idea fit only for theory.

Conclusion

Montesquieu's stature as a major figure in European thought remains secure and was already well established in his own day. Mme. de Tencin epitomized the contemporary adulation when she remarked shortly after publication of the work: "Here is, *mon cher Romain*, what I think about *L'Esprit des Lois*: Philosophy, Reason, Humanity have been brought together to compose this work, and the Graces have taken care to adorn it with erudition. I know of nothing that can compare to it. I have read it eagerly, and I would be vexed to be finished with reading a work that equally satisfies the heart, the wit, and good sense."[107] Even Voltaire,

---

[107] "Mme de Tencin to Montesquieu," December 2, 1748, in Nagel, III, 1148–49.

who frequently criticized the documentation and organization of the work, admitted that *The Spirit of Laws* "should always be precious to men," since Montesquieu "reminds men that they are free, shows mankind the rights it has lost in most of the world, combats superstition, and inspires good morals."[108]

As in the case of Marx a century later, Montesquieu's significance derives in large part from the methods he employed. If Marx was to emphasize the debilitating effects of the division of labor as one component of alienated labor, and the conflict between forces of production and relations of production as the key to explosive socio-economic change, Montesquieu stressed the diverse contributants to the "spirit" of any given legal system, as well as the equilibrium deriving from an historically conditioned balance of contributing elements to what he termed a society's general spirit. And Montesquieu divided these contributing elements into two broad categories: *causes physiques* and *causes morales*.[109] Depending on the particular society in question, the component elements of the *esprit général* will vary, as will the relative weight of physical and moral causes. The more highly developed a society, the less likely it is that climate and other physical causes will be the major factor accounting for that people's laws, government, life-style, and collective psychology. Where men still live in a primitive condition, however, virtually unable to direct and divert the forces of nature, *causes physiques* will exert the preponderant influence (XIX, 4 [2]).

Although not the climatological determinist some have judged him,[110] Montesquieu certainly helped to bring *causes physiques*

---

[108] *L' A, B, C* (1768), in *Philosophical Dictionary*, trans., with an Introduction and Glossary by Peter Gay (New York: Harcourt, Brace & World, Inc., 1962), p. 509.

[109] See above, pp. 26–27.

[110] See above, pp. 48–51.

into the maintream of sociological and historical analysis. Not content to envision societies as shaped exclusively by human will, he stressed the substantial — but not irreversible — influence of climate and other environmental factors upon human societies, and he thereby influenced a plethora of geophysical and climatological theories of the nineteenth and twentieth centuries.[111]

Montesquieu avoided the dogmatic systematizing that characterized the political and social thought of the next century. He made no attempt to strait-jacket the past into a progressist pattern culminating in a projected ideal condition for mankind. He sought not so much a universal solution to the riddle of history as explanations of individual societies observed from the vantage point of the contributing elements of their *esprits généraux*. His was a science of being, rather than a science of becoming, and to the extent that the twentieth century has revolted from the metaphysical systems of the nineteenth century — Kierkegaard's opposition to Hegel presaged the future — Montesquieu's method emerges as more modern, more objective, and more detached than that of the philosopher-metaphysicians of the next century who reduced the complexity of world history to oversimplified patterns.

Certainly part of Montesquieu's significance, in terms of the approaching age of the historical monograph, was his attention to concrete details, evident throughout *The Spirit of Laws*, but particularly in the analysis of feudal law in France in Books XXVIII, XXX, and XXXI, and in that remarkable twenty-first chapter of Book XXIII chronicling various Roman laws with regard to population growth. Montesquieu was no mere antiquarian recorder of

[111] For a very able summation of these developments, see Pitirim Sorokin, *Contemporary Sociological Theories through the First Quarter of the Twentieth Century* (New York: Harper & Row, 1928), pp. 99–193.

unimportant minutiae, however. He transcended that approach as a result of his conviction that facts are meaningless save as they provide the key to the overall structure of a society. And this is undoubtedly what Raymond Aron had in mind when he remarked: "One might say that Montesquieu, exactly like Max Weber, wanted to proceed from the meaningless fact to an intelligible order. This attitude is precisely the one peculiar to the sociologist."[112]

Equally significant in the context of eighteenth-century thought was Montesquieu's refusal to allow theology to define the contours of social and political truths.[113] In his *Defense of the Spirit of Laws* (1750), he found it necessary, time and again, to remind his Jansenist critic, the Abbé de La Roche, that his purpose in writing *The Spirit of Laws* had not been the winning of converts to Christianity. And it was with good reason that Montesquieu compared his Jansenist critic to the village curate who, upon looking through Galileo's telescope, saw only the steeple of a Church.[114] Jesuit and Jansenist opposition to Montesquieu's treatise, however, is certainly understandable. His ecclesiastical critics had a world-view to defend, and they rightly discerned a threat to orthodoxy within the methodology of *The Spirit of Laws*. Montesquieu claimed to regard Christianity as the one true, Divinely revealed faith (XXIV, 1 [4]), but he nevertheless consciously neglected Christianity to explore, with new sociological and psychological tools, the interesting question posed by the origin, practice, and utility of

[112] Raymond Aron, *Main Currents in Sociological Thought*, Vol. I, trans. by Richard Howard and Helen Weaver (Garden City, N.Y.: Anchor Books, 1968), p. 14.

[113] This aspect of *The Spirit of Laws* has been commented upon with particular skill by Louis Althusser in his *Montesquieu: La politique et l'histoire* (Paris: Presses Universitaires de France, 1974), pp. 15–18.

[114] *Défense*, Première Partie, "Neuvième Objection et Réponse."

other world religions. If the result of the new science of the sixteenth and seventeenth centuries had been the relegation of the Deity to the outskirts of the heavens, as a mere Designing Power needing, since the Creation, to intervene only occasionally to make adjustments in a universe largely self-running, the effect of *The Spirit of Laws* and other works of the new social science was to render the time-honored formulae of revealed religions peripheral to scientific, and hence legitimate, investigation of *les choses humaines*. The secularization of political thinking by no means began with *The Spirit of Laws*, but Montesquieu must be credited with accelerating a trend that would soon make it unnecessary to apologize for separating Church and State in political thought.

Characteristic of Montesquieu's methodology was his avoidance of an excessively mathematicizing approach to politics. He questioned the wisdom, in fact, of establishing the same laws and the same religion throughout a state, or even the same weights and measures (XXIX, 18). "If the people observe the laws," he remarked, "what signifies it whether these laws are the same?" (XXIX, 18).[115] It proved much more usual as the century progressed, to envision ideal political solutions based on the perfection of reason applicable *par tout*, and the Marquis de Condorcet, for one, found Montesquieu's approach unacceptable. "As truth, reason, justice, the rights of man, the interests of property, of liberty, of security, are in all places the same," he wrote in direct rebuttal of Montesquieu, "we cannot discover why all the provinces of a state, or even all states, should not have the same civil and criminal laws, and the same laws relative to commerce."[116]

---

[115] The American federal system, with its marked differences in some state laws, provides an interesting example of such a state of affairs.

[116] "Observations on the Twenty-Ninth Book of *The Spirit of Laws*," in Destutt de

And Condorcet saw no difficulty in establishing uniformity. "A good law should be good for all men," he continued. "A true proposition is true everywhere. . . . Uniformity in laws may be established without trouble, and without producing any evil effects by the change."[117]

Montesquieu disagreed. He was more sensitive than Condorcet to the potential danger of sweeping change in the name of abstract reason. Not content with the dream of blueprinting identical, "ideal" institutions for all realms, he had imbibed from the travel literature of his day a substantial dose of relativism, and this precluded his believing one constitution or set of laws could conceivably suit all peoples.[118] The best government, Montesquieu remarked, is that which suits the particular people for whom it is established (I, 3 [9]), and he vehemently denied having favored one form of government over another in *The Spirit of Laws*.[119]

Montesquieu made his share of errors, and his lack of self-conscious concern for methodology resulted in his failure to resolve the tension in his work between empiricism and rationalism and between conservatism and liberalism.[120] But perhaps a man who boldly remarked, "The bent of my mind is not to retrace what everyone knows,"[121] should be judged, not so much for his accuracy as for his originality. Whatever factual errors Montesquieu

Tracy, *A Commentary and Review of Montesquieu's Spirit of Laws* . . . (Philadelphia: Printed by William Duane, 1811), p. 274.

[117] *Ibid.*, p. 274.

[118] For a discussion of Montesquieu's relativism, see above pp. 34–40.

[119] See footnote 2* to Book III, chapter 5, of *The Spirit of Laws* for Montesquieu's contention, in response to his Jesuit critics, that all of Europe read his book and that there was general agreement that he had favored neither monarchy nor republicanism.

[120] See above, pp. 40–44; 30–34.

[121] *Pensée* 192 (1866. III. f. 112): 1749.

made, it can be said that his quest for the "spirit" of laws and his fascination with the relativity of morals, customs, and political and legal systems, coupled with his intense desire to seek the underlying causes of social and political phenomena and his keen appreciation of the interdependence of the contributing elements of a society's *esprit général*, contributed to a methodological revolution whose implications are still being explored and developed.

THE SPIRIT OF LAWS

Prolem sine matre creatam. OVID

PREFACE

[1] IF amidst the infinite number of subjects contained in this book, there is any thing, which, contrary to my expectation, may possibly offend, I can at least assure the public, that it was not inserted with an ill intention: For I am not naturally of a captious temper. Plato thanked the Gods, that he was born in the same age with Socrates: and for my part, I give thanks to the Almighty, that I was born a subject of that government under which I live; and that it is his pleasure I should obey those, whom he has made me love.

[2] I beg one favor of my readers, which I fear will not be granted me; this is, that they will not judge by a few hours reading, of the labour of twenty years; that they will approve or condemn the book intire, and not a few particular phrases. If they would search into the design of the author, they can do it no other way so completely, as by searching into the design of the work.

[3] I have first of all considered mankind; and the result of my thoughts has been, that amidst such an infinite diversity of laws and manners, they were not solely conducted by the caprice of fancy.

[4] I have laid down the first principles, and have found that the particular cases follow naturally from them; that the histories of all nations are only consequences of them; and that every particular law is connected with another law, or depends on some other of a more general extent.

[5]   When I have been obliged to look back into antiquity, I have
endeavoured to assume the spirit of the ancients, lest I should
consider those things as alike, which are really different; and lest I
should miss the difference of those which appear to be alike.

[6]   I have not drawn my principles from my prejudices, but from
the nature of things.

[7]   Here a great many truths will not appear, till we have seen the
chain which connects them with others. The more we enter into
particulars, the more we shall perceive the certainty of the principles on which they are founded. I have not even given all these
particulars, for who could mention them all without a most insupportable fatigue?

[8]   The reader will not here meet with any of those bold flights,
which seem to characterize the works of the present age. When
things are examined with ever so small a degree of extent, the
sallies of imagination must vanish; these generally arise from the
mind's collecting all its powers to view only one side of the subject, while it leaves the other unobserved.

[9]   I write not to censure any thing established in any country
whatsoever. Every nation will here find the reasons on which its
maxims are founded; and this will be the natural inference, that to
propose alterations, belongs only to those who are so happy as to be
born with a genius capable of penetrating into the entire constitution of a state.

[10]   It is not a matter of indifference, that the minds of the people be
enlightened. The prejudices of the magistrate have arisen from
national prejudice. In a time of ignorance they have committed
even the greatest evils without the least scruple; but in an enlighten'd age they even tremble, while conferring the greatest
blessings. They perceive the ancient abuses; they see how they
must be reformed; but they are sensible also of the abuses of the

reformation. They let the evil continue if they fear a worse; they are content with a lesser good, if they doubt of a greater. They examine into the parts, to judge of them in connection; they examine all the causes to discover their different effects.

[11]   Could I but succeed so as to afford new reasons to every man to love his prince, his country, his laws; new reasons to render him more sensible in every nation and government of the blessings he enjoys, I should think myself the most happy of mortals.

[12]   Could I but succeed so as to persuade those who command, to increase their knowledge in what they ought to prescribe; and those who obey, to find a new pleasure resulting from their obedience, I should think myself the most happy of mortals.

[13]   The most happy of mortals should I think myself, could I contribute to make mankind recover from their prejudices. By prejudices, I here mean, not that which renders men ignorant of some particular things, but whatever renders them ignorant of themselves.

[14]   It is in endeavouring to instruct mankind, that we are best able to practice that general virtue, which comprehends the love of all. Man, that flexible being, conforming in society to the thoughts and impressions of others, is equally capable of knowing his own nature, whenever it is laid open to his view; and of losing the very sense of it, when this idea is banished from his mind.

[15]   Often have I begun, and as often have I laid aside this undertaking. I have a thousand times given the leaves I have written to the winds: I every day felt my paternal hands fall. I have followed my object without any fixed plan: I have known neither rules nor exceptions; I have found the truth, only to lose it again. But when I had once discovered my first principles, every thing I sought for appeared; and in the course of twenty years, I have seen my work begun, grow up, advanced, and finished.

[16]   If this work meets with success, I shall owe it chiefly to the grandeur and majesty of the subject. However I do not think that I have been totally deficient in point of genius. When I have seen what so many great men both in France, England and Germany have said before me, I have been lost in admiration: but I have not lost my courage: I have said with Corregio, And I also am a painter.

❧ Part One

Books I through VIII constitute Part One of *The Spirit of Laws* as Montesquieu conceived it. He sets forth his ideas concerning law in general, in Book I; defines the nature and principle of the three basic forms of government, in Books II and III; and discusses the relations that various laws should bear to their particular principle of government, in Books IV to VII. Then in Book VIII he considers what constitutes the corruption of the principles of each of the three governments he has defined.

BOOK I: *Of Laws in General*

ANALYSIS

Book I presents Montesquieu's ideas on laws in general. Chapter 1 discusses the laws governing the universe, chapter 2, natural laws, and chapter 3, various types of man-made, or positive, laws. Laws in general, M begins, are "the necessary relations derived from the nature of things" (chap. 1, par. [1]). He thus borrows from natural science the concept of laws as descriptive of the constant relation between two variables and applies it to the relation between the Deity and all created beings. There exists a primitive reason, M asserts, "and laws are the relations which subsist between it and different beings, and the relations of these different beings among themselves" (chap. 1 [3]). The universe exhibits order — not chaos. "All beings have their laws" — including the Deity, the material world, the intelligences superior to man, the beasts, and man himself (chap. 1 [1]). If man adheres less strictly to his laws than do other beings, this results from his possessing free will and the capacity to err (chap. 1 [10]), and laws of religion and morality are designed to recall man to his duty (chap. 1 [14]).

However anticlerical the Persian Letters, *and however modern and unorthodox the utilitarian approach to religion in* The Spirit of Laws *(see Book XXIV and Introduction, pp. 51–54), Montesquieu clearly retained a belief in a Designing Deity, an Omniscient Architect responsible for the Creation. He rejects the Democritean-Epicurean doctrine of a creation void of an organizing principle of Divine Reason. Blind fatality, he remarks, could not have produced intelligent beings (chap. 1 [2]). There is a Designing Intelligence, and this "God," M writes, "is related to the universe as creator and preserver; the laws by which he has created all things, are those by which he preserves them. He acts according to these rules because he knows them; he knows them because he has made them; and he made them because they are relative to his wisdom and power" (chap. 1 [4]).*

An important source of order in the universe besides the laws bestowed on all beings by their Creator, is the existence of rules of justice antecedent to human societies and applicable to all men — regardless of the circumstances in which they find themselves (chap. 1 [9]). "Before laws were made," Montesquieu affirms, "there were relations of possible justice." Suggesting that positive laws alone determine the contours of right and wrong would be somewhat like asserting that prior to the drawing of a circle, all the radii are not equal (chap. 1 [8]). And M considered justice independent of the Deity. Even if there existed no God, he remarked in Persian Letter *83, men would have to love justice. And even if men were not bound by religion, they would be bound by the dictates of justice.*

In chapter 2 of Book I, Montesquieu discusses those natural laws deriving from man's frame and being. Some are physiological and others are psychological, and, by M's count, they are five in number: (1) awareness of God, (2) peaceful demeanor towards one's fellow man, (3) the need for nourishment, (4) the mutual attraction between the sexes, and (5) a desire to live in society with one's fellow man. These natural laws are basic to human behaviour, and systems of positive laws ought not to force men to violate them. (See Book XXVI, chap. 3). Particularly noteworthy in M's discussion of laws of nature is his rejection in the second of his natural laws, of the Hobbesian contention that the state of nature is a war of all against all (chap. 2 [4–5]). M posits no innate brutality in man, preferring to attribute aggression to man's life in society (chap. 2 [5]).

In the third and final chapter of Book I, Montesquieu discusses those positive laws men make for themselves. International law, political law, and civil law, he suggests, should combine to regulate the lives of men once they have joined together in societies (chap. 3 [1–7]. In terms of political law, M refrains from choosing between various modes of government, remarking that "the government most conformable to nature, is that whose particular disposition best agrees with the humour and disposition of the people in whose favour it is established" (chap. 3 [9]). And this relativistic perspective leads M to assert that if positive law should at all times mirror the primitive reason and justice writ large in the universe, it should also reflect the particular conditions of the society for which a given set of laws is designed. Laws should be so closely adapted, in fact, to the people to whom they apply, that "it should be a great chance if those of one nation suit another" (chap. 3 [12]). Hence in M's vision of law the absolute and the relative are reconciled. Societies will necessarily vary according to the historical, governmental, and climatological factors influencing their development — but only within certain carefully prescribed limits. And those limits are provided by reason, natural law, and justice.

The third chapter of Book I also contains Montesquieu's definition of the quest for the "spirit" of the laws as the search for the relations laws bear to all those factors influencing their character (chap. 3 [14]), chief among which is the nature and principle of government from which laws "appear to flow as from their source" (chap. 3 [17]). It is the nature and principle of government, therefore, that will concern M in Books II and III.

OF THE RELATION OF LAWS TO DIFFERENT BEINGS [Chapter 1]

[1]   LAWS in their most general signification, are the necessary relations derived from the nature of things.[1*] In this sense all beings have their laws,[a] the Deity has his laws, the material world its laws, the intelligences superior to man have their laws, the beasts their laws, man his laws.

[2]   Those who assert that *a blind fatality produced the various effects we behold in this world*, are guilty of a very great absurdity; for can any thing be more absurd than to pretend that a blind fatality could be productive of intelligent beings?

[3]   There is then a primitive reason; and laws are the relations

---

[a] *Law*, says Plutarch, *is the queen of the Gods and men*. In a treatise intitled, *That a prince ought to be a man of learning*.[2*]

which subsist between it and different beings, and the relations of these beings among themselves.

[4]   God is related to the universe as creator and preserver; the laws by which he has created all things, are those by which he preserves them. He acts according to these rules because he knows them; he knows them because he has made them; and he made them because they are relative to his wisdom and power.

[5]   As we see that the world, tho' formed by the motion of matter, and void of understanding, subsists notwithstanding thro' so long a succession of ages, its motions must certainly be directed by invariable laws: and could we imagine another world, it must also have constant rules, or must inevitably perish.

[6]   Thus the creation which seems an arbitrary act, supposeth laws as invariable as those of the fatality of the Atheists. It would be absurd to say, that the Creator might govern the world without those rules, since without them it could not subsist.[3*]

[7]   These rules are a fixt and invariable relation. In bodies moved the motion is received, increased, diminished, lost, according to the relations of the quantity of matter and velocity; each diversity is *uniformity*, each change is *constancy*.

[8]   Particular intelligent beings may have laws of their own making, but they have some likewise which they never made. Before there were intelligent beings, they were possible; they had therefore possible relations, and consequently possible laws. Before laws were made, there were relations of possible justice. To say that there is nothing just or unjust but what is commanded or forbidden by positive laws, is the same as saying that before the describing of a circle all the radii were not equal.

[9]   We must therefore acknowledge relations of justice antecedent to the positive law by which they are established: as for instance, that if human societies existed, it would be right to conform to

their laws; if there were intelligent beings that had received a benefit of another being, they ought to be grateful; if one intelligent being had created another intelligent being, the latter ought to continue in its original state of dependance; if one intelligent being injures another, it deserves a retaliation of the injury, and so on.

[10]   But the intelligent world is far from being so well governed as the physical. For tho' the former has also its laws which of their own nature are invariable, yet it does not conform to them so exactly as the physical world.[4*] This is because on the one hand particular intelligent beings are of a finite nature and consequently liable to error; and on the other, their nature requires them to be free agents. Hence they do not steadily conform to their primitive laws; and even those of their own instituting they frequently infringe.

[11]   Whether brutes be governed by the general laws of motion, or by a particular movement, is what we cannot determine. Be that as it will, they have not a more intimate relation to God than the rest of the material world; and sensation is of no other use to them, than in the relation they have either with other particular beings, or with themselves.

[12]   By the allurement of pleasure they preserve the being of the individual, and by the same allurement they preserve their species. They have natural laws, because they are united by sensations; positive laws they have none, because they are not connected by knowledge. And yet they do not conform invariably to their natural laws; these are better observed by vegetables, that have neither intellectual nor sensitive faculties.

[13]   Brutes are deprived of the high advantages which we have; but they have some which we have not. They have not our hopes, but they are without our fears; they are subject like us to death, but

without knowing it; even most of them are more attentive than we
to self-preservation, and do not make so bad a use of their passions.

[14]   Man, as a physical being, is, like other bodies, governed by
invariable laws. As an intelligent being, he incessantly transgresses
the laws established by God, and changes those which he himself
has established. He is left to his own direction, tho' he is a limited
being, subject like all finite intelligences, to ignorance and error;
even the imperfect knowledge he has, he loses as a sensible creature, and is hurried away by a thousand impetuous passions. Such
a being might every instant forget his Creator; God has therefore
reminded him of his duty by the laws of religion.[5*] Such a being
is liable every moment to forget himself; philosophy has provided
against this by the laws of morality. Formed to live in society, he
might forget his fellow creatures; legislators have therefore by
political and civil laws confined him to his duty.[6*]

OF THE LAWS OF NATURE [Chapter 2]

[1]   ANTECEDENT to all these laws are those of nature, so called
because they derive their force intirely from our frame and being.
In order to have a perfect knowledge of these laws, we must
consider man before the establishment of society: the laws received
in such a state would be those of nature.[7*]

[2]   The law which imprinting in our minds the idea of a Creator
inclines us to him, is the first in importance, tho' not in order, of
natural laws.[8*] Man in a state of nature would have the faculty of
knowing, before he had any acquired knowledge. Plain it is that
his first ideas would be far from being of a speculative nature; he
would think of the preservation of his being, before he would
investigate its origin. Such a man would feel nothing in himself at
first but impotency and weakness; his fears and apprehensions

would be excessive; as appears from instances (were there any necessity of proving it) of savages found in forests,[a] trembling at the motion of a leaf, and flying from every shadow.

[3]   In this state every man would fancy himself inferior, instead of being sensible of his equality. No danger would there be therefore of their attacking one another; peace would be the first law of nature.

[4]   The natural impulse or desire which Hobbes attributes to mankind of subduing one another, is far from being well founded. The idea of empire and dominion is so complex, and depends on so many other notions, that it could never be the first that would occur to human understandings.

[5]   Hobbes inquires, *For what reason do men go armed, and have locks and keys to fasten their doors, if they be not naturally in a state of war?* But is it not obvious that he attributes to man before the establishment of society, what cannot happen but in consequence of this establishment, which furnishes them with motives for hostile attacks and self-defence.

[6]   Next to a sense of his weakness man would soon find himself sensible of his wants. Hence another law of nature would prompt him to seek for nourishment.

[7]   Fear, I have observed, would incline men to shun one another; but the marks of this fear being reciprocal would soon induce them to associate. Besides, this association would quickly follow from the very pleasure one animal feels at the approach of another of the same species. Again, the attraction arising from the difference of sexes would enhance this pleasure, and the natural inclination they have for each other, would form a third law.

[8]   Beside the sense or instinct which man has in common with

---

[a] *Witness the savage found in the forests of Hanover, who was carried over to England under the reign of George I.*

brutes, he has the advantage of attaining to acquired knowledge; and thereby has a second tye which brutes have not. Mankind have therefore a new motive of uniting, and a fourth law of nature arises from the desire of living in society.[9]*

OF POSITIVE LAWS [Chapter 3]

[1] As soon as mankind enter into a state of society, they lose the sense of their weakness, the equality ceases, and then commences the state of war.

[2]   Each particular society begins to feel its strength, whence arises a state of war betwixt different nations. The individuals likewise of each society become sensible of their strength; hence the principal advantages of this society they endeavour to convert to their own emolument, which constitutes between them a state of war.

[3]   These two different kinds of military states give rise to human laws. Considered as inhabitants of so great a planet which necessarily implies a variety of nations, they have laws relative to their mutual intercourse, which is what we call the *law of nations*. Considered as members of a society that must be properly supported, they have laws relative to the governors and the governed; and this we call *politic law*. They have also another sort of laws relating to the mutual communication of citizens among themselves; by which is understood the *civil law*.

[4]   The law of nations is naturally founded on this principle, that different nations ought in time of peace to do one another all the good they can, and in time of war as little harm as possible, without prejudicing their real interests.

[5]   The object of war is victory; victory aims at conquest; conquest at preservation. From this and the preceding principle all those laws are derived which constitute the *law of nations*.

[6]   All countries have a law of nations, not excepting the Iroquois

themselves, tho' they devour their prisoners: for they send and receive ambassadors, and understand the rights of war and peace. The mischief is that this law of nations is not founded on true principles.

[7]   Besides the law of nations relating to all societies, there is a *politic law* for each particularly considered. No society can subsist without a form of government. *The conjunction of the particular forces of individuals*, as Gravina well observes,[10] *constitutes what we call a political state*.

[8]   The general force may be in the hands of a single person, or of many. Some have thought that nature having established paternal authority, the government of a single person was most conformable to nature.[11] But the example of paternal authority proves nothing. For if the power of a father is relative to a single government, that of brothers after the death of a father, or that of cousin-germans after the decease of brothers, are relative to a government of many. The political power necessarily comprehends the union of several families.

[9]   Better is it to say that the government most conformable to nature, is that whose particular disposition best agrees with the humour and disposition of the people in whose favour it is established.

[10]   The particular force of individuals cannot be united without a conjunction of all their wills. *The conjunction of those wills*, as Gravina again very justly observes, *is what we call the CIVIL STATE*.

[11]   Law in general is human reason, inasmuch as it governs all the inhabitants of the earth; the political and civil laws of each nation ought to be only the particular cases in which this human reason is applied.

[12]   They should be adapted in such a manner to the people for

whom they are made, as to render it very unlikely for those of one
nation to be proper for another.

[13]   They should be relative to the nature and principle of the actual,
or intended government; whether they form this principle, as in
the case of political laws, or whether they support it, as may be
said of civil institutions.

[14]   They should be relative to the climate, whether hot or cold, of
each country, to the quality of the soil, to its situation and bigness,
to the manner of living of the natives, whether husbandmen,
huntsmen, or shepherds; they should have a relation to the degree
of liberty which the constitution will bear; to the religion of the
inhabitants, to their inclinations, riches, number, commerce,
manners, and customs. In fine they have relations amongst themselves, as also with their origin, with the object of the legislator,
and with the order of things on which they are established, in all
which different lights they ought to be considered.

[15]   This is what I have undertaken to perform in the following
work. These relations I shall examine, which form all together
what we call the *Spirit of laws*.

[16]   I have not separated the political from the civil laws; for as I do
not pretend to treat of laws, but of their spirit, and as this spirit
consists in the various relations which the laws may have with
different things, 'tis not so much my business to follow the natural
order of laws, as that of these relations and things.

[17]   I shall first examine the relation which laws have with the
nature and principle of each government; and as this principle has
a strong influence on laws, I shall make it my business to understand it thoroughly; and if I can but once establish it, the laws will
soon appear to flow from thence as from their source. I shall
proceed afterwards to other more particular relations.

BOOK II: *Of Laws Directly Derived from the Nature of Government*

ANALYSIS

Having identified the nature and principle of government as the most impor-
tant factors influencing man-made, positive law (Book I, chap. 3, par.
[17]), Montesquieu devotes Books II and III of his work to definitions
of forms and principles of government. He defines three types of govern-
ments: republics, monarchies, and despotisms. Republican governments he
further subdivides into democracies and aristocracies, but since he regarded
the latter of these as imperfect forms of republican governments, the texts on
aristocracies have not been included. In republican governments the people,
or a portion of them, rule. In monarchical government one person rules "by
fixed and established laws," and in despotic governments one persons "directs
everything by his own will and caprice" (chap. 1 [1]).

Montesquieu's first concern is the fundamental nature of democracy
(chap. 2). Since the sovereign is elected, the laws governing the suffrage are
judged of paramount importance ([3, 5]). The populace is to possess the
right to choose their ministers as well as a senate, but this equal right to
choose is not equivalent to an equal right to serve ([6–9, 13]). And the
division of the populace into classes based on wealth is deemed an appropriate
method for determining eligibility for office ([14–16]). Except for offices
of great import, offices attended with great expense, or offices of a military
nature, use of a system of lots is recommended as the means of selecting among
those eligible to serve ([17–22]). And those chosen by lot should be subjected
to close scrutiny both before and after they have served ([23]). Voting for
those offices not determined by lot should be public so that the wisest will
influence the populace at large ([24–25]). Conflict within democratic

societies is affirmed a sign of health — not disease. Its absence, in fact, likely suggests corruption ([26]).

The heart of monarchical government as depicted by Montesquieu are the corps intermédiaires, *including nobility and clergy, situated between the sovereign and the populace, thereby precluding the despotic use of force (chap. 4 [1–7]). In monarchical governments there should exist a judicial body to safeguard the fundamental laws of the realm, and this body should be distinct from the prince's council (chap. 4 [10–11]).*

Montesquieu's depiction of the nature of despotic governments is rather brief, and one must look to Book V, chapters 14–15, for a fuller analysis. We do learn in chapter 5 of Book II, however, that the despot often commits his power to a chief subordinate ([1]), thereby freeing himself for a life of pleasure amid his concubines ([2]).

OF THE NATURE OF THE THREE DIFFERENT GOVERNMENTS [Chapter 1]

[1]   THERE are three species of government; *republican, monarchical,* and *despotic.* In order to discover their nature, 'tis sufficient to recollect the common notion, which supposes three definitions or rather three facts, that the *republican government is that in which the body or only a part of the people is possessed of the supreme power: monarchy that in which a single person governs but by fixt and established laws: a despotic government, that in which a single person directs every thing by his own will and caprice.*

[2]   This is what I call the nature of each government; we must examine now which are those laws that follow this nature directly, and consequently are the first fundamental laws.

OF THE REPUBLICAN GOVERNMENT, AND THE LAWS RELATIVE TO DEMOCRACY [Chapter 2][1]

[1]   WHEN the body of the people in a republic are possessed of the supreme power, this is called a *democracy.*

[2]   In a democracy the people are in some respects the sovereign, and in others the subject.

[3]   There can be no sovereign but by suffrages, which are their own will; and the sovereign's will is the sovereign himself. The laws therefore which establish the right of suffrage, are fundamental to this government. In fact, 'tis as important to regulate in a republic, in what manner, by whom, to whom, and concerning what, suffrages are to be given, as it is in a monarchy to know who is the prince and after what manner he ought to govern.

[5]   'Tis an essential point to fix the number of citizens that are to form the public assemblies; otherwise it might be uncertain whether the whole body or only a part of the people have voted. At Sparta the number was fixt to ten thousand. But at Rome, that had sometimes all its inhabitants without its walls, and sometimes all Italy and a great part of the world within them; at Rome, I say, this number was never fixed,[a] which was one of the principal causes of its ruin.[2]

[6]   The people in whom the supreme power resides, ought to do of themselves whatever conveniently they can; and what they cannot well do, they must commit to the management of ministers.

[7]   The ministers are not properly their's, unless they have the nomination of them: 'tis therefore a fundamental maxim in this government, that the people should chuse their ministers, that is, their magistrates.

[8]   They have occasion as well as monarchs, and even more than they, to be directed by a council or senate. But to have a proper confidence in them, they should have the chusing of the members; whether the election be made by themselves, as at Athens; or by some magistrate deputed for the purpose, as was customary at Rome on certain occasions.

[a] See the considerations on the causes of the grandeur and decline of the Romans.

[9]   The people are extremely well qualified for chusing those whom they are to intrust with part of their authority. They can tell when a person has been often in battle, and has had particular success; they are therefore very capable of electing a general. They can tell when a judge is assiduous in his office, when he gives general satisfaction, and has never been charged with bribery. These are all facts of which they can have better information in a public forum, than a monarch in his palace. But are they able to manage an affair, to find out and make a proper use of places, occasions, moments? No, this is beyond their capacity.

[13]   The public business must however be carried on, with a certain motion neither too quick nor too slow. But the action of the common people is always either too remiss or too violent. Sometimes with a hundred thousand arms they overturn all before them; and sometimes with a hundred thousand feet they creep like insects.

[14]   In a popular state the inhabitants are divided into certain classes. 'Tis in the manner of making this division that great legislators have signalized themselves; and 'tis on this the duration and prosperity of democracy have always depended.

[15]   Servius Tullius followed the spirit of aristocracy in the distribution of his classes.[3] We find in Livy[b] and in Dionysius Halicarnassus,[c] in what manner he lodged the right of suffrage in the hands of the principal citizens. He had divided the people of Rome into a hundred and ninety three centuries, which formed six classes; and ranking the rich, who were in smaller numbers, in the first centuries; and those in middling circumstances, who were more numerous, in the following centuries; he flung the indigent

[b] Lib. I.
[c] Lib. 4, Art, 15, & seq.

multitude into the last; and as each century had but one vote,[d] 'twas property rather than numbers that decided the elections.[4]

[16]   Solon divided the people of Athens into four classes. In this he was directed by the spirit of democracy, his intention not being to fix those who were to chuse, but those who were capable of being chosen; wherefore leaving to each citizen the right of election, he made the judges eligible from each of those four classes;[e] but the magistrates he ordered to be chosen only out of the three first, which consisted of citizens of easy fortunes.[5]

[17]   As the division of those who have a right of suffrage is a fundamental law in a republic, so the manner also of giving this suffrage is another fundamental law.

[18]   The suffrage by *lot* is natural to democracy; as that by *choice* is to aristocracy.[6]

[19]   The suffrage by *lot* is a method of electing that offends no one; it lets each citizen entertain reasonable hopes of serving his country.

[20]   But as this method is naturally defective, it has been the glorious endeavour of the most eminent legislators to regulate and amend it.

[21]   Solon made a law at Athens that military employments should be conferred by choice, but that senators and judges should be elected by lot.

[22]   The same legislator ordained, that civil magistracies, attended with great expence, should be given by choice; and the others by lot.

[23]   But in order to amend the suffrage by lot, he made a rule that none but those who presented themselves should be elected; that the

[d] See in the Considerations on the causes of the grandeur and decline of the Romans, how this spirit of Servius Tullius was preserved in the republic.

[e] Dionysius Halicarn. elogium of Isocrates, p. 97, tom. 2. Edit. Wechel. Pollux lib. 8. cap. 10. Art. 130.

person elected should be examined by judges,[f] and that every one should have a right to accuse him if he were unworthy of the office:[g] this participated at the same time of the suffrage by lot, and of that by choice. When the time of their magistracy was expired, they were obliged to submit to another judgment in regard to the manner they had behaved.[7] People who were utterly unqualified, must by this means have been extremely backward in giving in their names to be drawn by lot.

[24]   The law which determines the manner of giving the suffrages is likewise fundamental in a democracy. 'Tis a question of some importance, whether the suffrages ought to be public or secret. Cicero observes,[h] that the laws which rendered them secret towards the close of the republic, were the cause of its decline.[i] But as this is differently practiced in different republics, I shall offer here my thoughts concerning this subject.

[25]   The people's suffrages ought doubtless to be public;[j] and this should be considered as a fundamental law of democracy. The lower sort of people ought to be directed by those of higher rank, and restrained within bounds by the gravity of certain personages. Hence by rendering the suffrages secret in the Roman republic all was lost; it was no longer possible to direct a populace that sought its own destruction.

[26]   Intriguing in a senate is dangerous; dangerous it is also in a body of nobles; but not so in the people whose nature it is to act thro'

---

[f] See the oration of Demosthenes *de falsâ legat.* and the oration against Timarchus.

[g] They used even to draw two tickets for each place, one which gave the place, and the other which named the person who was to succeed, in case the first was rejected.

[h] Lib. I, & 3. de Leg.

[i] They were called *Leges Tabulares*; two tablets were presented to each citizen, the first marked with an *A*, for *Antiquo*, or *I forbid it*; and the other with an *U* and an *R*, for *Uti Rogas*, or *Be it as you desire*.

[j] At Athens the people used to lift up their hands.

passion. In countries where they have no share in the government, we often see them as much inflamed on the account of an actor, as they could possibly have been for state affairs. The misfortune of a republic is, when there are no more intrigues;[8] and this happens when the people are corrupted by dint of money: in which case they grow indifferent to public concerns, and passionately desirous of lucre. Careless of the government, and of every thing belonging to it, they quietly wait for their salary.

[27]   'Tis likewise a fundamental law in democracies, that the people should have the sole power to enact laws. And yet there are a thousand occasions on which 'tis necessary the senate should have a power of decreeing; nay it is frequently proper to make some trial of a law before it is established. The constitutions of Rome and Athens were extremely wise. The decrees of the senate had the force of laws for the space of a year,[k] and did not become perpetual till they were ratified by the consent of the people.

OF THE RELATION OF LAWS TO THE NATURE OF
MONARCHICAL GOVERNMENT [Chapter 4][9]

[1]   THE intermediate, subordinate and dependent powers, constitute the nature of monarchical government,[10] that is, of that in which a single person governs by fundamental laws. I said, *intermediate, subordinate* and *dependent powers*.[11] In fact, in monarchies the prince is the source of all power political and civil. These fundamental laws necessarily suppose the intermediate channels through which the power flows: for if there be only the momentary and capricious will of a single person to govern the state, nothing can be fixed, and, of course there can be no fundamental law.

[2]   The most natural, intermediate and subordinate power is that of the nobility.[12] This in some measure seems to be essential to a

[k] See Dionys. Halicarn. lib. 4, & 9.

monarchy, whose fundamental maxim is, *no monarch, no nobility; no nobility, no monarch;* but there may be a despotic prince.

[3]   There are men who have endeavoured in some countries in Europe to abolish all the jurisdiction of the nobility; not perceiving that they were driving at the very thing that was done by the parliament of *England*. Abolish the privileges of the lords, of the clergy, and of the cities in a monarchy, and you will soon have a popular state, or else an arbitrary government.

[4]   The courts of a considerable kingdom in Europe have been striking for many ages at the patrimonial jurisdiction of the lords and clergy.[13] We do not pretend to censure these sage magistrates; but we leave it to the public to judge, how far this may alter the constitution.

[5]   Far am I from being prejudiced in favour of the privileges of the clergy; however, I should be glad their jurisdiction were once fixed. The question is not whether their jurisdiction was justly established; but whether it be really established; whether it constitutes a part of the laws of the country, and is in every respect relative to those laws; whether between two powers acknowledged independent, the conditions ought not to be reciprocal; and whether it be not the same thing with respect to a good subject, to defend the prerogative of the prince, or the limits which from time immemorial he has prescribed to his authority.

[6]   Though the ecclesiastic power is so dangerous in a republic, yet it is extremely proper in a monarchy, especially of the absolute kind. What would become of *Spain* and *Portugal* since the subversion of their laws, were it not for this only barrier against the torrent of arbitrary power?[14] A barrier that is always useful when there is no other: for as a despotic government is productive of the most frightful calamities to human nature, the very evil that restrains it, is beneficial to the subject.

[7]   As the ocean which seems to threaten to overflow the whole earth, is stopped by weeds and by little pebbles that lie scattered along the shore; so monarchs whose power seems unbounded, are restrained by the smallest obstacles, and suffer their natural pride to be subdued by supplication and prayer.

[10]   It is not enough to have intermediate powers in a monarchy; there must be also a depositary of the laws. This depositary can be only the political bodies, who promulge the new laws, and revive the obsolete.[15] The natural ignorance of the nobility, their indolence, and contempt of civil government, require there should be a body invested with a power of reviving and executing the laws which would be otherwise buried in oblivion. The prince's council are not a proper depositary. They are naturally the depositaries of the momentary will of the prince, and not of the fundamental laws. Besides the prince's council continually changes; it is neither permanent, nor numerous; neither has it a sufficient share of the confidence of the people; consequently it is incapable to set them right in difficult conjunctures, or to reduce them to proper obedience.[16]

[11]   Despotic governments, where there are no fundamental laws, have no such kind of depositary. Hence it is that religion has generally so much influence in those countries, because it forms a kind of permanent depositary; and if this cannot be said of religion, it may of the customs that are respected instead of laws.

OF THE LAWS RELATIVE TO THE NATURE OF A
DESPOTIC GOVERNMENT [Chapter 5][17]

[1]   FROM the nature of a despotic power it follows that the single person invested with this power, commits the execution of it also to a single person. A man who his senses continually inform, that he himself is every thing, and his subjects nothing, is naturally

lazy, voluptuous, and ignorant. In consequence of this, he neg-
lects the management of public affairs. But were he to commit the
administration to many, there would be continual disputes between them; they would form intrigues to be his first slave; and the
prince would be obliged to take the reins into his own hands. It is
therefore more natural for him to resign it to a vizir,[a] and to invest
him with the same power as himself. The creation of a vizir is a
fundamental law of this government.

[2]   It is related of a pope, that he had raised an infinite number of
difficulties to prevent his election, from a thorough conviction of
his incapacity.[18] At length he was prevailed on to accept of the
pontificate; and resigned the administration intirely to his nephew.
He was soon struck with surprize, and said, *I should never have
thought that these things were so easy.* The same may be said of the
princes of the East. When from that prison, where eunuchs have
enervated both their hearts and understanding, and where they
frequently conceal from them their very condition, they are drawn
forth in order to be raised to the throne; they are at first amazed:
but as soon as they have got a vizir, and have abandoned themselves in their seraglio to the most brutal passions, pursuing, in the
middle of a prostituted court, the most capricious extravagancies,
they could never have dreamt to find matters so easy.

[3]   The greater the extent of an empire, the greater is the seraglio;
and consequently so much the more is the prince intoxicted with
pleasure. Hence the more nations such a prince has to govern, the
less he attends to the government; the greater his affairs, the less
he makes them the subject of his deliberations.

---

[a] The Eastern kings are never without vizirs, says Sir John Chardin.

BOOK III: *Of the Principles of the Three Kinds of Government*

ANALYSIS

Book III forms the close counterpart of Book II. Having surveyed the basic structure of the three distinct governmental types in Book II, Montesquieu discusses in Book III the underlying principle, or political psychology, activating otherwise lifeless institutions. And as chapter 8 reveals, M actually regarded the principle of government as even more important to the stability of a government than the institutional superstructure that principle supports.

The activating principle of democracy, the human passions that set it in motion, is virtue (chap. 3), by which Montesquieu means political virtue, that is, regard for the needs of the community above one's own egotistical desires. (See Introduction, pp. 60–61, and note 2 to Book III for a fuller discussion of M's definition of virtue.) In monarchies the role of virtue is filled by honor, an unwritten code of ethics activating the nobility both in support of the king and in defense of its own legitimate interests (chaps. 5–7). The principle of despotic government is fear. Citizens not cowed by fear would threaten a despotic government based exclusively on force and possessing no real hold on the loyalty of its subjects (chap. 9).

In the concluding chapter of Book III, Montesquieu revealed that he did not mean to imply that all democracies display virtue, or all monarchies honor, or all despotisms fear. His point rather was that the more perfect the democracy, monarchy, or despotism, the more it will display the psychologie politique *vital to its preservation (chap. 11).*

DIFFERENCE BETWEEN THE NATURE AND
PRINCIPLE OF GOVERNMENT [Chapter 1]

[1]   AFTER having examined the laws relative to the nature of each government, we must investigate those that relate to its principle.

[2]   There is this difference between the nature and principle of government, that its nature is that by which it is constituted, and its principle that by which it is made to act.[a] One is its particular structure, and the other the human passions which set it in motion.

[3]   Now laws ought to be no less relative to the principle than to the nature of each government. We must therefore inquire into this principle, which shall be the subject of this third book.

OF THE PRINCIPLE OF DIFFERENT
GOVERNMENTS [Chapter 2]

I HAVE already observed that it is the nature of a republican government, that either the collective body of the people, or particular families should be possessed of the sovereign power: of a monarchy, that the prince should have this sovereign power, but in the execution of it should be directed by established laws: of a despotic government, that a single person should rule according to his own will and caprice. No more do I want to enable me to discover their three principles; these are from thence most naturally derived. I shall begin with a republican government, and in particular with that of democracy.

OF THE PRINCIPLE OF DEMOCRACY [Chapter 3][1]

[1]   THERE is no great share of probity necessary to support a monarchical or despotic government. The force of laws in one, and the

---

[a] This is a very important distinction, from whence I shall draw a great many consequences; for it is the key of an infinite number of laws.

prince's arm in the other, are sufficient to direct and maintain the whole. But in a popular state, one spring more is necessary, namely *virtue*.

[2]   What I have here advanced, is confirmed by the unanimous testimony of historians, and is extremely agreeable to the nature of things. For it is clear that in a monarchy, where he who commands the execution of the laws generally thinks himself above them, there is less need of virtue than in a popular government, where the person intrusted with the execution of the laws, is sensible of his being subject to their direction, and that he must submit to their authority.

[3]   Clear it is also that a monarch, who through bad council or indolence ceases to enforce the execution of the laws, may easily repair the evil; he has only to change his council; or to shake off this indolence. But when in a popular government, there is a suspension of the laws, as this can proceed only from the corruption of the republic, the state is certainly undone.

[4]   A very droll spectacle it was in the last century to behold the impotent efforts the English made for the establishment of democracy. As those who had a share in the direction of public affairs were void of all virtue, as their ambition was inflam'd by the success of the most daring of their members,[a] as the spirit of a faction was suppressed only by that of a succeeding faction, the government was continually changing; the people amazed at so many revolutions fought every where for a democracy without being able to find it. At length after a series of tumultuary motions and violent shocks, they were obliged to have recourse to the very government they had so odiously proscribed.

[7]   When virtue is banished, ambition invades the hearts of those who are capable of receiving it, and avarice possesses the whole

[a] Cromwell.

community. Desires then change their objects; what they were fond of before, becomes now indifferent; they were free with laws, and they want to be free without them; every citizen is like a slave who has escaped from his master's house; what was maxim is called rigor; to rule they give the name of constraint; and of fear to attention. Frugality then, and not the thirst of gain, passes for avarice.

[8]   Athens was possessed of the same number of forces, when she triumphed with so much glory, and when with so much infamy she was enslaved. When Philip attempted to reign in Greece, and appeared at the gates of Athens, [b] she had even then lost nothing but time. We may see in Demosthenes how difficult it was to awake her: she dreaded Philip not as an enemy of her liberty, but of her pleasures. [c]

THAT VIRTUE IS NOT THE PRINCIPLE OF MONARCHICAL GOVERNMENT [Chapter 5][2]*

[1]   IN monarchies, policy makes people do great things with as little virtue as she can. Thus in the finest machines, art has contrived as few movements, springs, and wheels as possible.

[2]   The state subsists independent of the love of our country, of the thirst of true glory, of self-denial, of the sacrifice of our dearest interests, and of all those heroic virtues which we admire in the ancients, and which to us are known only by story.

[3]   The laws supply here the place of those virtues; they are by no means wanted, and the state dispenses with them: an action performed here in secret is in some measure of no consequence.

---

[b] She had then twenty thousand citizens. See Demosthenes in Aristog.

[c] They had passed a law which rendered it a capital crime for any one to propose applying the money designed for the theatres to the military service.

[4]   Though all crimes be of their own nature public, yet there is a distinction between crimes that are really public, and those that are private, which are so called, because they are more injurious to individuals than to the whole society.

[5]   Now in republics private crimes are more public, that is, they attack the constitution more than they do individuals; and in monarchies public crimes are more private, that is, they are more prejudicial to private people than to the constitution.

[6]   I beg that no one will take what I have said amiss; my observations are founded on the unanimous testimony of historians. I am not ignorant that virtuous princes are no such very rare sight; but I venture to affirm that in a monarchy it is extremely difficult for the people to be virtuous. [a]

[7]   Let us compare what the historians of all ages have said concerning the courts of monarchs; let us recollect the conversations and sentiments of people of all countries in respect to the abandoned character of courtiers; and we shall find, that these are not mere airy speculations, but things confirmed by a sad and melancholy experience.

[8]   Ambition with idleness, baseness with pride, the thirst of riches without labour, aversion to truth; flattery, treason, perfidy, violation of engagements, contempt of civil duties, fear of the prince's virtue, hope from his weakness, but above all, the perpetual ridicule of virtue; are, I think, the characteristic by which the courtiers of all ages and countries have been constantly distinguished. Now it is exceeding difficult for the leading men of the nation to be knaves and for the inferior sort of people to be honest;

[a] I speak here of political virtue, which is also moral virtue as it is directed to the public good; very little of private moral virtue; and not at all of that virtue which relates to revealed truths. This will appear better, Book V. chap. 2.

for the former to be cheats, and for the latter to consent to be duped.

[9]   But if there should chance to be some unlucky honest man among the people,[b] Cardinal Richelieu[3] in his political testament[c] seems to hint that a prince should take care not to employ him.[d] So true is it that virtue is not the spring of this government![4]

IN WHAT MANNER VIRTUE IS SUPPLIED IN A MONARCHICAL GOVERNMENT [Chapter 6][5]*

[1]   BUT it is high time for me to have done with this subject, lest I should be suspected of writing a satire against monarchical government. Far be it from me; if monarchy wants one spring, it is provided with another. Honor, that is, the prepossessions of every person and every rank, supplieth the place of virtue, and is every where her representative: here it is capable of inspiring the most glorious actions; and joined with the force of laws it may lead us to the end of government as well as virtue itself.

[2]   Hence in well policied monarchies, they are almost all good subjects, and very few honest men;[a] for to be an honest man, an honest intention is necessary.

OF THE PRINCIPLE OF MONARCHY [Chapter 7][6]

[1]   A MONARCHICAL government supposeth, as we have already observed, preeminences, ranks, and likewise a noble descent. Now as

---

[b] This is to be understood in the sense of the preceding note.

[c] This book was written under the inspection and from the memoirs of cardinal Richelieu by Messieurs de Bourseis, and de---- who were strongly his adherents.

[d] We must not, says he, employ people of mean extraction; they are too austere and difficult.

[a] See the note p. 120.

it is the nature of honor to aspire to preferments and distinguishing titles, it is therefore properly placed in this government.

[2]   Ambition is pernicious in a republic. But in a monarchy it has some good effects; it gives life to the government, and is attended with this advantage, that it is no way dangerous, because it may be continually checked.

[3]   It is with this kind of government as with the system of the universe, in which there is a power that constantly repels all bodies from the center, and a power of gravitation that attracts them to it. Honor sets all the parts of the body politic in motion; by its very action it connects them, and thus each individual advances the public good, while he only thinks of promoting his own particular interest.

[4]   True it is, that, philosophically speaking, it is a false honor which moves all the parts of the government; but even this false honor is as useful to the public, as true honor could possibly prove to private people.

[5]   Is it not a very great point, to oblige men to perform the most difficult actions, such as require a great degree of fortitude and spirit, without any other recompence, than the fame and reputation arising from the actions themselves?

THAT HONOR IS NOT THE PRINCIPLE OF DESPOTIC GOVERNMENTS [Chapter 8]

[1]   HONOR is far from being the principle of despotic governments; men being here all upon a level, no one can prefer himself to another; men being here all slaves, they can give themselves no preference at all.

[2]   Besides, as honor has its laws and rules, as it knows not how to submit, as it depends in great measure on a man's own caprice, and

not on that of another person; it can be found only in countries in which the constitution is fixed, and where they are governed by settled laws.

[3]   How can a despotic prince bear with any such thing as honor? Honor glories in contempt of life, and here the prince's whole strength consists in the power of taking it away. How can honor ever bear with a despotic prince? It has its fixed rules, and constant caprices; but a despotic prince is directed by no rule, and his own caprices destroy all others.

[4]   Honor therefore, a thing unknown in despotic governments, where very often they have not so much as a fit word to express it,[a] is the prevailing principle in monarchies; here it gives life to the whole body politic, to the laws, and even to the virtues themselves.

OF THE PRINCIPLE OF DESPOTIC GOVERNMENT [Chapter 9][7]

[1]   As virtue is necessary in a republic, and in a monarchy honor, so fear is necessary in a despotic government: with regard to virtue, there is no occasion for it at all, and honor would be extremely dangerous.

[2]   Here the immense power of the prince is devolved intirely upon those to whom he is pleased to intrust it. Persons capable of setting a value upon themselves would be likely to create revolutions. Fear must therefore depress all their spirits, and extinguish even the least sense of ambition.

[3]   A moderate government may, whenever it pleases, and without any danger, relax its springs. It supports itself by its laws, and by its own force. But when a despotic prince ceases one single moment to lift up his arm, when he cannot instantly demolish those

[a] See Perry, p. 447.

whom he has intrusted with the first posts and employments,[a] all is over: for as fear, the spring of this government, no longer subsists, the people are left without a protector.

DIFFERENCE OF OBEDIENCE IN MODERATE AND DESPOTIC GOVERNMENTS [Chapter 10]

[1]   IN despotic states the nature of the government requires the most passive obedience; and when once the prince's will is made known, it ought infallibly to produce its effect.

[2]   Here they have no limitations or restrictions, no mediums, terms, equivalents, parleys, or remonstrances; nothing equal or better to propose; man is a creature that submits to the absolute will of a creature like himself.

[3]   In a country like this they are no more allowed to represent their fears in respect to a future event, than to excuse their bad success by the capriciousness of fortune. Man's portion here, like that of beasts, is instinct, compliance and punishment.

[4]   Little does it then avail to plead the sentiments of nature, respect for a father, tenderness for a wife and children, the laws of honor, or an ill state of health; the orders are given, and that is sufficient.

[5]   In Persia when the king has condemned a person, it is no longer lawful to mention his name, or to intercede in his favor. Though he were drunk and beside himself, yet the decree must be executed;[a] otherwise he would contradict himself, and the law admits of no contradiction. This has been the way of thinking in this country in all ages.

[6]   There is one thing however that may be opposed to the prince's

---

[a] As it often happens in a military aristocracy.
[a] See Sir John Chardin.

will;[b] namely religion. They will abandon a parent, nay they will kill him, if the prince so commands; but he cannot oblige them to drink wine. The laws of religion are of a superior nature, because they bind the prince as well as the subject. But, with respect to the law of nature it is otherwise; the prince is no longer supposed to be a man.

REFLECTIONS ON THE FOREGOING [Chapter 11][8]

SUCH are the principles of the three sorts of government: which does not imply that in a particular republic they actually are, but that they ought to be, virtuous: nor does it prove, that in a particular monarchy they are actuated by honor, or in a particular despotic government by fear; but that they ought to be directed by these principles, otherwise the government is imperfect.

[b] Ibid.

BOOK IV: *That the Laws of Education Ought to Be in Relation to the Principles of Government*

ANALYSIS

Having defined the nature and principle of republics, monarchies, and despotisms, Montesquieu possessed the organizing principle of much of the remainder of his treatise and certainly of Books IV–XIII. He repeatedly returns to the three definitions of governmental types and principles as the starting point for his discussion of various aspects of state policy. (See Introduction, pp. 40–44, for how this relates to the rationalist component within M's method.)

The subject of Book IV is education, and given the stress placed on education in Part Two of the Essay on Causes *(see pars.* [1–43]*) plus Montesquieu's interest in the political ideas of Plato and Aristotle, it is not surprising that he should have given education such a prominent role in his treatise on laws.*

In Book IV, Montesquieu attributes to education a political role. The function of education is to produce citizens activated by the passion suitable to the particular form of government in which they reside. No matter what the form of government, education should instill in the citizen the mode of behavior supportive of the principle without which that government would collapse. In modern, sociological terms, education has a socializing function.

In monarchical governments, where honor is to be inculcated, the nobility are to be taught less what they owe to others than what they owe to themselves, less what makes them like their fellow citizens than what differentiates them from them (chap. 2, par. [3]). They are to learn, furthermore, that their actions are to be beautiful, great, and extraordinary (chap. 2 [4]) and that they are to display politeness motivated by pride (chap. 2 [12]). The aim of education in democratic governments should be to instill love of the fatherland and a capacity for renunciation of private interest for the sake of the goals of the community (chap. 5 [1–2]). The goal of education in despotic governments is to debase and induce fear among subjects, and education is thus very limited in this form of government (chap. 3 [1–5]).

OF THE LAWS OF EDUCATION [Chapter 1]

[1]   THE laws of education are the first impressions we receive; and as they prepare us for civil life, each particular family ought to be governed pursuant to the plan of the great family which comprehends them all.

[2]   If the people in general have a principle, their constituent parts, that is, the several families, will have one also. The laws of education will be therefore different in each species of government;[1] in monarchies they will have honor for their object, in republics virtue, in despotic governments fear.

OF EDUCATION IN MONARCHIES [Chapter 2]

[1]   IT is not from colleges or academies that the principal branch of education in monarchies is derived; it is when we set out in the world that our education in some measure commences. This is the school of what we call honor, that universal preceptor which ought every where to be our guide.

[2]   There it is that we constantly see and hear three things, *that we should have a certain nobleness in our virtues, a kind of frankness in our morals, and a particular politeness in our behaviour.*

[3]   The virtues we are there taught, are less what we owe to others, than to ourselves; they are not so much what assimilates us to, as what distinguishes us from, our fellow citizens.

[4]   There the actions of men are not judged as good, but as beautiful; not as just, but as great; not as reasonable, but as extraordinary.

[11]   In fine, the education of monarchies requires a certain politeness of behaviour. Men born for society, are born to please one another; and a person that would break thro' the rules of decorum, by shocking those he conversed with, would so far lose the public esteem as to become incapable of doing any good.

[12]   But politeness, generally speaking, does not derive its original from so pure a source. It rises from a desire of distinguishing our selves. It is pride that renders us polite: we feel a pleasing vanity in being remarked for a behaviour that shews in some measure we are not meanly born, and that we have not been bred up with those who in all ages have been considered as the scum of the people.

[19]   There is nothing so strongly inculcated in monarchies, by the laws, by religion, and honor, as submission to the prince's will; but this very honor tells us that the prince ought never to command a dishonourable action, because this would render us incapable to serve him.

[21]   There is nothing that honor more strongly recommends to the nobility, than to serve their prince in a military capacity. In fact this is their favourite profession, because its dangers, its success, and even its miscarriages are the road to grandeur.

[23]   Honor therefore has its supreme laws, to which education is obliged to conform. The chief of these are, that we are allowed to set a value upon our fortune, but it is absolutely forbidden to set any value upon our lives.[2*]

[24]   The second is, that when we are raised to a post or rank, we

should never do or permit any thing which may seem to imply that we look upon ourselves as inferior to the rank we hold.

[25]   The third is, that those things which honor forbids are more rigorously forbidden, when the laws do not concur in the prohibition; and those it commands are more strongly insisted upon, when they happen not to be commanded by law.

OF EDUCATION IN A DESPOTIC GOVERNMENT [Chapter 3]

[1]   As education in monarchies tends only to raise and ennoble the mind, so in despotic governments its only aim is to debase it.

[2]   Excessive obedience supposes ignorance in the person that obeys, the same it supposes in him that commands; for he has no occasion to deliberate, to doubt, to reason; he has only to will.

[3]   In despotic states each house is a separate government. As education therefore consists chiefly in social converse, it must be here very much limited; all it does is to strike the heart with fear, and to imprint in the understanding a very simple notion of a few principles of religion. Learning here proves dangerous, emulation fatal; and as to virtue, Aristotle cannot think there is any one virtue belonging to slaves;[a] if so, education in despotic countries is confined within a very narrow compass.

[4]   Here therefore education is in some measure needless; to give something one must take away every thing; and begin with making a bad subject in order to make a good slave.

[5]   For why should education take pains in forming a good citizen, only to make him share in the public misery? If he loved his country, he would strive to relax the springs of government; if he miscarried, he would be undone; if he succeeded, he would expose himself, the prince, and his country to ruin.

[a] Polit. lib. I.

OF EDUCATION IN A REPUBLICAN
GOVERNMENT [Chapter 5]

[1]   IT is in a republican government that the whole power of education is required. The fear of despotic governments rises naturally
of itself amidst threats and punishments; the honor of monarchies
is favoured by the passions, and favours them in its turn: but virtue
is a self-renunciation which is always arduous and painful.

[2]   This virtue may be defined, as the love of the laws and of our
country. As this love requires a constant preference of public to
private interest, it is the source of all the particular virtues; for
they are nothing more than this very preference it self.

[3]   This love is peculiar to democracies. In these alone the government is intrusted to private citizens. Now government is like every
thing else: to preserve it, we must love it.

[4]   Has it ever been heard that kings were not fond of monarchy, or
that despotic princes hated arbitrary power?

[5]   Every thing therefore depends on establishing this love in a
republic, and to inspire it ought to be the principal business of
education: but the surest way of instilling it into children, is for
parents to set them an example.

[6]   People have it generally in their power to communicate their
knowledge to their children; but they are still better able to transfuse their passions.

[7]   If this happens not to be the case, it is because the impressions
made at home are effaced by those they have received abroad.

[8]   It is not the young people that degenerate: they are not spoilt till
those of maturer age are already sunk in corruption.

BOOK V: *That the Laws Given by the Legislator Ought to be in Relation to the Principle of Government*

ANALYSIS

In Book V, Montesquieu explores the relation that laws — and particularly laws on landownership and inheritance — should bear to the principle of each of the three governmental types. He begins by stressing the need for equality and frugality in democracies (chap. 3) and suggests that, where possible, land should be equally distributed in small allotments (chaps. 5–6). And to insure the preservation of equality, equal attention need be given to the regulation of dowries, transfers of property, and laws of inheritance (chap. 5, par. [3]). The proper goal, says M, is a moderate degree of equality, extreme equality being usually beyond reach (5 [12]) and involving, in any case, disadvantages in placing all citizens too much on one level (see Book VIII, chap. 3).

Where the equal division of land is not practical, the political virtue of democracies can be supported by the presence of a senate adhering to ancient manners and institutions, a body of censors overseeing morals and preventing corruption, a healthy respect of youth for parental authority and for the aged, and a similar respect of citizens for their magistrates (chap. 7).

Montesquieu's comments on land and inheritance policies within monarchical states are rather brief. He emphasizes the need to enact laws preserving the wealth of the nobility undivided (chap. 9) and then, in two chapters disproving the charge that he denigrated monarchies while praising republics (see Book III, note 2), he digresses into a eulogy of the efficiency (chap. 10) and stability (chap. 11) of monarchy.

Chapters 13–15 of Book V present a detailed depiction of the nature of life in despotic governments, and as d'Alembert remarked, Montesquieu meant to satirize and ridicule what he described. One can expect to find in despotic governments, M reports, poverty, unstable landownership, usury, decline of commerce, and the embezzling of public funds (chap. 14 [17]; chap. 15 [5–7]).

Montesquieu concludes Book V with an important chapter (19) discussing whether each of the three principles of government is strengthened or weakened by such policies as compulsory eligibility for public office ([2]), compulsory duty among soldiers to serve a former inferior officer ([4–5]), the joining of civil and military posts ([6–10]), the sale of public offices ([12–14]), and the need for censors to oversee the behavior of the populace. Hence Book V contains key texts supplementing the discussion in Book II of the institutional nature of each of the three forms of government.

IDEA OF THIS BOOK [Chapter 1]

[1]   THAT the laws of education ought to be relative to the principle of each government, has been shewn in the preceding book. Now the same may be said of those which the legislator gives to the whole society. This relation of laws to this principle, strengthens the several springs of government, and this principle receives from thence, in its turn, a new degree of strength. Thus it is that in physical movements action is always followed by reaction.

[2]   Our design is to examine this relation in each government, beginning with the republican state whose principle is virtue.

WHAT IS MEANT BY VIRTUE IN A POLITICAL STATE [Chapter 2]

[1]   VIRTUE in a republic is a most simple thing; it is a love for the republic; it is a sensation, and not a consequence of acquired

knowledge: a sensation that may be felt by the meanest as well as
by the highest person in the state.

[2]   The love of our country is conducive to a purity of morals, and
the latter is again conducive to the love of our country. The less we
are able to satisfy our particular passions, the more we abandon
ourselves to those of a general nature. How comes it that monks
are so fond of their order? It is owing to the very cause that renders
the order insupportable. Their rule debars them of all those things
by which the ordinary passions are fed; there remains therefore
only this passion for the very rule that torments them. The more
austere it is, that is, the more it curbs their inclinations, the more
force it gives to the only passion it leaves them.

WHAT IS MEANT BY LOVE OF THE
REPUBLIC IN A DEMOCRACY [Chapter 3]

[1]   LOVE of the republic in a democracy, is a love of the democracy;
love of the democracy is that of equality.

[2]   Love of the democracy is likewise that of frugality. As every
individual ought to have here the same happiness and the same
advantages, they ought consequently to taste the same pleasures
and to form the same hopes; which cannot be expected but from a
general frugality.

[3]   The love of equality in a democracy limits ambition to the sole
desire, to the sole happiness of doing greater services to our country than the rest of our fellow citizens. They cannot all render her
equal services, but they ought all to serve her with equal alacrity.
At our coming into the world, we contract an immense debt to our
country, which we can never discharge.

[4]   Hence distinctions arise here from the principle of equality,
even when it seems to be removed by signal services, or superior
abilities.

[5]   The love of frugality limits the desire of having to the attention requisite for procuring necessaries to our family, and superfluities to our country. Riches give a power which a citizen cannot use for himself, for then he would be no longer equal. They likewise procure pleasures which he ought not to enjoy, because these would also subvert the equality.

[6]   Thus well policied democracies, by establishing domestic frugality, made way at the same time for public expences, as was the case at Rome and Athens, when magnificence and profusion arose from the very fund of frugality. And as religion requires us to have pure and unspotted hands when we make our offerings to the Gods, the laws require a frugality of life to enable us to be liberal to our country.

[7]   The good sense and happiness of individuals depend greatly on the mediocrity of their talents and fortunes. Therefore as a republic, where the laws have placed many in a middling station, is composed of wise men, it will be wisely governed, as it is composed of happy men, it will be extremely happy.

IN WHAT MANNER THE LOVE OF EQUALITY AND FRUGALITY IS INSPIRED [Chapter 4]

[1]   THE love of equality and of a frugal œconomy is greatly excited by equality and frugality themselves, in societies, where both these virtues are established by law.

[2]   In monarchies and despotic governments, no body aims at equality; this does not so much as enter their thoughts; they all aspire to superiority. People of the very lowest conditions desire to emerge from their obscurity only to lord it over their fellow subjects.

[3]   It is the same with respect to frugality. To love it we must

practice and enjoy it. It is not those who are enervated with
pleasure, that are fond of a frugal life.

[4]   A true maxim it is therefore, that in order to love equality and
frugality in a republic, these virtues must have been previously
established by law.

IN WHAT MANNER THE LAWS ESTABLISH
EQUALITY IN A DEMOCRACY [Chapter 5]

[1]   SOME ancient legislators, as Lycurgus and Romulus, made an
equal division of lands. A settlement of this kind can never take
place but upon the foundation of a new republic, or when the old
one is so corrupt, and the minds of the people so disposed, that the
poor think themselves obliged to demand, and the rich obliged to
consent to, a remedy of this nature.

[2]   If the legislator in making a division of this kind, does not enact
laws at the same time to support it, he forms only a temporary
constitution; inequality will break in where the laws have not
precluded it, and the republic will be utterly undone.

[3]   Hence for the preservation of this equality it is absolutely necessary there should be some regulation in respect to women's dowries, donations, successions, testamentary settlements, and all
other forms of contracting. For were it once allowed to dispose of
our property to whom and how we pleased, the will of each
individual would disturb the order of the fundamental law.

[4]   Solon, by permitting the Athenians upon failure of issue to
leave their estates to whom they pleased,[a] acted contrary to the
ancient laws by which the estates were ordered to continue in the
family of the testator;[b] and even contrary to his own laws, for by
abolishing debts he had aimed at equality.

        [a] Plutarch's life of Solon.   [b] Ibid.

[11]   Phaleas of Chalcedon contrived a very extraordinary method of rendering all fortunes equal, in a republic where there was the greatest inequality. His contrivance was, that the rich should give fortunes with their daughters to the poor, but should receive none themselves; and that the poor should receive money for their daughters, instead of giving them fortunes.[c] But I do not remember that a regulation of this kind ever took place in any republic. It lays the citizens under such hard and odious conditions, as would make them detest the very equality which they designed to establish. It is proper sometimes that the laws should not seem to tend so directly to the end they propose.

[12]   Tho' real equality be the very soul of a democracy, yet it is so difficult to establish, that an extreme exactness in this respect would not be always convenient. Sufficient it is to establish a census,[d] which should reduce or fix the differences to a certain point: it is afterwards the province of particular laws to level as it were the inequalities, by the duties laid upon the rich, and by the ease they afford to the poor. It is moderate riches alone that can give or suffer this sort of compensations; for as to men of overgrown estates, every thing which does not contribute to advance their power and honor, is considered by them as an injury.

[13]   All inequality in a democracy ought to be derived from the nature of the democracy, and even from the principle of equality. For example, it may be apprehended that people who are obliged to constant labour for their subsistence, would be too much impoverished by a public office, or neglect its duties; that artisans

---

[c] Aristot. lib. 2. cap. 7.

[d] Solon made four classes, the first, of those who had an income of 500 minas either in corn or liquid fruits; the second, of those who had 300 and were able to keep a horse; the third, of those who had only 200; the fourth, of all those who lived by their manual labor. *Plut.* Life of Solon.

would grow insolent; and that too great a number of freedmen would become more powerful than the ancient citizens. In this case the equality of the citizens may be suppressed in a democracy for the utility of the state.[e] But then it is only an apparent equality they remove: for a man ruined by a public office would be in a worse condition than the rest of his fellow citizens, and this same man being obliged to neglect his duty would reduce the other citizens to a worse condition than himself, and so on.

IN WHAT MANNER THE LAWS OUGHT TO MAINTAIN FRUGALITY IN A DEMOCRACY [Chapter 6]

[1]   IT is not sufficient in a regular policied democracy that the divisions of land be equal; they ought also to be small, as was customary among the Romans.

[2]   As the equality of fortunes supports frugality, frugality supports the equality of fortunes. These things, tho' in themselves different, are of such a nature as to be incapable of subsisting separately; each is the cause and the effect; if one withdraws it self from a democracy, it is surely followed by the other.

[3]   True it is that when a democracy is founded on commerce, private people may acquire vast riches without a corruption of morals. This is because the spirit of commerce is naturally attended with that of frugality, œconomy, moderation, labour, prudence, tranquillity, order, and rule. Wherefore as long as this spirit subsists, the riches it produces have no bad effect. The mischief is when excessive wealth destroys this spirit of commerce; then it is that the disorders of inequality which were yet unfelt, immediately arise.

[4]   In order to support the spirit of commerce, it is necessary it

[e] Solon excludes from public employments all those of the fourth class.

should be carried on by the principal citizens; that this spirit alone should prevail without being crossed by another; that all the laws should encourage it; that these very laws, by dividing the fortunes of individuals in proportion to the increase of commerce, should set every poor citizen so far at his ease as to be able to work like the rest, and every rich citizen in such a mediocrity as to be obliged to labour either to preserve or to acquire his wealth.

[5]   It is an excellent law in a trading republic, to make an equal division of the father's estate among the children. The consequence of this is, that how great soever a fortune the father has made, his children being not so rich as he, are induced to avoid luxury, and to follow the parent's industrious example. I speak here only of trading republics, for as to those that have no commerce, the legislator must pursue quite different measures. [a]

[6]   In Greece there was two sorts of republics: the one military, like Sparta; the other commercial, as Athens. In one the citizens were obliged to be idle; in the other endeavours were used to inspire them with the love of industry and labour. Solon made idleness a crime, and insisted that each citizen should give an account of his manner of getting a livelyhood. In fact, in a well policied democracy, where people's expences ought to extend only to what is necessary, every one ought to have as much as his necessities require; for how could his wants be otherwise supplied?

OTHER METHODS OF FAVOURING THE
PRINCIPLE OF DEMOCRACY [Chapter 7]

[1]   AN equal division of lands cannot be established in all democracies. Some circumstances there are in which a regulation of this

---

[a] In these the portions or fortunes of women ought to be very much limited.

nature would be impracticable, dangerous, and even subversive of the constitution. We are not always obliged to proceed to extremes.

[2]   If it appears that this division of lands, which was designed to preserve the people's morals, does not suit with the democracy, recourse must be had to other methods.

[3]   If a fixt body be established to serve as a rule and pattern of manners, a senate, to which age, virtue, gravity, and public services gain admittance; the senators exposed to public view like the statues of the Gods, must naturally inspire sentiments that will transfuse into the bosoms of every family.

[4]   Above all, this senate must steadily adhere to the ancient institutions, and mind that the people and the magistrates never swerve from them.

[5]   The preservation of the ancient customs is a very considerable point in respect to manners. As a corrupt people seldom perform any memorable actions; seldom establish societies, build cities, or enact laws, and on the contrary most institutions are derived from people of simple or severe morals; so to recall men to the ancient maxims is generally recalling them to virtue.

[10]   At Athens, besides the Areopagus,[1] there were guardians of the people's morals, and guardians of the laws.[a] At Sparta all the old men were censors. At Rome the censorship was committed to two particular magistrates. As the senate watched over the people, the censors were to have an eye over the people and the senate. Their office was to reform the corruptions of the republic, to stigmatize indolence, to judge irregularities, and to correct faults; and as for notorious crimes, they were left to the punishment of the laws.

[11]   That Roman law, which required the accusations of adultery to

_____

[a] Even the areopagus itself was subject to their censure.

be public, was admirably well calculated for preserving the purity of morals; it intimidated married women, as well as those who were to watch over their conduct.

[12]   Nothing contributes more to the preservation of morals, than an extreme subordination of the young to the old. Thus they are both restrained, the former by the respect they have for those of advanced age, and the latter by the respect they have for themselves. [2]

[13]   Nothing gives a greater force to the laws than a perfect subordination between the citizens and the magistrate. *The great difference which Lycurgus established between Sparta and the other cities,* says Xenophon, [b] *consists chiefly in the obedience the citizens shew to the laws; they run, when the magistrate calls them. But at Athens a rich man would be greatly displeased, to be thought dependent on the magistrate.* [3]

[14]   Paternal authority is likewise of great use towards the preservation of morals. We have already observed that in a republic there is not so coercive a force as in other governments. The laws must therefore endeavour to supply this deficiency by some means or other; which is done by paternal authority.

[15]   Fathers at Rome had the power of life and death over their children. [c] At Sparta every father had a right to correct another man's child.

[16]   Paternal authority ended at Rome together with the republic. In monarchies where such a purity of morals is not required, people are controlled by no other means than the authority of the magistrates.

---

[b] Republic of the Lacedaemonians.

[c] We may see in the Roman history, how useful this power was to the republic. I shall give an instance even in the time of its greatest corruption. Aulus Fulvius was set out on his journey in order to join Catiline; his father called him back, and put him to death. Sallust *de bello Catil.*

IN WHAT MANNER THE LAWS ARE RELATIVE TO
THEIR PRINCIPLE IN MONARCHIES [Chapter 9]

[1]   As honor is the principle of a monarchical government, the
laws ought to be relative to this principle.

[2]   They should endeavour to support the nobility, in respect to
whom honor may be, in some measure, deemed both child and
parent.

[3]   They should render the nobility hereditary, not as a boundary
between the power of the prince and the weakness of the people,
but as the bond and conjunction of both.

[4]   In this government, entails which preserve the estates of
families undivided, are extremely useful, though in others not so
proper.[4]

[5]   Here the power of redemption is of service, as it restores to
noble families the lands that had been alienated by the prodigality
of a parent.[5]

[6]   The lands of the nobility ought to have privileges as well as their
persons. The monarch's dignity is inseparable from that of his
kingdom; and the dignity of the nobles from that of their fief.

[7]   All these prerogatives must be particular to the nobility, and
incommunicable to the people, unless we intend to act contrary to
the principle of government, and to diminish the power of the
nobles together with that of the people.

OF THE EXPEDITION PECULIAR TO THE EXECUTIVE
POWER IN MONARCHIES [Chapter 10]

[1]   GREAT is the advantage which a monarchical government has
over a republic: as the state is conducted by a single person, the
executive power is thereby enabled to act with greater expedition.
But as this expedition might degenerate into rapidity, the laws

should use some contrivance to slacken it. They ought not only to favour the nature of each constitution, but likewise to remedy the abuses that might result from this very nature.

[2]   Cardinal Richelieu advises monarchs to permit no such thing as societies or corporations that raise difficulties upon every trifle.[a] If this man's heart had not been bewitched with the love of despotic power, still these arbitrary notions would have filled his head.

[3]   The bodies intrusted with the depositum of the laws, are never more obedient than when they proceed slowly, and when they use that reflection in the prince's affairs which can scarce be expected from ignorance of the laws in the court, nor from the precipitation of its counsels.[b]

[4]   What would have become of the finest monarchy in the world, if the magistrates by their delays, by their complaints, by their prayers, had not stopped the rapidity even of their princes' virtues, when these monarchs consulting only the generous impulses of great minds, wanted to give a boundless reward to services performed with a boundless courage and fidelity?

OF THE EXCELLENCE OF A MONARCHICAL GOVERNMENT
[Chapter 11]

[1]   MONARCHY has a great advantage over a despotic government. As it naturally requires there should be several orders belonging to the constitution under the prince, the state is more fixt, the constitution more steady, and the person of him that governs more secure.

[3]   In the commotions of a despotic government, the people hurried away of themselves, push things always as far as they can go. The

[a] Testam. Polit.

[b] *Barbaris cunctatio servilis, statim exequi regium videtur.* Tacit. Annal. lib. 5.

disorders they commit are all extreme; whereas in monarchies things are seldom carried to excess. The chiefs are afraid of themselves, they are afraid of being abandoned; and the intermediate dependent powers do not chuse that the people should have too much the upper hand. It rarely happens that the several orders of the state are intirely corrupted. The prince adheres to these, and the seditious who have neither will nor hopes to subvert the government, have neither power nor will to subvert the prince.

[4]   In these circumstances men of prudence and authority interfere; moderate measures are first proposed, then complied with, and things at length are redressed; the laws resume their vigor, and command submission.

[5]   Thus all our histories are full of civil wars without revolutions, while the histories of despotic governments abound with revolutions without civil wars.

[8]   As people who live under a good government, are happier than those who without rule or leaders wander about the forests; so monarchs who live under the fundamental laws of their country, are far happier than despotic princes, who have nothing to regulate either their own or their subjects' hearts.

THE SAME SUBJECT CONTINUED [Chapter 12]

[1]   LET us not look for magnanimity in despotic governments; the prince cannot impart a grandeur he has not himself: with him there is no such thing as glory.

[2]   'Tis in monarchies we see the subjects around the prince, receiving the influence of his beams; there it is that each person filling, as it were, a larger space, is capable of exercising those virtues that adorn the soul, not with independence, but with grandeur.

IDEA OF DESPOTIC POWER [Chapter 13]

WHEN the savages of Louisiana are desirous of fruit, they cut the tree to the root, and gather the fruit.[a] In this we behold an emblem of despotic government.

IN WHAT MANNER THE LAWS ARE RELATIVE TO THE PRINCIPLES OF A DESPOTIC GOVERNMENT [Chapter 14]

[1]   THE principle of despotic government is fear; but a timid, ignorant, and faint-spirited people have no occasion for a great number of laws.

[2]   Every thing ought to depend here on two or three ideas; therefore there is no necessity that any new notions should be added. When we want to break a horse, we take care not to let him change his master, his lesson, or his pace. Thus an impression is made on his brain by two or three motions, and no more.

[9]   Politics, with its several springs and laws, ought here to be very much limited, the political government should be every whit as simple as the civil.[a]

[10]   The whole is reduced to reconciling the political and civil government with the domestic management, the officers of state with those of the seraglio.

[12]   As fear is the principle of despotic government, its end is tranquillity: a tranquillity that cannot be called a peace; no, it is only the silence of those towns which the enemy is ready to invade.

[13]   As the strength does not lie in the state, but in the army that founded it; in order to defend the state, the army must be preserved, how formidable soever to the prince. How then can we reconcile the security of the government, with that of the prince's person?

[a] Edifying letters coll. 11. p. 315.

[a] According to Sir John Chardin there is no council of state in Persia.

[15]   In those states religion has more influence than any where else; it is a fear added to fear. In Mahometan countries it is partly from their religion that the people derive the surprizing veneration they have for their prince.

[17]   Of all despotic governments, there is none that labours more under its own weight, than that wherein the prince declares himself the proprietor of all the lands and heir to all his subjects. Thence the neglect of agriculture arises; and if the prince intermeddles likewise in trade, all manner of industry is ruined.

[18]   Under this sort of government nothing is repaired or improved.[b] Houses are built only for the necessity of habitation, there is no such thing as digging of ditches, or planting of trees, every thing is drawn from, but nothing restored to the earth; the land lies untilled, and the whole country becomes a desert.

[19]   Is it to be imagined that the laws which abolish the property of land and the succession of estates, will diminish the avarice and cupidity of the great? By no means. They will rather inflame this cupidity and avarice. The great men will be prompted to use a thousand vexatious methods, imagining they have no other property than the gold and silver which they are able to seize upon by violence or to conceal.

[20]   To prevent therefore the utter ruin of the state, the avidity of the prince ought to be moderated by some established custom.

[22]   In countries where there are no fundamental laws, the succession to the empire cannot be fixt. The crown is then elective by the prince either in his own or in some other family. In vain would it be to establish here the succession of the eldest son; the prince might always chuse another. The successor is declared by the prince himself, or by a civil war. Hence a despotic state is,

[b] See Ricaut, State of the Ottoman Empire, p. 196.

upon another account, more liable than a monarchical government to dissolution.

[23]   As every prince of the royal family has an equal capacity to be chosen, hence it follows that the prince who ascends the throne, strangles immediately his brothers, as in Turky; or puts out their eyes, as in Persia; or bereaves them of their understanding, as in the Mogul's country; or if these precautions are not used, as in Morocco, the vacancy of the throne is always attended with a horrid civil war.

[24]   By the constitutions of Russia the Czar may chuse who he has a mind for his successor, whether in his own or in a strange family.[c] Such a settlement produces a thousand revolutions, and renders the throne as tottering as the succession is arbitrary.

[28]   The princes of despotic governments have always perverted the use of marriage. They generally take a great many wives, especially in that part of the world where absolute power is in some measure naturalized, namely Asia. Hence they come to have such a multitude of children, that they can hardly have any great affection for them, nor the children for one another.

[29]   The reigning family resembles the state; it is too weak itself, and its head too powerful; it seems very numerous and extensive, and yet is suddenly extinct.

[30]   After what has been said, one would imagine that human nature should perpetually oppose a despotic government. But notwithstanding the love of liberty, so natural to mankind, notwithstanding their innate detestation of force and violence, most nations are subject to this very government. This is easily accounted for. In order to form a moderate government, it is necessary to combine the several powers, to rule, temper, and set them

---

[c] See the different constitutions, especially that of 1722.

in motion, to give, as it were, ballast to one in order to enable it to resist another. This is a master-piece of legislation, rarely produced by hazard, and seldom attained by prudence. On the contrary, a despotic government offers itself, as it were, at first sight; it is uniform throughout; and as passions only are requisite to establish it, this is what every capacity may reach.

THE SAME SUBJECT CONTINUED [Chapter 15]

[5]   POVERTY and uncertainty of property in a despotic state render usury natural, each person raising the value of his money in proportion to the danger he sees in lending it. Misery therefore pours in from all parts into those unhappy countries; they are bereft of every thing even of the resource of borrowing.

[6]   Hence it is that a merchant under this government is capable of carrying on a great trade; he lives from hand to mouth; were he to encumber himself with a large quantity of merchandises, he would lose more by the exorbitant interest he must give for money, than he could possibly get by the goods. Wherefore there are no laws here relating to commerce, they are all reduced to what is called the civil polity.

[7]   A government cannot be unjust without having hands to exercise its injustice. Now it is impossible but these hands will be grasping for themselves. The embezzling of the public money is therefore natural in despotic states.

NEW CONSEQUENCES OF THE PRINCIPLES
OF THE THREE GOVERNMENTS [Chapter 19]

[1]   I CANNOT conclude this book without making some applications of my three principles.

[2]   It is a question, whether the laws ought to oblige a subject to accept of a public employment. My opinion is that they ought in a

republic, but not in a monarchical government. In the former, public employments are attestations of virtue, depositums with which a citizen is intrusted by his country, for whom alone he ought to live, act, and think; consequently he cannot refuse them. [a] In the latter, public offices are testimonies of honor; now such is the capriciousness of honor, that it chuses to accept of none of those testimonies but when and in what manner it pleases.

[4]   Secondly, it is questioned whether a subject should be obliged to accept of a post in the army inferior to that which he held before? Among the Romans it was usual to see a captain serve the next year under his lieutenant. [b] This is because virtue in republics requires a continual sacrifice of our persons and of our repugnances to the state. But in monarchies, honor true or false will never bear with what it calls degrading itself.

[5]   In despotic governments where honor, posts and ranks are equally abused, they indiscriminately make of a prince, a scullion, and of a scullion a prince.

[6]   Thirdly it is a question, whether civil and military employments ought to be conferred on the same person? In a republic, I should think, they ought to be joined, but in monarchies separated. In republics it would be extremely dangerous to make the profession of arms a particular state, distinct from that of civil functions; and in monarchies no less dangerous would it be to confer these two employments on the same person.

[7]   In republics a person takes up arms only with a view to defend

---

[a] Plato in his Republic Book 8. ranks these refusals among the marks of the corruption of a republic. In his Laws, Book 6. he orders them to be punished by a fine; at Venice they are punished with banishment.

[b] Some centurions having appealed to the people for the employments which they had before enjoyed, *it is just, my comrades,* said a centurion, *that you should look upon every post as honourable in which you have an opportunity of defending the republic.* Decad. 5. lib. 42.

his country and its laws; it is because he is a citizen he makes himself for a while a soldier. Were there two distinct states, the person who under arms thinks himself a citizen, would soon be made sensible he is only a soldier.

[8]   In monarchies military men have nothing but glory, or at least honor or fortune, in view. To men therefore like these the prince should never give any civil employments; on the contrary they ought to be checked by the civil magistrates, and care should be taken that the same men may not have at the same time the confidence of the people and the power to abuse it.[c]

[9]   We have only to turn our eyes to a nation that may be justly called a republic disguised under the form of monarchy,[6] and there we shall see how jealous they are of a separate state of the gentle-men of the army, and how the military state is constantly allied with that of the citizen, and even sometimes of the magistrate, to the end that these qualities may be a pledge for their country, which should never be forgotten.

[10]   The division of civil and military employments, made by the Romans after the extinction of the republic, was not intirely arbi-trary. It was a consequence of the change which happened in the constitution of Rome; it was natural to a monarchical government, and what was only commenced under Augustus,[d] succeeding em-perors were obliged to finish,[e] in order to temper the military government.

[12]   Fourthly, it is a question, whether public employments should be venal? They ought not, I think, in despotic governments,

---

[c] Ne imperium ad optimos nobilium transferretur, Senatum militia vetuit Gallienus, etiam adire exercitum. *Aurelius Victor* de viris illustribus.

[d] Augustus deprived the senators, proconsuls, and governors of the privilege of wear-ing arms. Dio lib. 33.

[e] Constantine. See Zozimus lib. 2.

where the subjects must be instantaneously placed or displaced by the prince.

[13]   But in monarchies this venality is not at all improper, by reason it renders that a family employment which would never be undertaken through a motive of virtue; it fixes likewise every one to his duty, and renders the several orders of the kingdom more solid and permanent. [7]

[14]   Plato cannot bear with this venality. [f] *"This is exactly*, says he, *as if a person was to be made a mariner or pilot of a ship for his money. Is it possible that this rule should be bad in every other employment of life, and hold good only in the administration of a republic?"* But Plato speaks of a republic founded on virtue, and we of a monarchy. Now in monarchies (where though there was no such thing as a regular sale of public offices, still the indigence and avidity of the courtier would equally prompt him to expose them to sale) chance will furnish better subjects than the prince's choice. In fine, the method of attaining to honors through riches, inspires and cherishes industry, [g] a thing extremely wanting in this kind of government.

[15]   The fifth question is, in what kind of government censors are necessary? My answer is, that they are necessary in a republic, where the principle of government is virtue. It is not criminal actions only that are destructive of virtue; it is destroyed also by carelessness, by faults, by a certain coolness in the love of our country, by dangerous examples, by seeds of corruption, by whatever does not openly violate but eludes the laws, does not subvert but weakens them; all this ought to fall under the inquiry and correction of the censors. [8]

---

[f] Repub. lib. 8.

[g] We see the laziness of Spain, where all public employments are given away.

[17]   In monarchies there should be no censors; monarchies are founded on honor, and the nature of honor is to have the whole universe for a censor. Every man that fails in this respect is subject to the reproaches even of those that are void of honor.

[18]   Here the censors would be spoilt by the very people whom they ought to correct: they could not prevail against the corruption of a monarchy, the corruption rather would be too strong against them.

[19]   Hence it is obvious that there ought to be no censors in despotic governments. The example of China seems to derogate from this rule; but we shall see in the course of this work, the particular reasons of that institution.

BOOK VI

Consequences of the Principles of
Different Governments with Respect
to the Simplicity of Civil and
Criminal Laws, the Form of
Judgments, and the Inflicting of
Punishments

ANALYSIS

In Book VI, Montesquieu considers the nature of the civil and criminal laws,
judicial procedures, and forms of punishment best suited to preserving the
principles of democracies, monarchies, and despotisms. Its subject matter is
thus closely related to that of Book XII. M suggests that civil and criminal
laws need be far more complex in moderate governments than in despotisms
(chaps. 1–2). The general rule is that the greater the concern for the liberty
of the individual, the more extensive the legal system protecting him. In
moderate governments the judge should be separate from the sovereign and
should sentence in strictest possible accordance with the letter of the law
(chaps. 3–7). Equally important in moderate governments is the care taken
to avoid unjust accusations of innocent persons (chap. 8) and the scaling of
punishments to crimes (chaps. 9–20). Immoderate punishments, M contends,
are often desperate measures undertaken by despotic governments beset by
citizens possessing few motives for avoiding crime (chap. 9, pars. [1–3]).
And harsh punishments, M suggests, are not automatically efficient deterrents
to crime. Men soon grow accustomed to the threat of harsh punishments, so
that the state is left only with cruel and inhumane treatment of lawbreakers

rather than a substantially reduced level of crime (chap. 12 [1–2]). The
remedy to crime, according to M, is the creation of moderate governments
meting out moderate punishments while striving to produce a moral environ-
ment in which the shame attached to being regarded a tresspasser of the laws
is itself a substantial deterrent (chap. 12 [6–7]).

Montesquieu concludes Book VI with a chapter contending that clemency
is more necessary in monarchies than in either democracies or republics, since
honor frequently requires that the nobility do what the laws forbid, and since
in monarchies "disgrace is equivalent to chastisement" (chap. 21 [1]).

OF THE SIMPLICITY OF CIVIL LAWS IN
DIFFERENT GOVERNMENTS   [Chapter 1]

[1]   MONARCHIES do not permit of so great a simplicity of laws as
despotic governments. For in monarchies there must be courts of
judicature; these must give their decisions; the decisions must be
preserved and learnt, that they may judge in the same manner to
day as yesterday, and that the lives and property of the citizens may
be as certain and fixt as the very constitution of the state.

[3]   We must not therefore be surprized to find so many rules,
restrictions, and extensions in the laws of those countries; rules
that multiply the particular cases, and seem to make of reason
itself an art.

[4]   The difference of rank, birth and condition, established in
monarchical governments, is frequently attended with distinctions
in the nature of property; and the laws relative to the constitution
of this government, may augment the number of these distinctions.

[5]   In our governments, the fiefs are become hereditary. It was
necessary that the nobility should have a fixt property, that is, the
fief should have a certain consistency, to the end that the proprietor

of the fief might be always in a capacity of serving the prince. This must have been productive of great varieties; for instance, there are countries where fiefs could not be divided among the brothers; in others the young brothers may be allowed a more generous subsistence.

[8]   In governments where there are necessary distinctions of persons, there must likewise be privileges. This also diminishes the simplicity, and creates a thousand exceptions.

[10]   Far different is the case of people under despotic governments. In those countries I can see nothing that the legislator is capable to decree, or the magistrate to judge. As the lands belong to the prince, thence it follows, that there are scarce any civil laws concerning the property of lands.

[11]   Despotic power is of itself sufficient; round it there is an absolute vacuum. Hence it is, that when travellers favour us with the description of countries where arbitrary sway prevails, they seldom make mention of civil laws.[a]

[12]   All occasions therefore of rangling and law-suits are here removed. And to this in part it is owing that litigious people in those countries are so roughly handled: as the injustice of their demand is neither screened, palliated, nor protected by an infinite number of laws, it is of course immediately discovered.

OF THE SIMPLICITY OF CRIMINAL LAWS IN DIFFERENT GOVERNMENTS [Chapter 2]

[1]   WE hear it generally said that justice ought to be administered with us as in Turkey. Is it possible then that the most ignorant of

[a] In *Mazulipatan* it could never be found out that there was such a thing as written law. *See the collection of voyages that contributed to the establishment of the India company.* Tom. IV. Part I. p. 391. The Indians are regulated in their judgments by certain customs. The Vedas and such like books do not contain civil laws, but religious precepts. See Lettres éd. 14. collect.

all nations should be the most clear sighted in a point that it most behoves mankind to know?

[2]   If we examine the set forms of justice in respect to the trouble the subject undergoes in recovering his property, or in obtaining satisfaction for an injury or affront, we shall find them doubtless too many: but if we consider them in the relation they have to the liberty and security of the subject, we shall often find them too few; and we shall be convinced that the trouble, expence, delays, and even the very dangers of our judiciary proceedings, are the price that every subject pays for his liberty.

[3]   In Turkey where little regard is shewn to the estates, lives, or honor of the subjects, all manner of disputes are one way or other quickly decided. The method of determining them is a matter of indifference, provided they be determined. The bashaw[1] after a quick hearing orders which party he pleases to be bastinadoed,[2] and then sends them about their business.

[4]   Here every man ought to know that the magistrate must not hear his name mentioned, and that his security depends intirely on his being reduced to a kind of annihilation.

[5]   But in moderate governments, where the life of the meanest subject is deemed precious, no man is stript of his honor or property but after a long inquiry; and no man is bereft of life, 'till his very country has attacked him, an attack that is never made without leaving him all possible means of making his defence.

[6]   Hence it is that when a person renders himself absolute,[a] he immediately thinks of simplifying the laws. In a government thus constituted they are more affected with particular inconveniences, than with the liberty of the subject, which is very little minded.

[7]   In republics it is plain that as many formalities are necessary as in monarchies. In both governments they increase in proportion to

[a] Caesar, Cromwell, and many others.

the value which is set on the honor, fortune, life, and liberty of the subject.

[8]   In republican governments men are all equal; equal they are also in despotic governments: in the former because they are every thing, in the latter because they are nothing.

IN WHAT GOVERNMENTS AND IN WHAT CASES
THE JUDGES OUGHT TO DETERMINE ACCORDING
TO THE EXPRESS LETTER OF THE LAW   [Chapter 3]

[2]   In despotic governments there are no laws; the judge is himself his own rule. There are laws in monarchies; and where they are explicit, the judge conforms to them; where they are otherwise, he endeavours to investigate their spirit. In republics the very nature of the constitution requires the judges to follow the letter of the law. Here there is no possibility of interpreting a law against a subject, in cases where either his property, honor, or life is concerned.

[3]   At Rome the judges had no more to do than to declare that the person accused was guilty of a particular crime, and then the punishment was found in the laws, as may be seen in divers laws still extant. In England the jury determine whether the fact brought under their cognizance be proved or not; if it be proved, the judge pronounces the punishment inflicted by the law for such a fact, and for this he has only to open his eyes.

IN WHAT GOVERNMENTS THE SOVEREIGN
MAY BE JUDGE [Chapter 5]

[5]   In despotic governments the prince himself may be judge. But in monarchies this cannot be; the constitution by such means would be subverted, and the dependent intermediate powers annihilated; all set forms of judgment would cease; fear would take

possession of the people's minds, and paleness spread itself over
every countenance: the more confidence, honour, affection, and
security, the more widely extended is the power of the monarch.

[6]   We shall give here a few more reflections on this subject. In
monarchies the prince is the party that prosecutes the persons
accused, and causes them to be punished or acquitted; now were he
himself to sit as judge, he would be both judge and party.

[8]   Farther, by this means he would deprive himself of the most
beautiful attribute of sovereignty, namely, that of granting pardon;[a] for it would be quite foolish in him to make and unmake his
decisions: surely he would not chuse to contradict himself. Besides, this would be confounding all ideas; it would be impossible
to tell whether a man was acquitted, or received his pardon.

[10]   Again, sentences passed by the prince would be an inexhaustible
source of injustice and abuse; the courtiers by their importunity
would always be able to extort his decisions. Some Roman emperors were so mad as to sit as judges themselves; the consequence
was, that no reigns ever so surprized the universe with oppression
and injustice.

THAT IN MONARCHIES MINISTERS OUGHT
NOT TO BE JUDGES [Chapter 6]

[1]   IT is likewise a very great inconveniency in monarchies for the
ministers of the prince to be judges.

[2]   There is in the very nature of things a kind of contrast between
a prince's council and his courts of judicature. The king's council
ought to be composed of a few persons, and the courts of judicature
of a great many. The reason is, in the former, things should be
undertaken and pursued with a kind of warmth and passion, which

---

[a] Plato does not think it right that kings who, as he says, are priests, should preside at
judgments where people are condemned to death, exile, or imprisonment.

can hardly be expected but from four or five men who make it their sole business. On the contrary in courts of judicature a certain coolness is requisite, and an indifference in some measure to all manner of affairs.

OF THE SEVERITY OF PUNISHMENTS IN DIFFERENT GOVERNMENTS [Chapter 9]

[1]   THE severity of punishments is fitter for despotic governments whose principle is terror, than for a monarchy or republic whose spring is honor and virtue.

[2]   In moderate governments the love of one's country, shame and the fear of blame, are restraining motives, capable of preventing a great multitude of crimes. Here the greatest punishment of a bad action is conviction. The civil laws have therefore a softer way of correcting, and do not require so much force and severity.

[3]   In those states a good legislator is less bent upon punishing than preventing crimes; he is more attentive to inspire good morals than to inflict punishments.

[5]   It would be an easy matter to prove that in all or almost all the governments of Europe, punishments have increased or diminished in proportion as those governments favoured or discouraged liberty.

[7]   Men in excess of happiness or misery are equally inclinable to severity; witness monks and conquerors. It is mediocrity alone and a mixture of prosperous and adverse fortune that inspire us with lenity and pity.

[8]   Whatever we observe among particular men, is equally observable in different nations. In countries inhabited by savages who lead a very hard life, and in despotic governments, where there is only one person on whom fortune has lavished her favours, while the

miserable subjects lye exposed to her insults, people are equally cruel. Lenity reigns in moderate governments.

THAT WHEN A PEOPLE ARE VIRTUOUS FEW PUNISHMENTS ARE NECESSARY [Chapter 11]

[1]   THE people of Rome must be allowed to have had some share of probity. Such a force had this probity, that the legislator had frequently no farther occasion than to point out the right road, to induce them to follow it; one would imagine that instead of ordinances it was sufficient to give them counsels.

OF THE POWER OF PUNISHMENTS [Chapter 12]

[1]   EXPERIENCE shews that in countries remarkable for the lenity of penal laws, the spirit of the inhabitants is as much thereby affected, as in other countries with severer punishments.

[2]   If an inconveniency or abuse arises in the state, a violent government endeavours suddenly to redress it; and instead of putting the old laws in execution, it establishes some cruel punishment which instantly puts a stop to the evil. But the spring of government hereby loses its elasticity; the imagination grows accustomed to the severe as well as to the milder punishment; and as the fear of the latter diminishes, they are soon obliged in every case to have recourse to the other.

[5]   Let us follow nature, who has given shame to man for his scourge; and let the heaviest part of the punishment be the infamy attending it.

[6]   But if there be some countries where shame is not a consequence of punishment, this must be owing to tyranny, which has inflicted the same punishments on villains and honest men.

[7]   And if there are others where men are deterred only by cruel

punishments, we may be sure that this must in a great measure arise from the violence of the government, which has used such punishments for slight transgressions.

[11]   There are two sorts of corruption; one when the people do not observe the laws; the other when they are corrupted by the laws: an incurable evil, because it is in the very remedy itself.

IMPOTENCY OF THE LAWS OF JAPAN [Chapter 13]

[1]   EXCESSIVE punishments may even corrupt a despotic government; of this we have an instance in Japan.

[2]   Here almost all crimes are punished with death,[a] by reason that disobedience to so great an emperor, as that of Japan, is reckoned an enormous crime.[3] The question is not so much to correct the delinquent, as to avenge the prince. These notions are derived from servitude, and are owing especially to this, that as the emperor is universal proprietor, almost all crimes are directly against his interests.

[3]   They punish with death lies spoken before the magistrates;[b] a proceeding contrary to natural defence.

[4]   Even things which have not the appearance of a crime are severely punished; for instance, a man that ventures his money at play is put to death.

[7]   A wise legislator would have endeavoured to reclaim people's minds by a just temperature[4] of punishments and rewards, by maxims of philosophy, morality, and religion, adapted to these characters, by a just application of the rules of honor, and by the enjoyment of a constant happiness and soft tranquillity of life. But these are springs to which despotic power is a stranger; it may

---

[a] See *Kempfer*.

[b] Collection of voyages that contributed to the establishment of the East India Company. Tom. 3. p. 428.

abuse itself, and that is all it can do: in Japan it has made its utmost effort, and has surpassed even itself in cruelty.

[8]   As the spirits of the people by this means grew wild and intractable, they were obliged to be managed with the most horrid severity. This is the origin, this the spirit of the laws of Japan. They had more fury however than force. They succeeded in the extirpation of Christianity;[5] but such unaccountable efforts are a proof of their impotence. They wanted to establish a good polity, and they have only shewn greater marks of their weakness.

OF THE JUST PROPORTION BETWIXT PUNISHMENTS AND CRIMES [Chapter 16]

[1]   IT is an essential point that there should be a certain proportion in punishments, because it is essential that a great crime should be avoided rather than a lesser, and that which is more pernicious to society rather than that which is less.

[5]   It is a great abuse amongst us to subject to the same punishment a person that only robs on the high-way, and another that robs and murders. Obvious it is that for the public security some difference should be made in the punishment.

[6]   In *China* those that add murder to robbery, are cut into pieces;[a] but not so the others: to this difference it is owing that tho' they rob in that country, yet they never murder.

[7]   In Russia where the punishment of robbery and murder is the same, they always murder.[b] The dead, say they, tell no tales.

[8]   When there is no difference in the punishment, there should be some in the expectation of pardon. In England they never murder on the high-way, because robbers may have some hopes of transpor-

---

[a] Duhalde, Tom. I. p. 6.

[b] Present state of Russia by *Perry*.

tation,[6] which is never the case in respect to those that commit murder.

OF THE CLEMENCY OF THE PRINCE [Chapter 21]

[1] CLEMENCY is the peculiar characteristic of monarchs. In a republic whose principle is virtue, it is not so necessary. In a despotic government where fear predominates, it is less customary, because the great men of the state are to be restrained by examples of severity. More necessary it is in monarchies, where they are governed by honor, which frequently requires what the very law forbids. Disgrace is here equivalent to chastisement; and even the formalities of justice are punishments. This is because particular kinds of punishment are formed by shame which rushes from every quarter.

[2] The great men in monarchies are so heavily punished by disgrace, by the loss (tho' often imaginary) of their fortune, credit, acquaintances, and pleasures, that rigour in respect to them is needless. It can tend only to divest the subjects of the affection they have for the person of their prince, and of the respect they ought to have for public posts and employments.

[3] As the instability of the great is natural to a despotic government, so their security is interwoven with the nature of monarchy.

[4] So many are the advantages which monarchs gain by clemency, such love, such glory attends it, that it is generally a point of happiness with them to have an opportunity of exercising it; an opportunity which in our countries is seldom wanting.

BOOK VII: *Consequences of the Different Principles of the Three Governments with Respect to Sumptuary Laws, Luxury, and the Condition of Women*

ANALYSIS

Book VII treats laws regulating luxury (chaps. 1–7) and the conduct of women (chaps. 8–17). And in Montesquieu's view there is a close relationship between the two. Where luxury abounds, women are less likely to act virtuously.

In general, Montesquieu suggests, luxury stems either from the inequitable distribution of wealth within a society, or from the desire — more prevalent in cities than in agrarian areas — to distinguish oneself in the eyes of others (chap. 1, pars. [6–7]). The policy a state should adopt with regard to luxury will depend on its form of government. Luxury should be curtailed in democracies because it breeds concern for one's own selfish interests, thereby undermining regard for the needs of the community (chap. 2, [3]). In monarchies, however, luxury is beneficial. The pursuit of luxury is the counterpart to the inequality on which monarchies thrive, and the poor would starve if the rich did not spend their money freely (chap. 4 [2]).

Ever the sociologue *in search of general formulae, Montesquieu suggests, as a general rule, that luxury is admissible only where food is so abundant as to enable some of the population to engage in manufacturing without causing other citizens to be deprived of sufficient food (chap. 6 [1]).*

A second segment of Book VII considers the condition of women. In republics, Montesquieu contends, a loss of virtue signals decline (chap. 8), and he therefore praises that custom of the Samnites giving to the most virtuous youth who had done most for his country the first choice of a wife (chap. 16). In monarchies women act with relative freedom, particularly at court, and courtiers take advantage of this to advance their own status (chap. 9 [1]). In despotic governments, women are the object rather than the source of luxury (chap. 9 [2]). In general, M suggests later in the treatise, the freedom of women is an excellent index of the overall freedom characterizing any given society (see Book XVI, chap. 9, and Book XIX, chap. 15).

OF LUXURY [Chapter 1]

[1]   LUXURY is always in proportion to the inequality of fortunes. If the riches of a state are equally divided, there will be no luxury; for it is founded merely on the conveniences acquired by the labour of others.

[6]   Luxury is also in proportion to the bigness of the towns, and especially of the capital; so that it is in a compound proportion to the riches of the state, to the inequality of private fortunes, and to the number of people settled in particular places.

[7]   In proportion to the populousness of towns, the inhabitants are filled with vain notions, and actuated with an ambition of distinguishing themselves by trifles.[a] If they are very numerous, and most of them strangers to one another, the passion of distinguishing themselves redoubles, because there are greater hopes of success. As luxury inspires these hopes, each man assumes the marks of a superior condition. But by endeavouring thus at distinction,

[a] In a great city, *says the author of the Fable of the Bees*, tom. I. p. 133. they dress superior to their condition, in order to be esteemed more than what they really are by the multitude. This to a weak person is almost as great a pleasure as the accomplishment of his desires.

every one becomes equal and distinction ceases; as they are all
desirous of respect, no body is taken notice of.

OF SUMPTUARY LAWS IN A DEMOCRACY [Chapter 2]

[1]   The less luxury there is in a republic, the more it is perfect.
There was none among the old Romans, none among the
Lacedemonians;[1] and in republics where this equality is not quite
lost, the spirit of commerce, industry, and virtue, renders every
man able and willing to live on his own property, and consequently prevents the growth of luxury.

[2]   The laws concerning the new division of lands insisted upon so
eagerly in some republics, were of the most salutary nature. They
were dangerous only as they were sudden. By reducing instantaneously the wealth and riches of some, and increasing that of others,
they form a revolution in each family, and must produce a general
one in the state.

[3]   In proportion as luxury gains ground in a republic, the minds of
the people are turned towards their particular interests. Those who
are allowed only what is necessary, have nothing to wish for but
their own and their country's glory. But a soul depraved by luxury
has many other desires; and soon becomes an enemy to the laws
that confine it.

OF SUMPTUARY LAWS IN MONARCHIES [Chapter 4]

[2]   As riches, by the very constitution of monarchies, are unequally
divided, there is an absolute necessity for luxury. Were the rich
not to spend their money freely, the poor would starve. It is even
necessary here that the expences of the rich should be in proportion
to the inequality of fortunes; and that luxury, as we have already
observed, should increase in this proportion. The augmentation of

private wealth is owing to its having deprived one part of the citizens of their necessary support; this must therefore be restored to them.

[3]   For the preservation therefore of a monarchical state, luxury ought continually to increase and to grow more extensive, as it rises from the labourer to the artificers, to the merchants, to the magistrates, to the nobility, to the great officers of state, up to the very prince; otherwise the nation will be undone.

[8]   Hence arises a very natural reflexion. Republics end with luxury; monarchies with poverty. [a]

OF THE LUXURY OF CHINA [Chapter 6]

[1]   SUMPTUARY laws may, in some governments, be necessary for particular reasons. In order therefore to be able to judge whether luxury ought to be encouraged or proscribed, we should examine first what relation there is between the number of people and the facility they have of procuring subsistence. In England the soil produces more grain than is necessary for the maintenance of those who cultivate the land, and of those who are employed in the woollen manufactures. This country may be therefore allowed to have some trifling arts, and consequently luxury. In France likewise there is corn enough for the support of the husbandman, and of the manufacturer. Besides a foreign trade may bring in so many necessaries in return for toys, that there is no danger to be apprehended from luxury.

[2]   On the contrary, in China the women are so prolific, and the human species multiplies so fast, that the lands, tho' ever so much cultivated, are scarce sufficient to support the inhabitants. Here therefore luxury is pernicious, and the spirit of industry and

---

[a] Opulentia paritura mox egestatem. Florus lib. 3.

œconomy is as requisite, as in any republic.[a] They are obliged to pursue the necessary arts, and to shun those of luxury and pleasure.

[3]   This is the spirit of the excellent decrees of the Chinese emperors. "Our *ancestors*, says an emperor of the family of the Tangs,[b] *held it as a maxim, that if there was a man who did not work, or a woman that was idle, somebody must suffer cold or hunger in the empire.*" And on this principle he ordered an infinite number of monasteries of Bonzes[2] to be destroyed.

[4]   The third emperor of the one and twentieth Dynasty,[c] to whom some precious stones were brought that had been found in a mine, ordered it to be shut up, not chusing to fatigue his people with working for a thing that could neither feed nor cloath them.

OF PUBLIC CONTINENCY [Chapter 8][3]

[1]   So many are the imperfections that attend the loss of virtue in women, and so greatly are their souls degraded, when this principal guard is removed, that in a popular state public incontinency may be considered as the last of miseries, and as a certain forerunner of a change in the constitution.

[2]   Hence it is that the sage legislators of republican states have always required of women a particular gravity of manners. They have proscribed not only vice, but the very appearance of it, from their republics. They have banished even all commerce of gallantry, a commerce that produces idleness, that renders the women corrupters even before they are corrupted, that gives a value to trifles, and debases things of importance; a commerce, in fine, that

---

[a] Luxury has been here always prohibited.

[b] In an ordinance quoted by Father Du Halde, tom. 2, p. 497.

[c] History of China, 21st Dynasty in Father Du Halde's work, tom. I.

makes people act intirely by the maxims of ridicule, in which the women are so perfectly skilled.

OF THE CONDITION OR STATE OF WOMEN IN DIFFERENT GOVERNMENTS [Chapter 9]

[1]   IN monarchies women are subject to very little restraint, because as the distinction of ranks calls them to court, they repair thither in order to assume that spirit of liberty, which is the only one there tolerated. The aspiring courtier avails himself of their charms and passions, in order to advance his fortune; and as their weakness admits not of pride, but of vanity: luxury constantly attends them.

[2]   In despotic governments women do not introduce, but are themselves an object of luxury. They must be here in a state of the most rigorous servitude. Every one follows the spirit of the government, and adopts in his own family the customs he sees elsewhere established. As the laws are very severe and executed on the spot, they are afraid lest the liberty of women should involve them in dangers. Their quarrels, indiscretions, repugnancies, jealousies, piques, and that art, in fine, which little souls have of interesting great ones, would be attended there with fatal consequences.

[4]   In republics women are free by the laws, and constrained by manners; luxury is banished from thence, and with it corruption and vice.

AN EXCELLENT CUSTOM OF THE SAMNITES [Chapter 16]

[1]   THE Samnites had a custom which in so small a republic, and especially in their situation, must have produced admirable effects.[4] The young people were all convened in one place, and their

conduct was examined. He that was declared the best of the whole assembly, had leave given him to take which girl he pleased for his wife; the person that had been declared second best chose after him; and so on.[a] Admirable institution! The only recommendation that young men could have on this occasion, was that which was owing to virtue and to the services done their country. He that had the greatest share of these endowments, chose what girl he liked out of the whole nation. Love, beauty, chastity, virtue, birth, and even wealth itself, were all, in some measure, the dowry of virtue. A nobler, and grander recompence, less chargeable to a petty state, and more capable of influencing both sexes, could scarce be imagined.

[2]   The Samnites were descended from the Lacedemonians: and Plato,[5] whose institutes are only an improvement of those of Lycurgus, enacted very near the same law.[b]

---

[a] Fragment of Nicolaus Damascenus, taken from Stobeus in the collection of Constantine Porphyrogenitus.

[b] He even permits them to have a more frequent interview with one another.

BOOK VIII: *Of the Corruption of the Principles of the Three Governments*

ANALYSIS

Book VIII concludes Part One of The Spirit of Laws *according to Montesquieu's own plan for the work. Its most direct link is to Book III, in which M had spelled out the principles of government. After counseling various means in Books IV–VII by which lawgivers can support the principle of government in each of the three basic forms of government, M now advances the general proposition that the corruption of a government begins with the corruption of its principles (chap. 1). Once the dominant political psychology upholding a particular form of government is dissipated, corruption will soon set in (chaps. 1, 11, 12).*

Democracies are corrupted when the people fall into a state of either insufficient or extreme equality, or when citizens fail to accept the authority of their magistrates (chaps. 2–4). Monarchies are corrupted when the prince exerts too much power and usurps the rights of his subjects (chap. 6), or when he exchanges justice for severity (chap. 7, par. [3]), or when his subjects become so devoted to the person of the prince that they forget what they owe their country (chap. 7 [4]). Despotic governments are corrupt by their very nature, and they will only survive "when circumstances drawn from climate, religion, situation, or genius of the people, oblige it to follow some order, and to admit of some rule" (chap. 10).

Book VIII also contains the famous Montesquieu formulae for the proper size of each form of government, that is, the size most likely to insure the preservation of the principles of a government (chaps. 15–20). Republics need be small (chap. 16), monarchies of middling extent (chap. 17), and despotic governments very large (chap. 19).

GENERAL IDEA OF THIS BOOK [Chapter 1]

THE corruption of each government generally begins with that of the principles.[1]

OF THE CORRUPTION OF THE PRINCIPLE
OF DEMOCRACY [Chapter 2][2]

[1]   THE principle of democracy is corrupted, not only when the spirit of equality is extinct, but likewise when they fall into a spirit of extreme equality, and when every citizen wants to be upon a level with those he has chosen to command him. Then the people, incapable of bearing the very power they have intrusted, want to do every thing of themselves, to debate for the senate, to execute for the magistrate, and to strip the judges.[3]

[2]   When this is the case, virtue can no longer subsist in the republic. The people want to exercise the functions of the magistrates; who cease to be revered. The deliberations of the senate are slighted; all respect is then laid aside for the senators, and consequently for old age. If respect ceases for old age, it will cease also for parents; deference to husbands will be likewise thrown off, and submission to masters. This licentiousness will soon captivate the mind; and the restraint of command be as fatiguing as that of obedience. Wives, children, slaves, will shake off all subjection. No longer will there be any such thing as manners, order, or virtue.

[7]   Democracy hath therefore two excesses to avoid, the spirit of inequality which leads to aristocracy or monarchy; and the spirit of extreme equality, which leads to despotic power, as the latter is compleated by conquest.

OF THE SPIRIT OF EXTREME EQUALITY
[Chapter 3]

[1]   As distant as heaven is from earth, so is the true spirit of
equality from that of extreme equality.[4] The former does not
consist in managing so that every body should command, or that
no one should be commanded; but in obeying and commanding
our equals. It endeavours not to be without a master, but that its
masters should be none but its equals.

[2]   In the state of nature indeed, all men are born equal; but they
cannot continue in this equality. Society makes them lose it, and
they recover it only by means of the laws.

[3]   Such is the difference between a well and an ill policied democracy, that in the former men are equal only as citizens, but in the
latter they are equal also as magistrates, senators, judges, fathers,
husbands, masters.

[4]   The natural place of virtue is near to liberty; but it is not nearer
to extreme liberty than to servitude.

PARTICULAR CAUSE OF THE CORRUPTION
OF THE PEOPLE [Chapter 4]

GREAT success, especially when chiefly owing to the people,
swells them so high with pride, that it is impossible to manage
them. Jealous of their magistrates they soon become jealous
likewise of the magistracy; enemies to those that govern, enemies
they soon prove to the constitution. Thus it was the victory of
Salamine over the Persians[5] that corrupted the republic of
Athens;[a] and thus the defeat of the Athenians ruined the republic
of Syracuse.[b]

---

[a] Aristot. Polit. lib. 5. cap. 4.
[b] Ibid.

OF THE CORRUPTION OF THE PRINCIPLE
OF MONARCHY [Chapter 6]

[1]   As democracies are destroyed when the people despoil the senate, magistrates and judges of their functions; so monarchies are
corrupted when the prince insensibly deprives societies of their
prerogatives, or cities of their privileges.[6] In the first case the
multitude usurp a despotic power; in the second it is usurped by a
single person.

[3]   Monarchy is destroyed, when a prince thinks he shews a greater
exertion of power in changing than in conforming to the order of
things; when he deprives some of his subjects of their hereditary
employments to bestow them arbitrarily upon others, and when he
is fonder of being guided by his fancy than by his judgment.[7]

[4]   Monarchy is destroyed when the prince directing every thing
intirely to himself, calls that state to his capital, the capital to his
court, and the court to his own person.[8]

[5]   Monarchy is destroyed in fine, when the prince mistakes his
authority, his situation, and the love of his people; and when he is
not fully persuaded that a monarch ought to think himself secure,
as a despotic prince ought to think himself in danger.[9]

THE SAME SUBJECT CONTINUED [Chapter 7]

[1]   THE principle of monarchy is corrupted, when the first dignities
are marks of the first servitude, when the great men are stripped of
popular respect, and rendered the low tools of arbitrary power.

[2]   It is still more corrupted, when honor is set up in contradiction
to honors, and when men are capable of being loaded at the very
same time with infamy[a] and dignities.

[a] Under the reign of Tiberius statues were erected to, and triumphal ornaments
conferred on, informers; which debased these honors to such a degree, that those who

[3]   It is corrupted when the prince changes his justice into severity;
when he puts like the Roman emperors a Medusa's head on his
breast;[b] and when he assumes that menacing and terrible air which
Commodus ordered to be given to his statues.[c]

[4]   Again it is corrupted, when mean and abject souls grow vain of
the pomp attending their servitude; and imagine that the motive
which induces them to be intirely devoted to their prince, exempts
them from all duty to their country.

[5]   But if it be true, (and indeed the experience of all ages has
shewn it) that in proportion as the power of the monarch becomes
boundless and immense, his security diminishes; is the corrupting
this power, is the altering its very nature, a less crime than that of
high treason against the prince?

DANGER OF THE CORRUPTION OF THE
PRINCIPLE OF MONARCHICAL GOVERNMENT
[Chapter 8]

[1]   THE danger is not when the state passes from one moderate to
another moderate government, as from a republic to a monarchy,
or from a monarchy to a republic; but when it precipitates from a
moderate to a despotic government.

[2]   Most of the European nations are still governed by principles of
morality. But if through a long abuse of power, or through hurry
of conquest, despotic sway should prevail to a certain degree;

had merited them disdained to accept of them. *Fragm. of Dio, book* 58. taken from *the
extract of virtues and vices*, by Constantine Porphyrog. See in Tacitus in what manner
Nero on the discovery and punishment of a pretended conspiracy, bestowed triumphal
ornaments on Petronius Turpilianus, Nerva, and Tigellinus. *Annal. book* 14. See
likewise how the generals refused to serve, because they contemned the military honors,
pervulgatis triumphi insignibus, Tacit. Annal. book 13.

[b] In this state the prince knew extremely well the principle of his government.

[c] Herodian.

neither morals nor climate would be able to withstand its baleful influence: and then human nature would be exposed, for some time at least, even in this beautiful part of the world, to the insults with which she has been abused in the other three.

OF THE CORRUPTION OF THE
PRINCIPLES OF DESPOTIC GOVERNMENT
[Chapter 10]

THE principle of despotic government is subject to a continual corruption, because it is in its very nature corrupt. Other governments are destroyed by particular accidents which do violence to the principles of each constitution; this is ruined by its own intrinsic imperfection, when no accidental causes impede or corrupt the principles on which it is founded. It maintains itself therefore only when circumstances drawn from the climate, religion, situation, or genius of the people, oblige it to follow some order, and to admit of some rule. By these things its nature is forced without being changed; its ferocity remains; and it is made tame and tractable only for a time.

NATURAL EFFECTS OF THE GOODNESS AND
CORRUPTION OF THE PRINCIPLES
[Chapter 11]

[1]   WHEN once the principles of government are corrupted, the very best laws become bad and turn against the state; when the principles are sound, even bad laws have the same effect as good; the force of the principle draws everything to it.

THE SAME SUBJECT CONTINUED [Chapter 12]

[2]   WHEN once a republic is corrupted, there is no possibility of remedying any of the rising evils but by removing the corruption

and restoring its lost principles: every other correction is either useless or a new evil.

SURE METHODS OF PRESERVING THE THREE PRINCIPLES
[Chapter 15]

I SHALL not be able to make myself rightly understood, till the reader has perused the four following chapters.

DISTINCTIVE PROPERTIES OF A REPUBLIC [Chapter 16]

[1]   IT is natural to a republic to have only a small territory; otherwise it cannot long subsist.[10] In a large republic there are men of large fortunes, and consequently of less moderation; there are too great deposites to intrust into the hands of a single subject;[11] interests are divided; an ambitious person soon becomes sensible that he may be happy, great, and glorious, by oppressing his fellow citizens; and that he might raise himself to grandeur on the ruins of his country.

[2]   In a large republic the public good is sacrificed to a thousand views; it is subordinate to exceptions; and depends on accidents. In a small one, the interest of the public is easier perceived, better understood, and more within the reach of every citizen; abuses have a lesser extent, and of course are less protected.[12]

[3]   The long duration of the republic of Sparta was owing to its having always continued with the same extent of territory after all its wars. The sole aim of Sparta was liberty; and the sole advantage of its liberty, glory.

[4]   It was the spirit of the Greek republics to be as contented with their territories, as with their laws. Athens was first fired with ambition and gave it to Lacedemon;[13] but it was an ambition rather of commanding a free people, than of governing slaves;

rather of directing than of breaking the union. All was lost upon the starting up of monarchy, a government whose spirit is more turned to increase and advancement.

[5]   Excepting particular circumstances,[a] it is difficult for any other than a republican government to subsist long in a single town. A prince of so petty a state would naturally endeavour to oppress, because his power would be great while the means of enjoying it or of causing it to be respected, would be very inconsiderable. The consequence of this would be that he would trample upon his people. On the other hand, such a prince might be easily crushed by a foreign or even by a domestic force; the people might every instant unite and rise up against him. Now as soon as a prince of a single town is expelled, the quarrel is over; but if he has many towns, it only begins.[14]

DISTINCTIVE PROPERTIES OF A MONARCHY
[Chapter 17]

[1]   A MONARCHICAL state ought to be of a moderate bigness. Were it small, it would form itself into a republic: were it very large, the nobility, possessed of great estates, far from the inspection of the prince, with a private court of their own, and secure moreover from sudden executions by the laws and manners of the country, such a nobility, I say, might throw off their allegiance, having nothing to fear from too slow and too distant a punishment.

[2]   Thus Charlemain had scarce founded his empire when he was obliged to divide it; whether the governors of the provinces refused to obey; or whether in order to keep them more under subjection there was a necessity of parcelling the empire into several kingdoms.

[a] As when a petty sovereign supports himself betwixt two great powers by means of their mutual jealousy; but then he has only a precarious existence.

[3]   After the decease of Alexander his empire was divided. How was it possible for those Greek and Macedonian chiefs, who were each of them free and independent, or commanders at least of the victorious bands dispersed throughout that vast conquest, how was it possible, I say, for them to obey?

[4]   Attila's empire was dissolved soon after his death; such a number of kings, who were no longer under restraint, could not resume their fetters.

[5]   The sudden establishment of unlimited power is a remedy which in those cases may prevent a dissolution: but how dreadful the remedy, that after the inlargement of dominion, opens a new scene of misery!

[6]   The rivers hasten to mingle their waters with the sea; and monarchies lose themselves in despotic power.

DISTINCTIVE PROPERTIES OF A DESPOTIC GOVERNMENT
[Chapter 19]

A LARGE empire supposes a despotic authority in the person that governs. It is necessary that the quickness of the prince's resolutions should supply the distance of the places they are sent to; that fear should prevent the carelessness of the remote governor or magistrate; that the law should be derived from a single person, and should change continually according to the accidents which incessantly multiply in a state in proportion to its bigness.

CONSEQUENCE OF THE PRECEDING CHAPTERS
[Chapter 20]

IF it be therefore the natural property of small states to be governed as a republic, of middling ones to be subject to a monarch, and of large empires to be swayed by a despotic prince; the consequence is, that in order to preserve the principles of the established government, the state must be supported in the extent it has acquired, and that the spirit of this state will change in proportion as it contracts or extends its limits.

OF THE EMPIRE OF CHINA [Chapter 21]

[2] Our missionaries take notice of the vast empire of China, as of an admirable government, that has a proper mixture of fear, honor, and virtue. Consequently I must have given an idle distinction, in establishing the principles of the three governments.

[3] But I cannot conceive what this so much boasted honor can be among people that will not do the least thing without blows. [a]

[4] Again, our mercantile people are far from giving us any idea of that virtue so much talked of by the missionaries; we need only consult them in relation to the robberies and extortions of the mandarins. [b]

[5] Besides, Father *Parennin's* letters concerning the emperor's proceedings against some new-converted princes of the blood who had incurred his displeasure, [c] plainly shew us a continued plan of tyranny, and inhuman injuries committed by rule, that is in cool blood.

[6] We have likewise Monsieur *de Marian's*, and the same Father *Parennin's* letters on the government of China. After some pertinent questions and answers, the whole wonder vanishes.

[a] It is the cudgel that governs China, says Father Du Halde.
[b] Among others, *De Lange's* relation.
[c] Of the Family of Sourniama, Edifying Letters. 18th collection.

[manuscript page — folio 163]

Chapitre 6

Des principes de la liberté
politique et de ...
On les trouve dans la
Constitution d'Angleterre
sur la liberté politique.

est fondée sur ces
principes

de la Constitution
d'Angleterre

Il y a dans chaque état trois sortes

De pouvoir la puissance legislative, la puissance

executrice, des choses qui dependent du droit

des gens, et la puissance executrice de celles qui

Dependent du droit civil.

par la première le prince ou le magistrat

fait des loix pour un tems ou pour toujours

Esprit des Lois —Premier Jet
Book XI, chapter 6
Bibliothèque Nationale
Nouvelle Acquisition Francaise 12.833, f. 163

❧ Part Two

Books IX through XIII constitute Part Two of *The Spirit of Laws* as Montesquieu organized it. The unifying theme is liberty. Books IX and X discuss how each form of government best preserves its freedom from hostile powers, and Books XI–XIII discuss the preservation of liberty at home by means of proper constitutional law (Book XI), criminal law (Book XII), and taxation policy (Book XIII).

BOOK IX: *Of Laws in the Relation They Bear to a Defensive Force*

ANALYSIS

The subject of Book IX is national defense, and Montesquieu begins by assessing proper strategy within each of the forms of government he has described. Since republics are small by definition (see Book VIII, chap. 16), M recommends for the purpose of self-defense the formation of confederate republics, or associations of various republican states into one strong union (chap. 1). Within such confederate governments each of the component states should possess republican governments (chap. 2), and no individual government should possess the right to form an alliance without the consent of the other states (chap. 3). As a result of their vast territorial expanse, despotic governments provide for their safety, not by uniting with other states, but by sacrificing, if necessary, the outskirts of the country to safeguard the heart of the empire and by placing outlying provinces in the hands of a feudatory prince (chap. 4). Monarchical governments are not sufficiently large to enable them to sacrifice their borderlands in the event of a sudden invasion. Hence fortresses must be constructed along the frontiers, the same fortresses, that is, that would prove dangerous in despotic governments where the loyalty of troops cannot be guaranteed (chap. 5).

Having surveyed the problem of self-defense in each of the three forms of government he describes, Montesquieu states the general principle that a state will be safest when it is not so large that troops cannot be quickly dispatched to any frontier placed under attack (chap. 6). Thus Louis XIV, by seeking to enlarge France's borders, would actually have weakened his country had his military policies been a success (chap. 7). Furthermore, the ability of a state to defend itself may owe as much to the existence of neighboring states as

182

buffer zones as to its own military might (chap. 10). And power is relative,
M suggests. France was strong during the reign of Louis XIV in part because
Germany, Italy, England, Spain, and Russia were weak (chap. 9).

IN WHAT MANNER THE REPUBLICS PROVIDE
FOR THEIR SAFETY [Chapter 1]

[1]   IF a republic is small, it is destroyed by a foreign force, if it be
large, it is ruined by an internal imperfection.[a]

[2]   This twofold inconveniency is equally contagious to democracies and aristocracies, whether good or bad. The evil is in the
very thing itself; and no form can redress it.

[3]   Very probable it is therefore that mankind would have been at
length obliged to live constantly under the government of a single
person, had they not contrived a kind of constitution that has all
the internal advantages of a republican, together with the external
force of a monarchical, government. I mean a confederate republic.[1]

[4]   This form of government is a convention by which several
small states agree to become members of a larger one which they
intend to form. It is a kind of assemblage of societies, that constitute a new one, capable of increasing by means of new associations, till they arrive to such a degree of power, as to be able to
provide for the security of the whole united body.

[5]   It was these associations that contributed so long to the prosperity of Greece. By these the Romans attacked the universe, and by
these only the universe withstood them: for when Rome was arrived to her highest pitch of grandeur, it was the associations
behind the Danube and the Rhine, associations formed by terror,
that enabled the Barbarians to resist her power.

[a] Fato potentia, non suâ vi nixae. Tacit.

[6]   From hence it proceeds that Holland,[b] Germany, and the Swiss Cantons, are considered in Europe as perpetual republics.

[7]   The associations of cities were formerly more necessary than in our times. A weak defenceless town was exposed to greater dangers. By conquest it was deprived not only of the executive and legislative power, as at present, but moreover of all human property.[c]

[8]   A republic of this kind capable of withstanding an external force, may be able to support its greatness without any internal corruption; the form of this society prevents all manner of inconveniences.

[9]   The member that would attempt to usurp over the rest, could not be supposed to have an equal authority and credit in all the confederate states. Were it to have too great an influence over one, this would alarm the rest; were it to subdue another, that which would still remain free, might withstand it with forces independent of those which the other had usurped, and overpower it before it could be settled in its usurpation.

[10]   Should a popular insurrection happen in one of the confederate states, the others are able to quell it. Should abuses creep into one part, they are reformed by those that remain sound. The state may be destroyed on one side, and not on the other; the confederacy may be dissolved, and the confederates preserve their sovereignty.

[11]   As this government is composed of petty republics, it enjoys the internal happiness of each; and with respect to its external situation, it is possessed by means of the association, of all the advantages of large monarchies.

[b] It is composed of about fifty different republics. *State of the United Provinces* by M. Janisson.

[c] Civil liberty, goods, wives, children, temples, and even burying places.

THAT A CONFEDERATE GOVERNMENT OUGHT TO
BE COMPOSED OF STATES OF THE SAME NATURE,
ESPECIALLY OF THE REPUBLICAN KIND [Chapter 2]

[1]   THE Canaanites were destroyed, by reason they were petty monarchies, that had no union nor confederacy for their common defence: And indeed, a confederacy is not agreeable to the nature of
petty monarchies.[2]*

[2]   As the confederate republic of Germany consists of free cities,
and of petty states, subject to different princes, experience shews
us, that it is much more imperfect than that of Holland and
Switzerland.

[3]   The spirit of monarchy is war and enlargement of dominion:
peace and moderation is the spirit of a republic. These two kinds of
government cannot naturally subsist in a confederate republic.

OTHER REQUISITES IN A CONFEDERATE
REPUBLIC [Chapter 3]

[1]   IN the republic of Holland one province cannot conclude an alliance without the consent of the others. This law, which is an
excellent one and even necessary in a confederate republic, is
wanting in the Germanic constitution, where it would prevent the
misfortunes that may happen to the whole confederacy, thro' the
imprudence, ambition, or avarice of a single member. A republic
united by a political confederacy, has given it self intirely up, and
has nothing more to resign.

[2]   It is difficult for the united states, to be all of an equal bigness
and power. The Lycian republic was an association of twenty three
towns;[a] the large ones had three votes in the common council, the
middling ones two, the small towns one. The Dutch republic

[a] Strabo lib. 14.

consists of seven, great or small, provinces, that have each one voice.

IN WHAT MANNER DESPOTIC GOVERNMENTS PROVIDE FOR THEIR SECURITY [Chapter 4]

[1]   As republics provide for their security by uniting, despotic governments do it by separating, and by keeping themselves, as it were, single. They sacrifice part of the country, ravage and desolate the frontiers; and render by this means the heart of the empire inaccessible.

[4]   It preserves it self likewise by another kind of separation, which is by putting the most distant provinces in the hands of a feudatary prince.

IN WHAT MANNER A MONARCHICAL GOVERNMENT PROVIDES FOR ITS SECURITY [Chapter 5]

[1]   A MONARCHY never destroys it self like a despotic government; but a kingdom of a moderate extent is liable to sudden invasion. It must therefore have strong holds to defend its frontiers; and troops to garrison those holds. The least spot of ground is disputed with art, with courage, and obstinacy. Despotic states make incursions against one another; it is monarchies only that wage war.

[2]   Fortresses are proper for monarchies; despotic governments are afraid of them. They dare not intrust them to any body, for there is no one that has a love for the prince and his government.

OF THE DEFENSIVE FORCE OF STATES IN GENERAL [Chapter 6]

[1]   To preserve a state in its due force, it must have such an extent and magnitude, as to admit of a proportion between the quickness with which it may be invaded, and that with which it may render the

invasion abortive. As an invader may instantly appear on all sides, it is requisite that the state should be able to make on all sides its defence; consequently it should be of a moderate extent, proportioned to the degree of velocity that nature has given to man in order to move from one place to another.

[2]   France and Spain are exactly of a proper bigness. Their forces have so easy a communication, as to be able to convey themselves immediately to what part they have a mind; the armies unite and pass with rapidity from one frontier to another, without any apprehension of such difficulties as require time to remove.

[5]   The real power of a prince does not consist so much in the facility he meets with in conquering, as in the difficulty an enemy finds in attacking him, and, if I may so speak, in the immutability of his condition. But the increase of territory obliges a government to expose new sides by which it may be attacked.

[6]   As monarchs therefore ought to be endued with wisdom in order to increase, they ought likewise to have an equal share of prudence to limit, their power. Upon removing the inconveniences of too small a territory, they ought to have their eye constantly on the inconveniences that attend its immoderate enlargement.

A REFLECTION [Chapter 7]

[1]   THE enemies of a great prince,[3] whose reign was protracted to an unusual length, have very often accused him, rather, I believe, from their own fears, than upon any solid foundation, of having formed and carried on a project of universal monarchy. Had he succeeded, nothing would have been more fatal to Europe, to his ancient subjects, to himself, and to his family. Heaven that knows our true interests, served him more by his defeats, than it could have done by victories. Instead of making him the only sovereign

in Europe, it favoured him more by rendering him the most powerful.

OF THE RELATIVE FORCE OF STATES [Chapter 9]

[1]   ALL grandeur, force, and power is relative. Care therefore must be taken that in endeavouring to increase the real grandeur, the relative be not diminished.

[2]   Under the reign of Louis XIV, France was at its highest pitch of relative grandeur. Germany had not yet had such great monarchs as it has since produced. Italy was in the same case. England and Scotland were not yet formed into one united kingdom. Arragon was not joined to Castile; the distant parts of the Spanish monarchy were weakened by it, and weakened it in their turn; and Muscovy[4] was as little known in Europe, as Crim Tartary.[5]

OF THE WEAKNESS OF NEIGHBOURING STATES [Chapter 10]

WHENSOEVER a state lies contiguous to another that happens to be in its decline, the former ought to take particular care not to precipitate the latter's ruin, because in this respect it is in the happiest situation imaginable; nothing being so convenient for one prince as to be near another who receives for him all the rebuffs and insults of fortune. And it seldom happens that by subduing such a state, the real power of the conqueror is as much increased, as the relative is diminished.

BOOK X: *Of Laws in the Relation They Bear to Offensive Force*

ANALYSIS

Book X completes a two-book segment on military policy. Whereas Book IX discussed self-defense, Book X discusses offensive force. Montesquieu begins with the general proclamation that offensive strikes against other nations are subject to the law of nations (chap. 1), earlier defined as the principle "that different nations ought in time of peace to do one another all the good they can, and in time of war as little harm as possible, without prejudicing their real interests" (Book I, chap. 3, par. [4]). States, like men, have a right to defend themselves, and the right to strike first is sometimes closely related to the right of self-defense (chap. 2 [1–3]). War undertaken for reasons other than self-defense, however, that is, war motivated by glory, convenience, or utility, clearly violates the law of nations (chap. 2 [5]). And even when conquests can be justified by the law of nations, they are subject to rules of decency, conquest being at all times an acquisition carrying "with it the spirit of preservation and use, and not of destruction" (chap. 3 [2]). The right of conquerors to enslave captives is rejected (chap. 3 [7–9]) as it is in Book XV, chapter 2.

As was suggested by Montesquieu in several chapters of the preceding Book (IX, chaps. 6 and 7), conquests are only infrequently beneficial — even to the conqueror. Both republics and monarchies need be wary lest conquests enlarge their states beyond optimum size (see Book VIII, chap. 16). Conquests made by despotic princes already in control of substantial territory are less dangerous, but such conquests presuppose not only large forces in the conquered provinces but also substantial troops surrounding the prince himself lest provincial officers should be tempted to revolt against him (chap. 16).

OF OFFENSIVE FORCE [Chapter 1]

OFFENSIVE force is regulated by the law of nations, which is the political law of each country considered in its relation to every other.

OF WAR [Chapter 2]

[1]   THE life of governments is like that of man. The latter has a right to kill in case of natural defence; the former have a right to wage war for their own preservation.

[2]   In the case of natural defence I have a right to kill, because my life is in respect to me, what the life of my antagonist is to him: in the same manner a state wages war, because its preservation is like that of any other being.

[3]   Among citizens the right of natural defence does not imply a necessity of attacking. Instead of attacking they need only have recourse to proper tribunals. They cannot therefore exercise this right of defence, but in sudden cases, when immediate death would be the consequence of waiting for the assistance of the laws. But among societies the right of natural defence carries along with it sometimes the necessity of attacking; as for instance, when one nation sees that a longer peace will enable another to destroy it, and that to attack that nation instantly is the only way to prevent its own destruction.

[4]   From thence it follows, that small societies have oftener a right to declare war than great ones, because they are oftener in the case of being afraid of destruction.

[5]   The right therefore of war is derived from necessity and strict justice. If those who direct the conscience or councils of princes do not hold by this, all is undone: when they proceed on arbitrary principles of glory, conveniency, and utility; torrents of blood will overspread the earth.

[6]   But above all, let them not avail themselves of any such idle
plea as the glory of the prince: his glory is nothing but pride; it is a
passion and not a legitimate right.

[7]   It is true the fame of his power might increase the strength of
his government; but it might be equally increased by the reputation
of his justice.

OF THE RIGHT OF CONQUEST [Chapter 3]

[1]   FROM the right of war comes that of conquest; which is the
consequence of that right, and ought therefore to follow its spirit.

[2]   The right the conqueror has over a conquered people is directed
by four sorts of laws, the law of nature which makes every thing
tend to the preservation of the species; the law of natural reason,
which teaches us to do to others what we would have done to
ourselves; the law that forms political societies, whose duration
nature has not secured; and in fine the law derived from the nature
of the thing itself. Conquest is an acquisition; acquisition carries
with it the spirit of preservation and use, and not of destruction.

[5]   The authors of our common law, guided by ancient histories,
without confining themselves to cases of strict necessity, have
fallen into very great errors. They have adopted tyrannical and
arbitrary principles, by supposing the conquerors to be invested
with I know not what right to kill; from thence they have drawn
consequences as terrible as the very principle, and established
maxims which the conquerors themselves, when possessed of the
least grain of sense, never presumed to follow. Clear it is that
when the conquest is completed, the conqueror has no longer a
right to kill, because he has no longer the plea of natural defence
and self-preservation.

[6]   What has led them into this mistake, is that they imagined a
conqueror had a right to destroy the society; from whence they

inferred that he had a right to destroy the men that compose it; a wrong consequence from a false principle. For from the destruction of the society it does not at all follow that the people who compose it ought to be also destroyed. Society is the union of men, and not the men themselves; the citizen may perish, and the man remain.

[7]   From the right of killing in case of conquest, politicians have drawn that of reducing to slavery; a consequence as ill grounded as the principle.[1]

[8]   There is no such thing as a right of reducing people to slavery, but when it becomes necessary for the preservation of the conquest. Preservation, but never servitude, is the end of conquest; tho' servitude may happen sometimes to be a necessary means of preservation.

[9]   Even in that case it is contrary to the nature of things that the slavery should be perpetual. The people enslaved ought to be rendered capable of becoming subjects. Slavery in conquests is an accidental thing. When after the expiration of a certain space of time all the parts of the conquering state are connected with the conquered nation, by customs, marriages, laws, associations, and by a certain conformity of spirit; there ought to be an end of the slavery. For the rights of the conqueror are founded intirely on the want of those very things, and on the estrangement between the two nations which prevents their confiding in each other. A conqueror therefore who reduces the conquered people to slavery, ought always to reserve to himself the means (for means there are without number) of restoring them to their liberty.

OF CONQUESTS MADE BY A REPUBLIC [Chapter 6]

[1]   IT is also contrary to the nature of things, that in a confederate

government one state should make any conquest over another, as in our days we have seen in Switzerland.[a] In mixt confederate republics, where the association is between small republics and small monarchies, this is not so absurd.

[2]   Contrary it is also to the nature of things, that a democratical republic should conquer towns, that cannot enter into the sphere of its democracy. It is necessary that the conquered people should be capable of enjoying the privileges of sovereignty, as was settled in the very beginning among the Romans. The conquest ought to be limited to the number of citizens fixt for the democracy.

[3]   If a democratical republic subdues a nation in order to govern them as subjects, it exposes its own liberty, because it intrusts too great a power to the magistrates sent into the conquered provinces.

OF CONQUESTS MADE BY A MONARCHY [Chapter 9]

[1]   IF a monarchy can for a long time subsist before it is weakened by its increase, it will become formidable; and its strength will remain intire, while pent up by the neighbouring monarchies.

[2]   It ought not therefore to aim at conquests beyond the natural limits of its government. As soon as it has passed these limits, it is prudence to stop.

[3]   In this kind of conquest things must be left as they were found; the same courts of judicature, the same laws, the same customs, the same privileges: there ought to be no other alteration than that of the army and of the name of the sovereign.

[4]   When a monarchy has extended its limits by the conquest of some neighbouring provinces, it should treat those provinces with great lenity.

[a] With regard to Tockenburg.

OF THE MANNERS OF A CONQUERED PEOPLE [Chapter 11]

[1]   IT is not sufficient in those conquests to let the conquered nation enjoy their own laws; it is perhaps more necessary to leave them also their manners, because people generally know, love, and defend their manners better than their laws.

[2]   The French have been driven nine times out of Italy, because, as historians say,[a] of their insolent familiarities with the fair sex. It is too much for a nation to be obliged to bear not only with the pride of conquerors, but with their incontinence and indiscretion; these are, without doubt, most grievous and intolerable, as they are the source of infinite outrages.

CHARLES XII [Chapter 14][2]

[1]   THIS prince, who depended intirely on his own strength, hastened his fall by forming designs that could never be executed but by a long war; a thing which his kingdom was incapable of supporting.

[2]   It was not a declining state he undertook to subvert, but a rising empire. The Russians made use of the war he waged against them, as of a military school. Every defeat brought them nearer to victory; and losing abroad, they learnt to defend themselves at home.

[3]   *Charles* in the deserts of Poland imagined himself master of the universe: here he wandered, and with him in some measure wandered Sweden; whilst his capital enemy acquired new strength against him, locked him up, made settlements along the Baltic, destroyed or subdued Livonia.

[4]   Sweden was like a river whose waters are cut off at the fountain head in order to change its course. It was not the affair of *Pultova*

_____
[a] See Pufendorf's universal History.

that ruined Charles. Had he not been destroyed at that place, he would in another. The casualties of fortune are easily repaired; but who can be guarded against events that incessantly arise from the nature of things?[3]

[5]   But neither nature nor fortune were ever so much against him, as he himself.

[6]   He was not directed by the actual situation of things, but by a kind of a model he had formed to himself; and even this he followed very ill. He was not an Alexander; but he would have been Alexander's best soldier.

OF CONQUESTS MADE BY A DESPOTIC STATE [Chapter 16]

WHEN a conquest happens to be vastly large, it supposes a despotic power: and then the army dispersed in the provinces is not sufficient. There should be always a trusty body of troops around the prince, ready to fall instantly upon any part of the empire that might chance to waver. This military corps ought to awe the rest, and to strike terror into those who thro' necessity have been intrusted with any authority in the empire. The emperor of China has always a large body of Tartars near his person, ready upon all occasions. In India, in Turkey, in Japan, the prince has always a body-guard, independent of the other regular forces. This particular corps keeps the dispersed troops in awe.

BOOK XI: *Of the Laws Which Establish Political Liberty, With Regard to the Constitution*

ANALYSIS

Book XI is the first of three Books devoted to the problem of achieving liberty within the state. Montesquieu turns first to the subject of political liberty as established by the constitution. After mentioning the numerous definitions philosophers had attached to the word liberty *(chap. 2) and rejecting the identification of liberty with "unrestrained freedom," (chap. 3[1]), he defines freedom both as "the power of doing what we ought to will, and in not being constrained to do what we ought not to will" (chap. 3 [1]) and as the "right of doing whatever the laws permit" (chap. 3 [2]).*

Montesquieu declines to associate political liberty with any one form of government (chap. 4). Democracies, he contends, are no more automatically free than monarchies (chap. 4 [1]), and the Pensées *reveal his fear that republics are often plagued by factions. (See Introduction, p. 62.) Freedom, M is convinced, is found only in moderate governments where power is checked by power (chap. 4 [2]).*

In the famous sixth chapter of Book XI, M analyzes the components of English political liberty. A synopsis of this important chapter is provided below.

Distribution of Powers

Following a brief introductory segment ([1–3]), Montesquieu establishes the need to separate executive, legislative, and judicial power ([4–6]), or, failing this, to at least keep judicial power independent ([7]). (See Introduction, pp. 81–82, for a discussion of whether the English government actu-

196

ally displayed the degree of separation M attributed to it.) There follows a digression on the disastrous consequences of failing to separate the three sorts of power in the republics of Italy ([8–12]).

Judiciary Power

Montesquieu then undertakes an analysis of judiciary power ([13–20]), claiming that such power should be exercised by juries ([13–17]) and that those accused should possess the right both to be tried by their peers ([18]) and to exclude some persons from the jury ([15]). Only in rare instances, he adds, should the right of habeas corpus *be suspended ([19–20]).*

Legislative Power

Montesquieu next considers legislative power ([22–35; 38–51]). He begins by discussing the need within the legislative arm of government for representatives ([23–29]), a feature noticeably absent from the model of direct democracy provided in Book II. The advantage of the system of representatives is that it places in office those best qualified to discuss public affairs ([24]). M does not think representatives need consult their constituents on every issue ([25–26]).

In order to insure participation of the wealthy and well born in the legislative branch of government, Montesquieu recommends a bicameral legislature, with a lower house and "a separate upper chamber hereditary in nature" ([30–33]). The hereditary body will check the lower house ([30]), just as the lower house will check the power of the hereditary nobility by maintaining sole right to initiate financial legislation ([34–35]). The legislative bodies, M affirms, should neither remain too long out of session ([38]), nor too long in session ([39]), and new elections ought to be sufficiently frequent to induce optimism among a populace disenchanted with the legislative body currently sitting ([40]). In order to preclude legislative tyranny, the power to convene and prorogue the legislature ought to rest with the monarch, from whom, in M's view, there is less threat of tyranny ([41–46]).

Montesquieu concludes his discussion of legislative power by enumerating three instances in which the legislature should possess a portion of the judicial power ([47–50]). The upper house, M suggests, should possess the power both to try one of their own members accused of a crime ([48]) and to pardon and reduce sentences handed down by the courts ([49]). And the upper house should also hear the impeachment charges brought against a minister by the lower house ([50–51]).

Executive Power

Montesquieu next analyzes executive power ([52–64]). Having earlier maintained that, for the sake of efficiency, the executive power ought to be in the hands of one individual, a monarch ([36]), M now discusses the executive's right to veto bills enacted by the legislature ([52–56]). He excludes the executive from participating in debates or even proposing legislation, particularly financial legislation ([57–59]), and he discusses various means by which the power of the executive is restrained within reasonable limits ([60–64]).

Conclusion

In the final segment of Book XI, chapter 6 ([65–69]), Montesquieu traces the origins of English government to the forests of Germany ([65]), suggests that even the English system will not last forever ([66]), and claims to have described the potential for liberty established by their constitution rather than the actual degree of liberty enjoyed by the English ([67]). M concludes by asserting that he by no means intended to disvalue other forms of government ([68]; and see Book XI, chap. 7) and by criticizing Harrington for not realizing that liberty was all around him ([69]).

GENERAL IDEA [Chapter 1]

I MAKE a distinction between the laws that form political liberty with regard to the constitution, and those by which it is formed in respect to the citizen. The former shall be the subject of this book; the latter I shall examine in the next.

DIFFERENT SIGNIFICATIONS GIVEN TO THE
WORD LIBERTY [Chapter 2]

THERE is no word whatsoever that has admitted of more various
significations, and has made more different impressions on human
minds, than that of *Liberty*. Some have taken it for a facility of
deposing a person on whom they had conferred a tyrannical authority; others for the power of chusing a person whom they are
obliged to obey; others for the right of bearing arms, and of being
thereby enabled to use violence; others in fine for the privilege of
being governed by a native of their own country or by their own
laws.[a] A certain nation, for a long time thought liberty consisted
in the privilege of wearing a long beard.[b] Some have annexed this
name to one form of government, in exclusion of others: Those
who had a republican taste, applied it to this government; those
who liked a monarchical state, gave it to monarchies.[c] Thus they
all have applied the name of *liberty* to the government most conformable to their own customs and inclinations: and as in a republic people have not so constant and so present a view of the instruments of the evils they complain of, and likewise as the laws seem
there to speak more, and the executors of the laws less, it is
generally attributed to republics, and excluded from monarchies.
In fine as in democracies the people seem to do very near whatever
they please, liberty has been placed in this sort of government, and
the power of the people has been confounded with their liberty.

[a] I have copied, *says Cicero*, Scaevola's edict, which permits the Greeks to terminate
their differences among themselves according to their own laws; this makes them
consider themselves as a free people.

[b] The Russians could not bear that the Czar Peter should make them cut it off.

[c] The Cappadocians refused the condition of a republican state, which was offered
them by the Romans.

IN WHAT LIBERTY CONSISTS [Chapter 3]

[1]   IT is true that in democracies the people seem to do what they please; but political liberty does not consist in an unrestrained freedom. In governments, that is, in societies directed by laws, liberty can consist only in the power of doing what we ought to will, and in not being constrained to do what we ought not to will.

[2]   We must have continually present to our minds the difference between independence and liberty. Liberty is a right of doing whatever the laws permit; and if a citizen could do what they forbid, he would no longer be possest of liberty, because all his fellow citizens would have the same power.

THE SAME SUBJECT CONTINUED [Chapter 4]

[1]   DEMOCRATIC and aristocratic states are not necessarily free.[1] Political liberty is to be met with only in moderate governments: yet even in these it is not always met with. It is there only when there is no abuse of power: but constant experience shews us, that every man invested with power is apt to abuse it; he pushes on till he comes to the utmost limit. Is it not strange, tho' true, to say, that virtue itself has need of limits?

[2]   To prevent the abuse of power, 'tis necessary that by the very disposition of things power should be a check to power. A government may be so constituted, as no man shall be compelled to do things to which the law does not oblige him, nor forced to abstain from things which the law permits.

OF THE END OR VIEW OF DIFFERENT
GOVERNMENTS [Chapter 5]

[1]   THO' all governments have the same general end, which is that of preservation, yet each has another particular view. Increase of

dominion was the view of Rome; war, of Sparta; religion, of the Jewish laws; commerce, that of Marseilles; public tranquillity, that of the laws of China;[a] navigation, of the laws of Rhodes; natural liberty, that of the policy of the Savages; in general the pleasures of the prince, that of despotic states; that of monarchies, the prince's and the kingdom's glory; the independence of individuals is the end aimed at by the laws of Poland, and from thence results the oppression of the whole.[b]

[2]   One nation there is also in the world, that has for the direct end of its constitution political liberty. We shall examine presently the principles on which this liberty is founded: if they are found, liberty will appear as in a mirror.

[3]   To discover political liberty in a constitution, no great labour is requisite. If we are capable of seeing it where it exists, why should we go any further in search of it?

OF THE CONSTITUTION OF ENGLAND [Chapter 6]

[1]   In every government there are three sorts of power: the legislative; the executive in respect to things dependent on the law of nations; and the executive, in regard to things that depend on the civil laws.

[2]   By virtue of the first, the prince or magistrate enacts temporary or perpetual laws, and amends or abrogates those that have been already enacted. By the second, he makes peace or war, sends or receives embassies, establishes the public security, and provides against invasions. By the third, he punishes crimes, or determines the disputes that arise between individuals. The latter we shall call

---

[a] The natural end of a state that has no foreign enemies, or that thinks itself secured against them by barriers.

[b] Inconveniency of the *Liberum veto*.

the judiciary power, and the other simply the executive power of the state.

[3]   The political liberty of the subject is a tranquillity of mind, arising from the opinion each person has of his safety. In order to have this liberty, it is requisite the government be so constituted as one man need not be afraid of another.

[4]   When the legislative and executive powers are united in the same person, or in the same body of magistracy, there can be then no liberty; because apprehensions may arise, lest the same monarch or senate should enact tyrannical laws, to execute them in a tyrannical manner.

[5]   Again, there is no liberty, if the power of judging be not separated from the legislative and executive powers. Were it joined with the legislative, the life and liberty of the subject would be exposed to arbitrary control; for the judge would be then the legislator. Were it joined to the executive power, the judge might behave with all the violence of an oppressor.

[6]   Miserable indeed would be the case, were the same man, or the same body whether of the nobles or of the people, to exercise those three powers, that of enacting laws, that of executing the public resolutions, and that of judging the crimes or differences of individuals.

[7]   Most kingdoms of Europe enjoy a moderate government, because the prince who is invested with the two first powers, leaves the third to his subjects. In Turky, where these three powers are united in the Sultan's person, the subjects groan under the weight of tyranny and oppression.

[13]   The judiciary power ought not to be given to a standing senate; it should be exercised by persons taken from the body of the people,[a] at certain times of the year, and pursuant to a form and

[a] As at Athens.

manner prescribed by law, in order to erect a tribunal that should last only as long as necessity requires.[2]

[14]   By this means the power of judging, a power so terrible to mankind, not being annexed to any particular state or profession, becomes, as it were, invisible. People have not then the judges continually present to their view; they fear the office, but not the magistrate.

[15]   In accusations of a deep or criminal nature, it is proper the person accused should have the privilege of chusing in some measure his judges in concurrence with the law; or at least he should have a right to except against so great a number, that the remaining part may be deemed his own choice.

[16]   The other two powers may be given rather to magistrates or permanent bodies, because they are not exercised on any private subject; one being no more than the general will of the state, and the other the execution of that general will.

[17]   But tho' the tribunals ought not to be fixt, yet the judgments ought, and to such a degree, as to be always conformable to the exact letter of the law. Were they to be the private opinion of the judge, people would then live in society without knowing exactly the obligations it lays them under.[3]

[18]   The judges ought likewise to be in the same station as the accused, or in other words, his peers, to the end that he may not imagine he is fallen into the hands of persons inclined to treat him with rigour.[4]

[19]   If the legislature leaves the executive power in possession of a right to imprison those subjects who can give security for their good behaviour, there is an end of liberty; unless they are taken up, in order to answer without delay to a capital crime. In this case they are really free, being subject only to the power of the law.[5]

[20]   But should the legislature think itself in danger by some secret

conspiracy against the state, or by a correspondence with a foreign enemy, it might authorise the executive power, for a short and limited time, to imprison suspected persons, who in that case would lose their liberty only for a while, to preserve it for ever.

[22]   As in a free state, every man who is supposed a free agent, ought to be his own governor; so the legislative power should reside in the whole body of the people. But since this is impossible in large states, and in small ones is subject to many inconveniencies; it is fit that the people should act by their representatives, what they cannot act by themselves.

[23]   The inhabitants of a particular town are much better acquainted with its wants and interests, than with those of other places; and are better judges of the capacity of their neighbours, than of that of the rest of their countrymen. The members therefore of the legislature should not be chosen from the general body of the nation; but it is proper that in every considerable place, a representative should be elected by the inhabitants.

[24]   The great advantage of representatives is their being capable of discussing affairs. For this the people collectively are extremely unfit, which is one of the greatest inconveniences of a democracy.

[25]   It is not at all necessary that the representatives who have received a general instruction from their electors, should wait to be particularly instructed on every affair, as is practised in the diets of Germany. True it is that by this way of proceeding, the speeches of the deputies might with greater propriety be called the voice of the nation: but on the other hand this would throw them into infinite delays, would give each deputy a power of controlling the assembly; and on the most urgent and pressing occasions the springs of the nation might be stopped by a single caprice.

[26]   When the deputies, as Mr. Sidney well observes,[6] represent a

body of people as in Holland, they ought to be accountable to their constituents: but it is a different thing in England, where they are deputed by boroughs.

[27]   All the inhabitants of the several districts ought to have a right of voting at the election of a representative, except such as are in so mean a situation, as to be deemed to have no will of their own.

[28]   One great fault there was in most of the ancient republics; that the people had a right to active resolutions, such as require some execution, a thing of which they are absolutely incapable. They ought to have no hand in the government but for the chusing of representatives, which is within their reach.[7] For tho' few can tell the exact degree of men's capacities, yet there are none but are capable of knowing in general whether the person they chuse is better qualified than most of his neighbours.

[29]   Neither ought the representative body to be chosen for active resolutions,[8] for which it is not so fit; but for the enacting of laws, or to see whether the laws already enacted be duly executed, a thing they are very capable of, and which none indeed but themselves can properly perform.

[30]   In a state there are always persons distinguished by their birth, riches, or honors: but were they to be confounded with the common people, and to have only the weight of a single vote like the rest, the common liberty would be their slavery, and they would have no interest in supporting it, as most of the popular resolutions would be against them. The share they have therefore in the legislature ought to be proportioned to the other advantages they have in the state; which happens only when they form a body that has a right to put a stop to the enterprizes of the people, as the people have a right to oppose any encroachment of theirs.

[31]   The legislative power is therefore committed to the body of the

nobles, and to the body chosen to represent the people, which have each their assemblies and deliberations apart, each their separate view and interests.

[32]   Of the three powers above-mentioned the judiciary is in some measure next to nothing.[9] There remain therefore only two; and as these have need of a regulating power to temper them, the part of the legislative body composed of the nobility, is extremely proper for this very purpose.

[33]   The body of the nobility ought to be hereditary. In the first place it is so in its own nature; and in the next there must be a considerable interest to preserve its prerogatives; prerogatives that in themselves are obnoxious to popular envy, and of course in a free state are always in danger.

[34]   But as an hereditary power might be tempted to pursue its own particular interests, and forget those of the people; it is proper that where they may reap a singular advantage from being corrupted, as in the laws relating to the supplies,[10] they should have no other share in the legislation, than the power of refusing, and not that of enacting.[11]

[35]   By the *power of enacting*, I mean the right of ordaining by their own authority, or of amending what has been ordained by others. By the *power of refusing*, I would be understood to mean the right of annulling a resolution taken by another; which was the power of the tribunes at Rome. And tho' the person possessed of the privilege of refusing may likewise have the right of approving, yet this approbation passes for no more than a declaration, that he intends to make no use of his privilege of refusing, and is derived from that very privilege.

[36]   The executive power ought to be in the hands of a monarch; because this branch of government, which has always need of expedition, is better administered by one than by many: whereas,

whatever depends on the legislative power, is oftentimes better regulated by many than by a single person.

[37]   But if there was no monarch, and the executive power was committed to a certain number of persons selected from the legislative body,[12] there would be an end then of liberty; by reason the two powers would be united, as the same persons would actually sometimes have, and would moreover be always able to have, a share in both.

[38]   Were the legislative body to be a considerable time without meeting, this would likewise put an end to liberty. For of two things one would naturally follow; either that there would be no longer any legislative resolutions, and then the state would fall into anarchy; or that these resolutions would be taken by the executive power which would render it absolute.[13]

[39]   It would be needless for the legislative body to continue always assembled. This would be troublesome to the representatives, and moreover would cut out too much work for the executive power, so as to take off its attention from executing, and oblige it to think only of defending its own prerogatives and the right it has to execute.

[40]   Again, were the legislative body to be always assembled, it might happen to be kept up only by filling the vacant places of the deceased members with new representatives; and in that case, if the legislative body was once corrupted, the evil would be past all remedy. When different legislative bodies succeed one another, the people who have a bad opinion of that which is actually sitting, may reasonably entertain some hopes of the next: but were it to be always the same body, the people upon seeing it once corrupted, would no longer expect any good from its laws; and of course they would either become desperate or fall into a state of indolence.

[41]   The legislative body should not assemble of itself. For a body is

supposed to have no will but when it is assembled; and besides were it not to assemble unanimously, it would be impossible to determine which was really the legislative body, the part assembled, or the other. And if it had a right to prorogue itself, it might happen never to be prorogued; which would be extremely dangerous in case it should ever attempt to incroach on the executive power. Besides there are seasons, some more proper than others, for assembling the legislative body: it is fit therefore that the executive power should regulate the time of convening as well as the duration of those assemblies, according to the circumstances and exigencies of state known to itself.

[42]   Were the executive power not to have a right of putting a stop to the incroachments of the legislative body, the latter would become despotic; for as it might arrogate to itself what authority it pleased, it would soon destroy all the other powers.

[43]   But it is not proper on the other hand that the legislative power should have a right to stop the executive. For as the execution has its natural limits, it is useless to confine it; besides the executive power is generally employed in momentary operations. The power therefore of the Roman tribunes was faulty, as it put a stop not only to the legislation, but likewise to the execution itself; which was attended with infinite mischiefs.

[44]   But if the legislative power in a free government has no right to stay the executive, it has a right and ought to have the means of examining in what manner its laws have been executed.

[45]   But whatever may be the issue of that examination, the legislative body ought not to have a power of judging the person, nor of course the conduct of him who is intrusted with the executive power. His person should be sacred, because as it is necessary for the good of the state to prevent the legislative body from rendering

themselves arbitrary, the moment he is accused or tried, there is an end of liberty.

[46]   In this case the state would be no longer a monarchy, but a kind of republican, tho' not a free, government. But as the person intrusted with the executive power cannot abuse it without bad counsellors, and such as hate the laws as ministers, tho' the laws favour them as subjects; these men may be examined and punished.[14]

[47]   Tho' in general the judiciary power ought not to be united with any part of the legislative, yet this is liable to three exceptions founded on the particular interest of the party accused.

[48]   The great are always obnoxious to popular envy; and were they to be judged by the people, they might be in danger from their judges, and would moreover be deprived of the privilege which the meanest subject is possessed of in a free state, of being tried by their peers. The nobility for this reason ought not to be cited before the ordinary courts of judicature, but before that part of the legislature which is composed of their own body.

[49]   It is possible that the law, which is clear-sighted in one sense, and blind in another, might in some cases be too severe. But as we have already observed, the national judges are no more, than the mouth that pronounces the words of the law, mere passive beings incapable of moderating either its force or rigor. That part therefore of the legislative body, which we have just now observed to be a necessary tribunal on another occasion, is also a necessary tribunal in this; it belongs to its supreme authority to moderate the law in favour of the law itself, by mitigating the sentence.[15]

[50]   It might also happen that a subject intrusted with the administration of public affairs, may infringe the rights of the people, and be guilty of crimes which the ordinary magistrates either could

not, or would not punish. But in general the legislative power cannot judge; and much less can it be a judge in this particular case, where it represents the party concerned, which is the people. It can only therefore impeach. But before what court shall it bring its impeachment? Must it go and demean itself before the ordinary tribunals, which are its inferiors, and being composed moreover of men who are chosen from the people as well as itself, will naturally be swayed by the authority of so powerful an accuser? No: in order to preserve the dignity of the people, and the security of the subject, the legislative part which represents the people, must bring in its charge before the legislative part which represents the nobility, who have neither the same interests nor the same passions.

[51]   Here is an advantage which this government has over most of the ancient republics, where there was this abuse, that the people were at the same time both judge and accuser.

[52]   The executive power, pursuant to what has been already said, ought to have a share in the legislature by the power of refusing,[16] otherwise it would soon be stripp'd of its prerogatives. But should the legislative power usurp a share of the executive, the latter would be equally undone.

[53]   If the prince were to have a share in the legislature by the power of enacting, liberty would be lost. But as it is necessary he should have a share in the legislature for the support of his own prerogative, this share must consist in the power of refusing.

[54]   The change of government at Rome was owing to this, that neither the senate who had one part of the executive power, nor the magistates who were entrusted with the other, had the right of refusing, which was intirely lodged in the people.

[55]   Here then is the fundamental constitution of the government

we are treating of. The legislative body being composed of two parts, one checks the other, by the mutual privilege of refusing. They are both checked by the executive power, as the executive is by the legislative.

[56]   These three powers should naturally form a state of repose or inaction. But as there is a necessity for movement in the course of human affairs, they are forced to move, but still to move in concert.

[57]   As the executive power has no other part in the legislative than the privilege of refusing, it can have no share in the public debates. It is not even necessary that it should propose, because as it may always disapprove of the resolutions that shall be taken, it may likewise reject the decisions on those proposals which were made against its will.

[58]   In some ancient commonwealths, where public debates were carried on by the people in a body, it was natural for the executive power to propose and debate with the people, otherwise their resolutions must have been attended with a strange confusion.

[59]   Were the executive power to determine the raising of public money, otherwise than by giving its consent, liberty would cease; because it would become legislative in the most important point of legislation.

[60]   If the legislative power was to settle the subsidies, not from year to year, but for ever, it would run the risk of losing its liberty, because the executive power would no longer be dependent; and when once it was possessed of such a perpetual right, it would be a matter of indifference, whether it held it of itself, or of another.[17] The same may be said, if it should come to a resolution of intrusting, not an annual, but a perpetual command of the sea and land forces to the executive power.[18]

[61]   To prevent the executive power from being capable of oppressing, it is requisite that the armies, with which it is entrusted, should consist of the people, and have the same spirit as the people, as was the case at Rome till the time of *Marius*. To obtain this end, there are only two ways, either that the persons employed in the army, should have sufficient property to answer for their conduct to their fellow subjects, and be enlisted only for a year, as was customary at Rome: or if there should be a standing army, composed chiefly of the most despicable part of the nation, the legislative power should have a right to disband them as soon as it pleased; the soldiers should live in common with the rest of the people; and no separate camp, barracks, or fortress, should be suffered.

[62]   When once an army is established, it ought not to depend immediately on the legislative, but on the executive power; and this from the very nature of the thing; its business consisting more in action than in deliberation.

[63]   From a manner of thinking that prevails amongst mankind, they set a higher value upon courage than timorousness, on activity than prudence, on strength than counsel. Hence the army will ever despise a senate, and respect their own officers. They will naturally slight the orders sent them by a body of men, whom they look upon as cowards, and therefore unworthy to command them. So that as soon as the army depends on the legislative body, the government becomes a military one; and if the contrary has ever happened, it has been owing to some extraordinary circumstances. It is because the army was always kept divided; it is because it was composed of several bodies, that depended each on their particular province; it is because the capital towns were strong places, defended by their natural situation, and not garrisoned with regular troops.

[64]   Holland for instance, is still safer than Venice; she might
drown, or starve the revolted troops; for as they are not quartered
in towns that are capable to furnish them with necessary subsistence; this subsistence is of course precarious.[19]

[65]   Whoever shall read the admirable treatise of Tacitus on the
manners of the Germans,[b] will find that it is from them the
English have borrowed the idea of their political government.[20]
This beautiful system was invented first in the woods.

[66]   As all human things have an end, the state we are speaking of
will lose its liberty, will perish. Have not Rome, Sparta, and
Carthage perished? It will perish when the legislative power shall
be more corrupt than the executive.

[67]   It is not my business to examine whether the English actually
enjoy this liberty, or not. Sufficient it is for my purpose to observe, that it is established by their laws; and I inquire no further.[21]

[68]   Neither do I pretend by this to undervalue other governments,
nor to say that this extreme political liberty ought to give uneasiness to those who have only a moderate share of it. How should I
have any such design, I who think that even the excess of reason is
not always desirable, and that mankind generally find their account
better in mediums than in extremes?[22]

[69]   *Harrington* in his *Oceana* has also inquired into the highest point
of liberty to which the constitution of a state may be carried. But
of him indeed it may be said, that for want of knowing the nature
of real liberty, he busied himself in pursuit of an imaginary one,
and that he built a Chalcedon tho' he had a Byzantium before his
eyes.

---

[b] De minoribus rebus principes consultant, de majoribus omnes; ita tamen ut ea.
quoque quorum penes plebem arbitrium est apud principes pertractentur.

OF THE MONARCHIES WE ARE
ACQUAINTED WITH [Chapter 7]

[1]   THE monarchies we are acquainted with,[23] have not, like that we
have been speaking of, liberty for their direct view: their only aim
is the subject's, the state's, and the prince's glory. But from this
glory there results a spirit of liberty, which in those governments
may perform as great things, and may contribute as much perhaps
to happiness, as liberty itself.

[2]   Here the three powers are not distributed and founded on the
model of the constitution above-mentioned; they have each a particular distribution, according to which they border more or less on
political liberty; and if they did not border upon it, monarchy
would degenerate into despotic government.

BOOK XII: *Of the Laws That Form Political Liberty in Relation to the Subject*

ANALYSIS

Having concentrated in Book XI on political liberty as determined by the constitution, Montesquieu turns in Book XII to the political liberty of the subject. These two types of liberty, constitutional and personal, are related — but not identical. "The constitution may happen to be free, and the subject not. The subject may be free, and not the constitution" (chap. 1, par. [3]).

The liberty of the subject is primarily determined by the nature of the criminal laws and procedures to which he is subjected (chap. 2 [2]). The possible tyranny of manners and customs, however, is also considered (chap. 1 [4]). Particularly fatal to the liberty of the subject are criminal procedures sentencing men to death upon the deposition of a single witness (chap. 3). And as Montesquieu had argued in Book VI, chapter 16, punishments should fit the nature of the crime (chap. 4). The punishment for sacrilege, for instance, should be deprivation of the advantages conferred by religion — nothing more (chap. 4 [4–6]). Crimes prejudicial to morality, but not violating the rights of others, should be punished by fines and shame and, if necessary, expulsion from home and society (Book XII, chap. 4 [8]). Crimes that disturb the public tranquillity without, however, threatening anyone's security, should be punished by imprisonment, exile, or other means that will reform "turbulent spirits" (chap. 4 [10–11]). Only crimes that actually deprive another subject of his liberty are rightfully punished more severely. At a time when the death penalty was being inflicted for such crimes as smuggling, espionage, heresy, and counterfeiting, M argued that capital punishment is justified only when an individual has deprived, or attempted to deprive, another man of his life, and he quickly adds that even under these circumstances capital punishment "is the remedy, as it were, of a sick society" (chap. 4 [12]).

Certain crimes, chief among which are magic and heresy, should be prosecuted with extreme caution, Montesquieu counseled, since they often involve accusations against a person's character rather than his actions, and since the danger of being accused of one of these crimes grows in direct proportion to the ignorance of the people making the accusation (chap. 5 [1]). Similarly, prosecutions for the crime of treason are often prejudicial to the liberty of the subject, since the grounds for treason are often either indeterminate (chap. 7) or unjust (chap 8). Whatever the punishments eventually inflicted, care should be taken that no punishments debase the populace at large by infringing the rules of modesty (chap. 14).

IDEA OF THIS BOOK [Chapter 1]

[1]   IT is not sufficient to have treated of political liberty as relative to the constitution; we must examine it likewise in the relation it bears to the subject.

[2]   We have observed that in the first case it is formed by a certain distribution of the three powers: but in the second we must consider it under another idea. It consists in security, or in the opinion people have of their security.

[3]   The constitution may happen to be free, and the subject not. The subject may be free, and not the constitution.

[4]   It is the disposition only of the laws, and even of the fundamental laws, that constitutes liberty in its relation to the constitution. But as it relates to the subject; morals, customs, received examples may give rise to it, and particular civil laws may favour it, as we shall presently see in this book.

[5]   Farther, as in most governments, liberty is more checked or depressed than their constitution demands, it is proper to treat of the particular laws that in each constitution are apt to assist or check the principle of liberty, which each government is capable of receiving.

OF THE LIBERTY OF THE SUBJECT [Chapter 2]

[1]   PHILOSOPHICAL *liberty* consists in the exercise of our will, or at least (if we must speak agreeably to all systems) in the opinion we have of exercising our will. Political *liberty* consists in security, or at least in the opinion we have of security.

[2]   This security is never more dangerously attacked than in public or private accusations. It is therefore on the goodness of criminal laws that the liberty of the subject principally depends.

THE SAME SUBJECT CONTINUED [Chapter 3]

[1]   THOSE laws which condemn a man to death on the deposition of a single witness, are fatal to liberty. In right reason there should be two, because a witness who affirms, and the accused who denies, make an equal balance, and a third must incline the scale.

[2]   The Greeks[a] and Romans[b] required one voice more to condemn: but our French laws insist upon two. The Greeks pretend that their custom had been established by the Gods; but this more justly may be said of ours.

THAT LIBERTY IS FAVOURED BY THE NATURE AND PROPORTION OF PUNISHMENTS [Chapter 4][1]

[1]   LIBERTY is in its highest perfection, when criminal laws derive

[a] See Aristid. Orat. in Minervam.
[b] Dionys. Halicarn. on the judgment of Coriolanus, book 7.

each punishment from the particular nature of the crime. Then there are no arbitrary decisions; the punishment does not flow from the capriciousness of the legislator, but from the very nature of the thing; and man uses no violence to man.

[2]   There are four sorts of crimes. Those of the first species are prejudicial to religion, the second to morals, the third to the public tranquillity, and the fourth to the security of the subject. The punishments inflicted for these crimes ought to proceed from the nature of each of these species.

[3]   In the class of crimes that concern religion, I rank only those which attack it directly, such as all simple sacrileges. For as to crimes that disturb the exercise of it, they are of the nature of those which prejudice the tranquillity or security of the subject, and ought to be referred to those classes.

[4]   In order to derive the punishment of simple sacrileges from the nature of the thing,[a] it should consist in depriving people of the advantages conferred by religion, in expelling them out of the temples, in a temporary or perpetual exclusion from the society of the faithful, in shunning their presence, in execrations, detestations, and conjurations.

[5]   In things that prejudice the tranquillity or security of the state, secret actions are subject to human jurisdiction. But in those which offend the Deity, where there is no public action, there can be no criminal matter; the whole passes betwixt man and God, who knows the measure and time of his vengeance. Now if magistrates, confounding things, should inquire also into hidden sacrileges, this inquisition would be directed to a kind of action that does not at all require it; the liberty of the subject would be

---

[a] St. Louis made such severe laws against those who swore, that the pope thought himself obliged to admonish him for it. This prince moderated his zeal, and softened his laws. See his Ordinances.

subverted by arming the zeal of timorous as well as of presumptuous consciences against him.

[6]   The mischief arises from a notion some people have of reveng-
ing the cause of the Deity. But we must honor the Deity, and leave
him to avenge his own cause.[2]* In effect, were we to be directed
by such a notion, where would be the end of punishments? If
human laws are to avenge the cause of an infinite being, they will
be directed by his infinity, and not by the ignorance and caprice of
man.

[8]   The second class is of those crimes which are prejudicial to
morals. Such are the violation of public or private continency, that
is, of the policy directing the manner in which the pleasure annexed to the union of bodies is to be enjoyed. The punishment of
those crimes ought to be also derived from the nature of the thing;
the privation of such advantages as society has attached to the
purity of morals, fines, shame, necessity of concealment, public
infamy, expulsion from home and society, and in fine all such
punishments as belong to a corrective jurisdiction, are sufficient to
repress the temerity of the two sexes. In effect, these things are
less founded on malice, than on oblivion and self-contempt.

[9]   We speak here of none but crimes that relate merely to morals,
for as to those that are also prejudicial to the public security, such
as rapes and ravishments, they belong to the fourth species.

[10]   The crimes of the third class are those that disturb the public
tranquillity. The punishments ought therefore to be derived from
the nature of the thing, and to be relative to this tranquillity; such
as imprisonment, exile, corrections, and other-like chastisements,
proper for reclaiming turbulent spirits, and reducing them to the
established order.

[11]   I confine those crimes that injure the public tranquillity to
things that imply a simple transgression against the civil adminis-

tration: for as to those which by disturbing the public tranquillity attack at the same time the security of the subject, they ought to be ranked in the fourth class.

[12]   The punishments inflicted upon the latter crimes are what are properly distinguished by that name. It is a kind of retaliation, by which the society refuses security to a member, that either has actually, or intentionally deprived another of his security. This punishment is derived from the nature of the thing, founded on reason, and drawn from the very source of good and evil. A man deserves death when he has violated the security so far as to deprive, or to attempt to deprive another man of his life. This punishment of death is the remedy, as it were, of a sick society. When there is a breach of security in respect to property, there may be some reasons for inflicting a capital punishment: but it would be much better, and perhaps more natural, that crimes committed against the security of property should be punished with the loss of property; and this ought indeed to be the case if men's fortunes were common or equal. But as it is those who have no property that are generally the readiest to attack the property of others, it was found necessary to supply a pecuniary with a corporal punishment.

[13]   All that I have here advanced, is founded in nature, and extremely favourable to the liberty of the subject.

OF CERTAIN ACCUSATIONS THAT REQUIRE
PARTICULAR MODERATION AND PRUDENCE
[Chapter 5]

[1]   IT is an important *maxim*; that we ought to be extremely circumspect in the prosecution of magic and heresy. The accusation of these two crimes may be vastly injurious to liberty, and productive of an infinite number of oppressions, if the legislature knows

not how to set bounds to it. For as it does not aim directly at a person's actions, but at his character, it grows dangerous in proportion to the ignorance of the people; and then a man is always in danger, because the most unexceptionable conduct, the purest morals, and the constant practice of every duty in life, are not a sufficient security against the suspicion of those crimes.

OF THE CRIME OF HIGH TREASON [Chapter 7]

[1]   It is determined by the laws of China, that whosoever shews any disrespect to the emperor, is to be punished with death. As they do not mention what this disrespect consists in, every thing may furnish a pretext to take away a man's life, and to exterminate any family whatsoever.

[3]   If the crime of high treason be indeterminate, this alone is sufficient to make the government degenerate into arbitrary power. I shall descant more largely on this subject, when I come to treat[a] of the composition of laws.

OF THE BAD APPLICATION OF THE NAME OF SACRILEGE AND HIGH TREASON [Chapter 8]

[1]   It is likewise a shocking abuse to give the appellation of high treason to an action that does not deserve it. It was decreed by an imperial law,[a] that those who called in question the prince's judgment, or doubted of the merit of such as he had chosen for a public office, should be prosecuted as guilty of sacrilege.[b] Surely it was the cabinet and court favourites who invented that crime. By

---

[a] Book 29.

[a] Gratian, Valentinian, and Theodosius. This is the second in the Code de *Crimin. Sacril.*

[b] Sacrilegii instar est dubitare an is dignus sit quem elegerit Imperator. ibid. This law served as a model to that of Roger in the constitutions of Naples, Tit. 4.

another law it was determined, that whosoever made any attempt against the ministers and officers of the prince should be deemed guilty of high treason, as if he had attempted against the prince himself. [c]

OF INDISCREET SPEECHES [Chapter 12]

[1]   NOTHING renders the crime of high treason more arbitrary than declaring people guilty of it for indiscreet speeches. Speech is so subject to interpretation; there is so great a difference between indiscretion and malice, and so little is there of the latter in the expressions used; that the law can hardly subject people to a capital punishment for words, unless it expressly declares what words they are. [a]

[2]   Words do not constitute an overt act; they remain only in idea. For the greatest part of the time they have no signification of themselves, but by the tone in which they are pronounced. As there can be nothing so equivocal and ambiguous as all this; how is it possible to convert it into a crime of high treason? Wherever this law is established; there is an end not only of liberty, but even of its very shadow.

[4]   Not that I pretend to diminish the indignation people ought to have against those who presume to stain the glory of their prince; what I mean is, that if despotic princes are willing to moderate their power, a simple correction would be more proper on those occasions, than an accusation of high treason, a thing always terrible even to innocence itself. [b]

---

[c] The 5th law *ad leg. Jul. Maj.*

[a] *Si non tale sit delictum quod vel scriptura legis descendit vel ad exemplum legis vindican-dum est*, says Modestinus in the seventh law, *in ff. ad leg. Jul. Maj.*

[b] *Nec lubricum linguae ad poenam facile trahendum est.* Modestin. in the 7th law *in ff. ad leg. Jul. Maj.*

BREACH OF MODESTY IN PUNISHING CRIMES [Chapter 14]³

[1]   THERE are rules of modesty observed by almost every nation in the world; now it would be very absurd to infringe those rules in the punishment of crimes, whose principal view ought always to be the establishment of order.

[2]   Was it the intent of those oriental nations who exposed women to elephants trained up for an abominable kind of punishment, was it, I say, their intent to establish one law by the breach of another?

[3]   By an ancient custom of the Romans it was not permitted to put girls to death till they were ripe for marriage. Tiberius found out an expedient of having them debauched by the executioner before they were brought to the place of punishment:ª thus this bloody and subtle tyrant destroyed the morals of the people to preserve their customs.

[4]   When the magistrates of Japan caused women to be exposed naked in the market-places, and obliged them to go upon all four like beasts, modesty was shocked:ᵇ but when they wanted to compel a mother — when they wanted to force a son — I cannot proceed; even nature herself was struck with horror.

IN WHAT MANNER THE USE OF LIBERTY
IS SUSPENDED IN A REPUBLIC [Chapter 19]

IN countries where liberty is most esteemed, there are laws by which a single person is deprived of it, in order to preserve it for the whole community. Such are in England what they call *Bills of Attainder*.ª They are relative to those Athenian laws by which a

---

ª Suetonius in *Tiberio*.

ᵇ Collection of voyages that contributed to the establishment of the East India Company. Tom. 5. Part. 2.

ª The author of the Continuation of Rapin Thoyras defines *A Bill of Attainder*, a sentence which upon being approved by the two houses and signed by the king passes into

private person was condemned,[b] provided they were made by the unanimous suffrage of six thousand citizens. They are relative also to those laws which were made at Rome against private citizens, and were called *privileges*.[c] These were never passed but in the great meetings of the people. But in what manner soever they are enacted, Cicero is for having them abolished, because the force of law consists in its being made for the whole community.[d] Own I must, notwithstanding that the practice of the freest nation that ever existed, induces me to think that there are cases in which a veil should be drawn for a while over liberty, as it was customary to veil the statues of the Gods.[5]

OF LAWS FAVOURABLE TO THE LIBERTY OF THE SUBJECT IN A REPUBLIC [Chapter 20]

[1]   IN popular governments it often happens that accusations are carried on in public, and every man is allowed to accuse whomsoever he pleases. This rendered it necessary to establish proper laws in order to protect the innocence of the subject. At Athens if an accuser had not the fifth part of the votes on his side, he was obliged to pay a fine of a thousand drachms. Æschines who accused Ctesiphon, was condemned to pay this fine.[a] At Rome a false accuser was branded with infamy,[b] by marking the letter K on his forehead. Guards were also appointed to watch the accuser,

an act, whereby the party accused is declared guilty of high treason without any other formality, and without appeal, Tom. 2. p. 266.[4]

   [b] Legem de singulari aliquo ne rogato nisi sex millibus ita visum. *Ex Andocide de Mysteriis*. This is what they called Ostracism.

   [c] De privis hominibus latae. *Cicero*, de Leg. lib. 3.

   [d] Scitum est jussum in omnes, *Cicero* ibid.

   [a] See *Philostratus* book I. Lives of the Sophists. life of AEschines. See likewise *Plutarch* and *Phocius*.

   [b] By the Remnian Law.

in order to prevent his corrupting either the judges or the witnesses. ^c

OF THINGS THAT STRIKE AT LIBERTY IN MONARCHIES
[Chapter 22]

[1]   LIBERTY has been often weakened in our monarchies by a thing
of the least use in the world to the prince: this is the naming of
commissioners to try a private person. [6]

[2]   The prince himself derives so very little advantage from those
commissioners, [7] that it is not worth while to change for their sake
the common course of things. He is morally sure that he has more
of the spirit of probity and justice than his commissioners, who
always think themselves sufficiently justified by his orders, by an
obscure interest of state, by the choice that has been made of them,
and even by their very apprehensions.

[3]   Upon the arraigning of a peer under Henry VIII it was customary to try him by a committee of the house of lords: by this means
he put to death as many peers as he pleased.

OF SPIES IN MONARCHIES [Chapter 23] [8]

SHOULD I be asked whether there is any necessity for spies in
monarchies; my answer would be that the usual practice of good
princes is not to employ them. [9] When a man obeys the laws, he
has discharged his duty to his prince. He ought at least to have his
own house for an asylum, and the rest of his conduct should be
exempt from inquiry. The spying-trade might perhaps be tolerable, were it practised by honest men; but the necessary infamy of
the person is sufficient to make us judge of the infamy of the
thing. A prince ought to act towards his subjects with candor,

---

^c Plutarch in his treatise entitled, *How a person may reap advantage from his enemies.*

frankness, and confidence. He that has so much disquiet, suspicion, and fear, is an actor embarrassed in playing his part. When he finds that the laws are generally observed and respected, he may judge himself safe. The general behaviour of the public answers for that of every individual. Let him not be afraid: he cannot imagine how natural it is for his people to love him. And how should they do otherwise than love him? since he is the source of almost all the favours that are shewn, punishments being generally charged to the account of the laws. He never shews himself to his people but with a serene countenance; they have even a share of his glory, and they are protected by his power. A proof of his being loved is that his subjects have a confidence in him, and when the minister refuses, they generally imagine that the prince would have granted: even under public calamities they do not accuse his person; they are apt to complain of his being misinformed, or beset by corrupt men: *Did the prince but know*, say the people; these words are but a kind of invocation and a proof of the confidence they have in his person.

OF THE MANNER OF GOVERNING IN MONARCHIES [Chapter 25]

[1]   THE royal authority is a great spring that ought to move easily and without noise. The Chinese boast of one of their emperors, who governed, they say, like the heavens, that is, by his example.

[2]   There are some cases in which a sovereign ought to exert the full extent of his power; and others in which he ought to reduce it within its proper limits. The sublimity of administration consists in knowing perfectly the proper degree of power, great or small, that should be exerted on different occasions.

[3]   The whole felicity of our monarchies consists in the opinion people have of the lenity of the government. A wrong-headed minister wants constantly to remind us of our slavery. But grant-

ing even that we were slaves, he ought to endeavour to conceal our miserable condition from us. All he can say or write, is that the prince is uneasy, that he is surprised, that he will set things to rights. There is a certain ease in commanding; the prince ought only to exhort, and leave the menacing part to the laws. [a]

OF THE MANNERS OF THE MONARCH [Chapter 27]

THE manners of the prince contribute as much as the laws themselves to liberty; like them he may transform men into beasts, and beasts into men. If he likes free and noble souls, he will have subjects; if he likes base dastardly spirits, he will have slaves. Does he want to know the great art of ruling? Let him call honor and virtue around his person, let him invite personal merit. He may even sometimes cast an eye on talents and abilities. Let him not be afraid of those rivals who are called men of merit; he is their equal as soon as he loves them. Let him gain the hearts of his people without bringing their spirits into subjection. Let him render himself popular; he ought to be pleased with the affection of the lowest of his subjects, for they too are men. The common people require so very little deference, that it is fit they should be humoured; the infinite distance between the sovereign and them will surely prevent them from giving him any uneasiness. Let him be exorable to supplication, and resolute against demands; let him be sensible in fine, that his people have his refusals, while his courtiers enjoy his favors.

OF THE CIVIL LAWS PROPER FOR MIXING A
LITTLE LIBERTY IN A DESPOTIC GOVERNMENT [Chapter 29]

[1]   THO' despotic governments are of their own nature every where the same; yet from circumstances, from an opinion of religion,

[a] Nerva, *says Tacitus*, encreased the ease of the empire.

from prejudice, from received examples, from a turn of mind, from manners or morals, it is possible they may admit of a considerable difference.

[2]   It is useful that some particular notions should be established in those governments. Thus in China the prince is considered as the father of his people; and at the commencement of the empire of the Arabs, the prince was their preacher. [a]

[3]   It is proper there should be some sacred book to serve for a rule, as the Alcoran [10] among the Arabs, the books of Zoroaster among the Persians, the Vedam among the Indians, and the classic Books among the Chinese. The religious code supplies the civil one, and directs the arbitrary power.

[4]   It is not at all amiss that in dubious cases the judges should consult the ministers of religion. [b] Thus in Turky the Cadis [11] consult the Mollachs. But if it is a capital crime, it may be proper for the particular judge, if such there be, to take the governor's advice, to the end that the civil and ecclesiastic power may be tempered also by the political authority.

[a] The Caliphs.
[b] History of the Tartars, 3d part p. 277. in the remarks.

BOOK XIII: *Of the Relation Which the Levying of Taxes and the Greatness of the Public Revenues Bear to Liberty*

ANALYSIS

Book XIII concludes Part Two of The Spirit of Laws. *Having considered constitutional liberty (Book XI), and personal liberty (Book XII), Montesquieu now analyzes the influence of governmental economic policy on personal liberty. Economic tyranny, M was aware, can jeopardize the liberty of the subject just as readily as other forms of tyranny. Excessive taxes are not compatible with freedom. "The real wants of the people ought never to give way to the imaginary wants of the state" (chap. 1, par. [2]). Although the near total absence of taxes would likely be detrimental, heavy taxes are by no means automatically beneficial (chap. 2). Excessive taxes fail to inspire industry, and they weaken the tax base by depressing the fortunes of the individuals capable of supporting the government (chap. 7 [4]). Particularly pernicious in M's view are harsh and excessive taxes generated by inflated military spending (chap. 17). And to be equitable, M writes, taxes should be roughly, although not exactly, proportionate to an individual's income (chap. 7 [2]). Furthermore, taxes on merchandise are more conducive to liberty than forms of direct taxation (chap. 14 [1]), since they place much of the burden on those sufficiently wealthy to purchase the goods that are taxed.*

Montesquieu also incorporates in Book XIII a sociology of taxes based on the degree of liberty present in a given state. The greater the degree of liberty

enjoyed by the subject, the greater the taxes may be, since liberty is a
recompense for the burden of taxation (chap. 12 [1–2]). Taxes can more
easily be raised, therefore, in republics and monarchies than in despotic states
(chap. 13 [1–2]).

Montesquieu concludes Book XIII with two chapters (19 and 20) attack-
ing the system of tax-farming in France.

OF THE STATE REVENUES [Chapter 1]

[1]   THE *revenues of the state* are a portion that each subject gives of
his property, in order to secure, or to have the agreeable enjoyment
of the remainder.

[2]   To fix these revenues in a proper manner, regard should be had
both to the necessities of the state and to those of the subject. The
real wants of the people ought never to give way to the imaginary
wants of the state.

[3]   Imaginary wants are those which flow from the passions, and
from the weakness of the governors, from the charms of an extraordinary project, from the distempered desire of vain glory, and
from a certain impotency of mind incapable of withstanding the
attacks of fancy. Often has it happened that ministers of a restless
disposition, have imagined that the wants of the state were those of
their own little and ignoble souls.

[4]   There is nothing requires more wisdom and prudence than the
regulation of that portion which is taken from, and of that which
is left to, the subject.

[5]   The public revenues are not to be measured by what the people
are capable, but by what they ought, to give; and if they are
measured by what they are able to give, it ought to be at least by
what they are able to give for a constancy.

THAT IT IS BAD REASONING TO SAY THAT THE GREATNESS OF TAXES IS GOOD IN ITS OWN NATURE [Chapter 2]

[1]   THERE have been instances in particular monarchies, of small states exempt from taxes, that have been as miserable as the circumjacent places which groaned under the weight of exactions. The chief reason of this is; that the small state can hardly have any such thing as industry, arts, or manufactures, because in this respect it lies under a thousand restraints from the great state in which it is inclosed. The great state that surrounds it, is blessed with industry, manufactures, and arts; and establishes laws by which those several advantages are procured. The petty state becomes therefore necessarily poor, let it pay ever so few taxes.

[2]   And yet some have concluded from the poverty of those petty states, that in order to render the people industrious, it is necessary to load them with taxes. But it would be a much better conclusion to say that they ought to have no taxes at all. None live here but wretches who retire from the neighbouring parts to avoid working; wretches who disheartened by pain and toil make their whole felicity consist in idleness.

[3]   The effect of wealth in a country is to inspire every heart with ambition: the effect of poverty is to give birth to despair. The former is excited by labour, the latter is soothed by indolence.

[4]   Nature is just to all mankind; she rewards them for their industry; whilst she renders them industrious by annexing rewards in proportion to the greatness of their labour. But if an arbitrary power deprives people of the recompences of nature, they fall into a disrelish of industry, and then indolence and inaction seem to be their only happiness.

OF TAXES IN COUNTRIES WHERE PURE VILLENAGE[1]
IS NOT ESTABLISHED [Chapter 7]

[1]   WHEN the inhabitants of a state are all free subjects, and each
man possesses by his demain what the prince is possessed of by
dominion, taxes may then be laid either on persons, on lands, on
merchandises, on two of those things, or on all three together.

[2]   In the taxing of persons, it would be an unjust proportion to
conform exactly to that of property. At Athens the people were
divided into four classes.[a] Those who drew five hundred measures
of liquid or dry fruit from their estates, paid a talent[b] to the public;
those who drew three hundred measures, paid half a talent; those
who had two hundred measures paid ten minae; those of the fourth
class paid nothing at all. The tax was fair, tho' it was not propor-
tionable: if it did not follow the proportion of people's property, it
followed that of their wants. It was judged that every man had an
equal share of what was *necessary for nature*; that whatsoever was
necessary for nature, ought not to be taxed; that to this succeeded the
useful, which ought to be taxed, but less than the superfluous; and
that the largeness of the taxes on what was superfluous prevented
superfluity.

[4]   If some subjects do not pay enough, the mischief is not so great;
their convenience and ease turn always to the public advantage: if
some private people pay too much, their ruin redounds to the
public detriment. If the government proportions its fortune to that
of individuals, the ease and conveniency of the latter will soon
make its fortune rise. The whole depends upon a critical moment:
shall the state begin with impoverishing the subjects to enrich
itself? Or had it better wait to be enriched by its wealthy subjects?

[a] Pollux book 8th, chap. 10. art. 130.
[b] Or 60 minae.

Is it more adviseable for it to have the first, or the second advantage? Which shall it chuse, to begin, or to end, with being rich.

[5]   The duties on merchandize are felt least by the people, because they are not demanded of them in form. They may be so prudently managed, that the people themselves shall hardly know they pay them. For this purpose it is of the utmost consequence that the person who sells the merchandize should pay the duty. He is very sensible that he does not pay it for himself; and the consumer who pays it in the main, confounds it with the price.

[6]   There are two kingdoms in Europe where there are very heavy imposts upon liquors;[2] in one the brewer alone pays the duty, in the other it is levied indiscriminately upon all the consumers: in the first no body feels the rigor of the impost, in the second it is looked upon as a grievance. In the former the subject is sensible only of the liberty he has of not paying, in the latter he feels only the necessity that compels him to pay.

[7]   Farther, the obliging the consumers to pay, requires a perpetual rummaging and searching in their houses. Now nothing is more contrary than this to liberty; and those who establish these sorts of duties, have not surely been so happy in this respect, as to hit upon the best method of administration.

IN WHAT MANNER THE DECEIT IS KEPT UP [Chapter 8]

[1]   IN order to make the purchaser confound the price of the commodity with the impost, there must be some proportion between the impost and the value of the commodity; wherefore there ought not to be an excessive duty upon merchandizes of little value. There are countries in which the duty exceeds seventeen or eighteen times the value of the commodity.[3] In this case the prince removes the deceit: his subjects plainly see they are dealt with in an

unreasonable manner; which renders them most exquisitely sensible of their slavish situation.

[2]   Besides the prince to be able to levy a duty so disproportioned to the value of the commodity, must be himself the vender, and the people must not have it in their power to purchase it elsewhere: a practice subject to a thousand inconveniences.

[3]   Smuggling being in this case extremely lucrative, the natural and most reasonable penalty, namely the confiscation of the merchandize, becomes incapable to put a stop to it, especially as this very merchandize is intrinsically of an inconsiderable value. Recourse must be therefore had to extravagant punishments, such as those inflicted for capital crimes. All proportion then of punishments ceases. People that cannot really be considered as bad men, are punished like villains; which of all things in the world, is the most contrary to the spirit of a moderate government.

[4]   Again, the more the people are tempted to cheat the farmer of the revenues,[4] the more the latter is enriched, and the former impoverished. To put a stop to smuggling, the farmer must be invested with extraordinary means of oppressing, and then the country is ruined.

THAT THE GREATNESS OF TAXES DEPENDS
ON THE NATURE OF THE GOVERNMENT [Chapter 10]

[1]   TAXES ought to be very light in despotic governments; otherwise who would be at the trouble of tilling the land? Besides, how is it possible to pay heavy taxes in a government that makes no manner of return to the different contributions of the subject?

[2]   The exorbitant power of the prince, and the extreme depression of the people, require that there should not be even a possibility of the least mistake between them. The taxes ought to be so easy to

collect, and so clearly settled, as to leave no opportunity for the collectors to increase or diminish them. A portion of the fruits of the earth, a capitation, a duty of so much per cent on merchandizes, are the only taxes suitable to that government.

[3]   Merchants in despotic countries ought to have a personal safeguard, to which all due respect should be paid. Without this they would stand no chance in the disputes that might arise between them and the prince's officers.

RELATION BETWEEN THE GREATNESS OF TAXES AND LIBERTY [Chapter 12]

[1]   IT is a *general rule*, that taxes may be heavier in proportion to the liberty of the subject, and that there is a necessity for reducing them in proportion to the increase of slavery. This has always been and always will be the case. It is a rule derived from nature that never varies. We find it in all parts, in England, in Holland, and in every state where liberty gradually declines till we come to Turkey. Switzerland seems to be an exception to this rule, because they pay no taxes; but the particular reason for that exemption is well known, and even confirms what I have advanced. In those barren mountains provisions are so dear, and the country is so populous, that a Swiss pays four times more to nature, than a Turk does to the Sultan.

[2]   A conquering people, such as were formerly the Athenians and the Romans, may rid themselves of all taxes, as they reign over vanquished nations. Then indeed they do not pay in proportion to their liberty, because in this respect they are no longer a people, but a monarch.

[3]   But the general rule still holds good. In moderate governments there is an indemnity for the weight of the taxes, which is liberty.

In despotic countries there is an equivalent for liberty, which is the lightness of the taxes.[a]

IN WHAT GOVERNMENTS TAXES ARE CAPABLE OF INCREASE [Chapter 13]

[1]   TAXES may be increased in most republics, because the citizen, who thinks he is paying himself, willingly submits to them, and moreover is generally able to bear their weight thro' an effect of the nature of the government.

[2]   In a monarchy taxes may be increased, because the moderation of the government is capable of procuring riches: it is a recompence, as it were, of the prince for the respect he shews to the laws. In despotic governments they cannot be increased, because there can be no increase of the extremity of slavery.

THAT THE NATURE OF THE TAXES IS RELATIVE TO THE GOVERNMENT [Chapter 14]

[1]   A CAPITATION is more natural to slavery; a duty on merchandizes is more natural to liberty, because it has not so direct a relation to the person.

[3]   The natural tax of moderate governments, is the duty laid on merchandizes. As this is really paid by the consumer, tho' advanced by the merchant, it is a loan which the merchant has already made to the consumer. Wherefore the merchant must be considered on the one side, as the general debtor of the state, and on the other as the creditor of every individual. He advances to the state, the duty which the consumer will some time or other refund, and he has paid for the consumer the duty which he has paid

---

[a] In Russia the taxes are but small; they have been increased since the despotic power of the prince is exercised with more moderation. See the History of the Tartars, 2d part.

for the merchandize. In England a merchant lends really to the
state fifty or sixty pounds sterling for every tun[5] of wine he
imports. Where is the merchant that would dare do any such thing
in a country governed like Turky? And were he so presumptuous,
how could he do it with a dubious or shattered fortune?

OF THE AUGMENTATION OF TROOPS [Chapter 17]

[1]   A NEW distemper has spread itself over Europe; it has infected
our princes, and induces them to keep up an exorbitant number of
troops. It has its redoublings, and of necessity becomes contagious.
For as soon as one prince augments what he calls his troops, the
rest of course do the same; so that nothing is gained thereby but the
public ruin. Each monarch keeps as many armies on foot as if his
people were in danger of being exterminated; and they gave the
name of peace to this general effort of all against all.[a] Soon, by
thus augmenting our troops, we shall have nothing but soldiers,
and be reduced to the very same situation as the Tartars.[b]

[2]   Great princes not satisfied with hiring or buying troops of small
ones, make it their business on all sides to pay subsidies for
alliances, that is, almost generally, to throw away their money.

[3]   The consequence of such a situation is the perpetual augmentation of taxes; and the mischief which prevents all future remedies,
is that they reckon no more upon their revenues, but go to war
with their whole capital. It is no unusual thing to see governments
mortgage their funds even in time of peace, and to employ what
they call extraordinary means to ruin themselves; means so ex-

---

[a] True it is that this state of effort is the chief support of the balance, because it checks
the great powers.

[b] All that is wanting for this, is to improve the new invention of the militia established almost all over Europe, and carry it to the same excess as they do the regular troops.

traordinary indeed, that such are hardly thought on by the most extravagant young spendthrift.

WHICH IS MOST SUITABLE TO THE PRINCE AND TO THE PEOPLE, THE LETTING OUT TO FARM,[6] OR THE ADMINISTRATION OF THE REVENUES [Chapter 19]

[2]   By the administration of the revenues the prince is at liberty to press or to retard the levy of the taxes, either according to his own wants, or to those of his people. By this he saves to the state the immense profits of the farmers, who impoverish it a thousand ways. By this he spares the people the mortifying sight of sudden fortunes. By this the money collected passes thro' few hands; it goes directly to the treasury, and consequently makes a quicker return to the people. By this the prince avoids an infinite number of bad laws extorted from him continually by the importunate avarice of the farmers, who pretend to offer a present advantage for regulations pernicious to posterity.

[3]   As the moneyed man is always the most powerful, the farmer renders himself arbitrary even over the prince himself; he is not the legislator, but he obliges the legislator to give laws.

OF THE FARMERS OF THE REVENUES [Chapter 20][7]

[1]   ALL is lost when the lucrative profession of farmers obtains likewise by means of its riches to be a post of honor. This may do well enough in despotic states, where their employment is often-times a part of the functions of the governors themselves. But it is by no means proper in a republic; and a custom of that kind destroyed the republic of Rome. Nor is it better in monarchies; nothing being more opposite to the spirit of this government. All the other orders of the state are dissatisfied; honor loses its whole

value; the slow and natural means of distinction are no longer regarded; and the very principle of the government is subverted.

[3]   Every profession has its particular lot. The lot of those who levy the taxes is wealth, and the recompence of wealth is wealth itself. Glory and honor fall to the share of that nobility who neither know, see, nor feel any other happiness than honor and glory. Respect and esteem are for those ministers and magistrates, whose whole life is a continued succession of labour, and who watch day and night for the felicity of the empire.

❧ Part Three

Books XIV through XIX constitute Part Three of *The Spirit of Laws*, according to Montesquieu's plan. With Book XIV the question of the relations that laws should bear to the principle of government is left aside, and Montesquieu takes up the contrasting question of the influence on laws and governments of such *causes physiques* as climate, soil, topography, and terrain (Books XIV–XVIII). Then, in the final Book of Part Three, Book XIX, Montesquieu sets forth the important concept of the general spirit of a nation and analyzes the degree to which ingrained customs affect the character of a people.

BOOK XIV: *Of Laws in Relation to the Nature of the Climate*

ANALYSIS

Book XIV presents Montesquieu's famous theory of the influence of climate on human behavior. His basic premise is that if minds and characters vary from climate to climate, laws too should vary to accomodate those differences (chap. 1). And that climate does induce important differences he argues in chapters 2 and 10 within passages originally part of the Essay on Causes. *People are more vigorous, and hence more daring in cold climates than in hot, M suggests, because cold air contracts the fibres of their cardiovascular systems, causing their blood to flow more swiftly (chap. 2, pars. [1–2]). And climate also affects the nervous system. Nerve fibres close to the skin's surface contract in cold temperatures, causing northerners to display less imagination, taste, sensibility, as well as less sensitivity to pain, than those dwelling in southern climates (chap. 2 [4–13]). And this is owing in part to the coarser fibres of northerners (chap. 2 [3]). (See Introduction, pp. 45–47, for a discussion of fibre theory.)*

In spite of these statements, Montesquieu was not the climatological determinist some have judged him. (See Introduction, pp. 48–51.) As he was quick to point out in his Defense of the Spirit of Laws *(1750), he himself had countered the stress on climate so evident in Book XIV with emphasis elsewhere in the treatise on the influence on human behavior of education (Book IV), custom (Book XIX), religion (Books XXIV–XXV), and, most important, the dominant psychology engendered by a particular form of government (Book III). And even in Book XIV, M counseled a number of ways that legislators should counter the effects of climate when they prove detrimental. Where the climate is excessively hot, religion should encourage action rather than idleness (chap. 5), property distribution should favor widespread ownership as an incentive to labor (chap. 6), the practice of monasticism should be curbed (chap. 7), awards should be bestowed on the most productive farmers and artisans (chaps. 8–9), and the consumption of alcohol should be curtailed (chap. 10).*

In other important chapters of Book XIV, Montesquieu discusses the influence of climate on the inhabitants of India (chap. 3), analyzes how climate contributes to the immutability of Eastern religions, manners, customs, and laws (chap. 4), explores the effects of climate on the English people (chaps. 12 and 13), and suggests in a more general vein that where the effects of climate render individuals mild and gentle, harsh laws are unnecessary (chap. 15).

GENERAL IDEA [Chapter 1]

IF it be true that the character of the mind, and the passions of the heart are extremely different in different climates, the laws ought to be relative both to the difference of those passions, and to the difference of those characters.

OF THE DIFFERENCE OF MEN IN DIFFERENT CLIMATES [Chapter 2][1]

[1]   A COLD air constringes the extremities of the external fibres of the body;[a] this increases their elasticity, and favors the return of the blood from the extremities to the heart. It contracts those very fibres;[b] consequently it increases also their force. On the contrary a warm air relaxes and lengthens the extremes of the fibres; of course it diminishes their force and elasticity.

[2]   People are therefore more vigorous in cold climates. Here the

---

[a] This appears even in the countenance: in cold weather people look thinner.
[b] We know it shortens iron.

action of the heart and the reaction of the extremities of the fibres are better performed, the temperature of the humours is greater, the blood moves freer towards the heart, and reciprocally the heart has more power. This superiority of strength must produce a great many effects, for instance, a greater boldness, that is, more courage; a greater sense of superiority, that is, less desire of revenge; a greater opinion of security, that is, more frankness, less suspicion, policy, and cunning. In short this must be productive of very different characters. Put a man in a close warm place, and he will, for the reasons above given, feel a great faintness. If under this circumstance you propose a bold enterprize to him, I believe you will find him very little disposed towards it: his present weakness will throw him into a despondency of soul; he will be afraid of every thing, because he will feel himself capable of nothing. The inhabitants of warm countries are, like old men, timorous; the people in cold countries are, like young men, brave. If we reflect on the late wars,[c] which are more present to our memory, wherein we can better distinguish some slight effects that escape us at a great distance of time; we shall find that the northern people transplanted into southern countries,[d] did not perform such great actions as their countrymen, who fighting in their own climate possessed their full vigor and courage.

[3]   This strength of the fibres in northern nations is the cause that the coarsest juices are extracted from their aliments. From hence two things result: one that the parts of the chyle or lymph are more proper, by reason of their large surface, to be applied to, and to nourish, the fibres: the other, that they are less proper, because of their coarseness, to give a certain subtility to the nervous juice. Those people have therefore large bodies and little vivacity.

[c] Those for the succession to the Spanish Monarchy.

[d] For instance to Spain.

[4]   The nerves that terminate from all parts in the cutis, form each a bundle of nerves; generally speaking, the whole nerve is not moved, but a very minute part. In warm climates where the cutis is relaxed, the ends of the nerves are opened and exposed to the smallest action of the very weakest objects. In cold countries the cutis is constringed, and the papillae compressed; the miliary glands are in some measure paralytic; the sensation does not reach the brain but when it is very strong and proceeds from the whole nerve at once. Now imagination, taste, sensibility, and vivacity, depend on an infinite number of small sensations.

[5]   I have observed the outermost part of a sheep's tongue, where to the naked eye it seems covered with papillae. On these papillae, I have seen with a microscope, small hairs or a kind of down; between the papillae were pyramids which were shaped towards the ends like pincers. Very likely these pyramids are the principal organ of taste.

[6]   I caused the half of this tongue to be frozen, and observing it with the naked eye I found the papillae considerably diminished; even some rows of the papillae were sunk in their sheath. I examined the outermost part with the microscope, and I perceived no pyramids. In proportion as the frost went off, the papillae seemed to the naked eye to rise, and with the microscope the miliary glands began to appear.

[7]   This observation confirms what I have been saying, that in cold countries the nervous glands are less spread; they sink deeper into their sheaths, or they are sheltered from the action of external objects. Consequently they have not such lively sensations.

[8]   In cold countries, they have very little sensibility for pleasures; in temperate countries they have more; in warm countries their sensibility is exquisite. As climates are distinguished by degrees of latitude, we might distinguish them also, in some measure, by

degrees of sensibility. I have seen the operas of England and of Italy; they are the same pieces and the same performers; and yet the same music produces such different effects on the two nations, one is so cold and indifferent, and the other so transported, that it seems almost inconceivable.

[9]   It is the same with regard to pain; which is excited by the laceration of some fibre of the body. The author of nature has established, that this pain should be stronger in proportion as the laceration is greater: now it is evident that the large bodies and coarse fibres of the people of the north are less capable of laceration than the delicate fibres of the inhabitants of warm countries; consequently the soul is there less sensible of pain. You must flay a Muscovite alive to make him feel.

[10]   From this delicacy of organs peculiar to warm climates, it follows, that the soul is most sensibly moved by whatever has a relation to the union of the two sexes: here every thing leads to this object.[2]

[11]   In northern climates scarce has the animal part of love a power of making itself felt. In temperate climates, love attended by a thousand appendages, renders itself agreeable by things that have at first the appearance of love, tho' not the reality. In warmer climates love is liked for its own sake, it is the only cause of happiness, it is life itself.

[12]   In southern countries a delicate, weak, but sensible machine, resigns itself either to a love which rises and is incessantly laid in a seraglio; or to a love which leaves women in a greater independence, and is consequently exposed to a thousand inquietudes. In northern climates a strong but heavy machine, finds its pleasure in whatever is apt to throw the spirits into motion, such as hunting, travelling, war, and wine. In northern countries, we meet with a people who have few vices, many virtues, a great share of frank-

ness and sincerity. If we draw near the south, we fancy ourselves removed from all morality; the strongest passions multiply all manner of crimes, every one endeavouring to take what advantage he can over his neighbours, in order to encourage those passions. In temperate climates we find the inhabitants inconstant in their manners, in their very vices, and in their virtues: the climate has not a quality determinate enough to fix them.

[13]   The heat of the climate may be so excessive as to deprive the body of all vigor and strength. Then the faintness is communicated to the mind; there is no curiosity, no noble enterprize, no generous sentiment; the inclinations are all passive; indolence constitutes the utmost happiness; no punishment hardly is so severe as the action of the soul, and slavery is more supportable than the force and vigor of mind necessary for human conduct.

CONTRADICTION IN THE CHARACTERS OF
SOME SOUTHERN NATIONS [Chapter 3]

[1]   THE Indians are naturally a cowardly people; [a] even the children of the Europeans born in the Indies lose the courage peculiar to their own climate. [b] But how shall we reconcile this with their cruel actions, with their customs, and penances so full of barbarity? The men voluntarily undergo the greatest hardships; the women burn themselves: here we find a very odd compound of fortitude and weakness.

[2]   Nature having framed those people of a texture so weak as renders them timid, has formed them at the same time of an imagination so lively, that every object makes the strongest im-

---

[a] One hundred European soldiers, says Tavernier, would without any great difficulty beat a thousand Indian soldiers.

[b] Even the Persians, who settle in the Indies, contract in the third generation the indolence and cowardice of the Indians. See Bernier, on the Mogul, Tom. I. p. 182.

pression upon them. That delicacy of organs which renders them apprehensive of death, contributes likewise to make them dread a thousand things more than death: the very same sensibility makes them fly, and dare, all dangers.

[3]   As a good education is more necessary to children than to those who are arrived to a maturity of understanding, so the inhabitants of those climates have much greater need than our people of a wise legislator. The greater their sensibility, the more it behoves them to receive proper impressions, to imbibe no prejudices, and to let themselves be directed by reason.

[4]   At the time of the Romans the inhabitants of the north of Europe lived without art, education, and almost without laws: and yet by the help of the good sense annexed to the gross fibres of those climates, they made an admirable stand against the power of the Roman empire, till that memorable period in which they quitted their woods to subvert it.

CAUSE OF THE IMMUTABILITY OF RELIGION,
MANNERS, CUSTOMS, AND LAWS, IN THE
EASTERN COUNTRIES [Chapter 4]

IF that delicacy of organs which renders the eastern people so susceptible of every impression, is accompanied likewise with a sort of laziness of mind naturally connected with that of the body, by means of which they grow incapable of any action or effort; it is easy to comprehend, that when once the soul has received an impression it cannot change it. This is the reason, that the laws, manners [a] and customs, even those which seem quite indifferent,

---

[a] We find by a fragment of Nicolaus Damascenus, collected by Constantine Porphyrog., that it was an ancient custom in the East to send to strangle a governor who had given any displeasure; it was in the time of the Medes.

such as their manner of dress, are the same to this very day in eastern countries as they were a thousand years ago.

THAT THOSE ARE BAD LEGISLATORS WHO FAVOURED
THE VICES OF THE CLIMATE, AND GOOD LEGISLATORS
WHO OPPOSED THOSE VICES [Chapter 5][3]

[1]   THE Indians believe that repose and nothing are the foundation of all things, and the end in which they terminate. They consider therefore the state of intire inaction as the most perfect of all states, and the object of their desires. They give to the Supreme Being the title of Immoveable.[a] The inhabitants of Siam believe that their utmost happiness consists in not being obliged to animate a machine and to give motion to a body.[b]

[2]   In those countries where the excess of heat enervates and oppresses the body, rest is so delicious, and motion so painful, that this system of metaphysics seems natural; and Foe[4] the legislator of the Indies followed what he himself felt when he placed mankind in a state extremely passive: but his doctrine arising from the laziness of the climate, favoured it also in its turn; it has been the source of an infinite deal of mischief.[c]

[3]   The legislators of China had more sense, when considering men not in the peaceful state which they are to enjoy hereafter, but in the situation proper for discharging the several duties of life, they made their religion, philosophy, and laws all practical. The more

---

[a] Panamanack: See Kircher.

[b] La Loubère, Relation of Siam, p. 446.

[c] Foe wants to reduce the heart to a pure vacuum; "we have eyes and ears, but perfection consists in neither seeing nor hearing; a mouth, hands, & c. but perfection requires that these members should be inactive." This is taken from the dialogue of a Chinese philosopher, quoted by father Du Halde Tom. 3.

the physical causes incline mankind to inaction, the more the moral causes should estrange them from it.

OF THE CULTIVATION OF LANDS IN WARM CLIMATES [Chapter 6]

THE cultivation of lands is the principal labour of man. The more the climate inclines them to shun this labour, the more their religion and laws ought to excite them to it. Thus the Indian laws which give the lands to the prince, and destroy the spirit of property among the subjects, increase the bad effects of the climate, that is, their natural laziness.[5]*

OF MONACHISM [Chapter 7][6]*

[1] THE very same mischiefs result from monachism;[7] it had its rise in the warm countries of the east, where they are less inclined to action than to speculation.

[2]   In Asia the number of dervishes or monks seems to increase together with the heat of the climate. The Indies where the heat is excessive are full of them; and the same difference is found in Europe.

[3]   In order to surmount the laziness of the climate, the laws ought to endeavour to remove all means of subsisting without labour: But in the southern parts of Europe they do quite the reverse; to those who want to live in a state of indolence they afford retreats the most proper for a speculative life, and endow them with immense revenues. These men, who live in the midst of a plenty which they know not how to enjoy, are in the right to give their superfluities away to the common people. The poor are bereft of property; and these men indemnify them by supporting them in idleness, so as to make them even grow fond of their misery.

AN EXCELLENT CUSTOM OF CHINA [Chapter 8]

[1] THE historical relations of China[a] mention a ceremony of opening the grounds,[b] which the emperor performs every year. The
design of this public and solemn act is to excite the people to
tillage.[c]

[2]   Farther, the emperor is informed every year of the husbandman
who has distinguished himself most in his profession; and he
makes him a Mandarin of the eighth order.

[3]   Among the ancient Persians the kings quitted their grandeur
and pomp on the eighth day of the month called *Chorrem-ruz* to eat
with the husbandmen.[d] These institutions were admirably well
calculated for the encouragement of agriculture.

MEANS OF ENCOURAGING INDUSTRY [Chapter 9]

WE shall shew in the nineteenth book that lazy nations are generally proud. Now the effect might well be turned against the cause,
and laziness be destroyed by pride. In the south of Europe, where
people have such a high notion of the point of honor, it would be
right to give prizes to husbandmen who had cultivated best the
lands, or to artists who had made the greatest improvements in
their several professions. This practice has succeeded in our days in
Ireland, where it has established one of the most considerable linen
manufactures in Europe.

---

[a] Father Du Halde, history of China, tom. 2. p. 72.

[b] Several of the kings of India do the same; relation of the kingdom of Siam by La
Loubère p. 69.

[c] *Venty*, the 3d emperor of the 3d dynasty, tilled the lands himself, and made the
empress and his wives employ their time in the silk-works in his palace. History of
China.

[d] Hyde's religion of the Persians.

OF THE LAWS RELATIVE TO THE SOBRIETY
OF THE PEOPLE [Chapter 10]

[1]   IN warm countries the aqueous part of the blood loses itself greatly by perspiration;[a] it must therefore be supplied by a like liquid.
Water is there of admirable use; strong liquors would congeal the
globules of blood that remain after the transuding of the aqueous
humour.[b]

[2]   In cold countries the aqueous part of the blood is very little
evacuated by perspiration. They may therefore make use of
spirituous liquors, without which the blood would congeal. They
are full of humours; consequently strong liquors, which give a
motion to the blood, are proper for those countries.

[3]   The law of Mahomet, which prohibits the drinking of wine, is
therefore a law fitted to the climate of Arabia: and indeed before
Mahomet's time, water was the common drink of the Arabs. The
law which forbad the Carthaginians to drink wine,[c] was also a law
of the climate; in fact the climate of those two countries is pretty
near the same.

[4]   Such a law would be improper for cold countries, where the
climate seems to force them to a kind of national drunkenness,
very different from personal intemperance. Drunkenness predominates over all the world, in proportion to the coldness and
humidity of the climate. Go from the Equator to our Pole, and
you will find drunkenness increasing together with the degree of

    [a] Monsieur Bernier travelling from Lahor to Cachemir, wrote thus: My body is a
sieve; scarce have I swallowed a pint of water but I see it transude like dew out of all my
limbs, even to my fingers' ends. I drink ten pints a day, and it does me no manner of
harm. Bernier's travels. Tom. 2. p. 261.
    [b] In the blood there are red globules, fibrous parts, white globules, and water in which
the whole swims.
    [c] Plato Book 2. of laws; Aristotle of the care of domestic affairs; Eusebius's Evangeli-
cal preparation. Book 12. c. 17.

latitude. Go from the same equator to the opposite pole, and you will find drunkenness travelling south,[d] as on this side it travels towards the north.

[5]   It is very natural that where wine is contrary to the climate, and consequently to health, the excess of it should be more severely punished, than in countries where drunkenness produces very few bad effects to the person, and fewer to society, and where it does not make people mad, but only stupid and heavy. Hence laws[e] which punished a drunken man both for the fault he committed, and for his drunkenness, were applicable only to a personal, and not to a national ebriety. A German drinks thro' custom, and a Spaniard by choice.

[6]   In warm countries the relaxing of the fibres produces a great evacuation of the liquids, but the solid parts are less transpired. The fibres which have but a very weak action and little elasticity, are not much worn; a very small quantity of nutritious juice is requisite to repair them; for which reason they eat very little.

[7]   It is the difference of wants in different climates, that first formed a difference in the manner of living, and this difference of living gave rise to that of laws. Where people are very communicative, there must be particular laws; and others among people where there is very little communication.

OF THE LAWS AGAINST SUICIDES [Chapter 12]

[1]   WE do not find in history that the Romans ever killed themselves without a cause; but the English destroy themselves most unaccountably; they destroy themselves often in the very bosom of

---

[d] This is seen in the Hottentots and the inhabitants of the most southern part of Chily.

[e] As Pittacus did, according to Aristotle, polit. lib. I. c. 3. He lived in a climate where drunkenness is not a national vice.

happiness. This action among the Romans was the effect of education; it was connected with their principles and customs; among the English it is the effect of a distemper;[a] it is connected with the physical state of the machine, independent of every other cause.

[2]   In all probability it is a defect of the filtration of the nervous juice; the machine whose motive faculties are every moment without action, is weary of itself; the soul feels no pain, but a certain uneasiness in existing. Pain is a local thing, which leads us to the desire of seeing it cease; the burthen of life is an evil confin'd to no particular place, which prompts us to the desire of ceasing to live.

[3]   It is evident that the civil laws of some countries may have reasons for branding suicide with infamy: but in England it cannot be punished without punishing the effects of madness.[8*]

EFFECTS ARISING FROM THE CLIMATE
OF ENGLAND [Chapter 13]

[1]   IN a nation so distempered by the climate as to have a disrelish of every thing, nay even of life, it is plain that the government most suitable to the inhabitants, is that in which they cannot lay their chagrins to any single person's charge, and in which being under the direction rather of the laws than of the prince, they cannot change the government without subverting the laws themselves.

[2]   But if this nation had likewise derived from the climate a certain character of impatience which rendered them incapable of bearing the same train of things for any long continuance; it is obvious that the government above-mentioned is the fittest for them.

[3]   This character of impatience is not very considerable of itself; but it may become so when joined with courage.

---

[a] It may be complicated with the scurvy, which in some countries especially, renders a man whimsical and unsupportable to himself. See Pirard's voyages part 2, chap. 21.

[4]   It is quite a different thing from levity, which makes people
undertake or drop a project without cause; it borders more upon
obstinacy, because it proceeds from so lively a sense of misery, that
it is not weakened even by the habit of suffering.

[5]   This character in a free nation is extremely proper for discon-
certing the projects of tyranny,[a] which is always slow and feeble in
its commencements, as in the end it is active and lively; which at
first only stretches out a hand to assist, and exerts afterwards a
multitude of arms to oppress.

[6]   Slavery is ever preceded by sleep. But a people who find no rest
in any situation, who continually explore every part, and feel nothing but pain, can hardly be lulled to sleep.

[7]   Politics are a kind of a file; which wears out by use, and attains
its ends by a slow progression. Now the people of whom we have
been speaking, are incapable of bearing the delays, the details, the
coolness of negotiations: these are things in which they are more
unlikely to succeed than any other nation; wherefore they are apt
to lose by treaties what they obtain by their arms.

OF THE DIFFERENT CONFIDENCE WHICH THE LAWS
HAVE IN THE PEOPLE, ACCORDING TO THE
DIFFERENCE OF CLIMATES [Chapter 15]

[1]   THE people of Japan are so stubborn and perverse a temper, that
neither their legislators nor magistrates can put any confidence
in them: they set nothing before their eyes but judges, menaces,
and chastisements; every step they take is subject to the inquisition
of the civil magistrate. Those laws which out of five heads of families establish one as a magistrate over the other four; those laws

---

[a] Here I take this word for the design of subverting the established power, and
especially that of democracy; this is the signification in which it was understood by the
Greeks and Romans.

which punish a family or a whole ward for a single crime; those laws which find no one innocent where there may happen to be one guilty; are made with a design that the people should all mistrust one another, and that every one should be an inspector, witness and judge of every one's conduct.

[2]   On the contrary the people of India are mild, tender, and compassionate.[a] Hence their legislators repose a great confidence in them. They have established very few punishments;[b] these are not severe, nor are they rigorously executed. They have subjected nephews to their uncles, orphans to their guardians, as in other countries they are subjected to their fathers; they have regulated the succession by the acknowledged merit of the successor. They seem to think that every individual ought to place an intire confidence in the good nature of his fellow subjects.

[3]   They infranchise their slaves without difficulty, they marry them, they treat them as their children:[c] happy climate which gives birth to innocence, and produces a lenity in the laws![9]*

[a] See Bernier, tom. 2. p. 140.

[b] See in the 14th collection of *the edifying letters*, p. 403 the principal laws or customs of the inhabitants of the peninsula on this side of the Ganges.

[c] This is perhaps what made Diodorus say, that in the Indies there was neither master nor slave.

In What Manner the Laws of Civil Slavery Relate to the Nature of the Climate

ANALYSIS

Book XV on slavery is the second of the five books of The Spirit of Laws *that investigate the influence of* causes physiques *on human behavior, institutions, and government. Only two chapters, however, are specifically concerned with the possible effects of climate on the institution of slavery (chaps. 7–8). The remainder of the Book deals with slavery in more general terms.*

Montesquieu begins by affirming slavery to be bad of its own nature— beneficial to neither slave nor master (chap. 1, par. [1]). This initial contention is modified, however, by the assertion that the impact of slavery will necessarily vary from government to government. Slavery ought always to be avoided in moderate governments, since it is inimical to freedom. In despotic governments, however, the effects of slavery are less detrimental, political slavery having already debased the condition of men (chap. 1 [2–3], chap. 6).

In spite of this relativistic perspective, Montesquieu emerges in Book XV as a sharp critic of slavery and at a time when the institution remained largely unassailed. (M's antislavery argument was later further strengthened by the addition in the posthumous edition of 1757 of an additional chapter. See note 12 for an English translation of this chapter.) M vigorously denies —contra traditions of Roman law—the lawfulness of enslaving the captives of war, or debtors, or the children of men reduced to slavery (chap. 2). And with the satirical wit formerly unleashed in the Persian Letters, *M undermines such bigoted justifications of slavery as the seeming barbarity of the customs of those enslaved (chap. 3), or their failure to practice the Christian religion (chap. 4), or the color of their skin (chap. 5).*

*It is only in chapters 7 and 8 that the discussion focuses upon climate and slavery. Montesquieu seems at first to accept the idea that some climates are so hot that only slavery can induce men to labor (chap. 7), but he finally concludes that, given a system of proper rewards for hard labor and the use of "commodious machines" to augment human strength (chap. 8 [3]), there is possibly no climate on earth where the most difficult labor might not be performed by freemen (chap. 8 [4]). And to strengthen his antislavery argument, M rejects Aristotle's contention that some men are slaves by nature (chap. 7 [3]) and suggests that even if there exist some climates sufficiently hot for slavery to be founded on natural reason (*raison naturelle), *slavery will remain in any case unnatural (*contre la nature), *since all men are born equal (chap. 7 [4]).*

Since slavery was widespread in the eighteenth century—however contrary to nature it might be—and since Montesquieu was no utopian, he concluded Book XV with several chapters, not here reproduced, distinguishing among various types of slavery (chap. 9), arguing that slavery ought to be as humane as possible (chaps. 10–11; 16), and defining the relative danger posed by slavery to the three forms of government he had defined (chaps. 12–15).

OF CIVIL SLAVERY [Chapter 1]

[1]   SLAVERY, properly so called, is the establishment of a right which gives to one man such a power over another, as renders him absolute master of his life and fortune. The state of slavery is bad of its own nature: it is neither useful to the master nor to the slave; not to the slave, because he can do nothing thro' a motive of virtue; not to the master, because he contracts all manner of bad habits with his slaves; he accustoms himself insensibly to the want of all

moral virtues; he grows fierce, hasty, severe, choleric, voluptuous, and cruel.[1]

[2]   In despotic countries, where they are already in a state of political slavery, civil slavery is more tolerable than in other governments. Every one ought to be satisfied in those countries with necessaries and life. Hence the condition of a slave is hardly more burdensome than that of a subject.

[3]   But in a monarchical government, where it is of the utmost importance that human nature should not be debased, or dispirited, there ought to be no slavery. In democracies, slavery is contrary to the spirit of the constitution; it only contributes to give a power and luxury to the citizens which they ought not to have.

ORIGIN OF THE RIGHT OF SLAVERY
AMONG THE ROMAN CIVILIANS [Chapter 2]

[1]   ONE would never have imagined that slavery should owe its birth to pity, and that this should have been excited three different ways.[a]

[2]   The law of nations, to prevent prisoners from being put to death, has allowed them to be made slaves. The civil law of the Romans empowered debtors, who were subject to be ill used by their creditors, to sell themselves. And the law of nature requires, that children, whom a father reduced to slavery is no longer able to maintain, should be reduced to the same state as the father.

[3]   These reasons of the civilians are all false. It is false that killing in war is lawful, unless in a case of absolute necessity: but when a man has made another his slave, he cannot be said to have been under a necessity of taking away his life, since he actually did not

_____

[a] Justinian's Institutes, book 1.

take it away. War gives no other right over prisoners than to disable them from doing any further harm, by securing their persons. All nations concur[b] in detesting the murdering of prisoners in cold blood.[2]

[4]   Nor is it true, that a freeman can sell himself. Sale implies a price; now when a person sells himself, his whole substance immediately devolves to his master; the master therefore in that case gives nothing, and the slave receives nothing. You will say he has a *peculium*.[3] But this peculium goes along with his person: If it is not lawful for a man to kill himself, because he robs his country of his person, for the same reason he is not allowed to sell himself. The liberty of every citizen constitutes a part of the public liberty; and in a democratical state is even a part of the sovereignty. To sell one's citizenship[c] is so repugnant to all reason, as to be scarce supposeable in any man. If liberty may be rated with respect to the buyer, it is beyond all price to the seller.

[5]   The third way is birth; which falls with the two former. For if a man could not sell himself, much less could he sell an unborn offspring. If a prisoner of war is not to be reduced to slavery, much less are his children.

[8]   Nor is slavery less opposite to the civil law than to that of nature. What civil law can restrain a slave from running away, since he is not a member of society, and consequently has no interest in any civil laws? He can be retained only by a family law, that is, by the master's authority.

---

[b] Excepting a few Cannibals.

[c] I mean slavery in a strict sense, as formerly among the Romans, and at present in our colonies.

ANOTHER ORIGIN OF THE RIGHT OF SLAVERY [Chapter 3]

[1]   I WOULD as soon say, that the right of slavery proceeds from the contempt of one nation for another, founded on a difference in customs.

[2]   *Lopez de Gama* relates, "*that the Spaniards found near St. Martha, several baskets full of crabs, snails, grasshoppers and locusts, which proved to be the ordinary provision of the natives. This the conquerors turned to a heavy charge against the conquered.*"[a] The author owns that this, with their smoking and trimming their beards in a different manner, gave rise to the law by which the Americans became slaves to the Spaniards.

[3]   Knowledge humanises mankind, and reason inclines to mildness; but prejudices eradicate every tender disposition.

ANOTHER ORIGIN OF THE RIGHT OF SLAVERY [Chapter 4]

[1]   I WOULD as soon say that religion gives its professors a right to enslave those who dissent from it, in order to render its propagation more easy.

[2]   This was the notion that encouraged the ravagers of America in their iniquity.[a] Under the influence of this idea, they founded their right of enslaving so many nations; for these robbers, who would absolutely be both robbers and Christians, were superlatively devout.[4]

[3]   Louis XIII was extremely uneasy at a law, by which all the Negroes of his colonies were to be made slaves; but it being strongly urged to him as the readiest means for their conversion, he acquiesced without further scruple.[b]

[a] Biblioth. Angl. tom. 13. p. 2 art. 13.

[a] See Hist. of the conquest of Mexico, by Solis, and that of Peru, by Garcilasso de La Vega.

[b] Labat's new voyage to the isles of America, vol. 4, p. 114. 1722.

OF THE SLAVERY OF THE NEGROES [Chapter 5][5]

[1]   WERE I to vindicate our right to make slaves of the Negroes, these should be my arguments.

[2]   The Europeans, having extirpated the Americans,[6] they were obliged to make slaves of the Africans for clearing such vast tracts of land.

[3]   Sugar would be too dear, if the plants which produce it were cultivated by any other than slaves.

[4]   These creatures are all over black, and with such a flat nose, that they can scarcely be pitied.

[5]   It is hardly to be believed that God, who is a wise Being, should place a soul, especially a good soul, in such a black ugly body.

[6]   It is so natural to look upon colour as the criterion of human nature, that the Asiatics, among whom eunuchs are employed, always deprive the *Blacks* of their resemblance to us, by a more opprobrious distinction.

[7]   The colour of the skin may be determined by that of the hair, which among the Ægyptians, the best philosophers in the world, was of such importance, that they put to death all the red-haired men who fell into their hands.

[8]   The Negroes prefer a glass necklace to that gold, which polite nations so highly value: can there be a greater proof of their wanting common sense?

[9]   It is impossible for us to suppose these creatures to be men, because allowing them to be men, a suspicion would follow, that we ourselves are not Christians.

[10]   Weak minds exaggerate too much the wrong done to the Africans. For were the case as they state it, would the European powers, who make so many needless conventions among themselves, have failed to make a general one, in behalf of humanity and compassion?

TRUE ORIGIN OF THE RIGHT OF SLAVERY [Chapter 6]

[1]   IT is time to enquire into the true origin of the right of slavery. It ought to be founded on the nature of things; let us see if there be any cases where it can be derived from thence.

[2]   In all despotic governments, people make no difficulty in selling themselves; the political slavery in some measure annihilates the civil liberty.

[3]   According to Mr. Perry,[a] the Muscovites sell themselves very readily; their reason for it is evident; their liberty is not worth keeping.

[4]   At *Achim*[7] every one is for selling himself. Some of the chief lords have not less than a thousand slaves, all principal merchants, who have a great number of slaves themselves, and these also are not without their slaves. Their masters are their heirs, and put them into trade.[b] In those states, the freemen, being overpowered by the government, have no better resource than making themselves slaves to the tyrants in office.

[5]   This is the just and rational origin of that mild law of slavery, which obtains in some countries, and mild it ought to be, as founded on the free choice a man makes of a master, for his own benefit; which forms a mutual convention betwixt the two parties.

ANOTHER ORIGIN OF THE RIGHT OF SLAVERY [Chapter 7]

[1]   HERE is another origin of the right of slavery, and even of that cruel slavery, which is to be seen among men.

[2]   There are countries where the excess of heat enervates the body, and renders men so slothful and dispirited, that nothing but the fear of chastisement can oblige them to perform any laborious

[a] Present State of Russia.
[b] Dampier's voyages, Vol. 3.

duty: slavery is there more reconcileable to reason; and the master being as lazy with respect to his sovereign, as his slave is to him, this adds a political, to a civil slavery.

[3]   Aristotle endeavours to prove,[a] that there are natural slaves,[8] but what he says, is far from proving it. If there be any such, I believe they are those of whom I have been speaking.

[4]   But as all men are born equal, slavery must be accounted unnatural, tho' in some countries it be founded on natural reason; and a wide difference ought to be made betwixt such countries, and those where even natural reason rejects it, as in Europe, where it has been so happily abolished.

INUTILITY OF SLAVERY AMONG US [Chapter 8]

[1]   NATURAL slavery, then, is to be limited to some particular parts of the world. In all other countries, even the most laborious works of society may be performed, I think, by freemen.

[2]   Experience verifies my assertion. Before Christianity had abolished civil slavery in Europe,[9] working in the mines was judged too toilsom for any slaves or malefactors: but at present, there are men employed in them, who are known to live happily.[a] They have, by some small privileges, encouraged this profession; to an increase of labour, they have joined an increase of gain; and have gone so far as to make them better pleased with their condition than with any other which they could have embraced.

[3]   No labour is so heavy, but it may be brought to a level with the workman's strength, when regulated by equity, and not by avarice. The violent fatigues which slaves are made to undergo in other parts, may be supplied by commodious machines, invented by art,

---

[a] Polit. Lib. I. c. 1.

[a] As may be seen in the mines of Hartz in Lower Saxony, and in those of Hungary.

and skillfully applied. The Turkish mines in the Bannat of Temeswar,[10] tho' richer than those of Hungary, did not yield so much; because their invention, reached no further, than the arms of their slaves.

[4]   I know not whether this article be dictated by my understanding, or my heart.[11] Possibly there is not that climate upon earth, where the most laborious services might not, with proper encouragement, be performed by freemen. Bad laws having made lazy men; they have been reduced to slavery, because of their laziness.[12]

BOOK XVI: *How the Laws of Domestic Slavery Bear a Relation to the Nature of the Climate*

ANALYSIS

Book XVI is the third of the five books in Part Three that explore the influence of climate and other causes physiques *on human behavior, customs, and institutions. Having explored the influence of climate on slavery in Book XV, Montesquieu now analyzes the influence of climate on marital customs. And Book XVI was one of the most heavily censured of* The Spirit of Laws, *since instead of discussing the Divine origin of Christian, monogamous marriage, M preferred to seek the possible secular explanations of polygamous and polyandrous forms of marriage. The discovery of such causes by no means justified those marital customs in his view (see chap. 6), but it did at least disclose their* raisons naturelles.

It is in the opening chapters of the Book that Montesquieu analyzes various natural reasons that render polygamy and polyandry less contrary to reason in some climates than in others. Since women both mature early and age quickly in hot climates, their beauty has already declined by the time their reason is sufficiently developed to render them good intellectual companions. And therefore men residing in hot climates ought to be allowed more than one wife (chap. 2). The relative ease with which men gain a means of subsistence in hot climates provides an additional raison naturelle *for the absence of monogamy (chap. 3), as does the prevalence in some climates of a greater proportion of women than men, inclining that society toward polygamy, or a greater proportion of men than women, suggesting the practice of polyandry (chap. 4).*

Elsewhere in Book XVI Montesquieu returns to the correlation suggested in Book XIV between hot climates and heightened sensuality (see Book XIV, chap. 2, pars. [10–12]). He suggests that extremes of sensuality, when accompanied by the institution of polygamy, sometimes necessitate the confinement of women for the sake of both domestic (chap. 8) and societal order (chap. 11).

OF DOMESTIC SERVITUDE [Chapter 1]

SLAVES are established for the family; but they are not a part of it. Thus I distinguish their servitude from that of the women in some countries, and which I shall properly call domestic servitude.

THAT IN THE COUNTRIES OF THE SOUTH THERE IS A NATURAL INEQUALITY BETWEEN THE TWO SEXES [Chapter 2]

[1]   WOMEN, in hot climates, are marriageable at eight, nine, or ten years of age;[a] thus, in those countries, infancy and marriage almost always go together. They are old at twenty: Their reason therefore never accompanies their beauty. When beauty demands the empire, the want of reason forbids the claim; when reason is obtained, beauty is no more. These women ought then to be in a state of dependance; for reason cannot procure in old age, that empire, which even youth and beauty could not give. It is therefore extremely natural that in these places, a man, when no law opposes it,[1] should leave one wife to take another, and that polygamy should be introduced.

---

[a] Mahomet married Cadhisja at five, and took her to his bed at eight years old. In the hot countries of Arabia and the Indies, girls are marriageable at eight years of age, and are brought to bed the year after. *Prideaux's Life of Mahomet*. We see women in the kingdom of Algier [sic], pregnant at nine, ten and eleven years of age. *Hist. of the Kingdom of Algiers by Logiers de Tassis*, p. 61.

[2]   In temperate climates, where the charms of women are best preserved, where they arrive later at maturity, and have children at a more advanced season of life, the old age of their husband in some degree follows theirs; and as they have more reason and knowledge when married, if it be only on account of their having continued longer in life, it must naturally introduce a kind of equality between the two sexes, and, in consequence of this, the law of having only one wife.

[5]   Thus the law which permits only one wife, is physically conformable to the climate of Europe, and not to that of Asia. This is the reason why Mahometanism was established with such facility in Asia, and so difficultly extended in Europe; why Christianity is maintained in Europe, and has been destroyed in Asia; and in fine, why the Mahometans have made such progress in China, and the Christians so little.[2*]

THAT A PLURALITY OF WIVES DEPENDS GREATLY
ON THE MEANS OF SUPPORTING THEM [Chapter 3]

[1]   THO' in countries where polygamy is once established, the number of wives is principally determined by the riches of the husband; yet it cannot be said that riches established polygamy in these states; since poverty may produce the same effect, as I shall prove when I come to speak of the savages.

[2]   Polygamy in powerful nations, is less a luxury in itself, than the occasion of great luxury. In hot climates they have few wants,[a] and it costs little to maintain a wife and children; they may therefore have a great number of wives.

---

[a] At Ceylan a man may live on ten sols a month; they eat nothing there but rice and fish. *Collection of voyages made to establish an India Company.*

THAT THE LAW OF POLYGAMY IS AN AFFAIR
THAT DEPENDS ON CALCULATIONS [Chapter 4] [3]*

[1]   ACCORDING to the calculations made in several parts of Europe, there are here born more boys than girls;[a] on the contrary, by the accounts we have of Asia,[4] there are there born more girls than boys.[b] The law which in Europe allows only one wife, and that in Asia[5] which permits many, have therefore a certain relation to the climate.

[2]   In the cold climates of Asia, there are born as in Europe, more males than females; and from hence, say the Lamas,[c] is derived the reason of that law, which amongst them, permits a woman to have many husbands.

[3]   But it is difficult for me to believe that there are many countries,[6] where the disproportion can be great enough for any exigency to justify the introducing either the law in favour of many wives, or that of many husbands. This would only imply, that a majority of women, or even a majority of men, is more conformable to nature in certain countries than in others.

[4]   I confess, that if what history tells us be true, that, at Bantham[7] there are ten women to one man,[d] this must be a case particularly favourable to polygamy.

[5]   In all this I only give their reasons, but do not justify their customs.

[a] Dr. Arbuthnot finds that in England the number of boys exceeds that of girls; but people have been to blame to conclude that the case is the same in all climates.

[b] See Kempfer, who relates that upon numbering the people of Meaco, there were found 182072 males and 223573 females.

[c] Du Halde's Hist. of China, Vol. 4.

[d] Albuzeir-el-hassen, one of the two Mahometan Arabs, who, in the ninth century, went into India and China, thought this custom a prostitution. And indeed nothing could be more contrary to the ideas of a Mahometan.

THE REASON OF A LAW OF MALABAR [Chapter 5]

IN the tribe of the Naires,[a] on the coast of Malabar, the men can only have one wife, while a woman, on the contrary, may have many husbands. The origin of this custom is not I believe difficult to discover. The Naires are the tribe of nobles, who are the soldiers of all those nations. In Europe, soldiers are forbid to marry: in Malabar, where the climate requires greater indulgence, they are satisfied with rendering marriage as little burdensome as possible; they give a wife amongst many men, which consequently diminishes the attachment to a family, and the cares of houskeeping, and leaves them in the free possession of a military spirit.

OF POLYGAMY CONSIDERED IN ITSELF [Chapter 6][8]

[1]   WITH regard to polygamy in general, independently of the circumstances which may render it tolerable, it is not of the least service to mankind, nor to either of the two sexes, whether it be that which abuses, or that which is abused. Neither is it of service to the children; for one of its greatest inconveniencies is, that the father and mother cannot have the same affection for their offspring; a father cannot love twenty children with the same tenderness as a mother can love two. It is much worse when a wife has many husbands; for then paternal love is only held by this opinion,[9] that a father may believe, if he will, or that others may believe, that certain children belong to him.

[2]   May I not say that a plurality of wives leads to that passion which nature disallows? For one depravation always draws on

---

[a] See Francis Pirard, c. 27. Edifying Letters, 3d and 10th collection on the Malleami on the coast of Malabar. This is considered as an abuse of the military profession, as a woman, says Pirard, of the tribe of the Bramins never would marry many husbands.

another. I remember that in the revolution which happened at Constantinople, when sultan Achmet was deposed, history says, that the people having plundered the Chiaya's house, they found not a single woman; they tell us that at Algiers, in the greatest part of their seraglios, they have none at all.[a]

[3]   Besides, the possession of many wives does not always prevent their entertaining desires for those of others:[b] it is with lust as with avarice, whose thirst increases the acquisition of treasures.

OF THE SEPARATION OF WOMEN FROM MEN [Chapter 8]

[1]   THE prodigious number of wives possessed by those who live in rich and voluptuous nations, is a consequence of the law of polygamy. Their separation from men, and their close confinement, naturally follow from the greatness of this number. Domestic order renders this necessary; thus an insolvent debtor seeks to conceal himself from the pursuit of his creditors. There are climates where the impulses of nature have such strength that morality has almost none. If a man be left with a woman, the temptation and the fall will be the same thing; the attack certain, the resistance none. In these countries, instead of precepts, they have recourse to bolts and bars.[10*]

[2]   One of the Chinese classic authors considers the man as a prodigy of virtue, who finding a woman alone in a distant apartment, can forbear making use of force.[a]

---

[a] Hist. of Algiers by Logier de Tassis.

[b] This is the reason why women in the east are so carefully concealed.

[a] "It is an admirable touch-stone, to find by one's self a treasure whose matter is known, or a beautiful woman in a distant apartment, or the voice of an enemy who must perish without our assistance." Translation of a Chinese piece of morality which may be seen in Du Halde. Vol. 3. p. 151.

OF THE CONNEXION BETWEEN DOMESTIC
AND POLITICAL GOVERNMENT [Chapter 9]

[1]   IN a republic the condition of citizens is limited, equal, mild, and agreeable; every thing partakes of the benefit of public liberty. An empire over the women cannot amongst them be so well exerted; and where the climate demands this empire, it is most agreeable to a monarchical government. This is one of the reasons why it has always been difficult to establish a popular government in the east.

[2]   On the contrary the slavery of women is perfectly conformable to the genius of a despotic government, which delights in treating all with severity. Thus at all times have we seen in Asia domestic slavery and despotic government walk hand in hand with an equal pace.

THE PRINCIPLE ON WHICH THE MORALS
OF THE EAST ARE FOUNDED [Chapter 10]

[4]   We find the manners more pure in the several parts of the east, in proportion as the confinement of women is more strictly observed. In great kingdoms, there are necessarily great lords. The greater their wealth, the more enlarged is their ability of keeping their wives in an exact confinement, and of preventing them from entering again into society. From hence it proceeds, that in the empires of Turky, Persia, of the Mogulstan,[11] China, and Japan, the manners of their wives are admirable.

[5]   But the case is not the same with India.[12]

[7]   We may there see to what an extreme, the vices of a climate, indulged in full liberty, will carry licentiousness. It is there that nature has a strength, and modesty a weakness, that exceeds all

comprehension. At Patan [a] the wanton desires [b] of the women are so outragious, that the men are obliged to make use of a certain apparel to shelter them from their designs. In these countries, the two sexes lose even those laws which properly belong to each. [13]

OF DOMESTIC SLAVERY INDEPENDENTLY
OF POLYGAMY [Chapter 11]

[1]   IT is not only a plurality of wives, which in certain places of the east requires their confinement; but also the climate itself. Those who consider the horrible crimes, the treachery, the black villanies, the poisonings, the assassinations, which the liberty of women has occasioned at Goa, [14] and in the Portuguese settlements in the Indies, [15] where religion permits only one wife; and who compare them with the innocence and purity of manners of the women of Turky, Persia, Mogulstan, China, and Japan, will clearly see that it is frequently as necessary to separate them from the men, when they have but one, as when they have many.

[2]   These are things which ought to be decided by the climate. What purpose would it answer to shut up women in our northern countries, where their manners are naturally good; where all their passions are calm; and where love rules over the heart with so regular and gentle an empire, that the least degree of prudence is sufficient to conduct it?

[a] Collection of voyages for the establishment of an India Company. Vol. 2. p. 2.

[b] In the Maldivian isles the fathers marry their daughters at ten and eleven years of age, because it is a great sin, say they, to suffer them to endure the want of a husband, see Pirard, c. 12. At Bantham as soon as a girl is twelve or thirteen years old, she must be married if they would not have her lead a debauched life. Collection of Voyages for the establishment of an India Company, p. 348.

OF NATURAL MODESTY [Chapter 12]

[1]   ALL nations are equally agreed in fixing contempt and ignominy on the incontinence of women. Nature has dictated this to
all. She has established the attack, and she has established too the
resistance; and having implanted desires in both, she has given to
the one boldness, and to the other shame. She has given to individuals a long extent of years to preserve themselves; but to perpetuate themselves, only a momentary duration.

[2]   It is then far from being true, that to be incontinent is to follow
the laws of nature; since this is, on the contrary, a violation of
these laws, which can be followed only by modesty and discretion.

[3]   Besides, it is natural for intelligent beings to feel their imperfections. Nature has therefore fixed shame in our minds, a shame of
our imperfections.

[4]   When therefore the physical power of certain climates violates
the natural law of the two sexes, and that of intelligent beings; it
belongs to the legislature to make civil laws, to oppose the nature
of the climate, and to re-establish the primitive laws.[16]

BOOK XVII *How the Laws of Political Servitude Bear a Relation to the Nature of the Climate*

ANALYSIS

Book XVII is the fourth of the five books of Part Three devoted to the influence of causes physiques *on human behavior and institutions. Having explored the influence of climate on slavery, both civil (Book XV) and domestic (Book XVI), Montesquieu now turns to the influence of climate on political slavery, by which he means the subjection of men to tyrannical governments. Climate has no less a bearing on freedom for a society as a whole, M suggests, than on civil and domestic servitude. The maintenance of liberty requires an active citizenry sufficiently energetic to oppose tyranny, and liberty is, therefore, more likely to be found in cold climates than in hot (chap. 2). So influential does M judge climate to be on human strength that he suggests those who dwell in cold climates will readily subdue their southern neighbors (chap. 4). In Europe, M reports, the variation of climate from north to south is so gradual that there are no great differences in climate between countries bordering one another, and a rough balance of power is therefore insured (chap. 3).*

It is not just climate alone that influences the degree of freedom a society enjoys. Toward the end of Book XVII, Montesquieu touches on the influence of topography and terrain, a subject to which he will return in Book XVIII. The geography of Asia, he reports, favors despotism, since there are fewer natural borders such as mountain ranges and broad rivers, and since rule by law would not prevent kingdoms of such vast territorial extent from breaking up into smaller states (chap. 6, pars. [1–2]). In Europe, however, natural

boundaries suggest the establishment of smaller, more moderate states where
rule by law does not compromise the maintenance of the state in its present,
moderate size (chap. 6 [3]).

OF POLITICAL SERVITUDE [Chapter 1]

POLITICAL servitude does not less depend on the nature of the climate, than that which is civil and domestic, and this we are going to make appear.

THE DIFFERENCE BETWEEN NATIONS IN POINT
OF COURAGE [Chapter 2]

[1]   WE have already observed that great heat enervates the strength and courage of men,[1] and that in cold climates they have a certain vigor of body and mind which renders them capable of long, painful, great, and intrepid actions.

[2]   We ought not then to be astonished that the effeminacy of the people in hot climates, has almost always rendered them slaves; and that the bravery of those in cold climates has enabled them to maintain their liberties. This is an effect which springs from a natural cause.

[3]   This has also been found true in America; the despotic empires of Mexico and Peru were near the Line, and almost all the little free nations were, and are still, near the Poles.

OF THE CLIMATE OF ASIA [Chapter 3]

[2]   Asia has properly no temperate zone, as the places situated in a very cold climate immediately touch upon those which are exceedingly hot, that is Turkey, Persia, India, China, Korea, and Japan.

[3]   In Europe, on the contrary, the temperate zone is very exten-

sive, tho' situated in climates widely different from each other; there being no affinity between the climates of Spain and Italy, and those of Norway and Sweden. But as the climate grows insensibly cold upon our advancing from south to north, nearly in proportion to the latitude of each country; it thence follows that each resembles the country joining to it, that there is no very extraordinary difference between them, and that, as I have just said, the temperate zone is very extensive.

[4]   From hence it comes, that in Asia the strong nations are opposed to the weak; the warlike, brave, and active people touch immediately on those who are indolent, effeminate, and timorous: the one must therefore conquer, and the other be conquered. In Europe, on the contrary, strong nations are opposed to the strong; and those who join to each other have nearly the same courage. This is the grand reason of the weakness of Asia, and of the strength of Europe; of the liberty of Europe, and of the slavery of Asia: a cause that I do not recollect ever to have seen remarked. From hence it proceeds, that liberty in Asia never increases; whilst in Europe it is enlarged or diminished according to particular circumstances.

[5]   The Muscovite nobility have indeed been reduced to slavery by the ambition of one of their princes; but they have always discovered those marks of impatience and discontent which are never to be seen in the southern climates. Have they not been able for a short time to establish an aristocratical government? Another of the northern kingdoms has lost its laws; but we may trust to the climate that they are not lost in such a manner as never to be recovered.

THE CONSEQUENCES RESULTING FROM THIS [Chapter 4]

[1]   WHAT we have just said, is perfectly comformable to the events of history. Asia has been subdued thirteen times; eleven by the northern nations, and twice by those of the south.

[2]   In Europe, on the contrary, since the establishment of the Greek and Phoenician colonies we know but of four great changes; the first caused by the conquest of the Romans; the second by the inundation of barbarians who destroyed these very Romans; the third by the victories of Charlemain; and the last by the invasions of the Normans.

A NEW PHYSICAL CAUSE OF THE SLAVERY
OF ASIA, AND OF THE LIBERTY OF EUROPE [Chapter 6]

[1]   IN Asia they have always had great empires; in Europe these could never subsist. Asia has larger plains; it is cut out into much more extensive divisions by mountains and seas;[2] and as it lies more to the south, its springs are more easily dried up; the mountains are less covered with snow; and the rivers being not so large,[a] form smaller barriers.

[2]   Power in Asia ought then to be always despotic: for if their slavery was not severe, they would soon make a division, inconsistent with the nature of the country.

[3]   In Europe the natural division forms many nations of a moderate extent, in which the government of the laws is not incompatible with the maintenance of the state: on the contrary, it is so favourable to it, that without this the state would fall into decay, and become inferior to all others.

[4]   It is this which has formed a genius for liberty, that renders every part extremely difficult to be subdued and subjected to a

[a] The waters lose themselves, or evaporate before or after their streams are united.

foreign power, otherwise than by the laws and the advantage of commerce.

[5]   On the contrary there reigns in Asia a servile spirit, which they have never been able to shake off; and it is impossible to find, in all the histories of this country, a single passage which discovers a free soul: we shall never see any thing there but the heroism of slavery.

BOOK XVIII: *Of Laws in the Relation They Bear to the Nature of the Soil*

ANALYSIS

Book XVIII is the last of the five Books assessing the influence of causes physiques *on human behavior and institutions. Having concentrated primarily on the influence of climate in Books XIV–XVII, Montesquieu now turns to the condition of the soil and its influence on the form of government likely to develop in any given area. His basic premise is that fertile soil may actually prove a liability in terms of a society's potential for freedom. Farmers may be so distracted from public issues by the prospects of reaping profits as a result of good soil that they will cease to care about liberty (chap. 1, par. [1]). And since fertile lands are normally flat and less defensible than more barren, mountainous regions, there is greater likelihood that inhabitants of such areas will fall prey to a foreign power seeking to deprive them of their freedom in order to control their land (chaps. 2–3). Another liability of fertile land in terms of a society's potential for liberty is the possibility that crops will be so easily produced that men will become weak and timid and will lack the courage (chap. 4) necessary for the defense of freedom.*

Elsewhere in Book XVIII Montesquieu discusses the reasons why islands are conducive to liberty (chap. 5), advances the general proposition that the more complex the ways people earn their livings, the more intricate their code of laws (chap. 8), maintains that it is primarily the division of agricultural lands that increases the number of laws (chap. 13), and suggests a correlation between liberty and a nomadic existence (chap. 14). In chapter 17 he remarks that the lack of a monetary system among such nomadic peoples is an additional safeguard of liberty, and in chapter 18 he maintains that among such nomadic peoples superstition often replaces other forms of tyranny.

HOW THE NATURE OF THE SOIL HAS AN
INFLUENCE ON THE LAWS [Chapter 1]

[1]   THE goodness of the land, in any country, naturally establishes
subjection and dependance. The husbandmen who compose the
principal part of the people, are not very jealous of their liberty;
they are too busy and too intent on their own private affairs.

[2]   Thus monarchy is more frequently found in fruitful countries,
and a republican government in those which are not so; which is
sometimes a sufficient recompence.

[3]   The barrenness of the Attic soil, established there a popular
government; and the fertility of that of Lacedemonia an aristocratical form of government. For in those times, Greece was averse to
the government of a single person; and aristocracy had the nearest
resemblance to that government.

THE SAME SUBJECT CONTINUED [Chapter 2]

[1]   THESE fertile countries are always plains, where the inhabitants
are incapable of disputing against a stronger body: they are then
obliged to submit, and when they have once submitted, the spirit
of liberty cannot return; the wealth of the country is a pledge of
their fidelity. But in mountainous countries, as they have but
little, they may preserve what they have. The liberty they enjoy,
or in other words, the government they are under, is the only
blessing worthy of their defence. It reigns therefore more in
mountainous and difficult countries, than in those which nature
seems to have most favoured.

[2]   The mountaineers preserve a more moderate government; because they are not so liable to be conquered. They defend themselves easily, and are attacked with difficulty; ammunition and
provisions are collected and carried against them with great ex-

pence, for the country furnishes none. It is then more difficult to make war against them, a more hazardous enterprize; and all the laws that can be made for the safety of the people are there of least use.

WHAT COUNTRIES ARE BEST CULTIVATED [Chapter 3]

[1]   COUNTRIES are not cultivated in proportion to their fertility, but to their liberty; and if we make an imaginary division of the earth, we shall be astonished to see in most ages, deserts in the most fruitful parts, and great nations in those, where nature seems to refuse every thing.

[2]   It is natural for a people to leave a bad country to seek a better; and not to leave a good country to seek a worse. Most of the invasions have therefore been made in countries, which nature seems to have formed for happiness: and as nothing is more nearly allied than desolation and invasion, the best countries are most frequently depopulated; while the frightful countries of the north continue always inhabited, from their being almost uninhabitable.

NEW EFFECTS ON THE FERTILITY AND BARRENNESS OF COUNTRIES [Chapter 4]

THE barrenness of the earth renders men industrious, sober, inured to hardship, courageous and fit for war; they are obliged to procure by labour what the earth refuses to bestow. The fertility of a country gives ease, effeminacy, and a certain fondness for the preservation of life. It has been remarked that the German troops raised in those places where the peasants are rich, as, for instance, in Saxony, are not so good as the others. Military laws may provide against this inconvenience by a more severe discipline.

OF THE INHABITANTS OF ISLANDS [Chapter 5]

THE people of the isles have a higher relish for liberty than those of the continent. Islands are commonly of a small extent;[a] one part of the people cannot be so easily employed to oppress the other; the sea separates them from great empires; so that they cannot be countenanced by tyranny: conquerors are stopp'd by the sea, the islanders themselves are not involved in conquests, and more easily preserve their laws.

THE GENERAL RELATION OF LAWS [Chapter 8]

THE laws have a very great relation to the manner in which the several nations procure their subsistence. There should be a code of laws of a much larger extent, for a nation attached to trade and navigation, than for a people who are contented with cultivating the earth. There should be a much greater for these, than for a people who live by their flocks and herds. There must be a greater for this last, than for those who live by hunting.

OF THE SOIL OF AMERICA [Chapter 9]

[1]   THE cause of there being so many savage nations in America is the fertility of the earth, which spontaneously produces many fruits capable of affording them nourishment. If the women cultivate a spot of land round their cabins, the maiz grows up presently; and hunting and fishing put the men in a state of complete abundance. Besides, black cattle, as cows, buffaloes, &c. succeed there better than carnivorous beasts.

[2]   We should not, I believe, have all these advantages in Europe,

---

[a] Japan is an exception to this, by its great extent as well as by its slavery.

if the land was left uncultivated; it would produce scarce any thing besides forests of oaks and other barren trees.

OF THE LAW OF NATIONS AMONGST PEOPLE WHO DO NOT CULTIVATE THE EARTH [Chapter 12]

As these people do not live in limited and circumscribed boundaries, many causes of strife arise between them; they dispute the uncultivated land, as we dispute about inheritances. Thus they find frequent occasions for war, in defence of their hunting, their fishing, the pasture for their cattle, and the taking of their slaves; and having no territory, they have many things to regulate by the law of nations, and but few to decide by the civil law.

OF THE CIVIL LAWS OF THOSE NATIONS WHO DO NOT CULTIVATE THE EARTH [Chapter 13]

[1]   THE division of lands is what principally increases the civil code. Amongst nations where they have not made this division there are very few civil laws.

[2]   The institutions of these people may be called *manners* rather than *laws*.

[3]   Amongst such nations as these, the old men, who remember things past, have great authority; they cannot there be distinguished by wealth, but by wisdom and valour.

[4]   These people wander and disperse themselves in pasture grounds or in forests. Marriage cannot there have the security which it has amongst us, where it is fixed by the habitation, and where the wife continues in one house; they may then more easily change their wives, possess many, and sometimes mix indifferently like brutes.

[5]   Nations of herdsmen and shepherds cannot leave their cattle, which are their subsistence; neither can they separate themselves from their wives, who look after them. All this ought then to go

together, especially as living generally in great plains, where there
are few places of considerable strength, their wives, their children,
their flocks may become the prey of their enemies.

[6]   Their laws regulate the division of plunder; and have, like our
Salic laws, a particular attention to thefts.

OF THE POLITICAL STATE OF THE PEOPLE WHO DO
NOT CULTIVATE THE LANDS [Chapter 14]

THESE people enjoy great liberty. For as they do not cultivate
the earth, they are not fixed, they are wanderers and vagabonds;
and if a chief would deprive them of their liberty, they would
immediately go and seek it under another, or retire into the woods
and live there with their families. The liberty of the man is so
great among these people, that it necessarily draws after it the
liberty of the citizen.

OF POLITICAL LAWS AMONGST NATIONS WHO HAVE
NOT THE USE OF MONEY [Chapter 17]

[1]   THE greatest security of the liberties of a people who do not
cultivate the earth, is their not knowing the use of money. What is
gained by hunting, fishing, or keeping herds of cattle, cannot be
assembled in such great quantities, nor be sufficiently preserved,
for one man to find himself in a condition to corrupt many others:
but when, instead of this, a man has the sign of riches, he may
obtain a large quantity of these signs, and distribute them amongst
whom he pleases.

[2]   The people who have no money, have but few wants, and these
are supplied both with ease, and in an equal manner. Equality is
then unavoidable; and from hence it proceeds, that their chiefs are
not despotic.

OF THE POWER OF SUPERSTITION [Chapter 18]

[2]   The prejudices of superstition are superior to all other prejudices, and its reasons to all other reasons. Thus, tho' the savage
nations have naturally no knowledge of despotic tyranny, yet this
people feel it. They adore the sun; and if their chief had not
imagined that he was the brother of this glorious luminary, they
would have thought him a miserable wretch like themselves.

BOOK XIX: *Of Laws in Relation to the Principles Which Form the General Spirit, the Morals, and Customs of a Nation*

ANALYSIS

Book XIX completes Part Three of The Spirit of Laws. *Whereas the preceding five books in Part Three had dealt with the influence of various* causes physiques *on human behavior, laws, and customs, Book XIX focuses on the influence of less tangible but equally important* causes morales. *The prejudices and dispositions of various peoples East and West are deemed worthy of close analysis as Montesquieu explores how various national customs and psychological traits influence laws, institutions, and forms of government. The lighthearted Athenians are compared with the grave Spartans (chap. 7). The French are characterized as social, openhearted, cheerful, tasteful, communicative, indiscreet, courageous, generous, and frank (chap. 5), whereas the people of India are assessed as proud and lazy (chap. 9). And if we would doubt that widespread personality traits influence customs and institutions, we are told, on the authority of Dampier, that the people of Achim are so "proud and lazy" that they hire slaves if only to transport a quart of rice a few short steps (chap. 9, par. [6]).*

The important concept of the general spirit of a nation is presented in chapter 4. (See Introduction, pp. 23–30, for a thorough discussion of this concept.) In chapters 5–7, Montesquieu counsels against forcible alteration of the general spirit, and in chapters 14, 16, 21, and 22 he discusses the differences between written laws and unwritten customs. Chapter 14 stresses the tenacity with which people cling to custom as well as the tyranny involved in forcibly changing ingrained habits.

OF THE SUBJECT OF THIS BOOK [Chapter 1]

THIS subject is of a great extent. In that crowd of ideas which present themselves to my mind, I shall be more attentive to the order of things, than to the things themselves. I shall be obliged to wander to the right and to the left, that I may search into, and discover the truth.

THAT IT IS NECESSARY PEOPLE'S MINDS SHOULD BE PREPARED FOR THE RECEPTION OF THE BEST LAWS [Chapter 2]

[1]   LIBERTY itself has appeared insupportable to those nations who have not been accustomed to enjoy it. Thus a pure air is sometimes disagreeable to those who have lived in a fenny country.

[2]   Balbi, a Venetian, being at Pegu,[1] was introduced to the king.[a] When the monarch was informed that they had no king at Venice, he burst into such a fit of laughter, that he was seized with a cough, and had much ado to speak to his courtiers. What legislator could propose a popular government to a people like this?

OF TYRANNY [Chapter 3]

[1]   THERE are two sorts of tyranny; the one real, which arises from the oppressions of government; the other is seated in opinion, and is sure to be felt whenever those who govern, establish things shocking to the turn of thought, and inconsistent with the ideas of a nation.

[a] He has described this interview which happened in the year 1596 in the Collection of voyages for the establishment of an India company. Vol. 3. part. 1. p. 33.

[2]   Dio tells us,[2] that Augustus was desirous of being called
Romulus; but having been informed, that the people feared, that
he would cause himself to be crowned king, he changed his design.

OF THE GENERAL SPIRIT OF MANKIND [Chapter 4]

[1]   MEN are influenced by various causes, by the climate, the religion, the laws, the maxims of government; by precedents, morals
and customs, from whence is formed a general spirit that takes its
rise from these.[3]

[2]   In proportion, as in every nation any one of these causes acts
with more force, the others in the same degree become weak.
Nature and the climate rule almost alone over the savages; customs
govern the Chinese; the laws tyrannize in Japan; morals had formerly all their influence at Sparta; maxims of government, and the
ancient simplicity of manners, once prevailed at Rome.

HOW FAR WE SHOULD BE ATTENTIVE LEST THE GENERAL
SPIRIT OF A NATION SHOULD BE CHANGED [Chapter 5]

[1]   IF in any part of the world there had been a nation whose
inhabitants were of a sociable temper, open hearted, pleased with
life, possessed of judgment, and a facility in communicating their
thoughts; who were sprightly, agreeable, gay, sometimes imprudent, often indiscreet; and besides had courage, generosity, frankness, and a certain point of honor;[4] no one ought to endeavour to
restrain their manners by laws, unless he would lay a constraint on
their virtues. If in general the character is good, the little faults
that may be found in it, will be of small importance.

[2]   They might lay a restraint upon women, make laws to correct
their manners, and to limit their luxury: but who knows but that
by this means, they might lose that peculiar taste which would be

the source of the riches of the nation, and that politeness which would render the country frequented by strangers?

[3]   It is the business of the legislature to follow the spirit of the nation, when it is not contrary to the principles of government; for we do nothing so well as when we act with freedom, and follow the bent of our natural genius.

[4]   If an air of pedantry be given to a nation that is naturally gay, the state will gain no advantage from it, either at home or abroad. Leave it to do frivolous things in the most serious manner, and with gaiety things the most serious.

THAT EVERY THING OUGHT NOT TO BE CORRECTED [Chapter 6]

[1]   LET them but leave us as we are, said a gentleman of a nation which had a very great resemblance to that we have been describing, and nature will repair whatever is amiss. She has given us a vivacity capable of offending, and hurrying us beyond the bounds of respect: this same vivacity is corrected by the politeness it procures us, inspiring a taste for the world, and above all, for the conversation of women.

[2]   Let them leave us as we are: our indiscretions joined to our good nature, would make the laws which should constrain our sociable temper, not at all proper for us.

OF THE ATHENIANS AND LACEDEMONIANS [Chapter 7]

THE Athenians, this gentleman adds, were a nation that had some relation to ours. They mingled gaiety with business; a stroke of raillery was as agreeable in the senate, as in the theatre. This vivacity, which discovered itself in their councils, went along with them in the execution of their resolves. The characteristic of the Spartans was gravity, seriousness, severity, and silence. It would have been as difficult to bring over an Athenian by teazing, as it would a Spartan by diverting him.

EFFECTS OF A SOCIABLE TEMPER [Chapter 8]

[1]   THE more communicative a people are, the more easily they change their habits, because each is in a greater degree a spectacle to the other; and the singularities of individuals are better seen. The climate which makes one nation delight in being communicative, makes it also delight in change; and that which makes it delight in change, forms its taste.

[2]   The society of women spoils the manners, and forms the taste; the desire of giving greater pleasure than others, establishes the ornaments of dress; and the desire of pleasing others more than ourselves establishes fashions. The mode is a subject of importance: by giving a trifling turn of mind, it continually encreases the branches of its commerce.[a]

OF THE VANITY AND PRIDE OF NATIONS [Chapter 9]

[1]   VANITY is as advantageous to a government, as pride is dangerous.[5] To be convinced of this, we need only represent on the one hand, the numberless benefits which result from vanity; from thence arises luxury, industry, arts, fashions, politeness, taste; and on the other, the infinite evils which spring from the pride of certain nations, laziness, poverty, a universal neglect, the destruction of the nations which have accidentally fallen into their hands, as well as of their own. Laziness is the effect of pride;[a] labour a

[a] Fable of the bees.

[a] The people who follow the Khan of Malacamber, those of Carnataca and Coromandel, are proud and indolent; they consume little because they are miserably poor; while the subjects of the Mogul, and the people of Indostan, employ themselves and enjoy the

consequence of vanity: the pride of a Spaniard leads him to refuse labour; the vanity of a Frenchman to know how to work better than others.

[2]   All lazy nations are grave; for those who do not labour, regard themselves as the sovereigns of those who do.

[3]   If we search amongst all nations, we shall find that for the most part, gravity, pride, and indolence go hand in hand.

[4]   The people of Achim [6] are proud and lazy; [b] those who have no slaves hire one, if it be only to carry a quart of rice a hundred paces; they would be dishonoured if they carried it themselves.

[5]   In many places people let their nails grow, that all may see they do not work.

[6]   Women in the Indies [7] believe it shameful for them to learn to read: [c] this is, they say, the business of the slaves, who sing their spiritual songs in the temples of their pagodas. In one tribe they don't spin; in another they make nothing but baskets and mats; they are not even to pound rice; and in others they must not go to fetch water. These rules are established by pride, and the same passion makes them followed.

WHAT ARE THE NATURAL MEANS OF CHANGING THE MANNERS AND CUSTOMS OF A NATION [Chapter 14]

[1]   WE have said that the laws were the particular and precise institutions of a legislator, and manners and customs the institutions of a nation in general. From hence it follows, that when these manners and customs are to be changed, it ought not to be done by laws; this would have too much the air of tyranny: it

conveniences of life like the Europeans. Collection of Voyages for the establishment of an India Company. Vol 1. p. 54.

  [b] See Dampier, Vol. 3.

  [c] Edifying Letters, 12th Collect. p. 80.

would be better to change them by introducing other manners and other customs.

[2]   Thus when a prince would make great alterations in his kingdom, he should reform by laws what is established by laws, and change by customs what is established by customs; for it is very bad policy to change by laws, what ought to be changed by customs.

[3]   The law which obliged the Muscovites to cut off their beards, and to shorten their cloaths, and the rigour with which Peter I made them crop even to the knees, the long cloaks of those who entered into the cities, were instances of tyranny.[8] There are means that may be made use of to prevent crimes, these are punishments: there are those for changing our customs, these are examples.

[4]   The facility and ease with which this nation has been polished, plainly shews that this prince had a worse opinion of his people than they deserved, and that they were not brutes tho' he was pleased to call them so. The violent measures which he employed were needless; he would have attained his end as well by milder methods.

[5]   He himself experienced the easiness of bringing about these alterations. The women were shut up, and in some sort slaves; he called them to court; he sent them silks and stuffs, and made them dress like the German ladies. This sex immediately relished a manner of life which so greatly flattered their taste, their vanity, and their passions, and by their means it was relished by the men.

[6]   What rendered the change the more easy was, their manners being at that time foreign to the climate; and these having been introduced amongst them by conquest, and by a mixture of nations. Peter I, in giving the manners and customs of Europe to an European nation, found a facility which he did not himself expect.

The empire of the climate is the first, the most powerful of all empires.[9]* He had then no occasion for laws to change the manners and customs of his country; it would have been sufficient to have introduced other manners and other customs.

[7]   Nations are in general very tenacious of their customs; to take them away by violence is to render them unhappy: we should not therefore change them, but engage the people to make the change themselves.

[8]   All punishment which is not derived from necessity, is tyrannical. The law is not a mere act of power; things in their own nature indifferent are not within its province.

THE INFLUENCE OF DOMESTIC GOVERNMENT ON THE POLITICAL [Chapter 15]

THE changing the manners of women had, without doubt, a great influence in the government of Muscovy. One thing is very closely united to another: the despotic power of the prince is naturally connected with the servitude of women, the liberty of women with the spirit of monarchy.

HOW SOME LEGISLATORS HAVE CONFOUNDED THE PRINCIPLES WHICH GOVERN MANKIND [Chapter 16]

[1]   MANNERS and customs are those habits which are not established by the laws, either because they were not able, or were not willing to establish them.

[2]   There is this difference between laws and manners, that the laws are most adapted to regulate the actions of the subject, and manners to regulate the actions of the man. There is this difference between manners and customs, that the first principally relate to the interior conduct, the others to the exterior.

[3]   These things have been sometimes confounded.[a] Lycurgus made the same code for the laws, manners, and customs; and the legislators of China have done the same.

[4]   We ought to be surprized, that the legislators of China and Sparta should confound the laws, manners, and customs: the reason is, their manners produced their laws, and their customs their manners.

OF THE PECULIAR QUALITY OF THE
CHINESE GOVERNMENT [Chapter 17]

[1]   THE legislators of China went farther.[a] They confounded together their religion, laws, manners, customs; all those were morals, all these were virtue. The precepts relating to these four points were what they called rites; and it was in the exact observance of these that the Chinese government triumphed. They spent their whole youth in learning them, their whole life in their practice. They were taught by their men of learning, they were inculcated by the magistrates; and as they included all the ordinary actions of life, when they found the means of making them strictly observed, China was well governed.

A CONSEQUENCE DRAWN FROM THE
PRECEDING CHAPTER [Chapter 18]

[1]   FROM hence it follows that the laws of China are not destroyed by conquest. Their customs, manners, laws, and religion, being the same thing, they cannot change all these at once; and as it will

---

[a] Moses made the same code for laws and religion. The first Romans confounded the ancient customs with the laws.

[a] See the Classic books from which father Du Halde gives us some excellent fragments.

happen, that either the conqueror or the conquered must change, in China it has always been the conqueror. For the manners of the conquering nations not being its customs, nor its customs its laws, nor its laws its religion, it has been more easy for them to conform by degrees to the vanquished people, than the vanquished people to them.

[2]   There still follows from hence a very unhappy consequence, which is, that it is almost impossible for Christianity ever to be established in China.[a] The vows of virginity, the assembling of women in churches, their necessary communication with the ministers of religion, their participation in the sacraments, auricular confession, extreme unction, the marriage of only one wife, all these overturn the manners and customs of the country, and with the same blow strike at their religion and laws.[10]

HOW THE LAWS OUGHT TO HAVE A RELATION
TO MANNERS AND CUSTOMS [Chapter 21]

[1]   IT is only singular institutions which thus confound laws, manners, and customs, things naturally distinct and separate: but tho' they are things in themselves different, there is nevertheless a great relation between them.

[2]   Solon being asked if the laws he had given to the Athenians, were the best, he replied, "I have given them the best, they were able to bear."[11] A fine expression, that ought to be perfectly understood by all legislators.

THE SAME SUBJECT CONTINUED [Chapter 22]

[1]   WHEN a people have pure and regular manners, their laws

---

[a] See the reasons given by the Chinese magistrates in their decrees for proscribing the Christian religion. *Edifying Letters, 17th Collect.*

become simple and natural. Plato says that Rhadamanthus, who governed a people extremely religious, finished every process with an extraordinary celerity, administering only the oath on every accusation.[a] But says the same Plato, when a people are not religious, we should never have recourse to an oath, except on such occasions as those in which he who swears is entirely disinterested, as in the case of a judge and a witness.[b]

HOW THE LAWS ARE FOUNDED ON THE MANNERS OF A PEOPLE [Chapter 23]

[2]   At the time when the manners of the Romans were pure, they had no particular law against peculation. When this crime began to appear, it was thought so infamous, that to be condemned to restore[a] what they had taken, was considered as a sufficient disgrace: for a proof of this, see the sentence of L. Scipio.[b]

[a] Of Laws, lib. 12.
[b] Of Laws, lib. 12.
[a] In simplum.
[b] Livy, lib. 38.

❧Part Four

Books XX through XXIII form Part Four of *The Spirit of Laws*, according to Montesquieu's plan. In Books XX and XXI he discusses commerce, in Book XXII, monetary policy, and in Book XXIII, population. Books XX–XXII are not included in this edition.

BOOK XXIII: *Of Laws in the Relation They Bear to the Number of Inhabitants*

ANALYSIS

With Book XXIII Montesquieu returned to the questions of demography that had fascinated him in the Persian Letters. *He continued to believe that the ancient world had been more populous than the modern, and he therefore explores various factors contributing to population growth in the hope that European statesmen might be influenced by his recommendations.*

Montesquieu rejects the notion that poverty and the necessity to work hard to pay heavy taxes are a spur to population growth (chap. 11). Marriage, as opposed to concubinage (chaps. 2–4), however, as well as circumstances favoring the support of a wife and family (chap. 10), will augment popula- tion growth, as will a greater proportion of women than men (chap. 12), a diet heavy in protein (chap. 13), a wide variety of employment opportunities (chap. 14), and an equitable distribution of land (chap. 15). The concern of the legislator should be to do all in his power to further population growth within the limits imposed by climate and the quality of the soil (chap. 16). In some extreme situations even redistribution of the land may be called for (chap. 28, par. [3]), and as both a spur to population growth and a necessary humanitarian policy, M recommends that all men capable of work be given employment (chap. 29). Only in rare instances, such as among the ancient Greeks, is overpopulation the problem, and this eventually requires a wholly different approach (chap. 17).

Book XXIII also includes a discussion of the impact of Roman aggran- dizement on world population (chaps. 18–19), and of the necessity Rome faced during the reigns of Caesar and Augustus to introduce special laws favoring population expansion (chaps. 20–21). As for the problem of population in more recent times, Montesquieu judges feudalism to have been a healthy influence on population growth in Europe (chap. 14). The development of navigation and trade in the late Middle Ages he considers of little service (chap. 25), and he concludes that European legislators of his day need utilize strong measures to increase the birth rate within their realms (chaps. 26–28).

OF MEN AND ANIMALS WITH RESPECT TO THE MULTIPLICATION OF THEIR SPECIES [Chapter 1]

THE females of brutes have an almost constant fecundity. But in the human species, the manner of thinking, the character, the passions, the humour, the caprice, the idea of preserving beauty, the pain of child-bearing, and the fatigue of a too numerous family, obstruct propagation a thousand different ways.

OF MARRIAGE [Chapter 2]

[1]   THE natural obligation of the father to provide for his children has established marriage, which makes known the person who ought to fulfill this obligation.[1]*

[4]   Illicit conjunctions contribute but little to the propagation of the species. The father who is under a natural obligation to nourish and educate his children, is not then fixed; and the mother, with whom the obligation remains, finds a thousand obstacles from shame, remorse, the constraint of her sex, and the rigour of laws; and besides, she generally wants the means.

[5]   Women who have submitted to a public prostitution, cannot have the conveniency of educating their children: the trouble of education is incompatible with their station; and they are so corrupt, that they can have no protection from the law.

[6]   It follows from all this, that public continence is naturally connected with the propagation of the species.

OF FAMILIES [Chapter 4]

[1]   IT is almost every where a custom for the wife to pass into the family of the husband.

[2]   This law greatly contributes to the propagation of the human species. The family is a kind of property: a man who has children of a sex which does not perpetuate it, is never satisfied if he has not those who can render it perpetual.

[3]   Names, which give men an idea of a thing, which one would imagine ought not to perish, are extremely proper to inspire every family with a desire of extending its duration. There are people, amongst whom names distinguish families: there are others, where they only distinguish persons; these last have not the same advantage as the former.

OF THE SEVERITY OF GOVERNMENT [Chapter 11]

[2]   Some through a fluency of speech and an incapacity of examining, have pretended to say, that the greater the poverty of the subjects, the more numerous are their families; that the more they are loaded with taxes, the more industriously they endeavour to put themselves in a station in which they will be able to pay them: two sophisms, which have always destroyed, and will forever be the destruction of monarchies.

[3]   The severity of government may be carried to such an extreme, as to make the natural sensations destructive of the natural sensations themselves. Would the women of America have refused to bear children,[a] had their masters been less cruel?

[a] The Adventures of T. Gage, pag. 58.

OF THE NUMBER OF MALES AND FEMALES
IN DIFFERENT COUNTRIES [Chapter 12]

[1]   I HAVE already observed, that there are born in Europe rather
more boys than girls.[a] It has been remarked that in Japan there are
born rather more girls than boys:[b] all things compared, there must
be more fruitful women in Japan than in Europe, and consequently it must be more populous.

[2]   We are informed,[c] that at Bantam there are ten girls to one
boy.[2] A disproportion like this must cause the number of families
there, to be to the number of those of other climates as 1 to 5½;
which is a prodigious difference. Their families may be much
larger indeed; but there must be few men in circumstances
sufficient to provide for so large a family.

OF SEA-PORT TOWNS [Chapter 13]

IN sea-port towns, where men expose themselves to a thousand
dangers, and go abroad to live or die in distant climates, there are
fewer men than women: and yet we see more children there than
in other places. This proceeds from the great ease with which they
procure the means of subsistence. Perhaps even the oily parts of
fish are more proper to furnish that matter which contributes to
generation. This may be one of the causes of the infinite number
of people in Japan[a] and China,[b] where they live almost wholly on
fish.[c] If this be the case, certain monastic rules, which oblige the

[a] Book XVI. Chap. 4.

[b] See Kempfer, who gives a computation of the people of Meaco.

[c] Collection of Voyages that contributed to the establishment of the East India Company. Vol. I. Pag. 347.

[a] Japan is composed of a number of isles, where there are many banks, and the sea is
there extremely full of fish.

[b] China abounds in rivers.

[c] See Duhalde, Tom. ii. p. 139–142.

monks to live on fish, must be contrary to the spirit of the legislator himself.

OF THE PRODUCTIONS OF THE EARTH WHICH REQUIRE A GREATER OR A LESS NUMBER OF MEN [Chapter 14]

[1]   PASTURE-LANDS are but little peopled, because they find employment only for a few. Corn-lands employ a great many men,
and vineyards infinitely more.

[2]   It has been a frequent complaint in England that the increase of
pasture-land diminished the inhabitants;[a] and it has been observed
in France, that the prodigious number of vineyards is one of the
great causes of the multitude of people.

[3]   Those countries where coal-pits furnish a proper substance for
fuel, have this advantage over others, that not having the same
occasion for forests, the lands may be cultivated.

[4]   In countries productive of rice, they are at great pains in water-
ing the land; a great number of men must therefore be employed.
Besides, there is less land required to furnish subsistence for a
family, than in those which produce other kinds of grain. In fine,
the land which is elsewhere employed in raising cattle, serves
immediately for the subsistence of man; the labour, which in other
places is performed by cattle, is there performed by men; so that
the culture of the soil, becomes to man an immense manufacture.

OF THE NUMBER OF INHABITANTS WITH RELATION TO THE ARTS [Chapter 15]

[1]   WHEN there is an Agrarian law, and the lands are equally

---

[a] The greatest number of the proprietors of land, says Bishop Burnet, finding more
profit in selling their wool than their corn, inclosed their estates: the commons ready to
perish with hunger, rose up in arms; they insisted on a division of the lands: the young
king even wrote on this subject. And proclamations were made against those who
inclosed their lands. *Abridg. of the Hist. of the Reformation.*

divided, the country may be extremely well peopled, though there are but few arts; because every citizen receives from the cultivation of his land whatever is necessary for his subsistence, and all the citizens together consume all the fruits of the earth. Thus it was in some republics.

[2]   In our present situation, in which lands are so unequally distributed, they produce much more than those who cultivate them can consume; if the arts therefore should be neglected, and nothing minded but agriculture, the country could not be peopled. Those who cultivate, having corn to spare, nothing would engage them to work the following year; the fruits of the earth would not be consumed by the indolent; for these would have nothing with which they could purchase them. It is necessary then that the arts should be established, in order that the produce of the land may be consumed by the labourer and the artificer. In a word, it is now proper that many should cultivate much more than is necessary for their own use. For this purpose, they must have a desire of enjoying superficities; and these they can receive only from the artificer.

[3]   Those machines which are designed to abridge art, are not always useful. If a piece of workmanship is of a moderate price, such as is equally agreeable to the maker and the buyer, those machines which would render the manufacture more simple, or in other words, diminish the number of workmen, would be pernicious. And if water-mills were not every where established, I should not have believed them so useful as is pretended, because they have deprived an infinite multitude of their employment, a vast number of persons of the use of water, and great part of the lands of its fertility.

THE CONCERN OF THE LEGISLATOR IN THE
PROPAGATION OF THE SPECIES [Chapter 16]

[1]   REGULATIONS on the number of citizens depend greatly on circumstances. There are countries, in which nature does all: the
legislator then can do nothing. What need is there of inducing
men by laws to propagation, when a fruitful climate yields a
sufficient number of inhabitants? Sometimes the climate is more
favourable than the soil; the people multiply, and are destroyed by
famine: this is the case of China. Hence a father sells his
daughters, and exposes his children. In Tonquin, the same causes
produce the same effects;[a] so we need not, like the Arabian travellers mentioned by Renaudot, search for the origin of this in their
sentiments on the metempsychosis. [b]

[2]   For the same reason, the religion of the isle of Formosa does not
suffer the women to bring their children into the world, till they
are thirty-five years of age: the priestess before this age, by bruising
the belly, procures abortion. [c]

OF GREECE, AND THE NUMBER OF ITS INHABITANTS
[Chapter 17]

[1]   THAT effect which in certain countries of the east springs from
physical causes, was produced in Greece by the nature of the
government. The Greeks were a great nation, composed of cities,
each of which had a distinct government and separate laws. They
had no more the spirit of conquest and ambition, than those of
Switzerland, Holland, and Germany, have at this day. In every
republic the legislator had in view the happiness of the citizens at

[a] Dampiere's Voyages, Vol. II. Pag. 41.
[b] Ibid. Pag. 167.
[c] See the Collection of Voyages that contributed to the establishment of the East-India
Company, Vol. I. part 1. page. 182. & 188.

home, and their power abroad, lest it should prove inferior [a] to that of the neighbouring cities. Thus, with the enjoyment of a small territory and great happiness, it was easy for the number of the citizens to increase to such a degree as to become burthensome. This obliged them incessantly to send out colonies; and as the Swiss do now, to let their men out to war. Nothing was neglected that could hinder the too great multiplication of children.

[3]   The politics of the Greeks were particularly employed in regulating the number of citizens. Plato in his republic fixes them at five thousand and forty, and he would have them stop or encourage propagation, as was most convenient, by honours, shame, and the advice of the old men; he would even regulate the number of marriages, in such a manner, that the republic might be recruited without being overcharged. [b]

[4]   If the laws of a country, says Aristotle, forbid the exposing of children, the number of those brought forth ought to be limited. [c] If they have more than the number prescribed by law, he advises to make the women miscarry before the foetus be formed. [d].

[5]   The same author mentions the infamous means made use of by the Cretans, to prevent their having too great a number of children; a proceeding too indecent to repeat.

[6]   There are places, says Aristotle again, where the laws give bastards the privilege of being citizens; but as soon as they have a sufficient number of people, this privilege ceases. [e] The savages of Canada burn their prisoners: but when they have empty cottages to give them, they receive them into their nation.

[a] In valour, discipline, and military exercises.
[b] Republic. Lib. V.
[c] Polit. Lib. vii. Cap. 16.
[d] Ibid.
[e] Polit. Lib. iii. Cap. 3.

[7]   Sir William Petty, in his calculations, supposes that a man in England is worth what he would sell for at Algiers.[f] This can be true only with respect to England. There are countries where a man is worth nothing, there are others where he is worth less than nothing.

OF THE STATE AND NUMBER OF PEOPLE
BEFORE THE ROMANS [Chapter 18]

ITALY, Sicily, Asia Minor, Gaul and Germany, were nearly in the same state as Greece: full of small nations that abounded with inhabitants; they had no need of laws to increase their number.

OF THE DEPOPULATION OF THE UNIVERSE [Chapter 19]

[1]   ALL these little republics were swallowed up in a large one, and the universe insensibly became depopulated: in order to be convinced of this we need only consider the state of Italy and Greece, before and after the victories of the Romans.

THAT THE ROMANS WERE UNDER A NECESSITY OF
MAKING LAWS, TO ENCOURAGE THE PROPAGATION
OF THE SPECIES [Chapter 20]

[1]   THE Romans, by destroying others, were themselves destroyed; incessantly in action, in the heat of battle, and in the most violent attempts, they wore out like a weapon kept constantly in use.

[2]   I shall not here speak of the attention with which they applied themselves to procure citizens in the room of those they lost,[a] of the associations they entered into, the privileges they bestowed, and of that immense nursery of citizens their slaves. I shall men-

---

[f] Sixty pounds Sterling.

[a] A modern author has treated of this in his *Considerations on the causes of the rise and declension of the Roman grandeur.*

tion what they did to recruit the number, not of their citizens, but of their men; and as these were the people in the world, who knew best how to adapt their laws to their projects, an examination of what they did in this respect, cannot be a matter of indifference.

OF THE LAWS OF THE ROMANS RELATING TO THE PROPAGATION OF THE SPECIES [Chapter 21]

[1]   THE ancient laws of Rome endeavoured greatly to incite the citizens to marriage. The senate and the people made frequent regulations on this subject.

[3]   Independently of the laws, the censors had a particular eye upon marriages, and according to the exigencies of the republic engaged them to it by shame, and by punishments. [a]

[4]   The corruption of manners which began to take place, contributed vastly to disgust the citizens against marriage, which was painful to those who had no taste for the pleasures of innocence.

[5]   The corruption of manners destroyed the censorship, which was itself established to destroy the corruption of manners: for when this corruption became general, the censor lost his power. [b]

[6]   Civil discords, triumvirates, and proscriptions, weakened Rome more than any war she had hitherto engaged in. They left but few citizens, and the greatest part of them unmarried. To remedy this last evil, Caesar and Augustus re-established the censorship, and would even be censors themselves. [c] Caesar gave rewards to those who had many children. [d] All women under forty-five years of age, who had neither husband nor children, were forbid to wear jewels,

---

[a] See what was done in this respect in T. Livy, lib. xlv. The Epitome of T. Livy, lib. lix. Aulus Gellius, lib. i cap. 6. Valerius Maximus, lib. ii. cap. 19.

[b] See what I said in Book V, Chap. 19.

[c] See Dio, Lib. xliii. and Xiphilinus in August.

[d] Dio, Lib. xliii. Suetonius's Life of Caesar, Chap. xx. Appian, Lib. ii of the Civil War.

or to ride in litters;[e] an excellent method, thus to attack celibacy by
the power of vanity. The laws of Augustus were more pressing:[f] he
imposed new penalties on those who were not married,[g] and increased the rewards both of those who were married, and of those
who had children.

[14]   The married men who had the most children, were always
preferred,[h] whether in the pursuit, or in the exercise of honours.
The consul, who had the most numerous offspring, was the first
who received the fasces;[i] he had his choice of the provinces:[j] the
senator who had most children, had his name wrote first in the
catalogue of senators, and was the first in giving his opinion in the
senate.[k] They might even stand sooner than ordinary for an office,
because every child gave a dispensation of a year.[l] If an inhabitant
of Rome had three children, he was exempted from all troublesome offices.[m] The freeborn women who had three children, and
the freedwomen who had four, passed out of that perpetual tute-
lage,[n] in which they had been held by the ancient laws of Rome.[o]

[15]   As they had rewards, so they had also penalties.[p] Those who
were not married could receive no advantage from the will of any

[e] Eusebius in his Chronicle.
[f] Dio, Lib. liv.
[g] In the year of Rome 736.
[h] Tacitus, lib. ii. *Ut numerus liberorum in candidatis praepolleret, quod lex jubebat.*
[i] Aulus Gellius, Lib. ii. Cap. 15.
[j] Tacitus Annal. Lib XV.
[k] See Law 6. ¶5. *de Decurion.*
[l] See Law 2. ff. *de Minorib.*
[m] Law 1st and 2d, ff. *de Vacatione & excusat munerum.*
[n] Frag. of Ulpian, tit. 29. ¶3.
[o] Plutarch Life of Numa.
[p] See the fragments of Ulpian, tit. 14, 15, 16, 17, & 18. which compose one of the
finest pieces of the ancient civil law of the Romans.

person that was not a near relation;[q] and those who being married, had no children, could receive only half.[r] The Romans, says Plutarch, marry to *be* heirs, and not to *have* them.[s]

[18]   The law gave to a surviving husband or wife two years to marry again,[t] and a year and a half in case of a divorce. The fathers who would not suffer their children to marry, or refused to give their daughters a portion, were obliged to do it by the magistrates.[u]

[19]   They were not allowed to betroth, when the marriage was to be deferred for more than two years;[v] and as they could not marry a girl till she was twelve years old, they could not be betrothed to her till she was ten.

[20]   It was contrary to law, for a man of sixty to marry a woman of fifty.[w] As they had given great privileges to married men, the law would not suffer them to enter into useless marriages.

[28]   The sects of philosophers had already introduced in the empire a disposition that estranged them from business; a disposition which could not gain ground in the time of the republic,[x] when every body was employed in the arts of war and peace. From hence arose an idea of perfection, as connected with a life of speculation; from

---

[q] Sozom. lib. i. cap. 9. they could receive from their relations. Fragm. of Ulpian, tit. 16. ¶I.

[r] Sozom. lib. i cap. 9. & leg. unic. cod. Theod. *"de infirm. poenis caelib. et orbit."*

[s] *Moral works*, of the love of fathers towards their children.

[t] *Fragm. of Ulpian*, tit. 14. It seems the first Julian laws allowed three years. *Speech of Augustus* in Dio, lib. lvi. *Suetonius life of Augustus*, cap. 34. Other Julian laws granted but one year: the Papian law gave two. *Fragm. of Ulpian*, tit. 14. These laws were not agreeable to the people; Augustus therefore softened or strengthened them, as they were more or less disposed to comply with them.

[u] This was the 35th head of the Papian law. Leg. 19. ff. *de ritu nuptiarum.*

[v] See Dio lib. liv. anno 736. Suetonius in Octavio, cap. 34.

[w] Fragm. of Ulpian, tit. 16. the 27th law, Cod. *de nuptiis.*

[x] See in *Cicero's Offices*, his sentiments on this spirit of speculation.

hence an estrangement from the cares and embarrassments of a family. The Christian religion coming after this philosophy, fixed, if I may make use of the expression, the ideas which that had only prepared.

[29]   Christianity stamped its character on jurisprudence; for empire has always a connexion with the priesthood. This is visible from the Theodosian code, which is only a collection of the decrees of the Christian emperors.

[30]   A panegyrist of Constantine says to that emperor, *"Your laws were made only to correct vice, and to regulate manners: you have stripped the ancient laws of that artifice, which seemed to have no other aim than to lay snares for simplicity."*[y]

[31]   It is certain, that the alterations made by Constantine took their rise, either from sentiments relating to the establishment of Christianity, or from ideas conceived of its perfection. From the first, proceeded those laws which gave such authority to bishops, and which have been the foundation of the ecclesiastical jurisdiction: from hence those laws which weakened paternal authority,[z] by depriving the father of his property in the possessions of his children. To extend a new religion, they were obliged to take away the dependance of children, who are always least attached to what is already established.

[32]   The laws made with a view to Christian perfection, were more particularly those by which the penalties of the Papian laws were abolished;[a] those who were not married were equally exempt from them, with those who being married had no children.

---

[y] Nazarius in *Panegyrico Constantini*, anno 321.

[z] See Law, 1, 2, 3 in the Theodosian code, *de bonis maternis, maternique generis*, & c. and the only law of the code, *de bonis quae filiis famil. acquiruntur.*

[a] Leg. *unic.* cod. Theod. *de infirm. poen. caelib. et orbit.*

[33]   *"These laws were established*, says an ecclesiastic historian,[b] *as if the multiplication of the human species was an effect of our care, instead of being sensible that the number is increased or diminished, according to the order of providence."*

[34]   Principles of religion have had an extraordinary influence on the propagation of the human species. Sometimes they have promoted it as amongst the Jews, the Mahometans, the Gebres, the Chinese; at others, they have put a damp to it, as was the case of the Romans upon their conversion to Christianity.

[35]   They every where incessantly preached up continency; a virtue the more perfect, because in its own nature it can be practised but by very few.[3]*

THE CHANGES WHICH HAPPENED IN EUROPE, WITH REGARD TO THE NUMBER OF THE INHABITANTS [Chapter 24]

[1]   IN the state Europe was in, one would not imagine it possible for it to be retrieved; especially when under Charlemain it formed only one vast empire. But by the nature of government at that time, it became divided into an infinite number of petty sovereignties; and as the lord or sovereign who resided in his village, or city, was neither great, rich, powerful, nor even safe, but by the number of his subjects; every one employed himself with a singular attention to make his little country flourish. This succeeded in such a manner, that notwithstanding the irregularities of government, the want of that knowledge which has since been acquired in commerce, and the numerous wars and disorders incessantly arising, most countries of Europe were better peopled in those days, than they are even at present.

[b] Sozomenus, pag. 27.

[3]   'Tis the perpetual re-union of many little states that has
produced this diminution. Formerly every village of France was a
capital; there is at present only one large one: every part of the state
was a center of power, at present all has a relation to one center;
and this center is, in some measure, the state itself.

THE SAME SUBJECT CONTINUED [Chapter 25]

[1]   EUROPE, it is true, has for these two ages past greatly increased
its navigation: This has both procured and deprived it of inhabitants. Holland sends every year a great number of mariners to the
Indies; of whom not above two thirds return: the rest either perish
or settle in the Indies. The same thing must happen to every other
nation engaged in that trade.

[2]   We must not judge of Europe, as of a particular state engaged
alone in an extensive navigation. This state would increase in
people, because all the neighbouring nations would endeavour to
have a share in this commerce; and mariners would arrive from all
parts. Europe separated from the rest of the world by religion,[a] by
vast seas, and deserts, could not be repaired in this manner.

CONSEQUENCES [Chapter 26]

FROM all this we may conclude, that Europe is at present in a
condition to require laws to be made in favour of the propagation
of the human species. The politics of the ancient Greeks incessantly complain of the inconveniences that attend a republic from
the excessive number of citizens; but the politics of this age call
upon us to take proper means to increase ours.

[a] Mahometan countries surround it almost on every side.

OF THE LAW MADE IN FRANCE TO ENCOURAGE THE
PROPAGATION OF THE SPECIES [Chapter 27]

LOUIS XIV appointed particular pensions to those who had ten
children, and much larger to those who had twelve.[a] But it is not
sufficient to reward prodigies. In order to communicate a general
spirit which leads to the propagation of the species, it is necessary
for us to establish, like the Romans, general rewards, or general
penalties.

BY WHAT MEANS WE MAY REMEDY A
DEPOPULATION [Chapter 28]

[1]   WHEN a state is depopulated by particular accidents, by wars,
pestilence, or famine, there are still resources left. The men who
remain may preserve the spirit of industry; they may seek to repair
their misfortunes, and calamity itself may make them become
more industrious. The evil is almost incurable, when the depopulation is prepared before-hand by interior vice and a bad government. When this is the case, men perish with an insensible and
habitual sickness: born in misery and languishing weakness, in
violence or under the influence of a wicked administration, they
see themselves destroyed, and frequently without perceiving the
cause of their destruction. Of this we have a melancholy proof, in
the countries desolated by despotic power, or by the excessive
advantages of the clergy over the laity.

[2]   In vain shall we wait for the succour of children yet unborn, to
re-establish a state thus depopulated. There is not time for this;
men in their solitude are without courage or industry. With land
sufficient to nourish a people, they have scarcely enough to

[a] The Edict of 1666, in favour of marriages.

nourish a family. The common people have not even a property in the miseries of the country; that is, in the fallows with which it abounds. The clergy, the prince, the cities, the great men, and some of the principal citizens, insensibly become proprietors of all the land, which lies uncultivated: the families who are ruined have left their fields; and the labouring man is destitute.

[3]   In this situation they should take the same measures throughout the whole extent of the empire, which the Romans took in a part of theirs: they should practice in their distress, what these observed in the midst of plenty; that is, they should distribute land to all the families who are in want, and procure them the materials for clearing and cultivating it. This distribution ought to be continued as long as there is a man to receive it; and in such a manner, that not a moment for labour be lost.

OF HOSPITALS [Chapter 29]

[1]   A MAN is not poor because he has nothing, but because he does not work. The man who without any degree of wealth has an employment, is as much at his ease as he who without labour has an income of an hundred crowns a year. He who has no substance, and yet has a trade, is not poorer than he who possessing ten acres of land is obliged to cultivate it for his subsistence. The mechanic who gives his art as an inheritance to his children, has left them a fortune which is multiplied in proportion to their number. It is not so with him, who having ten acres of land, divides it amongst his children.

[2]   In trading countries, where many men have no other subsistence but from the arts, the state is frequently obliged to supply the necessities of the aged, the sick, and the orphan. A regular policied government draws this support from the arts themselves. It gives

to some such employment as they are capable of performing; others are taught to work, and this teaching of itself becomes an employment.

[3]   Those alms which are given to a naked man in the street do not fulfil the obligations of the state, which owes to every citizen a certain subsistence, a proper nourishment, convenient cloathing, and a kind of life not incompatible with health.

[4]   Aurengzebe being asked, why he did not build hospitals, said, *"I will make my empire so rich, that there shall be no need of hospitals."* [a] He ought to have said, I will begin by rendering my empire rich, and then I will build hospitals.

[5]   The riches of a state suppose great industry. Amidst the numerous branches of trade, it is impossible but some must suffer; and consequently the mechanics must be in a momentary necessity.

[6]   When this is the case, the state is obliged to lend them a ready assistance; whether it be to prevent the sufferings of the people, or to avoid a rebellion. In this case hospitals, or some equivalent regulations, are necessary to prevent this misery.

[7]   But when the nation is poor, private poverty springs from the general calamity; and is, if I may so express myself, the general calamity itself. All the hospitals in the world cannot cure this private poverty: on the contrary, the spirit of indolence which it constantly inspires, increases the general, and consequently the private misery.

[8]   Henry VIII, resolving to reform the church of England, ruined the monks, [b] of themselves a lazy set of people that encouraged laziness in others; [4*] because, as they practised hospitality, an infinite number of idle persons, gentlemen and citizens, spent their

---

[a] See Sir John Chardin's Travels thro' Persia, Vol. 8.

[b] See Burnet's *Hist. of the Reformation.*

lives in running from convent to convent. He demolished even the hospitals in which the lower people found subsistence, as the gentlemen did theirs in the monasteries. Since these changes, the spirit of trade and industry has been established in England.

[9]   At Rome, the hospitals place every one at his ease, except those who labour, except those who are industrious, except those who have land, except those who are engaged in trade.

[10]   I have observed, that wealthy nations have need of hospitals, because fortune subjects them to a thousand accidents: but 'tis plain that transient assistances are much better than perpetual foundations. The evil is momentary; it is necessary therefore, that the succour should be of the same nature, and that it be applied to particular accidents.

❧Part Five

Books XXIV through XXVI constitute Part Five of Montesquieu's plan for *The Spirit of Laws*. In Books XXIV and XXV he discusses religion, and in Book XXVI he returns to the general discussion of law that he first presented in Book I.

BOOK XXIV: *Of Laws in Relation to Religion Considered in Itself, and in Its Doctrines* [1]

ANALYSIS

Book XXIV is concerned with religion, and Montesquieu's approach is distinctly utilitarian. He begins by proclaiming himself a political writer— not a theologian—and although he refers to Christianity as the source of the best civil and political laws (chap. 1, par. [5]) and as the religion of moderate governments (chap. 3), he is not primarily concerned with the Christian religion. Rather, he surveys a wide range of faiths, both ancient and modern, to see which contribute most to the political and social welfare of the nations in which they are adopted. And in addition to assessing the impact of various theologies upon the peoples who adhere to them, M also examines the extent to which the bounds of a particular religion are circumscribed by limitations imposed by governmental type (chap. 5) or by climate (chaps. 24–26). For a more comprehensive discussion of Book XXIV, see Introduction, pp. 51–54.

OF RELIGION IN GENERAL [Chapter 1]

[1]   As amidst several degrees of darkness we may form a judgment of those which are the least thick, and among precipices, which are the least deep; so we may search among false religions for those that are most conformable to the welfare of society; for those, which, though they have not the effect of leading men to the

felicity of another life, may contribute most to their happiness in this.

[2]   I shall examine therefore the several religions of the world in relation only to the good they produce in civil society; whether I speak of that which has its root in heaven, or of those which spring from the earth.

[3]   As in this work I am not a divine, but a political writer, I may here advance things which are not otherwise true, than as they correspond with a wordly manner of thinking, not as considered in their relation to truths of a more sublime nature.

[4]   A person of the least degree of impartiality[2] must see that I have never pretended to make the interests of religion submit to those of a political nature, but rather to unite them: now, in order to unite, it is necessary that we should know them.

[5]   The Christian religion, which ordains that men should love each other, would without doubt have every nation blest with the best civil, the best political laws; because these, next to the religion, are the greatest good that men can give and receive.

A PARADOX OF MR. BAYLE'S [Chapter 2]

[1]   MR. Bayle has pretended to prove, that it is better to be an atheist than an idolater;[a] that is, in other words, that it is less dangerous to have no religion at all, than a bad one. This is only a sophism. To say that religion is not a restraining motive, because it does not always restrain, is equally absurd as to say that the civil laws are not a restraining motive. It is a false way of reasoning against religion, to collect in a large work a long detail of the evils it has produced, if we do not give at the same time an enumeration of the advantages which have flowed from it. Were I to relate all

---

[a] Thoughts on the Comet.

the evils that have arisen in the world from civil laws, from monarchy, and from republican government, I might tell of frightful things. Was it of no advantage for subjects to have religion, it would still be of some if princes had it, and if they whitened with foam the only rein which can restrain those who fear not human laws. A prince who loves and fears religion is a lion, who stoops to the hand that strokes, or the voice that appeases him. He who fears and hates religion, is like the savage beast that growls and bites the chain, which prevents his flying on the passenger.[3] He who has no religion at all, is that terrible animal, who perceives his liberty only when he tears in pieces, and when he devours.

[2]   The question is not to know, whether it would be better that a certain man, or a certain people had no religion, than to abuse what they have; but to know which is the least evil, that religion be sometimes abused, or that there be no such restraint as religion on mankind.

[3]   To diminish the horror of atheism, they lay too much to the charge of idolatry.

THAT A MODERATE GOVERNMENT IS MOST AGREEABLE
TO THE CHRISTIAN RELIGION, AND A DESPOTIC
GOVERNMENT TO THE MAHOMETANS [Chapter 3] [4]*

[1]   THE Christian religion is a stranger to mere despotic power. The mildness so frequently recommended in the gospel, is incompatible with the despotic rage with which a prince punishes his subjects, and exercises himself in cruelty.

[2]   As this religion forbids the plurality of wives, its princes are less confined, less concealed from their subjects, and consequently have more humanity: they are more disposed to be directed by

laws, and more capable of perceiving that they cannot do whatever they please.

[3]   While the Mahometan princes incessantly give or receive death, the religion of the Christians renders their princes less timid, and consequently less cruel. The prince confides in his subjects, and the subjects in the prince. How admirable the religion, which, while it seems only to have in view the felicity of the other life, constitutes the happiness of this!

[4]   'Tis the Christian religion, that in spite of the extent of the empire, and the influence of the climate, has hindered despotic power from being established in AEthiopia, and has carried into the heart of Africa the manners and laws of Europe.

[6]   We owe to Christianity, in government a certain political law, and in war a certain law of nations, benefits which human nature can never sufficiently acknowledge.

CONSEQUENCES FROM THE CHARACTER OF THE CHRISTIAN RELIGION, AND THAT OF THE MAHOMETAN [Chapter 4]

[1]   FROM the characters of the Christian and Mahometan religions we ought, without any further examination, to embrace the one, and reject the other: for it is much easier to prove that religion ought to humanize the manners of men, than that any particular religion is true.

[2]   It is a misfortune to human nature, when religion is given by a conqueror. The Mahometan religion, which speaks only by the sword, acts still upon men with that destructive spirit with which it was founded.

THAT THE CATHOLIC RELIGION IS MOST AGREEABLE TO A MONARCHY, AND THE PROTESTANT TO A REPUBLIC [Chapter 5]

[1]   WHEN a religion is introduced and fixed in a state, it is commonly such as is most suitable to the plan of government there established: for those who receive it, and those who are the cause of its being received, have scarcely any other idea of policy than that of the state in which they were born.

[2]   When the Christian religion two centuries ago, became unhappily divided into Catholic and Protestant, the people of the north embraced the Protestant; and those of the south adhered still to the Catholic.

[3]   The reason is plain: the people of the north have, and will forever have, a spirit of liberty and independence, which the people of the south have not; and therefore a religion, which has no visible head, is more agreeable to the independency of the climate than that which has one.[5]*

[4]   In the countries themselves where the Protestant religion became established, the revolutions were made pursuant to the several plans of political government. Luther having great princes on his side, would never have been able to make them relish an ecclesiastic authority that had no exterior pre-eminence; while Calvin, having to do with people who lived under republican governments, or with obscure citizens in monarchies, might very well avoid establishing dignities and pre-eminence.

[5]   Each of these two religions were believed to be the most perfect; the Calvinist judging his most conformable to what Christ had said, and the Lutheran to what the Apostles had practised.

ANOTHER OF MR. BAYLE'S PARADOXES [Chapter 6]

[1]   MR. Bayle, after having abused all religions, endeavours to

sully Christianity: he boldly asserts, that true Christians cannot form a government of any duration. Why not? The more they believe themselves indebted to religion, the more they would think due to their country. The principles of Christianity deeply engraved on the heart, would be infinitely more powerful than the false honour of monarchies, than the humane virtues of republics, or the servile fear of despotic states.

[2]   It is astonishing that this great man⁶* should not be able to distinguish between the orders for the establishment of Christianity, and Christianity itself; and that he should be liable to be charged with not knowing the spirit of his own religion. When the legislator, instead of laws has given counsels, this is because he knew, that if these counsels were ordained as laws, they would be contrary to the spirit of the laws themselves.

OF THE LAWS OF PERFECTION
IN RELIGION [Chapter 7]

[1]   HUMAN laws made to direct the will, ought to give precepts, and not counsels; those of religion made to influence the heart, ought to give many counsels and few precepts.

[2]   When, for instance, it gives rules not for what is good, but for what is better; not to direct to what is right, but to what is perfect; it is expedient, that these should be counsels, and not laws: for perfection can have no relation to the universality of men, or things. Besides, if these were laws, there would be a necessity for an infinite number of others to make people observe the first. Celibacy was advised by Christianity: when they made it a law in respect to a certain order of men, it became necessary to make new ones every day, in order to oblige those men to observe it.ᵃ The

---

ᵃ Dupin's Ecclesiastical Library of the 6th Century, Vol. 5.

legislator wearied himself, he wearied society, to make men execute by precept, what those who love perfection would have executed as counsel.[7]*

OF THE CONNECTION BETWEEN THE MORAL LAWS AND THOSE OF RELIGION [Chapter 8]

[1]   IN a country so unfortunate as to have a religion that God has not revealed, it is always necessary for it to be agreeable to morality; because even a false religion is the best security we can have of the probity of men.

[2]   The principal points of religion of the inhabitants of Pegu,[8] are not to commit murder, not to steal, to avoid uncleanness, not to give the least uneasiness to their neighbour, but to do him, on the contrary, all the good in their power.[a] With these rules they think they should be saved in any religion whatsoever. From hence it proceeds, that these people, though poor and proud, behave with gentleness and compassion to the unhappy.

OF THE ESSENES [Chapter 9][9]

THE Essenes made a vow to observe justice to mankind, to do no ill to any person, upon whatsoever account; to keep faith with all the world, to hate injustice, to command with modesty, always to side with truth, and to fly from all unlawful gain.[a]

OF THE SECT OF STOICS [Chapter 10][10]*

[1]   THE several sects of philosophy amongst the ancients, were a species of religion.[11] Never were any principles more worthy of human nature, and more proper to form the good man, than those

---

[a] Collection of Voyages that contributed to the establishment of the East-India Company, Vol iii. Part 1. pag. 63.

[a] Hist. of the Jews, by *Prideaux*.

of the Stoics; and if I could for a moment cease to think that I am a Christian, I should not be able to hinder myself from ranking the destruction of the sect of Zeno among the misfortunes that have befallen the human race.

[2]   It carried to excess only those things in which there is true greatness, the contempt of pleasure and of pain.

[3]   It was this sect alone that made citizens; this alone that made great men; this alone great emperors.

[4]   Laying aside for a moment revealed truths, let us search through all nature, and we shall not find a nobler object than the Antoninus's; even Julian himself, Julian: (a commendation thus wrested from me, will not render me an accomplice of his apostacy) no, there has not been a prince since his reign more worthy to govern mankind.[12]*

[5]   While the Stoics looked upon riches, human grandeur, grief, disquietudes, and pleasure, as vanity; they were entirely employed in labouring for the happiness of mankind; and in exercising the duties of society. It seems as if they regarded that sacred spirit, which they believed to dwell within them, as a kind of favourable providence watchful over the human race.

[6]   Born for society, they all believed that it was their destiny to labour for it; with so much the less fatigue, as their rewards were all within themselves. Happy by their philosophy alone, it seemed as if only the happiness of others could increase theirs.

OF CONTEMPLATION [Chapter 11]

[1]   MEN being made to preserve, to nourish, to clothe themselves, and to do all the actions of society, religion ought not to give them too contemplative a life.[a]

---

[a] This is the inconvenience of the doctrine of Foe and Laockium.[13]

[2]   The Mahometans become speculative by habit; they pray five times a day, and each time they are obliged to cast behind them every thing which has any concern with this world: this forms them for speculation. Add to this that indifference for all things which is inspired by the doctrine of unalterable fate.

[3]   If other causes besides these concur to disengage their affections, for instance, if the severity of the government, if the laws concerning the property of land, give them a precarious spirit; all is lost.

[4]   The religion of the Gebres[14] formerly rendered Persia a flourishing kingdom; it corrected the bad effects of despotic power. The same empire is now destroyed by the Mahometan religion.

OF PENANCE [Chapter 12]

PENANCES ought to be joined with the idea of labour, not with that of idleness; with the idea of good, not with that of supereminence; with the idea of frugality, not with that of avarice.

IN WHAT MANNER RELIGION HAS AN INFLUENCE
ON CIVIL LAWS [Chapter 14]

[1]   As both religion and the civil laws ought to have a peculiar tendency to render men good citizens, it is evident that when one of these deviates from this end, the tendency of the other ought to be strengthened. The less severity there is in religion, the more there ought to be in the civil laws.

[2]   Thus the reigning religion of Japan having few doctrines, and proposing neither future rewards nor punishments, the laws to supply these defects have been made with the spirit of severity, and are executed with an extraordinary punctuality.

[3]   When the doctrine of necessity is established by religion, the penalties of the laws ought to be more severe, and the magistrate

more vigilant; to the end that men, who would otherwise become
abandoned, might be determined by these motives: but it is quite
otherwise, where religion has established the doctrine of liberty.

[4]   From the inactivity of soul springs the Mahometan doctrine of
predestination, and from this doctrine of predestination springs the
inactivity of soul. This, they say, is in the decrees of God; they
must therefore indulge their repose. In a case like this, the magistrate ought to awaken by the laws, those who are lulled asleep by
religion.

[5]   When religion condemns things which the civil laws ought to
permit, there is danger lest the civil laws, on the other hand,
should permit what religion ought to condemn. Either of these is a
constant proof of a want of true ideas of that harmony and proportion, which ought to subsist between both.

[7]   The people of Formosa believe, that there is a kind of hell; but
it is to punish those who at certain seasons have not gone naked;
who have dressed in calico, and not in silk; who have presumed to
look for oysters, who have undertaken any business without consulting the song of birds: whilst drunkenness and debauchery are
not regarded as crimes. They believe, even that the debauches of
their children are agreeable to their gods. [a]

[8]   When religion absolves the mind by a thing merely accidental,
it loses its greatest influence on mankind. The people of India
believe, that the waters of the Ganges have a sanctifying virtue.
Those who die on its banks are imagined to be exempted from the
torments of the other life, and to be entitled to dwell in a region
full of delights; and for this reason the ashes of the dead are sent
from the most distant places to be thrown into this river. [b] Little

---

[a] Collection of Voyages that contributed to the establishment of the East-India Company, Vol. V. pag. 192.
[b] Edifying Letters, Collect. 15.

then does it signify whether they have lived virtuously or not, so they be but thrown into the Ganges.

[9]   The idea of a place of rewards has a necessary connection with the idea of the abodes of misery; and when they hope for the first without fearing the latter, the civil laws have no longer any influence. Men who believe that they are sure of the rewards of the other life, are above the power of the legislator; they look upon death with too much contempt: by what methods shall the man be restrained by laws, who believes that the greatest pain the magistrate can inflict will end in a moment, to begin his happiness?

HOW FALSE RELIGIONS ARE SOMETIMES CORRECTED BY THE CIVIL LAWS [Chapter 15]

[1]   SIMPLICITY, superstition, or a respect for antiquity, have sometimes established mysteries or ceremonies shocking to modesty: of this the world has furnished numerous examples. Aristotle says, that in this case the law permits the fathers of families to repair to the temple to celebrate these mysteries for their wives and children.[a] How admirable the civil law, which in spite of religion preserves the manners untainted!

[2]   Augustus excluded the youth of either sex from assisting at any nocturnal ceremony, unless accompanied by a more aged relation; and when he revived the *lupercalia*,[15] he would not allow the young men to run naked.[b]

HOW THE LAWS OF RELIGION CORRECT THE INCONVENIENCIES OF A POLITICAL CONSTITUTION [Chapter 16]

[1]   ON the other hand, religion may support a state, when the laws themselves are incapable of doing it.

[a] Polit. Lib. vii. Cap. 17.
[b] Suetonius *in Augusto*, cap. 31.

[2]   Thus when a kingdom is frequently agitated by civil wars, religion may do much by obliging one part of the state to remain always quiet. Among the Greeks, the Eleans, as priests of Apollo, enjoyed a perpetual peace. In Japan, the city of Meaco enjoys a constant peace, as being a holy city.[a]

[3]   In kingdoms where wars are not entered upon by a general consent, and where the laws have not pointed out any means either of terminating or preventing them, religion establishes times of peace, or cessation of hostilities, that the people may be able to sow their corn, and perform those other labours which are absolutely necessary for the subsistence of the state.

[4]   Every year all hostility ceases between the Arabian tribes for four months; the least disturbance would then be an impiety.[b] In former times, when every lord in France declared war or peace, religion granted a truce, which was to take place at certain seasons.

THE SAME SUBJECT CONTINUED [Chapter 17]

[1]   WHEN a state has many causes for hatred, religion ought to produce many ways of reconciliation. The Arabs, a people addicted to robbery, are frequently guilty of doing injury and injustice. Mahomet enacted this law:[a] *"If any one forgives the blood of his brother,[b] he may pursue the malefactor for damages and interest: but he who shall injure the wicked, after having received satisfaction, shall, in the day of judgment, suffer the most grievous torments."*

[2]   The Germans inherited the hatred and enmity of their near relations: but these were not eternal. Homicide was expiated by giving a certain number of cattle, and all the family received

[a] Collection of Voyages made to establish an India Company, Vol. iv. Pag. 127.
[b] See Prideaux's Life of Mahomet, Pag. 64.
[a] Alcoran, Book I Chap. of the cow.
[b] On renouncing the law of retaliation.

satisfaction. A thing extremely useful, says Tacitus, because en-
mities are most dangerous amongst a free people.[c] I believe indeed, that their ministers of religion who were held by them in so
much credit, were concerned in these reconciliations.

[3]   Amongst the Malays[16] where no form of reconciliation is established, he who has committed murder, certain of being assassi-
nated by the relations or friends of the deceased, abandons himself
to fury, wounds and kills all he meets.[d]

THAT IT IS NOT SO MUCH THE TRUTH OR FALSITY OF A
DOCTRINE WHICH RENDERS IT USEFUL OR PERNICIOUS
TO MEN IN CIVIL GOVERNMENT, AS THE USE OR ABUSE
WHICH IS MADE OF IT [Chapter 19]

[1]   THE most true and holy doctrines may be attended with the very
worst consequences, when they are not connected with the principles of society; and, on the contrary, doctrines the most false may
be attended with excellent consequences, when contrived so as to
be connected with these principles.

[2]   The religion of Confucius disowns the immortality of the soul,
and the sect of Zeno did not believe it. These two sects have drawn
from their bad principles consequences, not just indeed, but the
most admirable as to their influence on society. Those of the
religion of Tao, and of Foe,[a] believe the immortality of the soul;

[c] De moribus Germanorum.

[d] Collection of Voyages that contributed to the establishment of the East-India Company, Vol. vii. Pag. 303. See also Memoirs of the C. de Forbin, and what he says of the
Macassars.

[a] A Chinese philosopher reasons thus against the doctrine of Foe. "It is said in a book
of that sect, that the body is our dwelling place, and the soul the immortal guest which
lodges there: but if the bodies of our relations are only a lodging, it is natural to regard
them with the same contempt we should feel for a structure of earth and dirt. Is not this
endeavoring to tear from the heart the virtue of love to one's own parents? This leads us

but from this sacred doctrine they draw the most frightful consequences.

[3]   The doctrine of the immortality of the soul falsely understood,
has, almost throughout the whole world, and in every age, engaged women, slaves, subjects, friends, to murder themselves,
that they might go and serve in the other world the object of their
respect or love in this. Thus it was in the West-Indies; thus it was
amongst the Danes;[b] thus it is at present in Japan,[c] at Macassar,[d]
and many other places.[17]

[4]   These customs do not so directly proceed from the doctrine of
the immortality of the soul, as from that of the resurrection of the
body, from whence they have drawn this consequence, that after
death the same individual will have the same wants, the same
sentiments, the same passions. In this point of view the doctrine of
the immortality of the soul has a prodigious effect on mankind;
because the idea of only a simple change of habitation is more
within the reach of the human understanding, and more adapted to
flatter the heart, than the idea of a new modification.

[5]   It is not enough for religion to establish a doctrine, it must also
direct its influence. This the Christian religion performs in the
most admirable manner, particularly with regard to the doctrines
of which we have been speaking. It makes us hope for a state
which is the object of our belief; not for a state which we have

even to neglect the care of the body, and to refuse it the compassion and affection so
necessary for its preservation; hence the disciples of Foe kill themselves by thousands."
Work of an ancient Chinese philosopher, in the Collection of Du Halde, Vol III. pag.
52.
    [b] See Tho. Bartholin's Antiq. of the Danes.
    [c] An Account of Japan, in the Collection of Voyages that contributed to establish an
East India Company.
    [d] Forbin's Memoirs.

already experienced, or known: thus every article, even the resurrection of the body, leads us to spiritual ideas.

THE SAME SUBJECT CONTINUED [Chapter 20]

THE sacred books of the ancient Persians say, "*If you would be holy, instruct your children, because all the good actions which they perform, will be imputed to you.*" They advise them to marry betimes, because children at the day of judgment will be as a bridge, over which those who have none cannot pass.[a] These doctrines were false, but extremely useful.

THAT IT IS DANGEROUS FOR RELIGION TO INSPIRE
AN AVERSION FOR THINGS IN THEMSELVES
INDIFFERENT [Chapter 22]

[1]   A KIND of honour established in the Indies by the prejudices of religion, has made the several tribes conceive an aversion against each other. This honour is founded intirely on religion; these family distinctions form no civil distinctions; there are Indians who would think themselves dishonoured by eating with their king.

[2]   These sorts of distinctions are connected with a certain aversion for other men, very different from those sentiments which ought to proceed from difference of rank; which amongst us, comprehend a love for inferiors.

[3]   The laws of religion should never inspire an aversion to any thing but vice, and above all they should never estrange man from a love and tenderness for his own species.

[4]   The Mahometan and Indian religions embrace an infinite number of people: the Indians hate the Mahometans, because they

[a] Mr. Hyde.

eat cows; the Mahometans detest the Indians, because they eat hogs.

OF FESTIVALS [Chapter 23]

[1]   WHEN religion appoints a cessation from labour, it ought to have a greater regard to the necessities of mankind, than to the grandeur of the being it designs to honour.

[2]   Athens was subject to great inconveniencies from the excessive number of its festivals. [a] These powerful people, to whose decision all the cities of Greece came to submit their quarrels, could not but suffer in their affairs.

[3]   When Constantine ordained that the people should rest on the sabbath, he made this decree for the cities, and not for the inhabitants of the open country; [b] he was sensible, that labour in the cities was useful, and in the fields necessary.

[4]   For the same reason, in a country supported by commerce the number of festivals ought to be relative to this very commerce. Protestant and Catholic countries are situated in such a manner that there is more need of labor in the former, than in the latter; [c] the suppression of festivals is therefore more suitable to Protestant than to Catholic countries.

[5]   Dampierre observes, that the diversions of different nations vary greatly according to the climate. [d] As hot climates produce a quantity of delicate fruits, the barbarians, who easily find necessaries, spend much time in diversions. The Indians of colder countries have not so much leisure, being obliged to fish and hunt continually; wherefore they have less music, dancing, and festivals.

[a] Xenophon on the republic of Athens.
[b] Leg. 3. Cod, *de Feriis*. This law was doubtless made only for the Pagans.
[c] The Catholics lie more towards the south, and the Protestants toward the north.
[d] Dampierre's Voyages, Vol. II.

OF THE LOCAL LAWS OF RELIGION [Chapter 24]

[1]   THERE are many local laws in various religions; and when Montezuma with so much obstinacy insisted that the religion of the Spaniards was good for their country, and his for Mexico, he did not assert an absurdity; because, in fact, legislators could never help having a regard to what nature had established before them.[18*]

[2]   The opinion of the metempsychosis is adapted to the climate of the Indies. An excessive heat burns up all the country;[a] they can breed but very few cattle; they are always in danger of wanting them for tillage; their black cattle multiply but indifferently;[b] they are subject to many distempers: a law of religion which preserves them, is therefore most suitable to the policy of the country.

[3]   While the meadows are scorched up, rice and pulse by the assistance of water are brought to perfection: a law of religion which permits only this kind of nourishment, must therefore be extremely useful to men in these climates.

[4]   The flesh of beasts in that country is insipid, but the milk and butter which they receive from them serves for a part of their subsistence: therefore the law which prohibits the eating and killing of cows, is in the Indies not unreasonable.

[5]   Athens contained a prodigious multitude of people, but its territory was barren. It was therefore a religious maxim with this people, that those who offered some small presents to the gods, honoured them more than those who sacrificed an ox.[c]

---

[a] See Bernier's Travels, Vol. II. Pag. 137.

[b] Edifying Letters, Coll. XII. Pag. 95.

[c] *Euripides* in *Athenaeus*, lib. ii.

THE INCONVENIENCY OF TRANSPLANTING A RELIGION FROM ONE COUNTRY TO ANOTHER [Chapter 25]

[1]   IT follows from hence, that there are frequently many inconveniences attending the transplanting a religion from one country to another.[19]

[2]   *"The hog*, says Mr. de Boulainvilliers, *must be very scarce in Arabia, where there are almost no woods, and hardly any thing fit for the nourishment of these animals; besides, the saltness of the water and food renders the people most susceptible of cutaneous disorders."* [a] This local law could not be good in other countries,[b] where the hog is almost an universal, and in some sort a necessary nourishment.

[3]   I shall here make a reflection. Sanctorius[20] has observed that pork transpires but little,[c] and that this kind of meat greatly hinders the transpiration of other food; he has found that this diminution amounts to a third.[d] Besides it is known, that the want of transpiration forms or increases the disorders of the skin. The feeding on pork ought therefore to be prohibited, in climates where the people are subject to these disorders, as in Palestine, Arabia, Ægypt, and Lybia.

THE SAME SUBJECT CONTINUED [Chapter 26]

[1]   SIR John Chardin says, that there is not a navigable river in Persia, except the Kur, which is at the extremity of the empire.[a] The ancient law of the Gebres which prohibited sailing on rivers, was not therefore attended with any inconvenience in this country, though it would have ruined the trade of another.

[a] Life of Mahomet.
[b] As in China.
[c] Medicina Statica, Sect. 3. Aphor. 22.
[d] Ibid.
[a] Travels into Persia, Vol. II.

[2]   Frequent bathings are extremely useful in hot climates. On this account they are ordained in the Mahometan law, and in the Indian religion. In the Indies it is a most meritorious act to pray to God in the running stream:[b] but how could these things be performed in other climates?

[3]   When a religion adapted to the climate of one country clashes too much with the climate of another, it cannot be there established; and whenever it has been introduced, it has been afterwards discarded. It seems to all human appearance, as if the climate had prescribed the bounds of the Christian and the Mahometan religions.[21*]

[4]   It follows from hence, that it is almost always proper for a religion to have particular doctrines, and a general worship. In laws concerning the practice of religious worship, there ought to be but few particulars: for instance, they should command mortification in general, and not a certain kind of mortification. Christianity is full of good sense: abstinence is of divine institution; but a particular kind of abstinence is ordained by a political law, and therefore may be changed.

[b] Bernier's Travels, Vol. II.

BOOK XXV: *Of Laws in Relation to the Establishment of Religion and Its External Polity*[1]

ANALYSIS

If, in Book XXIV, Montesquieu was concerned with how various religious doctrines affect the welfare of society, he is now concerned with the consequences not of dogma but rather of various external practices and policies of religions. The dominant tone is again utilitarian. After setting forth various insights with regard to both the psychology of religion (chap. 2, and see Introduction, pp. 54–56) and the natural history of both temples (chap. 3) and ministers (chap. 4), M evaluates various aspects of Church policies from the vantage point of his Erastian conviction that the welfare of the state should be the legislator's chief concern. He denounces both excessive wealth among the clergy (chap. 5) and excessively lavish religious ceremonies, particularly in democratic states thriving on frugality (chap. 7). Similarly prejudicial to the welfare of a state, according to M, are the domination of secular politics by the Church (chap. 8), intolerance among competing faiths, leading to civil strife (chap. 9), competition between the punishments meted out by the Church and those established by civil law (chap. 12), and the brutal prosecution of those accused of heresy (chap. 13).

OF RELIGIOUS SENTIMENTS [Chapter 1]

THE pious man and the atheist always talk of religion; the one speaks of what he loves, and the other of what he fears.

OF THE MOTIVES OF ATTACHMENT TO DIFFERENT
RELIGIONS [Chapter 2]

[1]   THE different religions of the world do not give to those who
profess them equal motives of attachment: this depends greatly on
the manner in which they agree with the turn of thought and
perceptions of mankind.

[2]   We are extremely addicted to idolatry, and yet have no great
inclination for the religion of idolaters: we are not very fond of
spiritual ideas, and yet are most attached to those religions which
teach us to adore a spiritual being. This proceeds from the satisfaction we find in ourselves at having been so intelligent as to chuse a
religion, which raises the deity from that baseness in which he had
been placed by others. We look upon idolatry as the religion of an
ignorant people; and the religion which has a spiritual being for its
object, as that of the most enlightened nations.[2*]

[3]   When with a doctrine that gives us the idea of a spiritual
supreme being, we can still join those of a sensible nature, and
admit them into our worship, we contract a greater attachment to
religion; because those motives which we have just mentioned, are
added to our natural inclination for the objects of sense. Thus the
Catholics, who have more of this kind of worship than the Protestants, are more attached to their religion,[a] than the Protestants are
to theirs.

[4]   When the people of Ephesus were informed that the fathers of
the council had declared they might call the holy virgin the *mother
of God*, they were transported with joy, they kissed the hands of
the bishops, they embraced their knees, the whole city resounded
with acclamations.[b]

[a] They are more zealous for its propagation.
[b] St. Cyril's Letter.

[5]   When an intellectual religion superadds a choice made by the deity, and a preference of those who profess it to those who do not, this greatly attaches us to religion. The Mahometans would not be such good Mussulmans, if on the one hand there were not idolatrous nations who make them imagine themselves the champions of the unity of God; and on the other Christians, to make them believe that they are the objects of his preference.

[6]   A religion burthened with many ceremonies, attaches us to it more strongly than that which has a fewer number.[c] We have an extreme propensity to things in which we are continually employed: witness the obstinate prejudices of the Mahometans and the Jews;[d] and the readiness with which those barbarous and savage nations change their religion, who, as they are employed intirely in hunting, or war, have but few religious ceremonies.

[7]   Men are extremely inclined to the passions of hope and fear; a religion therefore, that had neither a heaven nor a hell, could hardly please them. This is proved by the ease with which foreign religions have been established in Japan, and the zeal and fondness with which they were received.[e]

[8]   In order to raise an attachment to religion, it is necessary that it should inculcate pure morals. Men who are knaves by retail, are extremely honest in the gross; they love morality. And were I not

---

[c] This does not contradict what I have said in the last chapter of the preceding book: I here speak of the motives of attachment to religion, and there of the means of rendering it more general.

[d] This has been remarked by the whole world. See as to the Turks, the missions of the Levant; the Collection of Voyages that contributed to the establishment of an East-India Company. Vol. iii. page 201, on the Moors of Batavia, and Father Labat on the Mahometan negroes, & c.

[e] The Christian and the Indian religions; these have a hell and a paradise, which the religion of *Sintos* has not.

treating of so grave a subject, I should say that this appears remarkably evident in our theatres: we are sure of pleasing the people
by sentiments avowed by morality; we are sure of shocking them
by those it disapproves.

[9]   When external worship is attended with great magnificence, it
flatters our minds, and strongly attaches us to religion. The riches
of temples, and those of the clergy, greatly affect us. Thus even
the misery of the people, is a motive that renders them fond of that
religion, which has served as a pretext to those who were the cause
of their misery.

OF TEMPLES [Chapter 3]

[1]   ALMOST all civilized nations dwell in houses: from hence naturally arose the idea of building a house for God, in which they
might adore and seek him amidst all their hopes and fears.

[2]   In fact, nothing is more comfortable to mankind, than a place
in which they may find the deity peculiarly present, and where
they may assemble together to confess their weakness and tell their
griefs.

[3]   But this natural idea never occurred to any but such as cultivated
the land; those who had no houses for themselves were never
known to build temples.

[4]   This was the cause that made Gengiskan discover such a prodigious contempt for mosques.[a] This prince examined the
Mahometans, he approved of all their doctrines, except that of the
necessity of going to Mecca: he could not comprehend why God
might not every where be adored.[b] As the Tartars did not dwell in
houses, they could have no idea of temples.

---

[a] Entering the Mosque of Bochara, he took the Alcoran, and threw it under the
horses' feet. *Hist. of the Tartars*, pag. 273.
[b] Ibid. pag. 342.

[5]   Those people who have no temples, have but a small attachment to their own religion. This is the reason why the Tartars have in all times given so great a toleration;[c] why the barbarous nations who conquered the Roman empire, did not hesitate a moment to embrace Christianity; why the savages of America have so little fondness for their own religion; why since our missionaries have built churches in Paraguay, the natives of that country are become so zealous for ours.

OF THE MINISTERS OF RELIGION [Chapter 4]

[1]   THE first men, says Porphyry, sacrificed only vegetables. In a worship so simple, every one might be priest in his own family.

[2]   The natural desire of pleasing the deity, multiplied ceremonies. From hence it followed, that men employed in agriculture became incapable of observing them all, and of filling up the number.

[3]   Particular places were consecrated to the gods; it then became necessary that they should have ministers to take care of them; in the same manner as every citizen took care of his house and domestic affairs. Hence the people who have no priests, are commonly barbarians: such were formerly the Pedalians,[a] [3] such are still the Wolgusky.[b]

[4]   Men consecrated to the deity ought to be honoured, especially amongst people who have formed an idea of a personal purity necessary to approach the places most agreeable to the gods, and for the performance of particular ceremonies.

[5]   The worship of the gods requiring a continual application, most

[c] This disposition of mind has been communicated to the Japanese, who, as is easily proved, derive their origin from the Tartars.

[a] Lilius Giraldus, pag. 726.

[b] A people of Siberia. See the account given by Mr. *Everard* Ysbrant-Ides, in the Collection of Travels to the North, Vol. viii.

nations were led to consider the clergy as a separate body. Thus amongst the Egyptians, the Jews, and the Persians,[c] they consecrated to the deity certain families who performed and perpetuated the service. There have been even religions, which have not only estranged ecclesiastics from business, but have also taken away the embarrassments of a family; and this is the practice of the principal branch of Christianity.

[7]   By the nature of the human understanding, we love in religion every thing which carries the idea of difficulty; as in point of morality we have a speculative fondness for every thing which bears the character of severity. Celibacy has been most agreeable to those nations to whom it seemed least adapted, and with whom it might be attended with the most fatal consequences. In the southern countries of Europe, where, by the nature of the climate, the law of celibacy is more difficult to observe, it has been retained; in those of the north, where the passions are less lively, it has been banished. Moreover, in countries where there are but few inhabitants, it has been admitted; in those that are vastly populous, it has been rejected. 'Tis obvious, that these reflections relate only to the too great extension of celibacy, and not to celibacy itself.

OF THE BOUNDS WHICH THE LAWS OUGHT TO PRESCRIBE
TO THE RICHES OF THE CLERGY [Chapter 5]

[1]   As particular families may be extinct, their wealth cannot be a perpetual inheritance. The clergy is a family which cannot be extinct; wealth is therefore fixed to it for ever, and cannot go out of it.

[2]   Particular families may increase, it is necessary then that their wealth should also increase. The clergy is a family, which ought not to increase; their wealth ought then to be limited.

[c] See Mr. Hyde.

[3]   We have retained the regulations of the Levitical laws as to the possessions of the clergy, except those relating to the bounds of these possessions: indeed, amongst us we must ever be ignorant of the bound, beyond which any religious community can no longer be permitted to acquire.

[4]   These endless acquisitions appear to the people so unreasonable, that he who should speak in their defence, would be regarded as an idiot.

[5]   The civil laws find sometimes many difficulties in altering established abuses; because they are connected with things worthy of respect: in this case an indirect proceeding would be a greater proof of the wisdom of the legislator, than another which struck directly at the thing itself. Instead of prohibiting the acquisitions of the clergy, we should seek to give them a distaste for them; to leave them the right, and to take away the deed.

OF THE LUXURY OF SUPERSTITION [Chapter 7]

[1]   "*THOSE are guilty of impiety towards the gods,* says Plato, *who deny their existence, or who, while they believe it, maintain that they do not interfere with what is done below; or, in short, who think that they can easily appease them by sacrifices: three opinions equally pernicious.*" [a] Plato has here said all that the clearest light of nature has ever been able to say, in point of religion.

[2]   The magnificence of external worship has a principal connection with the constitution of the state. In good republics, they have curbed not only the luxury of vanity, but even that of superstition. They have introduced frugal laws into religion. Of this number are many of the laws of Solon, many of those of Plato on

[a] Of Laws, Book X.

funerals adopted by Cicero; and, in fine, some of the laws of Numa on sacrifices.[b]

[3]   Birds, says Cicero, and paintings begun and finished in a day, are gifts the most divine. We offer common things, says a Spartan, that we may always have it in our power to honour the gods.

[4]   The desire of man to pay his worship to the deity, is very different from the magnificence of this worship. Let us not offer our treasures to him, if we are not proud of shewing that we esteem what he would have us despise.

[5]   *"What must the gods think of the gifts of the impious,* said the admirable Plato, *when a good man would blush to receive presents from a villain?"*

[6]   Religion ought not under the pretence of gifts to draw from the people, what the necessities of the state have left them: but, as Plato says, *"The chaste and the pious ought to offer gifts, which resemble themselves."*[c]

[7]   Nor is it proper for religion to encourage expensive funerals. What is there more natural, than to take away the difference of fortune in a circumstance, and in the very moment, which equals all fortunes?

OF THE PONTIFICATE [Chapter 8]

WHEN religion has many ministers, it is natural for them to have a chief, and for a sovereign pontiff to be established. In monarchies, where the several orders of the state cannot be kept too distinct, and where all powers ought not to be lodged in the same person; it is proper that the pontificate be distinct from the empire. The same necessity is not to be met with in a despotic government, the nature of which is to unite all the different

[b] *Rogum vino ne respergito.* Law of the twelve Tables.
[c] On Laws, lib. ii.

powers in the same person. But in this case it may happen, that the prince may regard religion as he does the laws themselves, as dependent on his own will. To prevent this inconveniency, there ought to be monuments of religion, for instance, sacred books, which fix and establish it. The king of Persia is the chief of the religion; but this religion is regulated by the alcoran. The emperor of China is the sovereign pontiff; but there are books in the hands of every body, to which he himself must conform. In vain a certain emperor attempted to abolish them; they triumphed over tyranny.

OF TOLERATION IN POINT OF RELIGION [Chapter 9] [4*]

[1]   WE are here politicians, and not divines: but the divines themselves must allow that there is a great difference between tolerating and approving a religion.

[2]   When the legislator has believed it a duty to permit the exercise of many religions, it is necessary that it should inforce also a toleration amongst these religions themselves. It is a principle that every religion which is persecuted, becomes itself persecuting: for as soon as by some accidental turn it arises from persecution, it attacks the religion which persecuted it; not as a religion, but as a tyranny.

[3]   It is necessary then that the laws require from the several religions, not only that they shall not embroil the state, but that they shall not raise disturbances amongst themselves. A citizen does not fulfil the laws, by not disturbing the government; it is requisite, that he should not trouble any citizen whomsoever.

THE SAME SUBJECT CONTINUED [Chapter 10] [4*]

[1]   As there are scarce any but persecuting religions that have an extraordinary zeal for being established in other places (because a

religion that can tolerate others seldom thinks of its own propagation), it must therefore be a very good civil law, when the state is already satisfied with the established religion, not to suffer the establishment of another.

[2]   This is then a fundamental principle of the political laws of religion: That when the state is at liberty to receive or to reject a new religion, it ought to be rejected; when it is received, it ought to be tolerated.

OF CHANGING A RELIGION [Chapter 11]

[1]   A PRINCE who undertakes to destroy or to change the established religion of his kingdom, must greatly expose himself. If his government is despotic, he runs the risk of seeing a revolution, which from some kind of tyranny or other is never a new thing in such states. The cause of this revolution is, that a state cannot change its religion, manners, and customs in an instant, and with the same rapidity as the prince publishes the ordinance which establishes a new religion.

[2]   Besides, the ancient religion is connected with the constitution of the kingdom, and the new one is not: the former agrees with the climate, and very often the new one is opposite to it. Moreover, the citizens, disgusted with their laws, look upon the government already established with contempt; they conceive a jealousy against the two religions, instead of a firm belief in one; and in a word, these revolutions give the state, at least for some time, both bad citizens, and bad believers.

OF PENAL LAWS [Chapter 12]

[1]   PENAL laws ought to be avoided, in respect to religion; they imprint fear, it is true; but as religion has also penal laws which

inspire fear, the one is effaced by the other: and between these two different kinds of fear, the mind becomes hardened.

[2]   The threatenings of religion are so terrible, and its promises so great, that when they actuate the mind, whatever efforts the magistrates may use to oblige us to renounce it, they seem to leave us nothing when they deprive us of the exercise of our religion; and to bereave us of nothing, when we are freely allowed to profess it.

[3]   It is not therefore in filling the soul with this great object, in hastening its approach to that important moment in which it ought to be of the highest importance, that they can succeed in detaching the soul from it. A more certain way is to attack religion by favours, by the conveniencies of life, by hopes of fortune; not by that which revives, but by that which extinguishes, the sense of its duty; not by that which shocks it, but by that which throws it into indifference, at the time when other passions actuate our minds, and those which religion inspires are hushed into silence. A general rule in changing a religion; the invitations should be much stronger than the penalties.

[4]   The temper of the human mind has appeared even in the nature of the punishments they have employed. If we take a survey of the persecutions in Japan,[a] we shall find that they were more shocked at cruel torments than at long sufferings, which rather weary than affright; which are the more difficult to surmount from their appearing less difficult.

[5]   In a word, history sufficiently informs us, that penal laws have never had any other effect but to destroy.

[a] In the Collection of Voyages that contributed to the establishment of an East India Company, Vol. 5.

A MOST HUMBLE REMONSTRANCE TO THE INQUISITORS OF SPAIN AND PORTUGAL [Chapter 13][5]

[1]   A Jewess of ten years of age, who was burnt at Lisbon at the last *Auto-da-fe*, gave occasion to the following little piece; the most idle, I believe, that ever was wrote. When we attempt to prove things so evident, we are sure never to convince.

[2]   The author declares, that though a Jew, he has a respect for the Christian religion; and that he should be glad to take away from the princes who are not Christians, a plausible pretence for persecuting this religion.

[3]   "You complain," says he to the inquisitors, "that the emperor of Japan caused all the Christians in his dominions to be burnt by a slow fire. But he will answer, we treat you who do not believe like us, as you yourselves treat those who do not believe like you: you can only complain of your weakness, which has hindered you from exterminating us, and which has enabled us to exterminate you.

[4]   "But it must be confessed, that you are much more cruel than this emperor. You put us to death, who believe only what you believe, because we do not believe *all* that you believe. We follow a religion, which you yourselves know to have been formerly dear to God. We think that God loves it still, and you think that he loves it no more: and because you judge thus, you make those suffer by sword and fire, who hold an error so pardonable as to believe that God still loves what he once loved.[a]

[5]   "If you are cruel to us, you are much more so to our children; you cause them to be burnt, because they follow the inspirations

---

[a] The source of the blindness of the Jews is, their not perceiving that the oeconomy of the gospel is in the order of the decrees of God; and that it is in this light a consequence of his immutability itself.

given them by those whom the law of nature, and the laws of all nations teach them to regard as gods.

[6]   "You deprive yourselves of the advantage you have over the Mahometans, with respect to the manner in which their religion was established. When they boast of the number of their believers, you tell them that they have obtained them by violence, and that they have extended their religion by the sword: why then do you establish yours by fire?

[7]   "When you would bring us over to you, we object a source from which you glory to descend. You reply to us, that though your religion is new, it is divine; and you prove it from its growing amidst the persecution of Pagans, and when watered by the blood of your martyrs: but at present you play the part of the Dioclesians, and make us take yours.

[8]   "We conjure you, not by the mighty God whom both you and we serve, but by that Christ who, you tell us, took upon him a human form, to propose himself for an example for you to follow; we conjure you to behave to us, as he himself would behave was he upon earth. You would have us be Christians, and you will not be so yourselves.

[9]   "But if you will not be Christians, be at least men: treat us as you would, if having only the weak light of justice which nature bestows, you had not a religion to conduct, and a revelation to enlighten you.

[10]   "If heaven has had so great a love for you, as to make you see the truth, you have received a great favour: but is it for children who have received the inheritance of their father, to hate those who have not?

[11]   "If you have this truth, hide it not from us by the manner in which you propose it. The characteristic of truth is its triumph

over hearts and minds, and not that impotency which you confess, when you would force us to receive it by your tortures.

[12]   "If you were wise, you would not put us to death for no other reason, but because we are unwilling to deceive you. If your Christ is the son of God, we hope he will reward us for being so unwilling to profane his mysteries; and we believe, that the God whom both you and we serve, will not punish us for having suffered death for a religion which he formerly gave us, only because we believe that he still continues to give it.

[13]   "You live in an age in which the light of nature shines more bright than it has ever done; in which philosophy has enlightened human understandings; in which the morality of your gospel has been more known; in which the respective rights of mankind, with regard to each other, and the empire which one conscience has over another, are best understood. If you do not therefore shake off your ancient prejudices, which whilst unregarded, mingle with your passions, it must be confessed, that you are incorrigible, incapable of any degree of light, or instruction; and a nation must be very unhappy that gives authority to such men.

[14]   "Would you have us frankly tell you our thoughts? You consider us rather as your enemies, than as the enemies of your religion: for if you loved your religion, you would not suffer it to be corrupted by such gross ignorance.

[15]   "It is necessary that we should advertise you of one thing, that is, if any one in times to come shall dare to assert, that in the age in which we live the people of Europe were civilized, you will be cited to prove that they were barbarians; and the idea they will have of you, will be such as will dishonour your age, and spread hatred over all your contemporaries."

OF THE PROPAGATION OF RELIGION [Chapter 15]

[1]   ALL the people of the east, except the Mahometans, believe all religions in themselves indifferent. They fear the establishment of another religion, not otherwise than as a change in government. Amongst the Japanese, where there are many sects, and where the state has had for so long a time an ecclesiastic superior, they never dispute on religion.[a] It is the same with the people of Siam.[b] The Calmucks do more, they make it a point of conscience to tolerate every species of religion:[c] at Calicut[6] it is a maxim of the state, that every religion is good.[d]

[2]   But it does not follow from hence, that a religion brought from a far distant country, and quite different in climate, laws, manners, and customs, will have all the success to which its holiness might entitle it. This is more particularly true in great despotic empires: here strangers are tolerated at first, because there is no attention given to what does not seem to strike at the authority of the prince: they are entirely immersed in ignorance. An European may render himself agreeable, by the knowledge he communicates: this is very well in the beginning. But as soon as he has any success, when disputes arise, when men who have some interest become informed of it, as their empire by its very nature, above all things requires tranquillity, and as the least disturbance may overturn it, they at first proscribe the new religion and those who preach it; disputes between the preachers breaking out, they begin to entertain a distaste for a religion on which even those who propose it are not agreed.

[a] See Kempfer.
[b] Forbin's Memoirs.
[c] History of the Tartars, part 5.
[d] Pirard's Travels, chap. 27.

BOOK XXVI: *Of Laws in Relation to the Order of Things Which They Determine*

ANALYSIS

Book XXVI concludes Part Five of The Spirit of Laws, *according to Montesquieu's plan for the work. Its subject matter links it to both Books I and XXIX, and it should perhaps have been placed elsewhere in the work. The purpose of Book XXVI is to identify and define the distinct spheres of natural, divine, canon, political, international, civil, and domestic law. M's basic premise is that each of these types of law must be allowed its proper sphere of influence so as "not to throw into confusion those principles which should govern mankind" (chap. 1). If a particular action is judged by an inappropriate type of law, injustice will likely result. Property, for example, is protected by civil law. Hence governments invoking political law to deprive citizens of their property would be guilty of tyranny (chap. 15). It would be similarly unjust, to cite another example, to convict of murder a slave who takes the life of a freeman in self-defense, since self-defense is governed not by civil law but by the laws of nature (chap. 3, par. [1]). Only in rare instances, M asserts, where individuals have forfeited the rights of nature, should civil laws be allowed precedence over the laws of nature (chap. 5).*

In passages reminiscent of the utilitarian tone of Book XXIV, Montesquieu also asserts that laws of religion ought not to conflict with the laws of nature. Excessive fasting, for example, might prove contrary to self-defense and so weaken a nation that it could not properly defend itself (chap. 7). Speaking generally, M asserts that, whereas religious laws may benefit the individuals who adhere to them, civil laws often benefit the society at large (chap. 9).

IDEA OF THIS BOOK [Chapter 1]

[1]   MEN are governed by several kinds of laws; by the law of nature; by the divine law, which is that of religion; by ecclesiastical, otherwise called canon law, which is that of religious polity; by the law of nations, which may be considered as the civil law of the universe, in which sense every nation is a citizen; by the general political law, whose object is that human wisdom which has been the foundation of all societies; by the law of conquest founded on this, that one nation has been willing and able, or has had a right to offer violence to another; by the civil law of every society, by which a citizen may defend his possessions and his life, against the attacks of any other citizen; in fine, by domestic law, which proceeds from a society's being divided into several families, all which have need of a particular government.

[2]   There are therefore different orders of laws, and the sublimity of human reason consists in perfectly knowing to which of these orders the things that are to be determined ought to have a principal relation, and not to throw into confusion those principles which should govern mankind.

OF LAWS DIVINE AND HUMAN [Chapter 2]

[1]   WE ought not to decide by the divine laws, what should be decided by human laws; nor determine by human, what should be determined by divine laws.

[2]   These two sorts of laws differ in their origin, in their object, and in their nature.

[3]   It is universally acknowledged, that human laws are in their own nature different from those of religion, and this is an important principle: but this principle is itself subject to others, which must be enquired after.

[4]   1. It is in the nature of human laws to be subject to all the accidents which can happen, and to vary in proportion as the will of man changes: on the contrary, by the nature of the laws of religion, they are never to vary. Human laws appoint for the good; those of religion for the better: the good may have another object, because there are many kinds of good: but the better is but one, it cannot therefore change. We may change laws, because they are reputed no more than good; but the institutions of religion are always supposed to be the best.

[5]   2. There are kingdoms, in which the laws are of no value, as they depend only on the capricious and fickle humour of the sovereign. If in these kingdoms the laws of religion were of the same nature as the human laws, the laws of religion too would be of no value. It is however necessary to the society, that it should have something fixed; and 'tis religion that has this stability.

[6]   3. The influence of religion proceeds from its being believed; that of human laws, from their being feared. Antiquity suits with religion, because we have frequently a firmer belief of things in proportion to their distance: for we have no ideas annexed to them drawn from those times, which can contradict them. Human laws, on the contrary, receive advantage from their novelty, which implies the actual and particular attention of the legislator to put them in execution.

OF CIVIL LAWS CONTRARY TO THE LAW OF NATURE [Chapter 3]

[1]   IF a slave, says Plato, defends himself, and kills a freeman, he ought to be treated as a parricide.[a] This is a civil law which punishes self-defence, tho' dictated by nature.

[2]   The law of Henry VIII which condemned a man, without

---

[a] Lib. IX. on Laws.

being confronted by witnesses, was contrary to self-defence. In fact, in order to pass sentence of condemnation, it is necessary that the witnesses should know whether the man against whom they make their deposition is he whom they accuse, and that this man be at liberty to say, I am not the person you mean.

[3]   The law passed under the same reign, which condemned every woman who having carried on a criminal commerce did not declare it to the king before her marriage, violated the regard due to natural modesty. It is as unreasonable to oblige a woman to make this declaration, as to oblige a man not to attempt the defence of his own life.

[4]   The law of Henry II which condemned the woman to death who lost her child, in case she did not make known her pregnancy to the magistrate, was not less contrary to self-defence. It would have been sufficient to oblige her to inform one of her nearest relations, who might watch over the preservation of the infant.[1*]

[6]   There has been much talk of a law in England, which permitted girls seven years old to chuse a husband.[b] This law was shocking two ways, it had no regard to the time when nature gives maturity to the understanding, nor to the time when she gives maturity to the body.

CASES IN WHICH WE MAY JUDGE BY THE PRINCIPLES
OF THE CIVIL LAW IN LIMITING THE PRINCIPLES
OF THE LAW OF NATURE [Chapter 5]

[1]   An Athenian law obliged children to provide for their fathers, when fallen into poverty;[a] it excepted those who were born of a

---

[b] Mr. Bayle, in his Criticism on the History of Calvinism speaks of this law, pag. 263.

[a] Under pain of infamy, another under pain of imprisonment.

courtezan,[b] those whose chastity had been infamously prostituted by their father, and those to whom he had not given any means of gaining a livelihood.[c]

[2]   The law considered that in the first case the father being uncertain, he had rendered the natural obligation precarious; that in the second, he had sullied the life he had given, and done the greatest injury he could do to his children in depriving them of their reputation; that in the third, he had rendered insupportable a life which had no means of subsistence. The law suspended the natural obligation of children, because the father had violated his.

THAT THE ORDER OF SUCCESSION OR INHERITANCE
DEPENDS ON THE PRINCIPLES OF POLITICAL AND CIVIL
LAW, AND NOT ON THOSE OF THE LAW OF NATURE [Chapter 6]

[2]   The law of nature ordains, that fathers shall provide for their children; but it does not oblige them to make them their heirs. The division of property, the laws of this division, the succession after the death of the person who has had this division, can be regulated only by the community, and consequently by political and civil laws.

[3]   True it is, that a political or civil order frequently demands that children should succeed to their father's estate; but it does not always make this necessary.

[5]   It was regulated in some of the Dynasties of China, that the brothers of the emperor should succeed to the throne, and that the children should not.

[6]   According to the custom of Numidia,[a] Delsace, brother of Gela, succeeded to the kingdom; not Massinissa, his son.

[b] Plutarch's life of Solon.

[c] Plutarch life of Solon, and *Gallienus* in exhort. ad art. c. 8.

[a] Livy Decad. iii. Lib. 9.

[8]   In countries where polygamy is established, the prince has
many children; the number of them is much greater in some of
these countries than in others. There are states, where it is impossible for the people to maintain the children of the king:[b] they
might therefore make it a law, that the crown shall devolve, not on
the king's children, but on those of his sister.

[11]   A general maxim: 'Tis an obligation of the law of nature, to
provide for our children; but to make them our successors, is an
obligation of the civil or political law. From hence are derived the
different regulations, with respect to bastards, in the different
countries of the world; these are according to the civil or political
laws of each country.

THAT WE OUGHT NOT TO DECIDE BY THE PRECEPTS OF RELIGION, WHAT BELONGS ONLY TO THE LAW OF NATURE [Chapter 7]

[1]   THE Abyssines have a most severe lent of fifty days, which
weakens them to such a degree, that for a long time they are
incapable of business: the Turks do not fail to attack them after
their lent.[a] Religion ought, in favour of the natural right of
self-defence, to set bounds to these customs.

[2]   The Jews were obliged to keep the sabbath; but it was an instance of great stupidity in this nation, not to defend themselves
when their enemies chose to attack them on this day. Cambyses
laying siege to Pelusium, set in the first rank a great number of
those animals, which the Ægyptians regarded as sacred; the consequence was, that the soldiers of the garrison durst not molest

---

[b] As at Lovengo in Africa. See the Collection of Voyages that contributed to the
establishment of an East-India Company. Vol. IV. Part. I. Pag. 114.

[a] Collection of Voyages that contributed to the establishment of an East-India Company, Vol. IV. pag. 35 & 103.

them. Who does not see that self-defence is a duty superior to every precept?

THAT THINGS WHICH OUGHT TO BE REGULATED BY THE PRINCIPLES OF CIVIL LAW CAN SELDOM BE REGULATED BY THOSE OF RELIGION [Chapter 9]

[1]   THE laws of religion have a greater sublimity, the civil laws a greater extent.

[2]   The laws of perfection drawn from religion have more in view the goodness of the person that observes them, than of the society in which they are observed: the civil laws, on the contrary, have more in view the moral goodness of men in general, than that of individuals.

[3]   Thus, venerable as those ideas are which immediately spring from religion, they ought not always to serve as a first principle to the civil laws; because these have another, the general welfare of society.

IN WHAT CASE WE OUGHT TO FOLLOW THE CIVIL LAW WHICH PERMITS, AND NOT THE LAW OF RELIGION WHICH FORBIDS [Chapter 10]

WHEN a religion which prohibits polygamy is introduced into a country where it is permitted, we cannot believe, (speaking only as politicans) that the laws of the country ought to suffer a man who has many wives to embrace this religion; unless the magistrate or the husband should indemnify them, by restoring them some way or other to their civil state. Without this their condition would be deplorable; no sooner would they obey the laws, than they would find themselves deprived of the greatest advantages of society.

IN WHAT CASES, WITH REGARD TO MARRIAGES, WE
OUGHT TO FOLLOW THE LAWS OF RELIGION, AND IN
WHAT CASES WE SHOULD FOLLOW THE CIVIL LAWS
[Chapter 13]

[1]   IT has happened in all ages and countries, that religion has been
blended with marriages. When certain things have been considered
as impure or unlawful, and were nevertheless become necessary,
they were obliged to call in religion, to legitimate in the one case,
and to reprove in others.

[2]   On the other hand, as marriage is of all human actions that in
which society is most interested, it became proper that this should
be regulated by the civil laws.

[3]   Every thing which relates to the nature of marriage, its form,
the manner of contracting it, the fruitfulness it occasions, a fruitfulness that has made all nations consider it as the object of a
particular benediction; which, not being always annexed to it,
depended on certain superior graces: all this, I say, is within the
ressort of religion.

[4]   The consequences of this union, with regard to property, the
reciprocal advantages, every thing which has a relation to the new
family, to that from which it sprung, to that which is expected to
arise; all this relates to the civil laws.

[5]   As one of the great objects of marriage is to take away that
uncertainty which attends unlawful conjunctions, religion here
stamps its seal, and the civil laws join theirs to it; to the end that it
may be as authentic as possible. Thus, besides the conditions
required by religion to make a marriage valid, the civil laws may
still exact others.

[6]   The civil laws receive this power from their being additional
obligations, and not contradictory ones. The law of religion insists

upon certain ceremonies, the civil laws on the consent of fathers, in this case they demand something more than that of religion, but they demand nothing contrary to it.

[7]   It follows from hence, that the religious law must decide whether the bond be indissoluble, or not; for if the laws of religion had made the bond indissoluble, and the civil law had declared it might be broken, they would be contradictory to each other.

IN WHAT INSTANCES MARRIAGES BETWEEN RELATIONS
SHOULD BE REGULATED BY THE LAWS OF NATURE;
AND IN WHAT INSTANCES BY THE CIVIL LAWS
[Chapter 14]

[1]   WITH regard to the prohibition of marriage between relations, it is a thing extremely delicate, to fix exactly the point at which the laws of nature stop, and where the civil laws begin. For this purpose we must establish some principles.

[2]   The marriage of the son with the mother confounds the state of things: the son ought to have an unlimited respect to his mother, the wife owes an unlimited respect to her husband; therefore the marriage of the mother to her son, would subvert the natural state of both.

[3]   Besides, nature has forwarded in women the time in which they are able to have children, but has retarded it in men; and, for the same reason, women sooner lose this ability, and men later. If the marriage between the mother and the son was permitted, it would almost always be the case, that when the husband was capable of entering into the views of nature, the wife would be incapable.

[4]   The marriage between the father and the daughter is contrary to nature, as well as the other; but it is less contrary, because it has not these two obstacles. Thus the Tartars, who may marry their

daughters,[a] never marry their mothers, as we see in the accounts we have of that nation.[b]

[5]   It has ever been the natural duty of fathers to watch over the chastity of their children. Intrusted with the care of their education, they are obliged to preserve the body in the greatest perfection, and the mind from the least corruption; to encourage whatever has a tendency to inspire them with virtuous desires, and to nourish a becoming tenderness. Fathers, always employed in preserving the morals of their children, must have a natural aversion to every thing that can render them corrupt. Marriage, you will say, is not a corruption: but before marriage they must speak, they must make their persons beloved, they must seduce: it is this seduction which ought to inspire us with horror.

[8]   These principles are so strong and so natural, that they have had their influence almost all over the earth, independently of any communication. It was not the Romans who taught the inhabitants of Formosa, that the marriage of relations of the fourth degree was incestuous:[c] it was not the Romans that communicated this sentiment to the Arabs;[d] it was not they who taught it to the inhabitants of the Maldivian islands.[e]

[9]   But if some nations have not rejected marriages between fathers and children, sisters and brothers; we have seen in the first book, that intelligent beings do not always follow the law of nature.

---

[a] This law is very ancient amongst them. Attila, says Priscus in his embassy, stopt in a certain place to marry Esca his daughter. *A thing permitted*, he adds, *by the laws of the Scythians*, pag. 22.

[b] Hist. of the Tartars, Part iii. Pag. 236.

[c] Collection of Voyages to the Indies, Vol. 5. Part I. An account of the state of the isle of Formosa.

[d] Alcoran, chap. *of women*.

[e] See Francis Pirard.

Who could have imagined it? Religious ideas have frequently made men fall into these mistakes.[2] If the Assyrians and the Persians married their mothers, the first were influenced by a religious respect for Semiramis, and the second did it because the religion of Zoroaster gave a preference to these marriages.[f] If the Ægyptians married their sisters, it proceeded from the wildness of the Ægyptian religion, which consecrated these marriages in honour of Isis. As the spirit of religion leads us to attempt whatever is great and difficult, we cannot infer that a thing is natural from its being consecrated by a false religion.

THAT WE SHOULD NOT REGULATE BY THE PRINCIPLES OF POLITICAL LAW THOSE THINGS WHICH DEPEND ON THE PRINCIPLES OF CIVIL LAWS [Chapter 15]

[1]   As men have given up their natural independence to live under political laws, they have given up the natural participation of property to live under civil laws.

[2]   By the first, they acquired liberty; by the second, property. We ought not to decide by the laws of liberty, which, as we have already said, is only the government of the community, what ought to be decided by the laws concerning property. 'Tis a paralogism to say, that the good of the individual ought to give way to that of the public: this can never take place, but when the government of the community, or, in other words, the liberty of the subject is concerned; this does not affect those cases which relate to private property, because the public good consists in every one's having that property which was given him by the civil laws, invariably preserved.

---

[f] They were considered as more honourable. See Philo *de specialibus legib. quae pertinent ad praecepta Decalogi*. Paris 1640. pag. 778.

[4]   Let us therefore lay down as a certain maxim, that whenever the
public good happens to be the matter in question, it is never for the
advantage of the public to deprive an individual of his property, or
even to retrench the least part of it by a law, or a political regulation. In this case we should follow the rigour of the civil law,
which is the *Palladium* of property.

[5]   Thus when the public has occasion for the estate of an individual, it ought never to act by the rigour of political law; it is here
that the civil law ought to triumph, who with the eyes of a mother
regards every individual as the whole community.

[6]   If the political magistrate would erect a public edifice, or make a
new road, he must indemnify those who are injured by it, the
public is in this respect like an individual, who treats with an
individual. It is full enough, that it can oblige a citizen to sell his
inheritance, and that it can strip him of this great privilege which
he holds from the civil law, the not being forced to alienate his
possessions.

THAT WE OUGHT NOT TO DECIDE THOSE THINGS BY THE
CIVIL LAW, WHICH OUGHT TO BE DECIDED BY
DOMESTIC LAWS [Chapter 19]

[1]   THE law of the Visigoths enjoins, that the slaves of the house
shall be obliged to bind the man and woman they surprise in
adultery, and to present them to the husband and to the judge: [a] a
terrible law, which puts into the hands of such mean persons the
care of public, domestic, and private vengeance!

[2]   This law can be no where proper but in the seraglios of the east,
where the slave who has charge of the inclosure, is deemed an
accomplice upon the discovery of the least infidelity. He seizes the

[a] Law of the Visigoths, lib. iii. tit. 4. ¶6.

criminals, not so much with a view to bring them to justice, as to do justice to himself, and to obtain a scrutiny into the circumstances of the action, in order to remove the suspicion of his negligence.

[3]   But, in countries where women are not guarded, it is ridiculous to subject those who govern the family, to the inquisition of their slaves.

[4]   This inquisition may, in certain cases, be at the most a particular domestic regulation, but never a civil law.

THAT WE OUGHT NOT TO DECIDE BY THE PRINCIPLES OF THE CIVIL LAWS, THOSE THINGS WHICH BELONG TO THE LAW OF NATIONS [Chapter 20]

[1]   LIBERTY consists principally in not being forced to do a thing where the laws do not oblige: People are in this state, only as they are governed by civil laws, and because they live under those civil laws, they are free.

[2]   It follows from hence, that princes who live not amongst themselves under civil laws, are not free; they are governed by force; they may continually force, or be forced. From hence it follows, that treaties made by force, are as obligatory as those made by free consent. When we who live under civil laws, are, contrary to law, constrained to enter into a contract, we may, by the assistance of the law, recover from the effects of violence: But a prince, who is always in that state in which he forces or is forced, cannot complain of a treaty which he has been obliged by violence to enter into. This would be to complain of his natural state; it would seem as if he would be a prince with respect to other princes, and as if other princes should be subjects with respect to him; that is, it would be contrary to the nature of things.

THAT WE SHOULD NOT DECIDE BY POLITICAL LAWS, THINGS WHICH BELONG TO THE LAW OF NATIONS
[Chapter 21]

[1]   POLITICAL laws demand that every man be subject to the criminal and civil courts of the Country where he resides, and to the censure of the sovereign.

[2]   The law of nations requires, that princes shall send ambassadors; and a reason drawn from the nature of things does not permit these ambassadors to depend either on the sovereign to whom they are sent, or on his tribunals. They are the voice of the prince who sends them, and this voice ought to be free; no obstacle should hinder the execution of their office; they may frequently offend, because they speak for a man entirely independent; they might charge them with crimes, if they were liable to be punished for crimes; if they could be arrested for debts, these might be forged. Thus a prince who has naturally a bold and enterprising spirit, would speak by the mouth of a man who had every thing to fear. We must then be guided with respect to ambassadors, by reasons drawn from the law of nations, and not by those derived from political law. But if they make an ill use of their representative character, a stop may be put to it, by sending them back. They may even be accused before their master, who by this means becomes either their judge or their accomplice.

THE UNHAPPY STATE OF YNCA ATHUALPA [Chapter 22]

THE principles we have just been establishing were cruelly violated by the Spaniards. Ynca Athualpa could not be tried by the law of nations;[a] they tried him by political and civil laws; they accused him for putting to death some of his own subjects, for

[a] See the Ynca *Garcilasso de la Vega*.

having many wives, &c. and to fill up the measure of their stupidity, they condemned him, not by the political and civil laws of his own country, but by the political and civil laws of theirs.

THAT WHEN BY SOME CIRCUMSTANCE THE POLITICAL
LAW BECOMES DESTRUCTIVE TO THE STATE, WE OUGHT
TO DECIDE BY SUCH A POLITICAL LAW AS WILL PRESERVE
IT, WHICH SOMETIMES BECOMES A LAW OF NATIONS
[Chapter 23]

[1]   WHEN that political law which has established in the kingdom a certain order of Succession, becomes destructive to the body politic for whose sake it was established, there is not the least room to doubt but another political law may be made to change this order; and so far would this law be from opposing the first, it would in the main be entirely conformable to it, since both would depend on this principle, that, THE SAFETY OF THE PEOPLE IS THE SUPREME LAW.

[2]   I have said, that a great kingdom becoming accessory to another, is itself weakened, and even weakens the principal.

[3]   It follows from hence, that if a great state has for its heir the possessor of a great state, the first may reasonably exclude him, because a change in the order of succession must be of service to both states.

[4]   But if a nation may exclude, it may with greater reason be allowed a right to oblige the prince to resign. If the people fear that a certain marriage will be attended with no other consequences, but such as will rob the nation of its independence, or dismember some of its provinces, it may very justly oblige both the contractors and their descendants to resign all right over them; while he who resigns, and those to whose prejudice he resigns, have the less reason to complain, as the state might originally have made a law to exclude them.

THAT THE REGULATIONS OF THE POLICE ARE OF A DIFFERENT CLASS FROM OTHER CIVIL LAWS [Chapter 24]

[2]   We ought not to confound a flagrant violation of the laws, with a simple breach of the *Police*; these things are of a different order.

[3]   From hence it follows, that the laws of that Italian republic[a] where bearing fire arms is punished as a capital crime, and where it is not more fatal to make an ill use of them than to carry them, is not agreeable to the nature of things.

[4]   It follows moreover, that the applauded action of that Emperor, who caused a baker to be empaled whom he had found guilty of a fraud, was the action of a sultan, who knew not how to be just, without committing an outrage on justice.

[a] Venice.

❧Part Six

The sixth and final Part of *The Spirit of Laws*, according to Montesquieu's organizational plan, consists of one Book on Roman laws of inheritance (Book XXVII), three Books on the development of civil and feudal law among the Franks (Books XXVIII, XXX, and XXXI), and one Book on how laws ought to be composed (Book XXIX). Had it not been for the composition in 1748 of Books XXX and XXXI, Book XXIX would have ended the work.

BOOK XXIX: *Of the Manner of Composing Laws*

ANALYSIS

Book XXIX contains important advice for legislators. Convinced that political good, like moral good, lies between two extremes, Montesquieu offers the general counsel that legislators ought to act moderately (chap. 1). More concrete suggestions are presented in chapter 16, where M asserts that laws ought to be concise and readily intelligible so that they mean the same thing to whoever reads them (chap. 16, par. [2]). Unnecessary alterations in existing laws, as well as laws that are easily eluded and laws that are actually unnecessary, ought to be avoided, since they weaken the authority of the legal system in general. The legislator's rule of thumb should be that "every law ought to have its effect, and no one should be . . . suffered to deviate from it by a particular convention" (chap. 16, [20]).

Book XXIX also contains an important chapter (18) warning legislators not to seek excessive uniformity in a legal system. Petty minds, Montesquieu suggests, are sometimes stricken with the idea of uprooting the existing nature of things in order to blueprint a new social and political order where exceptions have no place. "But is this always right?" M asks. There is often, he believes, a necessity for differences. Where one law cannot be made to apply to all men within a nation, then it is better to tolerate diversity than to impose a degree of uniformity that might be psychologically pleasing but harmful to those whose situation does not fit the mathematicized formulae the legislator has devised.

OF THE SPIRIT OF THE LEGISLATOR [Chapter 1][1]

[1]   I say it, and methinks I have undertaken this work with no other view than to prove it; the spirit of moderation ought to be that of the legislator; political, like moral evil, lying always between two extremes. Let us produce an example.

[2]   The set forms of justice are necessary to liberty; but the number of them might be so great as to be contrary to the end of the very laws that established them;[2] processes would have no end; property would be uncertain; the goods of one of the parties would be adjudged to the other without examining, or they would both be ruined by examining too much.

[3]   The subjects would lose both their liberty and security; the accusers would no longer have any means to convict, nor the accused to justify themselves.

THE SAME SUBJECT CONTINUED [Chapter 2]

Cecilius, in Aulus Gellius,[a] speaking of the law of the twelve tables, which permitted the creditor to cut the insolvent debtor to pieces, justifies it even by its cruelty, which hindered people from borrowing beyond their abilities.[b] Shall then the cruellest laws be the best? Shall goodness consist in excess, and all the relations of things be destroyed?

THAT THE LAWS WHICH SEEM TO DEVIATE FROM
THE VIEWS OF THE LEGISLATOR ARE FREQUENTLY
AGREEABLE TO THEM [Chapter 3]

[1]   The law of Solon, which declared those persons infamous who

---

[a] Book XX. Chap. I.

[b] Cecilius says, that he never saw nor read of an instance, in which this punishment had been inflicted; but 'tis likely, that no such punishment was ever established; the opinion of some civilians, that the law of the twelve tables meant only the division of the money arising from the sale of the debtor, seems very probable.

espoused no side in an insurrection, seemed very extraordinary; but we ought to consider the circumstances in which Greece was at that time. It was divided into very small states: and there was reason to apprehend, lest in a republic, torn by intestine divisions, the soberest part should keep retired, and things by this means should be carried to extremity.

[2]   In the seditions raised in those petty states, the bulk of the citizens either made or engaged in the quarrel. In our large monarchies, parties are formed by a few, and the people chuse to live quiet. In the latter case it is natural to call back the seditious to the bulk of the citizens, and not these to the seditious: in the other, it is necessary to oblige the small number of prudent people to enter among the seditious: 'tis thus the fermentation of one liquor may be stopt by a single drop of another.

THAT THE GREEK AND ROMAN LAWS PUNISHED SUICIDE, BUT NOT THRO' THE SAME MOTIVE [Chapter 9]

[1]   A MAN, says Plato, who has killed one nearly related to him, that is himself, not by an order of the magistrate, nor to avoid ignominy, but thro' faint-heartedness, shall be punished.[a] The Roman law punished this action when it was not committed thro' faint-heartedness, thro' weariness of life, thro' impatience in pain, but thro' a criminal despair. The Roman law acquitted where the Greek condemned, and condemned where the other acquitted.

[3]   During the time of the republic, there was no law at Rome against suicides: this action is always considered by their historians in a favourable light, and we never meet with any punishment inflicted upon those who committed it.

[4]   Under the first emperors, the great families of Rome were

[a] Book IX of laws.

continually destroyed by criminal prosecutions. The custom was then introduced of preventing judgment by a voluntary death. In this they found a great advantage: they had an honourable interment, and their wills were executed; because there was no law against suicides.[b] But when the emperors became as avaricious as cruel, they deprived those who destroyed themselves of the means of preserving their estates, by rendering it criminal for a person to make away with himself thro' a criminal remorse.[3*]

THAT WE MUST NOT SEPARATE THE LAWS FROM THE END FOR WHICH THEY WERE MADE: OF THE ROMAN LAWS ON THEFT [Chapter 13]

[7]   As the civil laws depend on the political institutions, because they are made for the same society; whenever there is a design of adopting the civil law of another nation, it would be proper to examine before-hand, whether they have both the same institutions, and the same political law.

[8]   Thus when the Cretan laws on theft were adopted by the Lacedemonians, as their constitution and government were adopted at the same time, these laws were equally reasonable in both nations. But when they were carried from Lacedemonia to Rome, as they did not find there the same constitution, they were always thought strange, and had no manner of connexion with the other civil laws of the Romans.

THAT WE MUST NOT SEPARATE THE LAWS FROM THE CIRCUMSTANCES IN WHICH THEY WERE MADE [Chapter 14]

[2]   The Roman laws ordained that physicians should be punished

[b] *Eorum qui de se statuebant humabantur corpora, manebant testamenta, pretium festinandi.* Tacit.

for neglect or unskilfulness.[a] In those cases, if the physician was a person of any fortune or rank, he was only condemned to *deportation*; but if he was of a low condition, he was put to death. By our laws it is otherwise. The Roman laws were not made under the same circumstances as ours: at Rome every ignorant pretender intermeddled with physic; but amongst us, physicians are obliged to go thro' a regular course of study, and to take their degrees; for which reason they are supposed to understand their art.

THINGS TO BE OBSERVED IN THE COMPOSING OF LAWS [Chapter 16]

[1]   THOSE who have a genius sufficient to enable them to give laws to their own, or to another nation, ought to be particularly attentive to the manner of forming them.

[2]   The style ought to be concise.

[3]   The style should also be plain and simple, a direct expression being always better understood than an indirect one.

[4]   'Tis an essential article that the words of the laws should excite in every body the same ideas.

[6]   When the law wants to fix a set rate upon things, it should avoid as much as possible the valuing it in money. The value of money changes from a thousand causes, and the same denomination continues without the same thing. Every one knows the story of that impudent fellow at Rome, who used to give those he met a box on the ear, and afterwards tendered them the five and twenty pence of the law of the twelve tables.[a]

[11]   The laws ought not to be subtle; they are designated for people of common understanding, not as an art of logic, but as the plain reason of a father of a family.

---

[a] The Cornelion law *de Sicariis*, Institut. lib. 4. tit. 3 de lege Aquilia, ¶7.
[a] Aulus Gellius, book 20. Chap. I.

[12]   When there is no necessity for exceptions and limitations in a law, it is much better to omit them: details of that kind throw people into new details.

[13]   No alteration should be made in a law without sufficient reason. Justinian ordained, that a husband might be repudiated without the wife's losing her portion, if for the space of two years he had been incapable of consummating the marriage.[b] He altered his law afterwards, and allowed the poor wretch three years.[c] But in a case of that nature two years are as good as three, and three are not worth more than two.

[14]   When a legislator condescends to give the reason of his law, it ought to be worthy of its majesty. A Roman law[d] decrees, that a blind man is incapable to plead, because he cannot see the ornaments of the magistracy. So bad a reason must have been given on purpose, when such a number of good reasons were at hand.

[20]   As useless laws debilitate such as are necessary, so those that may be easily eluded, weaken the legislation. Every law ought to have its effect, and no one should be ever suffered to deviate from it by a particular convention.

[24]   There ought to be a certain simplicity and candor in the laws: made to punish the iniquity of men, they themselves ought to have the most spotless innocence. We find in the law of the Visigoths[e] that ridiculous request by which the Jews were obliged to eat every thing dressed with pork, provided they did not eat the pork itself. This was a very great cruelty; they were obliged to submit to a law, contrary to their own; and they were allowed to retain

[b] Leg. I. Cod. de Repudiis.
[c] See the Authentic *Sed hodie*, in the code *de Repudiis*.
[d] Leg. i. ff. *de postulando*.
[e] Book xii. tit. 2, ¶16.

nothing more of their own, than what might serve as a mark to distinguish them.

OF THE IDEAS OF UNIFORMITY [Chapter 18]

THERE are certain ideas of uniformity, which sometimes strike great geniuses, (for they even affected Charlemain) but infallibly make an impression on little souls. They discover therein a kind of perfection, because it is impossible for them not to discover it; the same weights in the *police*, the same measures in commerce, the same laws in the state, the same religion in all its parts. But is this always right, and without exception? Is the evil of changing always less than that of suffering? And does not a greatness of genius consist rather in distinguishing between those cases in which uniformity is requisite, and those in which there is a necessity for differences? In China the Chinese are governed by the Chinese ceremonial; and the Tartars by theirs: And yet there is no nation in the world that aims so much at tranquillity. If the people observe the laws, what signifies it whether these laws are the same?

Editor's Notes to *The Spirit of Laws*

Notes with asterisks contain summaries of Jansenist and Jesuit objections and of Montesquieu's replies

BOOK I

1*. M's definition of laws as "necessary relations" led to the charge that he was a Spinozist and determinist adhering to Pope's dictum that "things cannot be other than they are and that whatever is, is right" (*Nouv. Ecclés*. Oct. 9, 1749: 161b). In his rebuttal (*Défense*, Première Partie, I, "Première Objection et Réponse") M stressed that his purpose in defining laws as the "necessary relations derived from the nature of things" had been to demonstrate that all beings have their laws and that there exist, even prior to the writing of positive laws, laws of justice and equity. The polemical intent of this definition, M remarked, had been to counter Hobbes's attempt to make virtue and vice solely dependent upon the positive laws men devise for themselves. (I, 1 [1])

2*. The Abbé de La Roche censured M for citing a pagan author (*Nouv. Ecclés*. Oct. 9, 1749: 161b). M's brief retort (*Défense*, Première Partie, I, "Seconde Objection et Réponse") consisted of simply admitting that he had indeed cited Plutarch, who had said law is the queen of mortals and immortals. (I, 1, note a)

3*. The Abbé de La Roche charged that M was here subjecting the Creation to the fatality of the atheists, i.e., suggesting that God had been bound to bring about the Creation (*Nouv. Ecclés*. Oct. 9, 1749: 161b–162a). M responded (*Défense*, Première Partie, I, "Troisième Objection et Réponse") that the whole of I, 1 [2] discounted this charge and that in I, 1 [6] his intention had been to suggest that the laws of motion God utilized in the Creation are invariable. "They are invariable," M said, "because God wished that they be invariable and because He desired to preserve the world." (I, 1 [6])

4*. According to the Abbé de La Roche, M was here denigrating God's Providential powers by maintaining that His control over the intelligent world was less perfect than his control over the physical world (*Nouv. Ecclés*. Oct. 9, 1749: 162b). In his reply (*Défense*, Première Partie, II, "Neuvième Objection et Réponse") M likened his critic's inability to read *The Spirit of Laws* objectively, without resorting to theology, to the village curate who, being invited to look at the moon through a telescope, could see nothing but a steeple. God's Providential powers, M remarked, did not fall within the scope and format of his treatise, and they had therefore gone unmentioned. (I, 1 [10])

5*. M's Jansenist critic attacked him for not specifying that it was the Christian religion to which he was here referring. "Is it the Christian religion?" he wrote. "Is it the religion of Mohammed? Is it that of the Chinese? It is apparently natural religion" (*Nouv. Ecclés*. Oct. 9, 1749: 162b). In his rebuttal (*Défense*, Première Partie, II, Introduction) M cited numerous quotations from *The Spirit of Laws* proving he was a Christian and hence no follower of natural religion. And he also contended that the Abbé de La Roche's charge that he was referring to natural religion rather than Christinity was completely illogical (*Défense*, Première Partie, II, "Septième Objection et Réponse"). (I, 1 [14])

6*. The Abbé de La Roche charged that M was here giving insufficient stress to Divine governance of the world. In his view, M should have attributed laws of morality to God—not philosophers—and he should have traced whatever wisdom legislators display to a Divine source. "According to the Author," wrote M's Jansenist critic, "the direction of the intelligent world is parcelled out between God, the Philosophers, and the Legislators" (*Nouv. Ecclés*. Oct. 9, 1749: 162b). In his reply (*Défense*, Première Partie, II, "Huitième Objection et Réponse") M readily admitted that the wisdom of philosophers and legislators derives from revelation when they are so favored and, otherwise, from "That law which, in impressing upon us the idea of a Creator leads us towards Him." M saw no reason, however, for objection to the passage as it stood. (I, 1 [14])

7*. The Abbé de La Roche contended that portraying man in an original state of nature was a pagan device that denigrated the biblical account of the Creation and the Fall of man through Original Sin (*Nouv. Ecclés.* Oct. 9, 1749: 162a). M's answer was that *The Spirit of Laws* was not a theological treatise and that, had he seen fit to mention original sin, he would then have been criticized for leaving out Redemption, etc. (*Défense*, Première Partie, II, "Troisième Objection et Réponse"). (I, 2 [1])

8*. The Abbé de La Roche censured this passage on the grounds that M should have treated those laws prescribing man's duty to God as first *both chronologically* and in order of importance (*Nouv. Ecclés.* Oct. 9, 1749: 162a). M replied (*Défense*, Première Partie, II, "Sixième Objection et Réponse") that it was no more unlawful for him than for other writers on philosophy and natural law to consider man from various points of view, including that of man's existing in a state of nature without education and prior to the formation of societies. M saw no reason to revise his psychology of primitive man. Sensations, he reiterated, would precede reflection among men dropped, as it were, from clouds and existing in a primitive condition. (I, 2 [2])

9*. For what he regarded as M's impious list of natural laws, the Abbé de La Roche desired to substitute only two: "Children learn in the Christian religion what the votaries of natural religion have proven unable to discover after twenty years of work, that the love of God is the first of all the Laws; that love of one's neighbour is the second; and that from these two primordial laws arise all the others" (*Nouv. Ecclés.* Oct. 9, 1749: 162b). (I, 2 [8])

10. Gian Vincenzo Gravina (1664–1718), author of *Origines juris civilis* (1701) and a professor of law at Rome.

11. M here alludes to Sir Robert Filmer's (1604–1688) *Patriarcha* (1680), a tract supporting Stuart absolutism through the argument that

royal power derives from paternal power traceable to Adam. Filmer's arguments were rebutted in Locke's *First Treatise*.

BOOK II

1. See also III, 3, 5; V, 2–7, 19; VII, 2, 8, 16; VIII, 1–4, 16, for other key discussions of the nature of democratic government.

2. M here alludes to the disruption in voting processes in the comitia of Rome following the granting of citizenship to the peoples of Italy in 90 B.C. See *Considérations*, chap. IX.

3. Servius Tullius was the sixth of Rome's seven kings. He is thought to have ruled from c. 578 B.C. until 535 B.C.

4. Modern historians attribute the class-centuriate organization not to Servius per se but to gradual military reorganization begun around 450 B.C. See also *Considérations*, chaps. I, VIII, and IX, for additional comment on Servius Tullius.

5. Solon was elected to the archonship of Athens in approximately 594 B.C. The four classes he established were the Pentacosiomedimni, the Hippês, the Zeugitae, and the Thêtes. The Helaea, a court of several thousand citizens, was open to the Thêtes, but, as M suggests, magistracies were reserved for the three highest classes. See V, 5 [12], for M's discussion of the economic basis of Solon's division.

6. A similar distinction was established by Aristotle (*Politics*, IV, 9, 1294b). Election by lot was more common at Athens than at Rome and may have been intended to reduce campaign intrigue.

7. At Athens this judgment was rendered by the Helaea.

8. For similar stress upon the positive value of political conflict within republics, see XXIX, 3 [1], and particularly *Considérations*, chap. IX.

9. See also III, 5–7; IV, 2; V, 9–11, 19; VI, 1, 5–6, 21; VII, 4; VIII, 6–8, 17; XII, 22, 23, 25, 27, for other key discussions of the nature of monarchical government.

10. The words "and dependent" were added during the course of printing and were intended to moderate the vigorous defense of the nobility presented in II, 4.

11. This sentence was added during the course of printing by means of a cancel.

12. The words "and subordinate power" were added during the course of printing.

13. The Paris MS. (I, f. 38) reveals that M was referring to France and, more particularly, to the reduction of seigneurial justice by an ordinance of 1667.

14. The allusion is to developments in Spain under Ferdinand and Isabella.

15. Implicit in this passage is a defense of the role of the parlements of France. See Introduction, p. 69. See also V, 10 [3–4]; VI, 1 [10]; VI, 5 [5], for additional discussion of the role of depositaries of laws in monarchical governments.

16. See also VI, 6, for M's concern that the law courts within monarchical states be separate from the prince and his ministers.

17. See also III, 8–10; IV, 3; V, 12–17; VI, 1, 10–12; VIII, 10, 19; XIII, 10, for other key discussions of the nature of despotic government.

18. The MS. (I, f. 45) identifies this Pope as Clement X (1670–1676).

BOOK III

1. See also IV, 5; V, 2, 19 [2, 4], and Appendix IV, for other important discussions of virtue as the principle of democratic government.

2*. This chapter was censured by both the Abbé de La Roche (*Nouv. Ecclés*. Oct. 9, 1749: 163a) and by the Sorbonne (Proposition XI). The basic issue was the definition M had given the word *virtue*. When read as Christian, or moral, virtue, it could be made to appear that M was suggesting the absence of morality within monarchical states. "Who would have believed," wrote the Abbé de La Roche, "that to make monarchical government perfect, the members of the state must be destitute of virtue and filled with vanity?" Such a claim was tantamount, in the Jansenist writer's view, to advocating the banishment from monarchical states of a religion such as Christianity that seeks to instill virtue and opposes vanity.

M's defense consisted largely of chiding his Jansenist critic for not paying proper attention to the definition he had given to virtue. In a special "Éclaircissements sur L'Esprit des Lois" appended to the *Défense de L'Esprit des Lois*, M referred the Abbé de La Roche to the note he had appended to III, 5, explicitly stating that the political virtue he had attributed to democratic governments should not be confused with moral virtue. And M also hinted that his Jansenist critic had perhaps read *The Spirit of Laws* too rapidly to be properly aware of this distinction.

The Faculty of Theology of the University of Paris censured paragraphs two and three of III, 5, and in his "Réponse et Explication à la Proposition XI" M spoke to the charge that his attribution of virtue to democratic governments implied a more favorable opinion of democracies than of monarchies and was therefore tantamount to disloyalty to his own native France. "Never has a citizen received such a cruel insult in his homeland," he wrote "and what consoles me is that no citizen has deserved it less. I will say it again here: 'Plato thanked the gods that he was born in the time of Socrates, and I myself give them thanks for being born under the government in which I live. . . .' All of Europe read my book and everyone agrees that it is not possible to tell if I give more support to republican government or to monarchy. And, indeed, it would have been narrow minded to choose, because in fact these two governments are very good, and the better of the two is that which gives greater satisfaction. But, although the Faculty gratuitously supposes that I hate monarchical government, they will note that in this particular case I do not in any way consider them my judge; they will note that I regard their decision as highly abusive, that I appeal to the public, and (no less important) I appeal to myself."

In order to preclude all future misunderstandings concerning his definition of virtue, M drafted an "Author's Explanatory Note" for the edition of 1757 (see Appendix IV), added an additional sentence to III,

5 [9] (see note 4 below), and made two changes in III, 6 (see note 5*
below). (III, 5)

3. As the chief minister of Louis XIII, Cardinal Richelieu was one of
the architects of Bourbon absolutism. He reduced the power of the
French nobility and of the Huguenots, and for these and other actions,
Montesquieu referred to him in the *Pensées* as one of France's two worst
citizens, Louvois being the other.

4. The 1757 edition added the following sentence: "It is not indeed
excluded, but it is not the spring of government."

5*. The Sorbonne's censure of M's discussions of the absence of virtue
from monarchical governments (see also note 2* above) included the
final sentence of III, 6 [1] and the whole of III, 6 [2]. In his "Réponse
et Explication à la Proposition XI" M indicated that two textual changes
would be made in the censured passages. The qualifying adjective "political" would be inserted prior to the word virtue in the final sentence of
III, 6 [1], and the following qualifying phrase would be added to III, 6
[2]: "and we should love our country, not so much on our own account,
as out of regard to the community." Both changes were incorporated in
the edition of 1757. (III, 6 [1])

6. See also IV, 2, for discussion of honor as the principle of monarchical government.

7. In the MS. (I, f. 63) this chapter contained a paragraph criticizing
Machiavelli for not pointedly restricting the policies of *The Prince* to
despotic states. In states other than despotisms, Montesquieu remarked,
Machiavelli's advice is "useless, dangerous, and even unmanageable."

8. This chapter provides important evidence for the view that the extent
of empiricism in M's discussion of forms of government is often exaggerated. See Introduction, pp. 58–59.

BOOK IV

1. Compare Aristotle, *Politics*, trans. by Ernest Barker (New York:
Oxford University Press, 1958), Book VIII, chap. 1, 2: "The citizens

of a state should always be educated to suit the constitution of their state."

2*. The Sorbonne censured this paragraph (Proposition XII) for exalting a purely secular principle of behavior. In his "Réponse et Explication à la Proposition XII" M pointed out that he was merely describing an existing situation without approving of it. To preclude all objections, he said he would add the following footnote: "We mention here what actually is, and not what ought to be; honor is a prejudice, which religion sometimes endeavors to remove, and at other times to regulate." The note was incorporated in the 1757 edition. (IV, 2 [23])

BOOK V

1. Originally an aristocratic council with pervasive legal and religious authority, the Areopagus declined in importance during the fifth century B.C., but by the mid-fourth century B.C. it was again influential and served as a court for the trial of premeditated homicide.

2. See also VIII, 2 [2], for M's belief that veneration of the aged helps sustain democratic governments.

3. See also VIII, 2 [1], for M's emphasis on the necessity for the people within a democratic state to accept the authority of the magistrates they have elected.

4. The disposition of an estate by entail involves the settling of the property on a whole line of successors rather than upon one particular heir. Montesquieu himself left his lands at La Brède, by entail, to his descendants through his son Jean-Baptiste de Secondat. See G, I, p. 273, for details concerning the will.

5. Redemption is the right of preemptive purchase that some legal systems have bestowed upon members of a family seeking to regain land they once held.

6. I.e., England.

7. The buying and selling of offices (*venalité des offices*) was introduced in France as early as the thirteenth and fourteenth centuries as a means

of increasing public revenue. Once purchased, a venal office became the property of its owner to be disposed of as that owner saw fit. (Peter Gay, *Voltaire's Politics. The Poet as Realist* [New York: Vintage Books, 1965; orig. ed. Princeton University Press, 1959], pp. 96–97.) The highest venal offices conferred nobility, and M had personally benefited from the practice through his grandfather's purchase of the parlementary office he himself inherited in 1716. For Voltaire's scathing attack on the whole system of venal offices and on M's defense of the practice, see the dialogue *L' A, B, C* (1768) included in Peter Gay's translation of Voltaire's *Philosophical Dictionary* (New York: Harcourt, Brace & World, Inc., 1962), pp. 497–606. For an excellent historical discussion of *venalité des offices*, see Franklin L. Ford, *Robe and Sword. The Regrouping of the French Aristocracy after Louis XIV* (Cambridge, Mass.: Harvard University Press, 1953), pp. 105–123; 148–155.

8. See also V, 7 [9–10], and VII, 8 [16], for M's stress on the need for morality within democratic governments.

BOOK VI

1. The Turkish bashaw, or pasha, was either a military commander or, as in this instance, the governor of a province.

2. I.e., beaten or caned on the soles of the feet.

3. One finds the same sentence in *Pensée* 1947 (Sp., f. 417v.) amplified by the following addition: "They [the Japanese] follow, accordingly, the same reasoning with respect to God: the mistake that offends an infinite being is itself infinite."

4. I.e., "moderation"; French text reads *tempérament*.

5. Christianity was introduced into Japan by St. Francis Xavier (1506–1552), but it was soundly persecuted in the seventeenth century and largely eliminated prior to its reintroduction in the middle of the nineteenth century (G, I, p. 297).

6. I.e., transportation to the colonies, either America or Australia depending upon the time period in question (G, I, p. 299).

BOOK VII

1. I.e., Spartans.
2. I.e., Buddhist monks.
3. This chapter constitutes, along with VII, 16, an important supplement to M's discussion of democratic government. Although M usually defined virtue in a political rather than a moral sense, he clearly believed moral virtue should also characterize democratic governments. See also V, 7 [4, 9, 10, 13], and V, 19 [15], for similar stress on morality in democratic governments.
4. The Samnites were an ancient tribe that settled in the mountainous regions of southern Italy in the fifth century B.C., subduing the Etruscans previously settled in that area. They later fought several unsuccessful wars against the Romans and were finally defeated in the 290s B.C. and again in the 80s B.C.
5. See *Republic*, V, 459E to 460C.

BOOK VIII

1. An earlier draft of this chapter in the MS. (II, f. 43) reveals M's fear that the result of the corruption of the principle of government would be tyranny: "Tyranny is less a specific state than the corruption of each particular state, and that corruption begins nearly always with that of its principles."
2. This chapter is an important expression of M's view that in democratic states citizens must revere parents, senators, judges, and the aged. Compare V, 7 [11–15], and Introduction, pp. 62–64.
3. Or rather, "despoil" the judges; French text reads *dépouiller*.
4. For M's advocacy of moderate rather than extreme equality, see also V, 5 [12], V, 7 [1], and VIII, 3 [1–4].
5. Or rather, the naval victory in September, 480 B.C., of the Greeks over the Persians in the waters off the island of Salamis.
6. The MS. (II, f. 56) reads "when the prince insensibly deprives intermediary bodies of their prerogatives, cities of their privileges, [and]

law courts of their functions." M apparently judged this wording too transparent an indictment of monarchical policy during the reign of Louis XIV.

7. The MS. (II, f. 56) contains a substantially longer third paragraph alluding more specifically to developments in France under Louis XIV: "Monarchy is destroyed when the prince wishes to do everything himself, or when his ministers use his power to do everything; or when the prince aspires to all details; or where, unable to act, he does not wish others to act; or where unable to scrutinize, he does not want others to scrutinize; or when he thinks he shows a greater exertion of power in changing than in conforming to the order of things; or when he takes away hereditary employments in order to bestow them arbitrarily on others; or when he is too jealous of his law-courts and of his nobility, and not enough of his council; in a word when he is fonder of being guided by his fancy than by his judgment."

8. M's eighteenth-century readers must have understood this passage as a clear indictment of Louis XIV's structuring of court life at Versailles and of his "L'État, c'est moi" policy (G, I, p. 314).

9. In the MS. (II, f. 56) the final paragraph of VIII, 6, reads: "Monarchy is destroyed in fine, when the prince mistakes his authority, and believes himself attacked when he is not."

10. M's correlation of republics and limited territorial expanse was a much debated point in eighteenth-century America. In *Federalist Paper* No. 14 James Madison argued that "the great principle of representation" developed in modern Europe enabled republican states to grow to substantially greater size than M had envisioned. Madison remained sufficiently concerned with the issue of size, however, to point out that "the Atlantic Coast is the largest side of the union" and that no representative would have to travel any farther than a representative from the northernmost point of the British isles travels to the English Parliament.

11. Less literally translated in later editions as: "there are trusts too considerable to be placed in any single subject."

12. Compare the contrasting view of Madison, in *Federalist Paper* No. 10, that a large representative republic is the best safeguard against the evil of factions.

13. I.e., Sparta.

14. *Pensée* 1708 (777. I, p. 507): 1734, reveals that M's ideas in this paragraph were suggested to him by his reading of Pufendorf (G. I, p 317).

BOOK IX

1. In *Federalist Paper* No. 9 Hamilton praised this portion of *The Spirit of Laws* and reminded his readers that a confederate republic such as America could be substantially larger than a republic that did not consist of separate states.

2*. The Sorbonne censured this passage (Proposition XVII) for its neglect of the Biblical, Providential explanations for Joshua's success in overthrowing the Canaanites. In his "Réponse et Explication à la Proposition XVII" M stressed the orthodoxy of his own Providentialism, referring his critics to his characterization in Book I, chap. 1 [4], of God as both creator and preserver of the world. To object to his analysis of the defeat of the Canaanites, M remarked, it was necessary to believe he rejected both the Old and the New Testament, and there was, he observed, no basis for that view. And M saw no difficulty in reconciling his analysis with Providential explanations. If the Canaanites did not possess a political organization conducive to their defeat of the Jews, then surely this was as much a part of God's plan for the Jews as were the Jordan River, and the mountains, valleys, and topography of Canaan. (IX, 2 [1])

3. The reference is to Louis XIV.

4. I.e., Russia.

5. I.e., the Crimea.

BOOK X

1. Compare XV, 2 [3].

2. This chapter became number 13 in the edition of 1757.

3. Pultowa, or Poltava, was the decisive defeat of Charles XII of Sweden (1682–1718) in June, 1709, by the forces of Peter the Great of Russia (1672–1725). Prior to that defeat Charles had enjoyed remarkable military success, often against seemingly overwhelming odds. M's discussion reflects the interest in determinism evident in his *De la politique* (1725) (see Introduction, pp. 24–25) and in the *Considérations* wherein he had remarked (chap. 18) that general causes, moral and physical, rather than chance occurences, generally shape world history. Voltaire was also intrigued by Charles's career, and in his *Histoire de Charles XII* (1731) he maintained that Charles's heroic virtues eventually became heroic vices.

BOOK XI

1. For M's belief that republican governments are prone to factions that destroy liberty, see Introduction, p. 62.

2. This paragraph provides a rough description of the English jury system. M ignores the role of the prerogative courts.

3. See also VI, 3, for similar emphasis on the need for judges to adhere to the strict letter of the law.

4. As Jean Brèthe de La Gressaye has pointed out (II, p. 335), eighteenth-century England did not conform to this rule, since the juries were drawn from the propertied citizens.

5. In this paragraph M is referring to the right of habeas corpus reaffirmed in the Stuart period both in the Petition of Right (1628) and in the Habeas Corpus Act of 1679. A writ of habeas corpus ad subiiciendum requires that a person accused be brought into court so that the lawfulness of his detainment can be ascertained.

6. Algernon Sidney (1617–1683), English opponent of Stuart absolutism executed after being implicated in the imaginary Rye House

Plot against Charles. His *Discourses on Government* (1698), translated into French in 1702, are known to have influenced Montesquieu.

7. Compare II, 2 [6, 9 and 13], for similar skepticism concerning the political capacities of the common people.

8. I.e., for executive actions that would violate the principle of distinct executive, legislative, and judicial powers.

9. See Introduction, p. 78.

10. I.e., Parliamentary appropriations of tax money for use by the Crown.

11. The power of the House of Lords even to refuse financial legislation was significantly reduced in 1911 when their power of rejecting money bills was reduced to a suspensive veto. As of 1911, the Lords were left with the power to suspend money bills for one month and all other bills for two years. In 1949 another Act of Parliament reduced the Lords' suspensive veto on nonmoney bills to only a year.

12. Montesquieu fails to note that this was precisely the effect of the emerging "inner" Cabinet system in the period of Walpole's ascendancy. See Introduction, p. 81.

13. Rule without Parliament had been a weapon of Stuart absolutism in the seventeenth century. With the exception of the short-lived "Addled Parliament" of 1614, James I ruled from 1611 to 1621 without summoning Parliament, and his son and successor, Charles I, ruled from 1629 until 1640 without convening Parliament. The Bill of Rights of 1689 accordingly proclaimed that "Parliaments ought to be held frequently," and the Triennial Act of 1694 decreed that the English Crown could neither govern without nor continue the same Parliament for more than three years in succession. This was revised to seven years by the Septennial Act of 1716.

14. Montesquieu here refers to the Parliament's powers of impeachment.

15. As Gressaye has pointed out, (II, p. 347), M was incorrect in attributing to the House of Lords the power of lessening a sentence or moderating the application of the law.

16. In her veto of the Scottish Militia Bill of 1708, Queen Anne was the last monarch to exercise the power of veto.

17. The reigns of James I (1603–1625) and Charles I (1625–1649) particularly demonstrated this fact, since only the necessity to go to Parliament for the voting of supplies forced these two Divine Right monarchs to deal with Parliaments that were bent on curbing monarchical power.

18. As noted by Gressaye (II, p. 349), one of the provisions of the English Bill of Rights (1689) was the *annual* voting of military power to the Crown.

19. In the edition of 1757 two additional paragraphs were added to the text at this point:

> But if, in the case where the army is governed by the legislative body, particular circumstances prevent the government from becoming military, the state will fall into other inconveniences; from two things one: the army will have to destroy the government, or the government will have to weaken the army.
>
> And that weakness will have an entirely fatal cause: it will spring from the very weakness of the government.

20. Other theorists, such as Jean de Lolme, suggested that English governmental institutions were no more ancient than the Norman conquest. For two eighteenth-century defenses of M's point of view, see Gilbert Stuart, *An Historical Dissertation concerning the Antiquity of the English Constitution* (1768), and Francis Sullivan, *Lectures on the Feudal Law of England* (1772).

21. This paragraph supports the view that M's analysis of the English government was not strictly empirical. See Introduction, pp. 81–82.

22. This paragraph should be read in light of M's relativism. See Introduction, pp. 34–40.

23. I.e., France in particular.

BOOK XII

1. This chapter constitutes an important supplement to the discussion of crime and punishment in VI, 9, 11, 12, and 16.

2*. The Faculty of Theology of the University of Paris characterized this passage as "scandalous, impious, erroneous, and heretical." In his "Réponse et Explication à la Proposition IV," M indicated he had deleted the passage. The change was not included, however, in the edition of 1757. (XII, 4 [6])

3. Although modesty is absent from the discussion of laws of nature in Book I, chap. 2, this chapter reveals that M placed moral virtue in the same category as such basic human instincts as cognizance of a Creator, innate timidity, the need for nourishment, mutual attraction between the sexes, and man's desire to live together in societies.

4. The edition of 1757 replaced this footnote with this longer note: "It is not sufficient in the courts of justice of that kingdom that the evidence be of such a nature as to satisfy the judges; there must be a legal proof; and the law requires the deposition of two witnesses against the accused. No other proof will do. Now, if a person who is presumed guilty of high treason should contrive to secrete the witnesses, so as to render it impossible for him to be legally condemned, the government then may bring a bill of attainder against him; that is, they may enact a particular law for that single fact. They proceed then in the same manner as in all other bills brought into parliament; it must pass the two houses, and have the King's consent, otherwise it is not a bill: that is, a sentence of the Legislature. The person accused may plead against the bill by counsel, and the members of the house may speak in defence of the bill."

5. *Pensée* 1965 (1665. III, f. 13v.): 1749, presents a lengthier discussion of Bills of Attainder and reveals that Charles Yorke, a son of the English Lord Chancellor, Lord Hardwicke, was M's source of information.

6. In the MS. (III, f. 75) this first paragraph is considerably longer and includes M's criticisms of the *lettres de cachet*: "Two things of the least use in the world to the prince have weakened liberty in our monarchies:

the commissioners that the prince sometimes names to try a private person and the letters that he gives in order to commit to prison those he judges deserving of it." The MS. (III, f's 76–78) also printed four additional paragraphs suggesting reforms in the use of *lettres de cachet*. During the course of the printing of his work, however, M decided to suppress these passages, fearing, no doubt, that they were too blatantly critical of the Bourbon monarchy.

7. The commissioners to which M here refers circumvented the usual legal procedures and were outlawed by the Estates-General in 1579. They were revived by Richelieu, however, and were known during the period of Louis XIV as *Chambres de justice* (G, II, p. 382).

8. Montesquieu refers in this chapter to domestic surveillance such as that undertaken by the *cabinet noir* of Louis XIV and Louis XV (G, II, p. 382).

9. In the MS. (III, f. 79) this opening sentence was considerably bolder: "Seeking to know the secrets of families and having spies to accomplish this is a thing that good princes have never done."

10. I.e., the Koran.

11. The Cadis were civil judges.

BOOK XIII

1. Villenage was the system of feudal land tenure wherein the peasant did not own his land outright, but was merely granted limited tenure by a feudal lord in return for certain services.

2. Gressaye, II, p. 388, identifies these two countries as England and France.

3. Among M's French contemporaries, this paragraph no doubt brought to mind the *gabelle*, or salt-tax, levied disproportionately throughout France and to great excess in some areas.

4. Since the time of Colbert, the collection of indirect taxes had been in the hands of approximately forty *Fermiers Généraux*, or Farmers General, who purchased every six years the right to collect indirect taxes. They paid the Crown a fixed sum every year out of what they collected,

and by indulging in rigorous methods of collection, they often turned a profit. For M's hostility toward the Farmers General, see XIII, 19, 20.

5. I.e., cask.

6. "Letting out to farm" refers to the system of tax-farming. See note 4 above.

7. This chapter was not part of the MS. Its presence in the published work was one reason the Fermier Général Claude Dupin wrote his critical *Observations sur un livre intitulé de L'Esprit des Lois* (1752). For other comments by M on tax-farming, see *Pensées* 300 (1878. III, f. 116v.): 1749, and 301 (1877. III, f. 115v.): 1749.

BOOK XIV

1. Paragraphs 1–13 of this chapter and paragraphs 1, 2, and 7 of XIV, 10, were originally part of the *Essay on Causes*. See notes 3, 6, and 7 to the translation of this treatise, p. 456.

2. See also XVI, 10 [7], for M's correlation of hot climates and sensuality.

3. This chapter, along with XIV, 6, 8, and 9, provides important evidence that M believed the effects of climate can be counteracted. See Introduction, pp. 48–51.

4. I.e., Buddha.

5*. The Sorbonne included this passage in its censure of M's correlation of monasticism with hot climates (Proposition XV). M's lengthy "Réponse et Explication à la Proposition XV" did not specifically allude to this portion of the censure. See XIV, 7, and XXIII, 29, for other texts censured in Proposition XV. (XIV, 6)

6*. This chapter was censured by both the Abbé de La Roche (*Nouv. Ecclés.* Oct. 9, 1749: 163a–163b) and by the Sorbonne (Proposition XV). According to M's Jansenist critic, the anticlerical pen of the author of the *Persian Letters* was clearly evident. And in addition to objecting generally to M's correlation of monasticism with hot climates more conducive to speculation than to action, the Abbé de La Roche criticized

M for failing to differentiate monasticism as practiced by Christians from monasticism as practiced by followers of Islam and adherents of idolatrous sects. *The Defense of the Spirit of Laws* contained no specific response to this portion of the Jansenist attack. M did respond at some length, however, to the Sorbonne's censure of this passage. Far from retracting anything he had said, he maintained that although the church has the right to establish monastic orders, a prince should be able to limit their number and their wealth as best serves the welfare of his state. And if princes can do this, then "political writers" ought not to be censured for discussing such things. All that is necessary, M contended, is that one speak wisely and with proper respect for those institutions the Church considers useful for the care of souls. This he believed he had done ("Réponse et Explication à la Proposition XV"). (XIV, 7)

7. I.e, monasticism.

8*. The Church's prohibition of suicide led to the censure of this passage by both the Abbé de La Roche (*Nouv. Ecclés.* Oct. 9, 1749: 163b) and by the Sorbonne (Proposition X). The Abbé de La Roche accused M of attempting to "pass a sponge" over the crime of suicide in England precisely because England was the cradle of natural religion of which he was an adherent. M's response (*Défense*, Première Partie, II, Dixième Objection et Réponse) was that while he did not know that England was the cradle of natural religion, he knew it was not his cradle. He was most definitely, he remarked, not a follower of natural religion, but he would be pleased, he said, to have a critic who was a follower of natural logic.

In response to the censure of XIV, 12, by the Faculty of Theology of the University of Paris, M indicated that he would add the following note to the title of the chapter: "Suicide is contrary to the law of nature and to revealed religion." (This note was added to the edition of 1757, although it has not previously been printed in English-language editions of M's work.) Having indicated he would alter his text, M did nevertheless add that he saw no more harm in reasoning about the English physiological malady leading to suicide than in reasoning about mad persons who jump out of windows in France ("Réponse et Explication à la Proposition X"). (XIV, 12 [3])

9*. In his censure of this passage as tending to reduce morality to a mere offshoot of climate (*Nouv. Ecclés.* Oct. 19, 1749: 163b), the Abbé de La Roche accused M of inconsistency, since, in XIV, 3, M had indicated that, far from being rendered innocent by climate, the people of India cling to such barbarous customs as suicide on the part of wives who lose their husbands. In his rebuttal (*Défense*, Seconde Partie, "Climat") M belittled the charge, stating that all peoples display contradictory traits and that the barbarous practises mentioned in XIV, 3, do not change the basic truth that, overall, climate renders the people of India "mild, tender, and compassionate." (XIV, 15 [3])

BOOK XV

1. One finds an even stronger antislavery judgment in *Pensée* 1935 (174. I, p. 154): 1728–29, wherein M affirms: "Slavery is contrary to natural law by which all men are born free and independent."

2. See also X, 3 [7–9], for M's argument that slavery cannot be deduced from the right of conquest.

3. In Roman law the *peculium* was the property a father allowed his child, or a master his slave.

4. The prospect of widespread conversions did often figure in European rationalizations of slavery. It was on religious grounds, for example, that King Ferdinand of Spain sanctioned the enslavement of the Lucayan Indians of the Bahamas for work in Hispaniola (See Sir Alan Burns, *History of the British West Indies* [London: Allen & Unwin, 1954], p. 122).

5. Voltaire correctly asserted that this chapter was written "with the touch of a Molière" (Art. "Slaves" in *Philosophical Dictionary*).

6. European slave practices did actually result in the extermination of whole races of Caribbean Indians. Both the Arawaks of the Greater Antilles and the Caribs of the Lesser Antilles were made extinct. M also

discussed European cruelty to the Indians in *Persian Letters* 118 and 121.

7. An ancient kingdom in the northwest corner of the island of Sumatra.

8. Cf. *Politics*, Bk. I, chs. 5, 8, 1254b: ". . . all men who differ from others as much as the body differs from the soul, or an animal from a man (and this is the case with all whose function is bodily service, and who produce their best when they supply such service)—all such are by nature slaves, and it is better for them . . . to be ruled by a master" (*The Politics of Aristotle*, trans. by Ernest Barker [Oxford University Press, 1958], p. 13).

9. For the view that the Catholic Church actually did little to abolish slavery, see David B. Davis, *The Problem of Slavery in Western Culture* (Ithaca, 1966), pp. 85–106.

10. Temeswar was a village in South Hungary that fell to the Turks in 1552 and was recaptured in 1716.

11. This final paragraph was not present in the manuscript and was added for the edition of 1748.

12. Chapters nine through eighteen of the 1748 edition are not included in this compendium. A new ninth chapter, however, which was added to the 1757 edition and has not previously appeared in an English-language edition of *The Spirit of Laws*, is translated below:

Of Nations in Which Civil Liberty is Generally Established

Every day one hears people say that, were there slaves among us, it would be advantageous.*

But to judge rightly of this, one must not explore whether such a thing would be useful to the small, rich, and voluptuous part of each nation. No doubt slavery would be useful to them. But, adopting another point of view, I do not believe that any of those who make up

---

* Jean Melon, a friend of M and fellow member of the Academy of Bordeaux, had written a book (*L'Essai politique sur le commerce*, 1734) recommending use of Asiatics and Turks as slaves in Europe.

this group would consent to drawing lots to see who should constitute the free portion of the nation and who should be the slaves. Those who speak the most in favor of slavery would most abhor that condition, and the most destitute would likewise abhor it. Hence the clamor for slavery is the cry of luxury and voluptuousness, not of love for the public happiness. Who can doubt that, privately, each man would be very happy to be master of the wealth, the honor, and the lives of others and that all our passions awaken at this idea? In these matters, if you wish to assess the legitimacy of the desires of each particular individual, then examine the desires of all individuals collectively.

BOOK XVI

1. Changed to "when no religion opposes it" in the 1757 edition.

2*. Objecting that M's reasoning reduced the present status and potential progress of Christianity to a by-product of climate, the Abbé de La Roche censured this paragraph in both of his attacks on *The Spirit of Laws* (*Nouv. Ecclés.* Oct. 9, 1749: 163b, and Oct. 16, 1749: 166a). M's message, as the Jansenist writer perceived it, was that where the climate inclines men toward polygamy, Christianity will necessarily make little headway. In order to reduce the emphasis on climate within the paragraph in question, M made three changes that were included in the edition of 1757: (1) "is physically conformable to the climate of Europe, and not to that of Asia" was changed to "corresponds more to the climate of Europe than to the climate of Asia"; (2) "This is the reason why" was altered to "This is one of the reasons why"; and (3) a final sentence was added to the paragraph: "Human reasons, however, are subordinate to that Supreme Cause who does whatever He pleases, and renders everything subservient to His will." XVI, 2 [5] was not censured by the Sorbonne. (XVI, 2 [5])

3*. This chapter was censured by both the Abbé de La Roche (*Nouv. Ecclés.* Oct. 9, 1749: 163b–164a) and the Sorbonne (Proposition VI). From the vantage point of his Jansenist and Jesuit critics, M was guilty of transforming polygamy—a clear-cut moral offense—into a matter of mathematical calculation dependent on demographical considerations. And the Abbé de La Roche was particularly distressed by the absence in XVI, 4, of a clear statement that polyandry is even more morally offensive than polygamy.

In his response to his Jansenist critic, M began by quoting the whole of XVI, 6, as evidence that he had opposed polygamy on moral grounds. He then explained that in the chapter in question he had only taken up the question of population in order to assess those conditions under which polygamy is *least pernicious*. Polygamy, M contended, is undesirable in and of itself, but it is less reprehensible where women considerably outnumber men. Hence polygamy *is* an affair of population calculation "when one wishes to know if polygamy is more or less pernicious in certain climates, countries or circumstances than in others. It is not an affair of calculation when one must decide whether it is good or bad in and of itself." As for the charge that he had justified polygamy, M said his Jansenist critic should have paid closer attention to the concluding sentence of the chapter: "In all this I only give their reasons, but do not justify their customs." (*Défense*, Seconde Partie, "De la Polygamie").

In reply to the censure of XVI, 4, by the Sorbonne, M said he had altered the title and had changed "is more conformable to nature" ([3]) to "is less distant from nature." Both changes were made in the 1757 edition, and the title was altered to "Concerning Polygamy. Its Diverse Circumstances," although it has not previously been printed as such in an English-language edition of *The Spirit of Laws*. In concluding his response to the Sorbonne, M added the following reflection for good measure: "To hear the *Nouvelliste ecclésiastique* exclaim concerning polygamy, it would seem Hannibal is at the gates and that we are now threatened with the introduction of the plurality of women. One has to greatly love dispute and agitation to pounce on this subject" ("Réponse et Explication à la Proposition VI"). (XVI, 4)

4. 1757 edition: "Asia and Africa." M added the reference to Africa as

a result of the charge in the *Journal de Trévoux* (April, 1749) that he had provided insufficient data supporting his contention that in hot climates women outnumber men. He also added the following footnote: "See *The Voyage to Guinea* by Mr. Smith, Second Part concerning the County of Ante."

5. 1757 edition: "Asia and Africa."

6. 1757 edition: "But I do not believe that there are many countries. . . ."

7. Once the flourishing capital of the sultanate of Bantam, a kingdom converted to Islam in the sixteenth century and conquered by the Dutch in the seventeenth century, the city of Bantam lies on the extreme northwest coast of what is today Java, Indonesia. Djakarta has now replaced Bantam as a major port.

8. In the 1757 edition the order of the paragraphs within this chapter was altered somewhat and the following new paragraph was added: "They say that the Emperor of Morocco has women of all colors, white, black, and tawny, in his seraglio. But the wretch has scarcely need of a single color."

9. 1757 edition: "holds no further than this opinion. . . ."

10*. This passage was censured by the Sorbonne (Proposition I) as attributing too much influence to *causes physiques* in the realm of morality. In his reply ("Réponse et Explication à la Proposition I") M said he should be the last to be accused of ignoring moral causes. If, he remarked, he had admittedly spoken at great length concerning climate in the relevant portions of his treatise, he had also spoken a great deal about moral causes elsewhere in the treatise. Nor was he content to rest his case there. "It can be said," he proclaimed, "that the book *The Spirit of Laws* constitutes a perpetual triumph of morality over climate, or rather, in general, over physical causes." The comment that "there are climates where the impulses of nature have such strength that morality has *almost none*" (my italics) had been based on "facts," M contended, and to deny it, it would be necessary to burn all the books that indicate men are more inclined toward sensual and alcoholic excesses in some countries than in others. And for good measure M reminded his Jesuit critics that he had qualified his argument by saying "*almost* none" (my italics) and had recommended in XVI, 10, the confinement of women as a suitable remedy for immoral behaviour in hot climates. (XVI, 8 [1])

11. Mogulstan was the name given the dynasty of the Mongol rulers of India (1526–1857). For a time the Mogul empire embraced central and northern India and much of Afghanistan. Decline can be dated from around the death of Aurengzeg in 1707, and the last Mogul emperor was Bahadur Shah II, deposed by the British in 1857. Nearly a century earlier, the Moguls had been forced to cede the administration of Bayal, Bengal, Bihar, and Orissa to the British.

12. The French text reads "des Indes," and as Gressaye (II, p. 431) has noted, M refers not just to India but to the islands of the Indian Ocean, to Java and Sumatra, and to Indo-China.

13. 1757 edition: "At Patan the wanton desires of the women are so outragious [*sic*], that the men are obliged to make use of a certain apparel to shelter them from their designs. According to Mr. Smith, things are not better conducted in the petty kingdoms of Guinea. It seems that in these countries, the two sexes lose even those laws which properly belong to each." The following footnote was also included, following the allusion to Guinea: "Voyage to Guinea," part second. "When the women happen to meet with a man, they lay hold of him, and threaten to make a complaint to their husbands if he slight their addresses. They steal into a man's bed, and wake him; and if he refuses to comply with their desires, they threaten to suffer themselves to be caught in flagranti." Patan, or Anhilwar, is a city in Nepal, approximately two miles S.E. of Katmandu.

14. Annexed by India in 1961, and now part of a union territory, Goa was formerly the stronghold of the Portuguese empire in the east. It is located on the Malabar Coast of western India.

15. For Indies read India. See note 12 above.

16. Compare XIV, 5, 6, 8, and 9 for similar stress on the legislator's ability to counteract the effects of climate when they are detrimental, and see also Introduction, pp. 48–51.

BOOK XVII

1. See Book XIV, chap. 2.
2. In the edition of 1757 "mountains and seas" was altered to just "seas."

BOOK XIX

1. City in lower Burma, approximately fifty miles northeast of Rangoon, that gave its name to the surrounding area and was famous for its Buddhist culture in the late fourteenth through the early sixteenth centuries.
2. I.e., Dio Cassius, author of a Roman history owned by M in a Latin edition of 1592 (*Catalogue*, 2828).
3. For a discussion of the important concept of the general spirit, see Introduction, pp. 23–30.
4. The allusion is to France.
5. In response to Grosley's suggestion that the success of the Romans proved that pride is advantageous rather than dangerous, M responded that pride has diverse effects depending upon other components of a nation's character ("M to Grosley," April 8, 1750, in Nagel, III, p. 1295). Grosley's comment also prompted M to add the following sentence to the sixth paragraph of this chapter in the edition of 1757: "There is no necessity for mentioning that the moral qualities, according as they are blended with others, are productive of different effects; thus pride, joined to a vast ambition and notions of grandeur, produced such effects among the Romans as are known to all the world."
6. Achim is an ancient kingdom in the northwest corner of the island of Sumatra.
7. For *Indies* read *India*. See Book XVI, n. 12.

8. Desirous of Westernizing Russia, and convinced that the bearded Old Believers constituted a potential political opposition, Peter the Great shaved the beards of his principal noblemen following the Streltsi uprising of 1698. Ukases of 1700 and 1701 ordered that all save clergy and peasants dress in Western style, and ukases of 1705 and 1715 taxed beards and moustaches, save among the clergy and among peasants who remained in their villages. Like other Petrine reforms, these measures were prompted by both economic and political considerations (Vasili Klyuchevsky, *Peter the Great*, trans. by Liliana Archibald (New York St. Martin's Press, 1958), pp. 162, 267–268). The Old Believers were vigorously opposed to shaving their beards, since the Eastern Church regarded them as aspects of Divinity, and some deemed them necessary for salvation. Peter was so unpopular as a result of the measures M discusses that it was rumored among the peasantry that he must be the bastard son of a foreign woman. Peter himself, unlike other Tsars, was beardless, and he often dressed in the Western clothes of a ship's captain or a shipwright (Ian Grey, *Peter the Great: Emperor of all Russia* [Philadelphia: J. B. Lippincott, 1960], pp. 137, 258).

9*. This sentence was censured by the Sorbonne (Proposition I) for attributing excessive influence to climate in human affairs (see also XVI, 8 [1]; XXIV, 26 [3]). In his rebuttal M expressed surprise that the Sorbonne should have censured a passage having nothing to do with religion, and he minimized the importance of the passage by referring to it as a "metaphorical expression" ("Réponse et Explication à la Proposition I"). (XIX, 14 [6])

10. Strangely enough, this passage was not censured by either the Abbé de La Roche or the Sorbonne even though it denigrated the power of missionaries to establish the Christian religion wherever they chose. See XXIV, 26 [3], for a passage of similar import that did not escape censure by M's ecclesiastical critics.

11. Gressaye, III, p. 334, identifies the source of this passage as Plutarch's *Life of Solon*, XIX.

BOOK XXIII

1*. The Abbé de La Roche censured this passage as follows: "A Christian would refer the institution of Marriage to God Himself, who gave a companion to Adam and who joined the first man and the first woman by an indissoluble bond before they had any children to nourish. But the Author evades all that treats of Revelation, although he wishes to sometimes pass for a Christian" (*Nouv. Ecclés*. Oct. 9, 1749: 164a–164b). In his reply (*Défense*, Seconde Partie, "Mariage") M said he was "a Christian but not an imbecile" and that there was no reason why revealed truths, however true, should enter into his work. And for good measure he mentioned that no one had seen fit to censure Justinian for similarly defining marriage without resort to theology. (XXIII, 2 [1])

2. For Bantam, see Book XVI, note 7 (p. 399).

3*. For these comments on the tendency of Christian ideas on celibacy to reverse Roman customs and laws favoring population growth, M was criticized by both the Abbé de La Roche (*Nouv. Ecclés*. Oct. 9, 1749: 164b) and the Sorbonne (Proposition IX). A key point in M's rebuttal (*Défense*, Seconde Partie, "Célibat") was that nowhere in *The Spirit of Laws* had he discussed the merits of celibacy as a religious institution. He had only sought to consider, he explained, as a political writer rather than a theologian, those demographic circumstances under which the effects of celibacy might prove detrimental. The question of the merit of celibacy in a religious context had not concerned him. And he reiterated his consistent complaint that the Abbé de La Roche, instead of letting him treat his subject, was always demanding that he treat questions of theology instead.

In response to the censure of XXIII, 21 [34–35] by the Faculty of Theology of the University of Paris, M stressed the difficulty he experienced in discovering what had offended them. The Catholic Church's advocacy of celibacy was a fact, he remarked, as was the suitability of celibacy for only very few men. M did indicate, however, that he would alter the text as follows: "can be practised but by very few" would be changed to "can be practised but by few" (par. 35) and "at others they have put a damp to it" would be moderated to "at others they have slowed its pace" (par. 34). Neither of these changes was incorporated in the 1757 edition. (XXIII, 21 [35])

4*. The Sorbonne censured this passage (Proposition XV), and in his "Réponse et Explication à la Proposition ⟨XV," M indicated that the passage would be altered to read: "Henry VIII, resolving to reform the church of England, ruined the monks, whom he regarded as a lazy set of people etc." The change, however, was not made.

BOOK XXIV

1. Title altered in edition of 1757 to: "Of Laws in Relation to the Religion Established in Each Country Considered in Itself, and in Its Observances."

2. Altered in 1757 edition to: "With regard to the true religion, a person of the least degree of impartiality."

3. I.e., passers-by; French text reads *ceux qui passe*.

4*. The Abbé de La Roche censured this chapter on the grounds that M was counseling Mohammedan princes to avoid converting to Christianity lest the principle of their despotic governments be undermined (*Nouv. Ecclés*. Oct. 16, 1749: 165a–165b). In his rebuttal (*Défense*, Seconde Partie, "Idée Générale") M stressed that suggesting a connection between Mohammedanism and despotism was by no means equivalent either to approving Mohammedanism or to abandoning Christianity. And he chided his Jansenist critic for failing to understand that *The Spirit of Laws* was not conceived as an apologia for Christianity and that its author should not, therefore, be expected to proselytize for Christianity, however much that same author loved and respected Christianity, adored Christian truths, and placed Christianity in a separate category as a Divinely revealed religion. (XXIV, 3 [1])

5*. The Abbé de La Roche censured M's climatological correlation of Protestantism with the freedom of the cold, northern republics and Catholicism with the less free monarchies of the hot South on the grounds that it encouraged republics that had adopted Protestantism to remain outside the Catholic fold (*Nouv. Ecclés*. Oct. 16, 1749: 165a). M did not specifically rebut the censure of this passage, but the *Defense of the Spirit of Laws* did contain the following passage relevant to the point M had been attempting to establish: "I know very well that religion is, in and of itself, independent of all physical effects whatsoever, that what is good in one country is good in another, and that a religion cannot be bad in one country without being bad in all. But I say that, since a religion is practised by men and for men, there are some places where some religion or other can be practiced more easily, whether in whole or in part in one country than in another and under some circumstances rather than others. And as soon as someone asserts the contrary, he will surrender all claim to common sense" (*Défense*, Seconde Partie, "Climat"). (XXIV, 5 [3])

6*. The Abbé de La Roche censured M for referring to the skeptical and anticlerical Bayle as a "great man" (*Nouv. Ecclés*. Oct. 16, 1749: 165a). M responded (*Défense*, Première Partie, II, Seconde Objection) that Bayle's *ill use* of his faculties did not negate his having possessed admirable capacities. (XXIV, 6 [2])

7*. The Sorbonne censured this passage (Proposition VIII) for its implication that Catholic priests do not take willingly to celibacy. In his "Réponse et Explication à la Proposition VIII" M indicated that the last two sentences of the chapter would be deleted. The change was not made in the 1757 edition, however. (XIV, 7 [2])

8. For Pegu, see Book XIX, note 1 (p. 404).

9. The Essenes were a Jewish, communal sect residing in Palestine near the Dead Sea between approximately 200 B.C. and A.D. 100. Reference is made to them by both Josephus and Philo, and it is now thought the Dead Sea Scrolls may have belonged to a member of this sect.

10*. In his censure of this chapter (*Nouv. Ecclés*. Oct. 16, 1749: 165b–166a), the Abbé de La Roche charged both that no Christian could have written such a eulogy of the Stoics and that this chapter revealed that M was an adherent of the Stoic view of nature and hence a follower of natural religion. In his response (Défense, Première Partie, II, Première Objection), M said he had praised only the ethics—not the metaphysics—of the Stoics and that I, 1 [2], provided sufficient evidence of his disenchantment with Stoic natural philosophy. (XXIV, 10)

11. Altered in the edition of 1757 to: "The several sects of philosophy amongst the ancients could be considered a species of religion."

12*. The Sorbonne censured M's assessment of Julian the Apostate, who had during his brief reign (A.D. 361–363) written a tract against the Christians and had contemplated the restoration of paganism. In his "Réponse et Explication à la Proposition V" M simply indicated: "I have removed that." The change was not incorporated, however, in the edition of 1757. (XXIV, 10 [4])

13. I.e., Buddha (Foe) and Tao-Tsen (Lackium), the founder of Taoism in China.

14. I.e., Zoroastrianism, the dominant religion of Persia prior to the conquest of Persia by the Muslims in the seventh century.

15. Taking its name from the Lupercal, a cave in the Palatine hill, the Lupercalia was an ancient Roman festival supervised by priests called Luperci and held on February 15. The sacrifice of goats and a dog was followed by the cutting of these animal skins into strips with which the Luperci struck any women they met as they ran around the walls of the city. The touch of one of these thongs was believed to cure sterility.

16. M's footnote reveals he was referring particularly to the inhabitants of Malacca on the western Malayan coast.

17. Situated near the southwest tip of the island of Celebes, Macassar is now a major seaport of Indonesia. It was settled by the Portuguese in the sixteenth century and captured by the Dutch in 1667. Prior to Indonesian independence, it had both a Dutch and a Malay section.

18*. This paragraph was censured by both the Abbé de La Roche (*Nouv. Ecclés*. Oct. 16, 1749: 166a) and the Sorbonne (Proposition III) as destructive to the spread of Christianity. In response to the Sorbonne censure, M indicated he would delete the passage ("Réponse et Explication à la Proposition III"), but the change was not made. (XXIV, 24 [1])

19. The following footnote to this paragraph was added to the edition of 1757: "It is not the Christian religion that is being spoken of here because, as had been said at the conclusion of Book XXIV, chap. 1, the Christian religion is the greatest good."

20. Sanctorius, or Santorio de' Santori (1561–1636), was an Italian doctor and professor of theoretical medicine at the University of Padua. M refers in his note to his *De Statica medicina et de responsione ad staticomasticem* (1624), a work of several hundred aphroistic judgments on the effects of air, water, aliments, and sleep on the body. A French translation was issued in Paris in 1722 with the title: *La Médicine statique de Sanctorius, ou l'Art de se conserver la santé par la transpiration*, and an English translation had earlier been published in London in 1712.

21*. This paragraph was censured by both the Abbé de La Roche (*Nouv. Ecclés*. Oct. 16, 1749: 166a) and the Sorbonne (Proposition I) on the grounds that it denigrated the conversion prospects of Christianity. In his reply to his Jansenist critic (*Défense*, Seconde Partie, "Climat") M stressed that whereas the doctrines of religion are themselves independent of climate, the diverse ceremonies of various religions render them sufficiently different to insure that a given religion is more easily practiced in some areas than in others. In his reply to the Sorbonne censure ("Réponse et Explication à la Proposition I") M said he had deleted the passage. The change, however, was not made. (XXIV, 26 [3])

BOOK XXV

1. Title altered in edition of 1757 to: "Of Laws as Relative to the Establishment of Religion in Each Country and Its External Polity."

2*. The Abbé de La Roche censured this passage for presenting a psychological rather than a theological account of the development of Christian monotheism (*Nouv. Ecclés*. Oct. 16, 1749: 166a). "A follower of natural religion," he wrote, "traces everything back to nature." And speaking of what he regarded as M's resort to pride rather than the coming of Christ to explain man's progress from idolatry to monotheism, the Jansenist critic complained: "He pretends not to know that the whole world was idolatrous when Jesus Christ appeared, that the Jews were the only People who knew God, and that this People had possessed up until the Captivity a frightful penchant for idolatry." In his response (*Défense*, Seconde Partie, "Erreur Particulière du Critique"), M stressed that he had focused on the pride of adherents of monotheistic religions solely to explain why Jews and Mahometans cling as tenaciously to their religions as do Christians, in spite of their religions possessing fewer advantages than Christianity. Nowhere had he spoken, M remarked, of the transition from polytheism to monotheism, or, more specifically, of the origins of Christian monotheism. And M concluded his rebuttal with the comment that if a Christian experiences satisfaction in contemplating the glory and grandeur of a monotheistic Deity and one wishes to call this pride, then it is a form of pride that is entirely praise worthy. (XXV, 2 [2])

3. In *Pensée* 2134 (870. II, f. 2v): 1734–1735 M reports that the Pedalians were a nation of India without priests. M owned the *OEuvres complètes* of Lilius Giraldus, the Latinised name of Lilio Gregorio Giraldi (1479–1552), and *Pensées* 2134–2145 (Pléiade) are based on his writings (G, III, p. 434).

4*. M's Jansenist critic censured both XXV, 9, and XXV, 10 (*Nouv. Ecclés*. Oct. 16, 1749: 166b) as "arming infidel Princes versus Christianity" by enumerating situations in which Christianity should not be tolerated. In his rebuttal (*Défense*, Seconde Partie, "Tolérance"), M stressed that his remarks had not been meant to apply to Christianity, a religion he placed in a special category as Divinely revealed. And to prove his point he referred his critic to his praise of Christianity in XXIV, 1 [4–5]. The Christian religion, he went on to remark, possesses heavenly rather than earthly origins, and it is therefore established wherever God sees fit.

XXV, 10, was also censured by the Sorbonne (Proposition II) as detrimental to the cause of Christianity, and in his "Réponse et Explication à la Proposition II," M indicated that he would add the following footnote to the chapter, lest there be any question that he had intended to make an exception of Christianity: "I do not speak here of the Christian religion because, as I have said elsewhere, the Christian religion is the greatest good. See the end of chapter 1 of the preceeding Book [i.e., Book XXIV] and the *Defense of The Spirit of Laws*, Part II." This footnote was incorporated in the edition of 1757. (XXV, 9)

5. Voltaire considered this denunciation of the Inquisition one of the triumphs of *The Spirit of Laws* and in his *L' A, B, C* (1768) (see note 7 to Book V for information concerning a modern translation), he compared its ironical tone to XV, 5 on slavery, while remarking that both chapters were better than Callot.

6. Situated on the Malabar coast of India, Calicut (now Kozhikade, part of Kerala State, India) was the base of an East India company trading establishment as of 1664. Both the French and the Danes later established trade connections in Calicut.

BOOK XXVI

1*. Since this law of Henry II had been intended to discourage abortions, the Sorbonne censured XXVI, 3 [4] (Proposition XVI), on the grounds that Montesquieu's argument was detrimental to the welfare of children. In his "Réponse et Explication à la Proposition XVI," M said the censured passage conveyed neither approval of abortion nor disapproval of the punishment of that crime. There is a substantial difference, M remarked, between approving a crime and judging the punishment for that crime excessive. And M affirmed that the law of Henry II was contrary to self-defense since it condemned to death (i.e., among those women who had not reported their pregnancies) not only those who had aborted their children, but also those who had lost their children through disease or natural causes. (XXVI, 3 [4])

2. M's ecclesiastical critics either overlooked this passage or believed M had rendered the passage innocuous by restricting himself to pagan, false religions.

BOOK XXIX

1. The MS. (V, f. 332) contains a different first chapter, entitled "Idea of this Book" and beginning with the sentence: "The subject of this book is so immense that I will be content with reporting several examples." And in the MS. this first chapter also contained the important methodological statement: "This should not be regarded as a treatise on jurisprudence. It is rather a sort of method for studying jurisprudence. It is not the body of the laws that I am seeking, but their soul."

2. See VI, 1–2, however, for M's concern that the other extreme of too few laws also be avoided.

3*. The Sorbonne censured this fourth paragraph of chapter 9 (Proposition X), along with Book XIV, chap. 12 [1–3], as revealing an attitude insufficiently critical of suicide. In his "Réponse et Explication à la Proposition X," M maintained that the passage in question referred to the absence of civil laws against suicide. He had said nothing, M pointed out, about those natural laws that prohibit suicide. In order to clarify his true meaning, he altered the phrase "there was no law against suicides" in [4] to read "there was no civil law at Rome against suicides" in the edition of 1757. (XXIX, 9 [4])

An Essay on

CAUSES AFFECTING
MINDS
AND CHARACTERS[1]

PART ONE: *Physical Causes Affecting Minds and Characters* ²

[1] These causes become less arbitrary as they have a more general effect. Thus we know better what gives a certain character to a nation than what gives a particular mentality to an individual, what modifies one of the sexes than what affects a man, what forms the spirit of societies that have embraced a way of life than what forms the character of a single person.

[HOW CLIMATE AND TEMPERATURE CAN AFFECT MINDS AND CHARACTERS]

. . . . .³

[2] Several effects must follow from this physical constitution. The peoples of the North will not have that immediate insight, that mental quickness, that facility for receiving and communicating all sorts of impressions that people in other climates have. But if they have not the advantage of quickness, they have that of composure. They adhere better to their decisions, and they make fewer mistakes carrying them out.

[3] The Dutch ⁴ are famous for the slowness with which their ideas are formed. It is to this that they owe the consistency of their political principles and that steadfastness of their passions that has enabled them to accomplish such great things.

[4] Accordingly, the imaginations of Northern peoples will be more tranquil. ⁵ They will be less capable of what are called creative

works than works of compilation, and, for the same reason, they will be more suited than other peoples for making discoveries in the arts that demand assiduous effort and sustained research.

                                                        [6]

. . . .

[5]   It is these differences in the constitution of the machine that give rise to differences in the strength of the passions. In a country where love is the greatest concern, jealousy is the greatest passion.

. . . . [7]

[HOW FOODS CAN AFFECT MINDS AND CHARACTERS]

[6]   People in hot countries, as we have said, need to eat watery foods.[8] Now these foods are the lightest. Besides, they must have delicate food because their fibres are weak, and their fibres become weak because they eat delicate food.

[7]   People in cold countries need coarse food to sustain themselves. The attrition of their solid parts needs to be counteracted.[9] Besides, their food must be coarse because their fibres are strong, and their fibres are strong because their food is coarse.

[8]   Those in charge of training the athletes and young men who exercised in the palestra found that the athletes' strength depended entirely on the coarseness of the food they were given, namely, pork seasoned with dill and a type of very heavy bread that was kneaded with cheese. If the athletes were given lighter food, regardless of the quantity, their strength was observed to immediately diminish. The coarse food must therefore have thickened their fibres and given them a sturdier contexture. When the thickening and toughness of the fibres reaches the point of excess, the brain is perpetually sluggish. The fibres and animal spirits[10] then prove incapable of receiving the infinite number of varied, unexpected, and distinct movements they require. The athletes of

whom we have spoken are proof of this.[a] All authors agree on the
dullness of their minds.

[HOW THE CONDITION OF THE FIBRES OF THE NERVOUS
SYSTEM CAN AFFECT MINDS AND CHARACTERS]

[9]   Although it would appear that impressions are communicated to
the soul by means of an animal spirit or a fluid contained in the
nerves, it is nevertheless necessary that the fibres be flexible and
that they be capable of moving and being moved.[b] These are
reciprocal things. The nerve fluid cannot be transported without
some tension in the fibres, nor can the fibres be made taut, or be
moved without the nerve fluid being transported in them.[c]

[10]   The soul will be able to call its ideas back to consciousness when
it can reproduce in the brain the movements the brain has had, and
when it makes the nerve fluid flow to the brain. The flexibility of
the fibres can therefore render the soul able to easily reproduce
ideas.

[11]   The thinner the string of a musical instrument, the better suited
it is for making a high-pitched sound. That is, it vibrates more in
the same space of time than a string whose sound is pitched lower.
On the other hand, the thicker the string, the lower pitched the

---

[a] Gorgus Messenius, says Polybius, was an exception to this stupidity characteristic of
athletes (*Excerpta ex Polybio*. Libro VII).[11]

[b] When the nerve diameters are larger, there is a broader column of liquid contained
between the extremity of the nerve and its inner part, and the impressions could be
weaker. It appears that the neural ganglia, attached in various places along the pathways
of the nerves, contradict the vibration-theory.[12]

[c] Monsieur Bertin[13] reports having made a fine experiment. Tying the diaphragmatic
nerve of a dog, he squeezed it above the ligature and found that movement was restored as
if he had squeezed it below the ligature. Thus the experiment that was cited against
vibrations supports vibrations.[14]

sound. That is to say, it vibrates less in the same space of time than other cords whose sound is pitched higher. Consequently, when the fibres that the soul moves are thick, their vibrations are less frequent and slower.[d]

[12]   External objects give sensations to the soul. The soul cannot exactly reexperience them, but it can recall that it has had them. Suppose the soul has felt a pain. It surely does not give itself that pain again, but it feels that it has previously had the pain. That is, it places itself again, as much as it possibly can, in the state of the previous sensation. In order for the soul to actually experience that sensation, the pain must return to it along the path it had already taken. An idea is thus simply anything that we feel as a result of a sensation we have once had, a present situation occasioned by a past situation.

[13]   When, by means of the senses, the soul has felt a pain, the irritation of the affected part has communicated pressure to the point of origin of the nerve[16] and excited a commotion felt in proportion to the strength of the irritation. Now the soul, which has the ability to make the animal spirits pass wherever it wants (as the experience of all voluntary movements shows), can cause them to pass again over the paths they had previously traversed when they were stimulated by an external cause.[e] They therefore pass again into the brain, or they press on it, which amounts to the

[d] Our brain fibres, incessantly in motion, must be like those fibres in a harpsichord player's fingers, which appear, by force of habit, to move completely unaided, that is, without dependence on the will.[15]

[e] The soul can do three things: (1) hold back the animal spirits and use them to renew its sensations; (2) use the animal spirits to bring about the various movements that it wishes to give to the body; and finally, allow them to flow through the cerebellum[17] for vital movements.[18]

same thing.^{f} Now, this new feeling is only an idea or a representation, since the soul is well aware that this is not the sensation itself and that this commotion, unlike the other, does not come to it from the whole length of the nerve, nor from a real external action, but merely by means of its own will-power. Feelings need no further explanation. Perception, ideas, memory involve always the same operation, stemming only from the soul's faculty of feeling. But one sees how necessary it is that the fibres of the brain be flexible.

[14]   Too much rigidity or thickness of the brain fibres[22] can produce a sluggish mind. But then too much flexibility, when accompanied by slackening, can produce a weak mind; and when this delicateness and slackening of the fibres happens to be accompanied by a great abundance of animal spirits, then inconstancy, capriciousness, and eccentricity naturally result. The brain is briskly moved by the present object and ceases to be moved by others.

[15]   We do not know what particular disposition of the brain is requisite for mental alertness, but we can conjecture something on the subject. For instance, we know that liveliness of the eyes often indicates an alert mind. Now people of cold countries rarely have

---

^{f} Monsieur Sénac[19] says that the reverse action of the animal spirits is inexplicable. Why is this so? I am well aware that they do not circulate from the outer parts to the brain, and that they appear to continue their course. But why can't they exert pressure from the extremities of the body towards the brain, since they are inside completely filled tubes? From this I conclude, by functional analogy, that the soul receives sensations through the ministry of the nerves only by means of pressure, and that a canal full of liquid, pressed at one end, affects the other end and must, likewise, when pressed at the opposite end, have a similar effect. If, then, the soul, by pressing the fibres in the region of the medulla oblongata, sends animal spirits toward the legs, the nerves that extend from the brain to the legs, when pressed in the area of the legs, must likewise exert pressure in the brain.[20][21]

lively eyes. Since they have superfluous humidity in the brain, the motor nerves, being perpetually wet, slacken and become incapable of producing the quick and lively vibrations in the eyes that make them bright. So, since I have just said that mental alertness and lively eyes generally go together, it seems to follow that superfluous humidity is almost as adverse to one as to the other. Thus, the Ancients had made a good point, although without being conscious of what they were saying, when they regarded intelligence as resulting from a moderate dryness of the brain.

[HOW BONE FIBRES AND BONE MARROW CAN AFFECT MINDS AND CHARACTERS]

[16]   It has been observed in England that the bones of a thoroughbred horse, that is, one born of a Barbary stallion and an English mare, weigh more, by a half, than those of an ordinary English horse with bones of the same size. The bones of the thoroughbred have less marrow, their fibres are more compact, and the texture of these fibres is less sparse. I would like to do the same experiment with the bones of a Dutchman and a man from the Pyrenees. If the difference proved to be the same, we could surmise that the condition of the fibres, whether more or less dry, or more or less compact, would contribute to creating the differences between their characters.

[HOW THE AIR WE BREATHE CAN AFFECT MINDS AND CHARACTERS]

[17]   Upon entering our lungs, air inflates the vesicles covered by tiny branches of the pulmonary artery and pulmonary vein.[23] These vesicles, ceasing to be collapsed, allow the blood to traverse the whole of the lungs. When the air has a lot of elasticity, there occur an infinite number of small impacts on the walls of these vesicles,

and, as a result, on the coatings of the blood vessels covering them. This causes further degrees of movement to be continually added to the blood. The blood is portioned out better, and it becomes more suited to an abundant secretion of animal spirits.

[18] The intelligence of the Athenians has been attributed to the fineness of the air in Athens,[24] and it appears that this was indeed one of the major causes, since, although the Athenians are now, as subjects of the Turkish empire, enslaved and without education, having scarcely anything in their favor but the air, their genius is still noteworthy.[25]

[19] We often hear about the intelligence of the Canarins, the people who inhabit the territory of Goa. They have such innate advantage over the Portuguese that they make more progress in school in six months, regardless of the subject, than Europeans do in a year. And this superiority is so noteworthy that it offends the dominant nation. The Portuguese prevent the Canarins from participating in the shipping trade. They weaken them in heart and mind[26] by a kind of slavery. They allow them no profession other than that of trial lawyer, and there they exercise their art so shrewdly that they surpass the hopes of the litigants.

[20] And, from this, we can conclude two things: first, that the climate contributes immeasurably to modifying the mind; and second, that the effect is not immediate. A long sequence of generations must be necessary to produce it,[27] since the Portuguese still remain almost as they were prior to the conquest of Goa.[28]

[HOW SOILS CAN AFFECT MINDS AND CHARACTERS]

[21] In every country the food consumed has a quality analagous to the nature of the soil. We find iron in honey. The particles of this metal must therefore have been absorbed by the plants and flowers

from which the bees extracted it. Iron is found in blood, too. Accordingly, the plants and animals eaten by men must contain such metallic particles. The same can be said of the other metals and minerals.^g Thus we see minds and characters veritably subjected to differences of soils.²⁹

[HOW WINDS CAN AFFECT MINDS AND CHARACTERS]

[22]   If the air in every country acts on the mind, the winds, which are transports of air, do so no less. There is very remarkable proof of this all over the world. The peoples who live along the Pyrenees on this side are quite different from those who live along them on the other side. The peoples who have the Apennines to the north are very different from those who have them to the south, and so forth.

[23]   Winds affect us by transporting air that is heavier or thinner, drier or more humid, than that of our own climate, or by transporting air charged with particles more peculiar to the country through which they have passed, or finally by giving greater buoyancy to the air. But whatever the specific case, the degree of the wind's effect is greatly augmented by its quickness, for winds lay hold of us suddenly and produce changes in us instantaneously.

[24]   There is, in Italy, a southern wind^h called the Sirocco, which has passed over the African sands. It rules Italy. It casts the spell of its power over all minds. It produces sluggishness and a general uneasiness. A man can sense, even while in bed, when the Sirocco is blowing. He behaves differently than he did the day before. In short, the Sirocco is the power that controls the national psychology of the Italians, and I am tempted to believe that the difference

^g Enough of them enter to influence the body, but not enough to harm it.
^h It is actually southeastern. According to Father Ansted's account of Egypt, that country is subject to the ravages of the same southern wind.

existing between the mentality and character of the inhabitants of
Lombardy[i] and that of other Italians stems from Lombardy having
the Apennines, on her southern flank, protecting her inhabitants
from the ravages of the Sirocco.

[25]   The English also have their easterly wind. But the difference is
that whereas the maladies attacking Italian minds incline them
toward self-preservation, those attacking the English mind incline
them toward their ruin. The English malady, however, is not
simply the effect of a passing cause. It is rather the cumulative
effect of several other, long-standing causes.[30]

[HOW THE DIFFERENCE BETWEEN THE SEXES CAN AFFECT
MINDS AND CHARACTERS]

[26]   The difference between the two sexes must also diversify
minds. The periodic upheaval that occurs in women has very
extensive effects. It must lay hold of the mind itself. We know
that its cause lies in a kind of fullness that increases continuously
during approximately one month, whereupon the blood discharges
as a result of being present in too great a quantity. Now, since this
quantity changes daily in women, their temperament and disposition must similarly change.

[27]   Women's fibres are softer, slacker, more flexible, and more
delicate than those of men. This is because a portion of their blood
vessels are less compressed, since the cavity formed by the sacrum,
the coccyx, pubic, and innominate bones is larger in women. The
womb, with the innumerable blood vessels that run through it, can
dilate better, and just as veins have a weaker contexture than
arteries (for they can be dilated more), it will be the same with
these vessels. Besides, the blood, being overly abundant, is able to

---

[i] Lombardy is a triangle, of which the apex is in Piedmont, the base is on the Adriatic
sea, and the sides are formed by the Alps and the Apennines.

force open a passage, and the blood vessels do not need to contract so strongly to propel the blood from the extremities of the womb toward its center.[31]

[28]   Furthermore, men have an organ that, through a function beginning at puberty, soon changes the contexture of their fibres, which were previously as delicate as those of women. We cannot explain how the liquid that is separated, filtered, and stored in these organs produces these effects, but we observe them, and we see no such thing hapening to women or eunuchs.[32] We know, moreover, that this liquid is so active that the meat of female animals changes in taste after they have conceived. Considering the manner in which our sense of taste is produced, this implies an extraordinary disturbance in their fibres. All these things make us quite aware of the physical difference of character between the two sexes.

[HOW THE STRUCTURAL MAKEUP OF THE BODY CAN AFFECT MINDS AND CHARACTERS]

[29]   Anatomical observations reveal a prodigious variety from one person to another. This variety is so great that there perhaps never were two men whose organic parts have been similarly arranged in all respects.

[30]   If we look at works on anatomy and take veins, for example, we will see that there are few that follow the same pattern in one subject as in another. One person will have only one vein of a certain name, whereas another will have two of this type. What is found in regard to veins will also be found in regard to arteries, nerves, lymphatic vessels. I will not go into details. They would be endless, and even the observations which have been made are nothing compared with those lying beyond our limited powers.

[31]   These variations that are clearly visible in the readily discerni-

ble portions of the human body are no less great in the imperceptible blood vessels of the brain.

[32]   If with the onset of circulation,[33] it happened that the blood for some reason found more resistance in passing through the descending aorta than through the branches of the thoracic aorta,[j] it would rise to the brain in greater quantity, and the filtration of the animal spirits would undoubtedly be very different from what it would be in the opposite case. And this effect would be permanent because the blood vessels would have to contain more liquid and would thereby increase in diameter.

[33]   The parts of the body cannot adequately fulfill their intended functions unless their size corresponds to what the mechanism of the body requires. The head must accommodate six lobes of the brain and two of the cerebellum. Its shape must therefore correspond to this purpose. If we do not see that the head has such a shape, there must be some irregularity in the shape of the brain.

[34]   Although, when we think, we feel that the action takes place in the head, and not in the feet or in the hands, it is nevertheless not only the fibres of the brain that affect the mind.[k] An example will illustrate this.

[35]   The portio dura of the auditory nerve[35] forms what is called the chorda tympani, which ends in the lingual nerve of the third branch of the fifth pair. The hard portion is further divided into

---

[j] There are persons in whom two external jugular veins are found on each side. The blood empties more easily from the brain, and, as a result, rises to the brain more easily.

[k] The more necessary the sensation, the more it is clear, strong, and common to all. Thus the senses of sight, hearing, and touch are very clear. The nerves that occasion them are as alert and sensitive in one climate as in another. It is the milder sensations, unessential to the well-being of the machine, that are not given to everyone and occur only in refined persons. It is necessary that everyone hear sounds but not that everyone be sensitive to the beauties of music. In a word, the strong and unrefined sense operations are bestowed on all men. The delicate ones are bestowed on only a few.[34]

three branches: the lower, the middle, and the upper. These are in communication with the three branches[1] of the fifth pair, which send two branches to the intercostal nerve. Furthermore, this hard portion joins the cervical nerves which communicate with the intercostal nerve.[m] This intercostal is the great instrument of involuntary movements because it goes to the heart and the lungs and all the parts contained in the chest and the lower abdomen. Whence I conclude that when we hear singing or declamation, two equally mechanical things happen. First, we hear the sounds clearly, and second, we are moved by these sounds. And it is a daily occurence that, of two persons, the one who hears better is nevertheless less moved. To hear well, it is sufficient that the ear be well formed, but to be moved while hearing, there must be good communication between the nerves of the ear and the nerves which go to other parts of the body to produce involuntary movements. For then the heart is moved, as are most of the internal parts, and emotion, which, it seemed, would arrive at the brain solely from the ear, actually arrives there from almost every part of the body.

[36]   Since the feelings we have almost always result from the various movements produced in the different organs of our body, men in whom the communication of these motions takes place easily have more refinement of feeling and more acute minds than those in whom such communication is difficult.

[37]   The soul in our body is like a spider in its web. The spider

---

[1] The upper branch of the trunk of the portio dura is connected to the first branch of the fifth pair, called the opthalmic nerve; the middle branch joins the second branch of the fifth pair, or the upper maxillary nerve, and the lower branch is connected to the third branch of the fifth pair, or the lower maxillary nerve.

[m] Sometimes the seven cervical nerves are connected to the intercostal.

cannot move without disturbing one of the threads which stretch out from it, and, similarly, none of these threads can be moved without disturbing the spider. Nor can any of the threads be touched without making another connected to it move as well. The more taut the threads, the better informed the spider. If some of the threads are slack, then there will be less communication from the thread to the spider, or from one thread to another, and the fate of the spider will be almost hanging in the balance in its web.

[38]   Just as those who play a musical instrument are careful, in order to insure that no interruption of sound occurs, to use strings that have no knots and no places thicker or thinner, tighter or looser than others, it is also necessary for the easy communication of movements in our machine, that all parts of the nerves be uniform and smooth, that there be no places tighter, or drier, or less suited to receiving the activating fluid[36] than others, that each part be joined to all the rest, that the whole constitute a unified system, and that there be no break in the network of the nerve fibres.

[39]   Nothing in nature is entirely uniform, but each thing has uniformity to a certain degree, and this greater or lesser uniformity in each fibre produces great differences in movements.

[40]   One cannot imagine on how many things the state of our minds depends. It is not just the disposition of the brain that modifies the mind. The machine as a whole and almost all of its parts, often, in fact, even those parts one would not suspect, contribute to modifying the mind.

[41]   There is a type of person who is usually sad, angry, capricious, weak, spiteful, eccentric and timid. This person is the eunuch. Whether the semen reenters the bloodstream or does not separate out from it,[37] it is certain that they become different from other

people. This failure of separation exists also in women and is the reason eunuchs resemble women, at least bodily. For example, the physical constitution of eunuchs becomes weak, like that of women, and, like women, they have no beards.

[42]   Those who, without the permission of Nature or a true vocation from above, devote themselves to celibacy are placed by perpetual continence in much the same situation as eunuchs. They indeed have the capacity but it is not used, and this very capacity can contribute to further distressing them. The liquid is separated in the seminal vesicles, but it stays there too long. It irritates these vesicles, signaling the soul to dispatch animal spirits, but the soul does not dare obey.[38]

[HOW DIVERSE PASSIONS AND BEHAVIOR PATTERNS CAN AFFECT MINDS AND CHARACTERS]

[43]   Emotions act greatly on us. Life is but a series of passions, sometimes stronger, sometimes weaker, now of one kind, now of another. It cannot be doubted that the combination of these passions during the whole of life, a combination which is different in every individual, produces a great variety of minds.

[44]   There are some emotions that give elasticity to the fibres and others that slacken them. This is proved, on the one hand, by the strength and power of anger, and, on the other, by the effects of fear. The arms sag, the legs bend, the voice fails, the muscles slacken.[39] Thus a life lived timidly or courageously over a long period of time will be that way always.

[45]   We must make extremely careful use of our brain fibres. As moderate movements permit us to continue them indefinitely, violent movements restrict those that follow. The Orientals distract themselves with a concoction of hemp that gives them such

agreeable ideas and such lively pleasures that for a few hours they are completely transported. The final result is total dejection and a virtually lethargic condition. The effect of this liquid [n] is to stretch the fibres, [o] which consequently become unresponsive to slighter movements. One dose stupefies only for a while. Extensive use stupefies forever. Great joy is a state as far removed from good health as is great sorrow. For someone who is in good health, the mere pleasure of being alive is sufficient.

[46]   The immoderate use of wine stupefies little by little. The fibres are excited, but only for a short time. They slacken and it takes more alcohol to stir them. Soon the same quantity will not suffice, and, in order to produce the very same result, stronger doses will become necessary day by day.

[47]   Great nobles who exhaust themselves with sensual pleasures sink into dejection, boredom, and dull-wittedness, and such ills are inherited by their offspring. These noblemen grow bored because they can no longer receive new impressions. They are dejected because their nerve fibres are no longer capable of lively movements. They sometimes have weak minds because, receiving nothing but the impressions of present objects, their minds are necessarily enslaved to passing and momentary movements.

[48]   Too much sleep stupefies greatly. [p] The fibres remain for too long immobile. The animal spirits thicken and remain in their reservoirs. Athletes slept the most, [q] and they were the stupidest of all men. [43]

[n] It produces heat, strengthens the heart, and increases the movement of the blood. [40]

[o] This stretching is the cause of the loss of ideas that takes place in certain illnesses.

[p] According to Aulus Gellius, it has been noticed that children who sleep too long become slow-witted. See my extract. [41]

[q] Plato, *Republic*, Book I. [42]

[49]   Excessive sleeplessness may not produce stupidity, but it does cause foolishness and even madness,[r] especially if it is accompanied by long fasts. The animal spirits become hyperactive, as in moments of intense emotion, and they rush impetuously to the brain where they leave deep traces.

[50]   No one could suspect the Fathers of the Desert[45] of having been imbeciles. The great reputation they enjoyed in their time, the homage people paid their wisdom by coming from all over the world to consult them, show that they were not held in contempt—and not just because they were holy. Nevertheless, these Fathers, by their fasts and sleepless vigils, carried to excess, did pitiful harm to their minds, and the ceaseless combats they imagined themselves having with the Demons were one of the weaknesses that seemed attached to their way of life.

[51]   Excessively prolonged singing, especially shouting also stupefies. We see in Livy[s] that the sect of profligates who celebrated the Bacchanalia and gathered in secret places, where amid the mysteries of the most impious superstition, they depraved or slaughtered young persons to the sound of singing and musical instruments, were entirely stupefied by their vigils and their continual yelling.

[52]   We know that the Mohammedans who, in order to put themselves in an ecstatic state, place themselves in tombs where they remain awake and scream unceasingly, always emerge with weaker minds. Mahmut,[t] one of the conquerors of Persia, who, as a result of some misfortune, wanted to take counsel with God in

---

[r] Read in Boerhaave, *De Vigilia* (*Institutiones medicae*), and, in addition, in his *Pathologie*. It is the same volume.[44]

[s] Fourth Decade, Book IX.

[t] *Histoire de la dernière Révolution de Perse* (Paris, 1728), Vol. II, p. 295.

that fashion, lapsed into a kind of madness from which he never recovered.

[53]   Screaming benumbs the fibres and creates irregular movements within them. The animal spirits run about in all directions without any order. All traces are mixed together. Some are imprinted more vividly, others are erased, and the brain is beset by confusion.

[54]   The effects of solitude on the mind are no less dangerous than those of fasts, sleeplessness, and screaming. The brain fibres are left in a state of repose, and they become almost incapable of movement. It has been noted that those Indian contemplatives who pass their lives contemplating the void, become veritable idiots. There is no portion of our body whose functions can be preserved without exercise. Teeth not used for chewing decay, and were one to use only one eye, the other would become blind.

[55]   I believe that, in a subject as complicated as this, one must avoid going into much detail. Huarte,[46] a Spaniard who has treated this subject before me, tells us that Francis I, disgusted with his Christian doctors and with the uselessness of their remedies, sent word to Charles V for a Jewish doctor. The good fellow then tries to discover why the Jews have more aptitude for medicine than Christians have, and he finds that this comes from the enormous quantity of manna the Israelites ate in the Desert.[47]

PART TWO: *Moral Causes Affecting Minds and Characters*

[1]   Those who begin to use their reason live either among barbarous peoples, where there is no education whatsoever, or among civilized peoples where one receives a general education in society.[1]

[HOW LIVING AMONG BARBAROUS, UNEDUCATED PEOPLES CAN AFFECT MINDS AND CHARACTERS]

[2]   Those raised among a barbarous people quite understandably possess only those ideas related to self-preservation. They live in eternal darkness with regard to all the rest. Among barbarous peoples, differences between one man and another and between one mind and another are less great. The general crudeness and paucity of ideas somehow equalizes the differences.

[3]   Proof of their relative lack of ideas is the barreness of the languages they use. Not only do they have few words, since they have few things to express, but they also have only a few ways of conceiving ideas and of feeling.

[4]   Their brain fibres, little accustomed to being exercised, have become rigid. One can compare men living among these peoples to those old persons among us who have never learned anything. Perhaps I may put it as follows. Their brains not having had to work, the fibres are not trained in the required movements. They are incapable of adding any new ideas to the few they already have,

and this weakness is not restricted to their brains. It would also be found in their throats if one wished to make them sing, and in their fingers if one wished to have them play a musical instrument.

[5]   It has been discovered[2] that the savages of America are immune to discipline, incorrigible, and incapable of any enlightenment or instruction. Indeed, trying to teach them something, trying to bend their brain fibres, is like trying to make totally crippled people walk.

[6]   Coarseness can reach such a point among these peoples that they are sometimes little different from beasts. Witness those slaves that the Turks take from Circassia and Mingrelia,[3] who pass the whole day with their heads bent over their stomachs, saying nothing and doing nothing, completely uninterested in anything that transpires around them.

[7]   Brains left thus idle lose their capacity to function. These brains do not enjoy the use of their souls, nor the soul that of its union with the body.

[HOW LIVING AMONG CIVILIZED, EDUCATED PEOPLES AND AFFECT MINDS AND CHARACTERS]

[8]   It is education that renders this union [of soul and body] perfect. We find it among civilized peoples. There, as I have already said, we receive a particular education in our family and a general one in society.

[HOW INDIVIDUAL EDUCATION CAN AFFECT MINDS AND CHARACTERS]

[9]   Individual education consists of (1) acquiring ideas and (2) proportioning them to the real nature of things. Now the number

of ideas one has and the degree of accuracy with which these ideas are interrelated must greatly diversify minds.

[10]   Those who raise us are, in a manner of speaking, manufacturers of our ideas. They multiply them. They teach us to fashion them and to make abstractions. They constantly give us new ways of being and perceiving.[a]

[11]   Old people, on the other hand, lapse gradually into imbecility by the daily loss of their ideas: they return to childhood by losing their ideas, just as children outgrow childhood by acquiring ideas.

[12]   Men with few ideas necessarily err in almost all their judgments. Ideas are interrelated. The soul's principal faculty is that of making comparisons, and it cannot exercise this faculty unless it is supplied with ideas.

[13]   Education does not multiply our ideas without also multiplying our ways of feeling. Education heightens the soul's awareness, refines its faculties, and leads us to detect those slight and delicate differences that are imperceptible to people born with less than perfect organs or to people of less than perfect upbringing.

[14]   It is not sufficient to have many ideas and types of sensation. It is also essential that there be harmony between them and the objects they represent. It is foolish to be affected either too much or too little by an object.

[15]   But men seldom receive impressions of objects in a manner commensurate with their value. The first impression we receive strikes us with a lasting force, and this is quite understandable. The first ideas are always accepted because, owing to the mind's inability to compare them with others, it has no grounds upon which to reject them. And so the second idea can scarcely make the mind turn away from the first, nor the third from the second, for it

[a] See the difference between a language in which there have been no writers at all, and another in which great geniuses have written.[4]

is only by the first that it judges the second, and by the second that it judges the third. Thus, regardless of their value, the first things that have affected the mind seem somehow indestructible.

[16]   They say that old people who forget what they did the previous day recall very well what happened to them thirty years earlier. Hence the strength of an impression depends more on the time of the action than on the action itself, more on the circumstances in which we are affected than on the importance of the thing that affects us.

[17]   After impressions are received in childhood, our soul successively receives a great number of others, which are joined together with the first group, but in a thousand and one different patterns.

[18]   Do we place our confidence in someone who addresses us or in a philosopher whom we read? If so, we create for ourselves an order of things true, good, and appropriate, namely, the things that this one has written or that one has told us. We take from something outside us the grounds for our opinions.

[19]   Do we like someone very much? Here again is an order of things true, good, and appropriate, namely, the things that this person has approved, advised, prescribed, or done, things that immediately dominate our thinking.

[20]   In order to be more aware of our soul's capacity for being differently affected by the same objects at different times, we need only picture to ourselves the moments when we are enraptured by love and those when our passion subsides. How the entire soul is transformed! How all that affected it does so no longer! How all that had ceased to affect it moves it once again! Our soul is very limited, and it cannot respond to several emotions at the same time. When it has several, the least of them must follow the main one and be swept along with it, as by a common movement. Thus, in the furor of love, all other ideas take on the coloring of that

passion that grips the soul to the exclusion of all others. Hatred, jealousy, fear, hope, are all like glasses of distinct colors, through which we see an object that appears always equally red, or green, etc., and differs only in shade.

[21]   Moreover, our human machine is normally constituted so that our brain is physically disposed to receiving the impressions of one order of things rather than another.

[22]   A man who has imagination, and another who has not, see things as differently as two fictional heroes, one of whom is captivated by what he sees and the other not. The first would see crystal walls, ruby roofs, silver streams, diamond tables. The other would perceive only hideous rocks and an arid countryside.

[23]   The physical constitution of our machine is such that we are too much or too little struck by things that come to us through the senses or through a certain sense, by relations based on exact reason or on moral feeling, by general or specific concepts, by facts, or by reasoning. One person will be convinced by rhetoric and another only by plain logic. One person will be struck by mere words and another only by evidence. One person will never see a proposition without also visualizing various objections to it and will be uncertain. Another will see the proposition better than the objections to it and will believe all. Finally, another, always visualizing the objections better than the proposition, will believe nothing. One person will perceive things separately without seeing their interconnections and will not possess an orderly understanding. Or else, this person will believe he has found everything interconnected, and will be confused. One person will want always to create, another always to destroy. One person will have an active mind, while another will merely take things in like a purse yielding nothing but the money placed therein.[5] Ideas that will only

brush against the brain of one man will pierce that of another through and through, as it were, even to the point of engendering madness.

[24]   All is lost when, in addition to the particular disposition of the brain, which is rarely constructed so as to receive ideas in just proportion, education is also inadequate. Our teachers only communicate impressions to us as they themselves have received them, and if these impressions are not appropriately proportioned to objects, they diminish our capacity for comparison, which is the soul's key faculty.

[25]   Education, as I have said, consists in giving us ideas, and a good education in attaching proper significance to each one. A dearth of ideas results in stupidity, lack of harmony among one's ideas leads to foolishness, and extreme disharmony causes madness.

[26]   A man is intelligent when things make the appropriate impression on him, whether putting him in a position to judge well, or to please others. Hence two kinds of education: one we receive from our teachers and one we receive in society. We must have both because all things have two values, an intrinsic value and a value based on opinion. These two types of education impart to us precisely these two values, and intelligence enables us to make use of one or the other, depending upon the time, persons, and place.

[27]   An intelligent man perceives and acts as he should perceive and act — and without delay or reflection. He conducts himself, at each moment, according to the present need. He both perceives and senses the exact relationship between his surroundings and himself. An intelligent man senses intuitively what others can only know through experience. All that is mute for most people speaks to him and instructs him. There are some who read the lines of a face; others interpret facial expressions; and still others

see right into the soul. One could say that a fool lives only among physical objects, whereas an intelligent man dwells in the realm of the mind as well.

[28]   An intelligent man does not always have flashes of wit, because three-fourths of the time they are out of place. Nor is having intelligence equivalent to being always exact, because exactness is also often inappropriate as, for example, in playful conversations that are only webs of false reasoning, pleasing by their very false-ness and uniqueness. Conversation would not be varied, and would no longer amuse, if one looked only for truth in it.

[29]   An intelligent man has a more general grasp of things, but such a person (in the strict sense) is quite rare. He must combine two qualities nearly incompatible physically, for there is really as much difference between a man thought witty in society and one thought intelligent among philosophers as there is between an intelligent man and a stupid one.[b] According to people in society, brilliance consists of reconciling ideas that are quite different. According to philosophers, it consists of keeping ideas distinct. With the former type of intelligence, all ideas that are somewhat related, no matter how distantly, are set in play. With the latter, all ideas are kept so distinct that nothing can confound them.

[30]   Here is a song of the Greeks.[c] "The foremost of all blessings is health, the second, beauty, the third, wealth amassed without fraud, the fourth, youth spent with friends." Wit, which is the principal attribute of our times, is not mentioned at all.[9]

[b] Among the Greeks the very idea of a man of wit was scarcely known. See the song at the end of the extract from the *Journal des Savants*.[6]
[c] See this song in *l'Histoire de l'Académie des Inscriptions*, Vols. IX and X.[7] [8]

[HOW GENERAL EDUCATION CAN AFFECT MINDS AND CHARACTERS; THE CONCEPT OF THE GENERAL CHARACTER OF A PEOPLE]

[31]   We have just spoken of the particular education that shapes the character of each man. There is also a general education that we receive in the society in which we live. For there is in every people a general character that more or less leaves its stamp on the character of each individual. It is produced in two ways: by physical causes depending on climate, of which I will say no more, and by moral causes, which are the combined result of laws, religion, customs, manners, and that sort of emanation of the general way of thinking and of the mannerisms and foolishness of the court and the capital that spreads far afield.

[32]   The laws that prescribe ignorance to Mohammedans, like the customs that prevent them from communicating with one another, leave their minds sluggish. The works of Confucius, which confuse an immense detail of civil ceremonies with moral precepts, thereby putting the most trifling things on the same plane as the most essential, greatly affect the Chinese mind. The Scholastic logic greatly modifies the minds of peoples who apply themselves to it. The great freedom of speech and expression that exists in certain countries results in a countless number of unique minds. The extraordinary importance bestowed on unessential details in the Talmud, as opposed to a similar importance given to essential matters in the Holy Scriptures, has very much narrowed the minds of the Jewish doctors.

[33]   The intricacy of causes that shape the general character of a people is quite great. Let a man in Constantinople enter the house of a Turk; he will hear the latter speak only the bare minimum of words. Let him enter the house of a Greek; he will find the whole

family talking incessantly. The Turkish nation is solemn because it knows that it rules. The nation that obeys, on the other hand, has a more natural character.[10] Moreover, the Turk's house is a monarchy, whereas the Greek's is a popular state. Having only one wife, the Greek savors that joy which always accompanies moderation. Having a great number of wives, the Turk is habitually sad and lives under the heavy burden of his pleasures.

[34]   When one sees some of our young men go running about, bantering, laughing, eager to do all the foolish things they see others have done, compensating for their lack of reflection by their flashes of wit, who would not say that these are people of a very lively wit?[11] Most of the time, however, this is not the case. It is only that their bodily mechanisms are adapted to such behavior, either by a penchant we have for imitating what we see, or by a prejudice in favor of what is fashionable, or by a desire to please women, or seem to please them. For, while in countries where women are constrained one makes headway with them through a reserved mien, in those countries where they are free one pleases them with a frivolous bearing, whether because reflection is in itself boring or because impetuosity better suits the nature of passion.

[35]   The great importance that has been attached among the Spanish to the honor of ladies has established there a serious and respectful chivalry. Because they place their women on pedestals, the gaiety produced by familiar manners has been forbidden the Spanish. Moreover, as the code of honor has been extended to all social classes — each member of the nation desiring to be respected by all the others — solemnity has become universal, and all the more so because it is easier to come by than true merit, people being able to judge the solemnity of a man more easily than the quality of his mind and talents. Finally, so many petty officials sent into all four

corners of the world where, like Chinese mandarins, they have done nothing but command, have come back to Spain more solemn than when they left.[12]

[36]   Thus, even independently of the climate, which acts greatly on the Spaniards in this respect,[d] they could have acquired a phlegmatic manner as we French have acquired vivacity. A Spaniard, born lively, could restrain the commotion of his bodily mechanism, and a Frenchman, born sluggish, could excite his.

[37]   Everybody knows that in Sparta they spoke very little. That had to have been so, for, on the one hand, respect for old age must have kept young people in silence, and gravity of manners, on the other hand, must have had the same effect on the old.

[38]   Moral causes shape the general character of a nation and determine the quality of its mind more than do physical causes. A great proof of this is found among the Jews, who, dispersed over the whole globe, born in all times and places, have had a lot of authors, though hardly two could be cited that possess a modicum of common sense.

[39]   One could, however, believe that rabbis had some advantage, with respect to intelligence over the rest of their people, just as one assumes that those who in Europe enjoy the reputation of men of letters have some advantage, in regard to intelligence over other Europeans. Among that crowd of rabbis who have written, however, there is not a single one who had more than mediocre ability. The reason for this is natural. The Jews coming back from Assyria were very much like captives delivered from Algiers who are paraded in the streets; but they were more uncouth because they, like their fathers, had been born into slavery. Although they had a limitless respect for their sacred books, they had little knowledge

[d] See Strabo.[13]

of them. They no longer understood the language in which these books were written. They had merely oral traditions of the great miracles that God had brought about in favor of their fathers. Ignorance, which is the mother of oral tradition, that is to say, of popular superstition, created new legends, but these sprang up bearing the character of the minds that produced them and took on, in addition, the hue of all the minds through which they passed. Scholars, that is, people whose heads were full of these vulgar traditions, collected them, and, since the earliest writers of all peoples, whether they are good or bad, have always had a very great reputation because they have always been, at least for a time, superior to all those who read them, it happened that these first, miserable works were regarded by the Jews as perfect models, upon which they formed, as they have ever since, their tastes and their distinctive character.

[40]   I am not talking about the Sacred Books written since the captivity. The style in them is very different from that of the rabbinical works. They are divinely inspired, and, even if they were not, their authors would scarcely have been able to put anything of their own invention into purely historical writings.

[41]   Here is another example that shows clearly the extent to which the moral cause overrides the physical cause. The peoples who live, like the Asiatics, toward the South have a certain timidity, which leads them naturally to obey, and the peoples who live toward the North, like the Europeans, have a boldness which inclines them to scorn life and wealth in order to command others. Now this timidity, which in the South induces everyone to obey, makes for tyrannical authority, and that boldness, which in cold countries causes everyone to want to command, makes for moderate authority. For the exercise of power carries with it a continual lust for more power unless externally stopped. Those who exercise

authority do not respect the limits prescribed by reason, but only those fixed by exhausted patience.

[42]   It must be admitted, however, that these timid peoples of the South who shun death to enjoy real blessings, such as life, tranquillity, and pleasure, are born with better brains than the foolish people of the North, who sacrifice their lives for vainglory, that is, who would rather insure their fame than enjoy life. But, since the sound minds of the Southern peoples are subjected, by chance, to servitude, whereas the imperfect minds of Northerners benefit from liberty, it turns out that slavery debases, weakens, and destroys minds in the South, whereas liberty educates, improves, and fortifies minds in the North. The moral cause destroys the physical cause, and Nature is so greatly betrayed that the people whom she created with better minds have less sense, and those to whom she gave less sense have better minds.

[43]   In Europe, there are two kinds of religion: the Catholic, which calls for submission, and the Protestant, which requires independence. From the start, peoples of the North embraced Protestantism, whereas those of the South kept Catholicism.[14] Now the independence of Protestant peoples insures that they are perfectly instructed in human knowledge, whereas the submission of Catholic peoples, in itself very reasonable and essential to a religion founded on mysteries, causes them to know precisely what is necessary for salvation but to be entirely ignorant of everything else. The result is that the peoples of the South, who have a sounder understanding of the great truths, and even more natural intelligence, have yet a very great disadvantage compared with the peoples of the North.

[ADDITIONAL REFLECTIONS ON HOW DIVERSE PHYSICAL
AND SOCIAL CAUSES CAN AFFECT MINDS AND CHARACTERS]

[44]   There are many contributing elements to the education we have
received, some deriving from certain physical circumstances,
others from certain customs, professions, or styles of life that
we embrace. And all these factors can greatly modify our minds.
We must enter into a bit of detail.

[45]   Our character is very much shaped by that of the people whose
company we keep. Interaction with intelligent people is for us a
perpetual education, whereas a different sort of interaction makes
us lose the education we already have. With some people we are
enriched. With others we become impoverished. Character is
communicated from one person to another. Human machines are
invisibly linked; the springs that make one of them move influence
others. Whereas moderate people train us to be calm, impetuous
people tend to make us vivacious.

[46]   Books are a kind of society that one provides for oneself, but
each person chooses them after his own fashion. Those who read
good books are like those who keep good company. Those who
read bad books are like those who keep bad company and who, at
the very least, waste their time.

[47]   Knowledge gives much breadth to the mind. Philosophers of
former times lacked knowledge. Although they had good minds,
they made little use of them. They never touched upon the real
questions. They attempted to explain the inexplicable and passed
their time explaining spurious facts with principles just as false.

[48]   Traveling also greatly expands the mind. The narrow circle of
national prejudices is left behind, and those prejudices of foreign-
ers are scarcely apt to be acquired.

[49]   Certain fortunate circumstances accompanying our entry into
the world give us the confidence that can be useful for the remain-

der of our lives. Reputation has two good effects: it establishes our credibility, and it gives us courage. But the despondency that results from contempt suspends all the functions of the soul.

[50]   People claim to have noticed that hunchbacks are ordinarily clever. One might say that if deformed people have not bodily graces, they also do not have the insipidness and foolishness characteristic of those who believe themselves likeable. Their minds are thus not so easily spoiled. Besides, a high opinion of one's mind is less ridiculous than a similar opinion concerning one's looks. Finally, hunchbacks are ordinarily destined to a condition of life that leaves them scarcely any concerns other than the cultivation of their minds and the development of their talents.

[51]   There is another popular belief, containing perhaps some truth, that most deformed people have malicious minds. The reason for this is natural enough. Having a deformity which they know everybody sees, they constantly have to avenge small insults, and if they have some intelligence, they feel their strength lies therein and they make merciless use of that ability.

[52]   Certain practices can affect our minds. Engravers see figures on the walls which are not there, because their brains have received the impressions of figures they have carved. Those who have been frightened by a ghost continue to be disturbed by such an apparition because the same movements are repeated in their brain. In like fashion we can say that those who have accustomed their minds to see numerical or geometrical relationships see and find such relationships everywhere, and measure and calculate everything. One who accustoms himself to a problematic way of thinking accustoms his mind to always receive two equally strong impressions simultaneously, while he who has always adopted a decisive tone, has trained himself to receive the first idea that comes to him. Still another, who has familiarized himself with Scholastic

terminology at first feels no ideas awaken in him, but by repeating such terms, he succeeds little by little in forming a vague idea. Finally, in the same manner, we can say that a man who has long told himself, or has long been told, that metaphysical concepts are solid, but not the principles of physics, that Greek histories are true, but modern ones are not, will in the end be convinced of it. We create for ourselves the type of mind that pleases us; we are its true artisans.

[53]   It is not the mind that shapes opinions. It is the heart. And religious orders offer striking proof of this. Each has its particular philosophy that is embraced in its totality by all the members of the order. If you see a man's clothing, you see into his soul. If his clothing is gray, you can count on the wearer having a mind well furnished with ideas. Do not imagine that you will find the same kind of brain in a man whose clothes are white and black. But it will be something else again if the clothing is black.

[54]   All our ideas are linked to one another and to ourselves. If one knew in how many different ways an opinion adheres to a man's brain, one would no longer be astonished by his obstinacy in defending it.

[55]   Why are all authors so enchanted with their writings? It will be said it is because they are vain. I agree. But why is such vanity always uniformly misplaced? The reason is that what we have put in our writings is bound up with all our other ideas and relates to things that we have taken pleasure in, since we have troubled to learn about them. Our masterpieces enchant us less after a certain time has elapsed because, as a result of changes occurring in our brains, they are no longer so closely linked to our way of thinking as they were initially.

[56]   Different professions can greatly affect our minds. For in-stance, a man who teaches can easily become opinionated because

in his profession a man is supposed never to be wrong. A philosopher can easily lose intellectual charm because he becomes used to viewing and judging everything with too much precision and exactness. A Don Juan can become foolishly vainglorious because he overvalues the taste women display for him. Such taste proves only the women's weakness, and not his merit, being merely a mechanical consent rather than a considered judgment. Lawyers and magistrates can become extremely vain because, dealing only with people who need them, they imagine that their wisdom settles all questions. A soldier can become a boring storyteller because he is overly impressed with all the little things that have happened to him as a result of the connection he has drawn between them and great events. And besides, a certain boldness makes him want to be heard at all costs. Finally, as big talkers are those people whose minds are struck by many things, and so forcefully that they believe everything equally important, a scholar can succeed in becoming a very great talker, for he occupies his mind with an infinite number of ideas, and he can even believe them all important. He has acquired them laboriously, and the value of things is judged by the amount of effort their acquisition has cost.

[57]   The Persians call courtiers "*d'ellal*," or big talkers, and, generally, all people whose business is persuading others, talk a great deal because it is in their interest to prevent others from thinking and to fill other minds with their own reasoning. The same is not true of people who seek to persuade themselves.

[58]   Those who have little to do are very big talkers. The less cause one has to reflect, the more one talks. Thinking is speaking to oneself, and when one speaks to oneself, one hardly intends to speak to others.

[59]   Generally, all occupations destroy the harmonious balance of

our ideas. We are inclined to regard as very important those things that constitute our worth and that people like us do every day. Our vanity bestows on these things a most eminent rank among all the things that are done in the universe. There is a story of a priest in charge of ceremonial at the Vatican who cried with sorrow because the cardinal[e] whom he served had made a bow at the wrong time. In the mind of this man a bow had more importance than a battle in the mind of Prince Eugene.[16]

[e] Cardinal d'Estrées.[15]

[MATERIALS]¹

[This has not been added to the new correction.
When I turn this work to account, I will see what use
ought to be made of these materials.]²

[1]   The qualities of the child, being thus relative to those of the father and mother, derive from both, and from father and mother a third kind of character results that will pass from generation to generation,³ if the causes that contribute to its preservation are stronger than those contributing to its destruction.⁴ Histories teach us that all the princes of the Carolingian line had weak minds. There is scarcely any country where the hereditary stupidity of some princely house is not evident. Such remarks could hardly be made except about families on view to other men.

[2]   From conception to birth, and from birth to the time when a child stops growing, the brain develops gradually, and Nature is so prudent that the termination of the brain's growth comes ordinarily at the point when it is in the most perfect state for receiving ideas. But if, by chance, it happened that the brain were perfectly formed before the body as a whole stopped growing, you can see that its fibres would become thicker, and it would lose the perfect condition it had already acquired. Thus it can be said that there is no surer sign of future stupidity in children than precocious intelligence.

.   .   .   .   ⁵

[3]   Work thickens the fibres of the body and makes them considerably stronger. When the body is at rest, the branched and
oleaginous parts of the blood stop in the fatty cells, which are
always open to receive them. But when the body is in motion, the
nutritive parts are sent to the extremities of the fibres. The force of
the blood's circulation deposits and inserts them in the fibres and in
the spaces between these fibres. The fibres must accordingly become thicker, more solid, and more compact.

[4]   We notice that, of two parts of the body having the same
functions, those which are used more are better nourished and
stronger. It has also been observed that working people are more
difficult to purge than other people and that various medical remedies have less effect on them. Therefore, their fibres must be
harder, more massive, and tougher; and these fibres better resist
remedies that irritate or prick them.

[5]   In addition to thickening the fibres, work also gradually hardens
them. Here is how I conceive of this happening. Muscular action
is a movement of contraction. The nerve fluid, on entering the
muscular vesicles, renders them harder and more taut. The fleshy
fibres are pressed; the blood they contain is driven out, and no new
blood can enter. Soon the blood, after having filled the neighboring vesicles, presses on the muscular vesicles even more strongly
than does the nerve fluid, and this blood forces a passage. And it
reenters with all the more force the longer it has been held back.
There is therefore a kind of battle between the blood which abounds
in the muscle and presses the nerves, and the nerve fluid contained
in the same muscular fibres; or rather there are two battles: one
for the entry of animal spirits, that blocks the inflow of blood;
the other for the entry of the blood, that blocks the inflow of
the animal spirits.[6] Thus, in addition to the action and reaction

of the two liquids, there is also the action and reaction of the solid parts,[7] which is in proportion to the action of the liquids.

[6]   It happens, therefore, that the liquids forcefully strike the walls of the solids, and that the solids, whose fibres are thickened by a heavy fluid, rub against each other and harden, almost like a worker's hand that has rubbed for a long time against a wooden handle.

[7]   A certain moistness of the air, certain foods, or the use of certain drinks thickens the fibres of some peoples. This results, in part, in their having, as I have said, less vivacity.

. . . . [8]

[8]   Much more blood rises to the brain through the carotid and vertebral arteries than the ratio between the size of the head and the rest of the body seems to require. It is therefore carried there for a particular use, namely, to filter or separate the nerve fluid or spirits. It is in the cortex of the brain that this separation takes place. From there the nerve fluid can pass into the medullary substance,[9] and then into the nerves.

[9]   This must be a major reason for the variety found in the characters and minds of peoples living in different climates, and it will depend on the greater or lesser suitability of the blood for the filtration of the nerve fluid.

[10]   The quickness of our minds, our inconstancy, the frivolity of our characters, the joy which reigns among us, leads us to believe that we are as well provided with animal spirits as any nation in the world.[10]

[11]   Besides that, the sap of plants proper to each country, and those that nourish us in particular, can cause even greater changes.[11]

[12]   It must, however, be admitted that little of the metals or minerals the plant sap contains enters the bloodstream. They would work

too much havoc and cause the illnesses to which so many artisans are subject, as seen in the treatise of Bernard Ramazzini.[a] It is necessary that, in mining countries, only as much mineral and metallic substance enters the blood as is needed to sustain the body, and not enough to damage it to any degree.[13]

[13]   It is true that when one has often changed climates, one eventually does so without danger, for the solids have never assumed an absolutely fixed state,[b] and they are ready for whatever change happens either to them or to the blood.

[14]   The air, being charged with particles of earth, has in each climate specific qualities analogous to medical remedies, which consist of metals, minerals, and plant saps. Thus it is only seldom that a change of air does not have on us the effect of some remedy. But the trouble is that the remedy, when provided by chance, is almost always inappropriate.

[a] *De Morbis Artificum.*[12]

[b] Besides, the blood is not composed of the sap of plants from a single country. The change is thus less great.[14]

Editor's Notes to *An Essay on Causes*

PART ONE

1. The translation of the *Essai sur les causes* . . . (1736–1743) follows the text and paragraphing of its first printing in the *Mélanges inédits de Montesquieu* (Bordeaux, 1892). The original manuscript, sold at auction in 1939 and lost during World War II, consisted of seven *cahiers* totaling 124 pages, the first four containing Part One and the final three containing Part Two of the *Essay*. In addition, nine fragments of paper, attached by pins to the relevant page, or sometimes simply placed between the relevant pages, bore a portion of Montesquieu's twenty-five footnotes to the treatise. And finally, another group of pages, very likely fragments of the earlier "De la différence des Génies" (1717) (see "Materials," footnote 1 for evidence) comprised the "Materials" portion of the *Essay*. The *écriture* within the manuscript was that of a copyist, but most of the corrections, marginal notations, and footnotes were autograph, as is indicated in several of the notes below.

Following what has become accepted practice, the term *causes morales* has been consistently rendered "moral causes," although the full range of Montesquieu's meaning is perhaps better conveyed by "social causes." The term is etymologically traceable to *mos, moris*, pl. *mores*, and it therefore means, quite literally, that which concerns the manners, customs, and rules of conduct of a given people. For Montesquieu this includes politics, education, and religion, as well as customs and manners. No single English word conveys the full range of Montesquieu's meaning.

2. At the top of the first page of the MS. Montesquieu wrote the following note: "Shorten as much as possible those things generally known concerning air, food, etc."

3. The next seven paragraphs of the MS. were deleted by Montesquieu, and they became XIV, 2 [1–7] of *The Spirit of Laws*. In the margin of the deleted paragraphs Montesquieu three times wrote: "Placed in the Laws," and he also drafted the following, longer marginal notation: "We have seen in Book XIV of *The Spirit of Laws* (chap. 1) [*sic*] how cold and hot climates give diverse nations such different characters. We will not repeat here what we said there."

The following three footnotes to the seven deleted paragraphs were written on separate pieces of paper placed between the pages of the MS. They were neither deleted nor moved to Book XIV of *The Spirit of Laws*:

"Do an experiment on a tendon, on a nerve. Place it lengthwise in a long tube of glass closed off by two stoppers. Freeze it. See if the nerve shortens. Likewise, if the tendon."

"*Ext. Hist. univ.*—Constitution du climat de l'Espagne ancienne, p. 193."

"Extrait d'Hérodote, p. 424, vol. *Hist. universelle:* "*Caricae gentis omnium illius temporis ingeniosissimae.*"—*Vide hic tria inventa.*

4. Marginal note, autograph: "Placed" [in *The Spirit of Laws*].

5. Marginal note, autograph: "I have not placed this article."

6. The MS. here originally contained what became XIV, 2 [8–11] of *The Spirit of Laws*. In the margin of three of the four deleted paragraphs Montesquieu wrote: "Placed."

7. The MS. here originally contained six paragraphs that became, following some modification, XIV, 2 [12–13], and XIV, 10 [1, 2, 7], of *The Spirit of Laws*. In the margin of the deleted paragraphs Montesquieu five times noted: "Placed," and he also drafted the following longer, marginal notation: "Take a look at blood mixed with water to which alcohol is added."

8. Marginal note, autograph: "Not yet placed."

9. I.e., the wearing away of the solid parts of the body by friction or by the action of the body's fluids must be counteracted by diet. Long a medical concern, this process had been called Anachoresis and Pleurosis

by Plato, consumption and repletion by Hippocrates, depredation and reparation by Bacon, and decrement and increment by Boerhaave. See Thomas S. Hall, "Life as Opposed Transformation," *Journal of the History of Medicine and Allied Sciences*, XX (1965), pp. 262–275.

10. As opposed to a competing theory of nerve transmission involving vibrations, an idea traceable to Newton and popularized by David Hartley in his *Observations on Man* (1749), the ancient theory of animal spirits held, in its eighteenth-century form, that a subtle nerve fluid, so subtle in fact as to be invisible (Boerhaave, *Institutiones medicae*, II [289]; Haller, *First Lines*, CCCLXXXI), was filtered out of the blood in the cortex of the brain on its way to the medulla oblongata, where it entered the hollow nerve system to effect muscular contraction, when flowing from the brain into the muscles, and sensation, when flowing in the opposite direction, or when simply pressing on the brain as a result of pressure within the nerve tube, as Montesquieu himself suggests in note f. (Boerhaave, II [274]; Haller, CCCLXXXIII–CCCLXXXIV). While Montesquieu adopted the idea of transmission of nerve impulses by the animal spirits, rather than by vibrations, notes b. and c. to his treatise indicate his awareness of the theory of vibrations. He made no attempt to combine the two theories, however, as did David Hartley, who suggested that the vibrations are conveyed to the brain by means of an aether residing within the pores of the nerves.

11. I.e., *Polybii, Diodori Siculi, Nicolai Damasceni. . . . Excerpta ex collectaneis constantini Augusti Porphyrogenetae* (Paris, 1634), a volume edited by Henri de Valois (*Mélanges*, p. 266).

12. Autograph, on a fragment of paper pinned to page 21 of the MS.

13. Exupère Joseph Bertin (1712–1781), a celebrated French anatomist.

14. Experiments with ligatures were quite common and were generally thought to prove the existence of animal spirits, since the lack of sensation beyond the ligature could be attributed to the blocked flow of the nerve fluid. Bertin's experiment purported to show the contrary, how-

ever, and Montesquieu therefore cites it as possible support for the theory of transmission by vibrations that could continue their course beyond a ligature.

15. Autograph, on a fragment of paper pinned to page 23 of the MS.

16. I.e., in the brain.

17. The cerebellum was known to play a key role in the coordination and regulation of muscular activity (Boerhaave, *Institutiones medicae*, II [273], Haller, note 1).

18. Autograph, on a fragment of paper placed between the pages of the MS. without reference to a specific passage. The placement of the note has been altered slightly in this translation.

19. I.e., Jean-Baptiste Sénac (1693–1770), physician to Louis XV.

20. Autograph, on a fragment of paper placed between the pages of the MS. without reference to a specific passage. The placement of the note has been altered slightly in this translation.

21. Albrecht von Haller advanced a very similar argument: "If it be asked," he wrote, "What Change is made in the sentient Nerve; I answer that the Spirits propel forward those which lie next adjacent; and these again move the next, till the last but one moves the very last; and therefore the Change in the common Sensory can be nothing more than a Repulse of the Spirits against their Origin. This is certainly a very simple Explanation, but we know not of any other." (Boerhaave, *Institutiones medicae*, IV [568], Haller, note 3.)

22. Marginal note, autograph: "Perhaps delete this."

23. Montesquieu is referring to the three or four hundred million pulmonary air sacs, now called alveoli, and known in his day either as *vesiculae pulmonales*, or Malpighi's vesicles. By the eighteenth century it was understood that it was by means of these air sacs that pulmonary, arterial blood is oxygenated prior to delivery into the atrium of the left side of the heart. Montesquieu's chief interest in the *vesiculae pulmonales* was the effect of the air they contain on the blood's secretion of animal spirits in the cortex of the brain.

24. Marginal note, autograph: "Give the source."

25. The Greeks were ruled by the Ottoman Turks from the late Middle Ages up until 1830 when their partial independence was recognized by The London Protocol.

26. Marginal note, autograph: "Delete this, or make the point less forcefully."

27. In margin, autograph: "Delete this."

28. Goa was conquered by the Portuguese in the early sixteenth century, and it remained a Portuguese outpost in India until 1961.

29. A fuller discussion of trace elements and their effect on national character appeared in the "De la différence des Génies" (1717). See *Pensée* 2265 (Nagel, II, pp. 675–676), discovered at La Brède in 1950 and labeled by Montesquieu as page 13 of the 1717 essay.

In the original MS. of the *Essay on Causes* paragraph 21 was followed by two additional paragraphs, one on the influence of air and the other on the influence of voyages. A marginal note to these two paragraphs read: "Put these deleted articles elsewhere." The "De la différence des Génies" would have been a likely repository.

30. In margin, autograph: "Place with laws relative to climate."

Montesquieu deleted the next paragraph in the MS. to make it XIV, 12 [2] of *The Spirit of Laws*. It explains suicide among the English in terms of a defect in the filtration of their nerve fluid.

31. In Montesquieu's day, the influence of the estrogenic hormone estradiol in thickening the endometrium, followed by the constriction of the spiral arteries leading to desquamation of a portion of the endometrium was not as yet understood, and it was generally thought that the uterine blood vessels bleed easily because the fibres of women are softer, the descending trunk of the aorta is larger in women, and the blood vessels of the womb are not surrounded by muscles or fat.

32. At the time Montesquieu composed the *Essay on Causes*, it was erroneously believed that semen is derived from the blood by a process of filtration in the testes and stored in the seminal vesicles (Boerhaave, *Institutiones medicae*, V [649] and also Haller, note 2). The secretion of androgen in the testes, creating secondary sexual characteristics

at puberty was not yet understood, and such bodily changes, experienced neither in women nor eunuchs, were commonly attributed to the reabsorption by the blood of a portion of the semen (Boerhaave, V [647]).

33. I.e., fetal circulation.

34. Autograph, on a fragment of paper attached to page 47 of the MS.

35. The auditory nerve has both a hard portion (*portio dura*), or vestibular nerve, and a soft portion (*portio mollis*), or cochlear nerve. The portio dura to which Montesquieu refers controls balance rather than hearing, but his error does not substantially alter the main point he makes.

36. I.e., the animal spirits.

37. See note 32 above.

38. The seminal vesicles were thought to store the semen prior to venery. They are now known to contribute the bulk of the seminal plasma. For an eighteenth-century analysis of their functioning, see Haller, *First Lines*, DCCXXII–DCCCXXIII.

39. Compare paragraph three of *Pensée* 182 (1192. II, f. 90v.): 1736–1737, labeled by Montesquieu as originally intended for the "De la différence des Génies" (1717).

40. Autograph.

41. Cf., *The Attic Nights*, Book IV, chap. 19 (*Mélanges*, p. 267).

42. Autograph.

43. Montesquieu employed the past tense because he was referring to the athletes of classical antiquity.

44. Autograph, on a fragment of paper pinned to page 60 of the MS.

45. Montesquieu here alludes to the early Christian monks of the third through fifth centuries A.D., the first of whom was St. Anthony (c. 251–c. 356), who gave up his worldly possessions to live a life of extreme asceticism in the mountains of Egypt and who thought himself many times tempted by the devil in various guises.

46. I.e., Juan Huarte de San Juan (c. 1529–c. 1588), a medical doctor trained at the University of Alcalá and author of *Examen des esprits propres et naiz aux sciences* (Paris, 1645) [*Catalogue*, 1474]; first French

trans. Lyon, 1580; orig. edition, Pamplona, 1578. There were seventy editions of this work by 1700, and an English translation was issued in London in 1594.

47. A fuller discussion of Huarte's idea appeared in the "De la différence des Génies" (1717). See *Pensée* 181 (1191. II. f. 89v.): 1736–1737, labeled by Montesquieu as originally intended for the essay of 1717.

PART TWO

1. An autograph note at the bottom of the page reads: "It seems to me that what concerns education is being neglected. For who doubts that education is doing little good?"

2. Montesquieu wrote two words in the margin of this passage, but they are indecipherable.

3. Circassia, or Cherkessia, in the Greater Caucasus Mountains, was subjected to the rule of the Crimean Tatars in 1725. In the eighteenth century, many Circassian women, notable for their beauty, were found in Turkish harems. Mingrelia is the Black Sea region that was known as Colchis in ancient times.

4. Autograph.

5. This sentence, autograph, was written in the margin of page 83 of the MS.

6. Autograph.

7. Autograph.

8. I.e., La Nauze, *Histoire de l'Académie royale des Inscriptions . . .* , Vol. IX, p. 330 (*Mélanges*, p. 267).

9. This whole paragraph, autograph, was written at the top of page 90 of the MS.

10. See Part One, note 25, above.

11. Marginal note, autograph: "Don't state this in absolute terms; suggest only that their wit is aided."

12. Marginal note, autograph: "They were already solemn before this."

13. I.e., *Geography*, Book III, chap. 4 (*Mélanges*, p. 267).

14. See **XXIV**, 5 [2–3] of *The Spirit of Laws*.

15. I.e., César, Cardinal d'Estrées (1628–1714), who won his cardinal's hat by skillful negotiating between the pope and the Jansenists.

16. I.e., Prince François-Eugène of Savoy (1663–1736), commander of the imperial armies of Austria in the War of the Spanish Succession and a notably successful general whose battles were studied and praised by Napoleon.

MATERIALS

1. The "Materials" segment consists of pages 9–10, 37–44, and 49–50 of what has previously been considered an early draft of the *Essay on Causes (Mélanges*, p. 267, Nagel, III, p. 427). Reference to *Pensée* 181 (1191. II, f. 89v.): 1736–1737, *Pensée* 182 (1192. II, f. 90v.): 1736–1737, *Pensée* 183 (2035. III, f. 328): 1750, and particularly *Pensée* 2265 (Nagel, II, pp. 675–676), discovered at La Brède in 1950, suggests, however, that these pages are fragments of the "De la différence des Génies" (1717).

2. This autograph note by Montesquieu was written on page 37 of the "Materials" and moved to its present position when the *Essay on Causes* was first printed in the *Mélanges inédits* (Bordeaux, 1892), p. 149.

3. In the original MS. this whole portion of the first sentence on page 9 was deleted by Montesquieu.

4. In the original MS. this first sentence was preceded by the following words completing a sentence begun on page 8: ". . . will remind one of the face of the father or mother, that is to say, will look like them."

5. End of pages 9–10.

6. The original MS. contained an uncorrected error, and the latter portion of this sentence read: ". . . one for the entry of animal spirits, by blocking the inflow of blood; the other for the entry of animal spirits by blocking the inflow of blood."

7. I.e., the muscles and nerves.

8. End of pages 37–44.

9. I.e., the medulla oblongata.

10. Montesquieu is here referring to the French nation.

11. This whole paragraph appeared as a marginal note, autograph.

12. I.e., *De morbis artificum diatriba* . . . (1700), trans. into French as *Essai sur les maladies des artisans* . . . (Paris, 1777) and into English as *A Treatise of the Diseases of Tradesmen, shewing the various influences of particular trades upon the state of health* (London, 1705). Bernardo Ramazzini (1633–1714) was a professor of medicine, first at Modena and then at Padua. Montesquieu owned a copy of his *Opera omnia, medica et physica (Geneva, 1716)* [*Catalogue*, 1184].

13. This whole paragraph, autograph, was written on a fragment of paper pinned to page 49 of the MS.

14. Autograph.

APPENDIXES

APPENDIXES

APPENDIX I: *Jansenist and Jesuit Censures of The Spirit of Laws*

This Appendix lists by Book, chapter, and paragraph number (in brackets) those passages of *The Spirit of Laws* censured by the Abbé de La Roche in the Jansenist periodical *Nouvelles Ecclésiastiques* (Oct. 9, 1749, and Oct. 16, 1749) and by the Faculty of Theology of the University of Paris in their *projet de censure* of August 1, 1752. For summaries of the Jansenist and Jesuit objections and of Montesquieu's replies see the textual notes accompanied by asterisks.

PASSAGES CENSURED BY THE ABBÉ DE LA ROCHE

I, 1 [1]	XIV, 7	XXIV, 3
I, 1, M's footnote	XIV, 12	XXIV, 5 [3]
I, 1 [6]	XIV, 15 [3]	XXIV, 6 [2]
I, 1 [10]		XXIV, 10
I, 1 [14]	XVI, 2 [5]	XXIV, 24 [1]
I, 2*	XVI, 4	XXIV, 26 [3]
I, 2 [2]		
I, 2 [2–8]	XXII, 19 [2]**	XXV, 2 [2]
	XXIII, 2 [1]	XXV, 9, 10
III, 5	XXIII, 21 [28–35]	

*Where no paragraph number has been indicated, the whole chapter has been censured.
** Absent from this edition.

PASSAGES CENSURED BY THE FACULTY OF THEOLOGY OF
THE UNIVERSITY OF PARIS, AUGUST 1, 1752

III, 5	XVI, 4	XXIII, 29 [8]
III, 6	XVI, 8 [1]	
	XVI, 15 [5]*	XXIV, 7 [2]
IV, 2 [23]		XXIV, 10 [4]
	XIX, 14 [6]	XXIV, 24 [1]
IX, 2 [1]		XXIV, 26 [3]
XII, 4 [6]	XXI, 16*	XXV, 10
XIV, 6	XXII, 19 [2]*	XXVI, 3 [4]
XIV, 7		
XIV, 12	XXIII, 21 [34–35]	XXIX, 9 [4]

PASSAGES CENSURED BY BOTH THE ABBÉ DE LA ROCHE AND
THE FACULTY OF THEOLOGY OF THE UNIVERSITY OF PARIS

III, 5	XVI, 4	XXIV, 24 [1]
		XXIV, 26 [3]
XIV, 7	XXII, 19 [2]*	
XIV, 12	XXIII, 21 [34–35]	XXV, 10

*Absent from this edition.

APPENDIX II: *Travel Literature*

This appendix lists alphabetically the travel literature to which Montesquieu referred in his footnotes to those texts included in this edition. Works available to Montesquieu in his library at La Brède are preceded by an asterisk and are cited in the edition he owned. In the case of works not listed in the *Catalogue* of the library at La Brède, titles are cited in the first edition, with information concerning French translations cited where relevant.

Bernier, François. *Voyages, contenant la description des États du Grand Mogul, de l'Hindoustan; du royaume de Cachemire*. 2 vols. Amsterdam, 1709, 1710; orig. ed. 1670–71.

Chardin, Jean. *Voyages en Perse et aux Indes orientales*. 2 vols. Lyon, 1687.

Dampier, William. *Nouveau voyage autour du monde*. 5 vols. Amsterdam, 1711; orig. ed. London, 1697.

Du Halde, Jean Baptiste. *Description géographique, historique, chronologique et physique de l'Empire de la Chine et de la Tartarie Chinoise*. 4 vols. Paris, 1735.

Forbin, Claude, Comte de. *Mémoires de Claude, Comte de Forbin*. 2 vols. Amsterdam, 1730.

Gage, Thomas. *Survey of the West Indies, Containing a Journal of 3,300 Miles within the Main Land of America*. London, 1648; French trans. Paris, 1676.

Gomara, Francesco-Lopez de. *La Historia general de las Indias, con la Conquista del Mexico y de la Nueva-España*. 2 vols. (Caragoza, Anvers, 1552, 1554; French trans. Paris. 1569, 1584).

———. *Histoire généalogique des Tartars, traduite du manuscrit tartare d'Abulgazi Bayadur Chan, et enrichie de remarques sur l'état présent de l'Asie septentrionale.* Leyde, 1726.

Hyde, Thomas. *Historia religionis veterum Persarum.* Oxford, 1700.

Kaempfer, Englebert. **Historia imperii japonici.* . . . 2 vols. London, 1727; issued simultaneously in English, London, 1727; French trans. 1729.

Kircher, Athanasius. **La Chine . . . illustrée . . . avec un Dictionnaire Chinois et Francois.* Amsterdam, 1670.

Labat, Jean-Baptiste. **Nouveau voyage aux isles de l'Amérique, contenant l'histoire naturelle de ces pays, l'origine, . . . la religion et la gouvernement des habitans anciens et modernes.* 6 vols. Paris, 1722.

————. *Lettres édifiantes et curieuses, écrites des Missions Etrangères par quelques missionnaires de la compagnie de Jésus.* 1703–1741.

La Loubère, Simon de. **Du Royaume de Siam.* 2 vols. Paris, 1691.

Perry, John. *The State of Russia under the present Czar: in Relation to the Several Great and Remarkable Things He has Done.* London, 1716; French trans. 1717.

Pyrard, François. *Discours du voyage des François aux Indes Orientales, ensemble des divers accidens, adventures et dangers de l'auteur en plusieurs royaumes des Indes et du séjour qu'il y a fait par dix ans, depuis l'an 1601 jusques en cette année 1611.* Paris, 1611.

————. *Recueil des voyages qui ont servir à l'établissement et aux progrès de la Compagnie des Indes orientales, formée dans les Provinces-Unises des Pays-Bas.* 5 vols. Amsterdam, 1710.

————. *Recueil de Voyages au Nord, contenant divers Mémoires trés utiles au Commerce et à la Navigation.* Amsterdam, 1715.

Rycaut, Paul. *The Present State of the Ottoman Empire. Containing the Maxims of the Turkish Politie, the Most Material Points of the Mahometan Religion.* . . . London, 1668; French trans., 1670.

Shaw, Thomas. *Travels, or Observations Relating to Several Parts of Barbary and the Levant.* Oxford, 1738; French trans. 2 vols. 1743.

Smith, William. *A New Voyage to Guinea: Describing Whatever . . . is*

Memorable among the Inhabitants. . . . London, 1744; French trans. 1751.

Solis y Ribadaneyra, Antonio de. *Histoire de la conquête du Mexique par Fernand Cortez, traduite de l'espagnol.* 2 vols. Paris, 1714; orig. ed. Madrid, 1684; orig. French trans. Paris, 1691.

Tassy, Logier de. *Histoire du royaume d'Alger avec l'état présent de son gouvernement, de ses forces de terre et de mer, de ses revenus, police, justice, politique, et commerce.* 2 vols. Amsterdam, 1725.

Tavernier, Jean-Baptiste. *Les Six Voyages de J.-B. Tavernier . . . en Turquie, en Perse et aux Indes.* . . . 6 vols. Rouen, 1713; orig. ed. 2 vols. Paris, 1676–77.

La Vega, Garcias Lasso de. *Primera parte de los Commentarios reales que tratan del origen de los Yncas, reges que fueron del Peru.* . . . Lisbon, 1609; French trans. 2 vols. Paris, 1744. M owned the second part of this work (orig. ed. Cordoue, 1616) in the four-volume French translation listed in the two titles immediately following.

———. *Histoire des guerres civiles des Espagnols dans les Indes.* 2 vols. Paris, 1658; orig. ed. Cordoue, 1616.

———. *Le Commentaire royal, ou l'histoire des Incas, rois du Pérou, contenant leur origine.* 2 vols. Paris, 1633; orig. ed. Cordoue, 1616.

APPENDIX III: *The Manuscript of*
The Spirit of Laws*

In spite of a thorough search undertaken in 1948 in the Bibliothèque Nationale Suisse in Berne and in both the Bibliothèque Publique and the Archives d'État in Geneva, the manuscript from which the Genevan printer Barillot set the type for the first edition of *The Spirit of Laws* has not been located.** An earlier manuscript copy is extant, however. Purchased at public auction in 1939 by the Bibliothèque Nationale, this 2,700-page manuscript is now bound in five volumes (Nouvelle Acquisition française 12.832–12.836) the contents of which are listed immediately below:

    I. (N.A. Fr. 12.832); 270 folios comprising Books I–VI, of which 19 folios are in Montesquieu's hand

    II. (N.A. Fr. 12.833); 274 folios comprising Books VII–XI, of which 61 folios are in Montesquieu's hand

    III. (N.A. Fr. 12.834); 249 folios comprising Books XII–XV, of which 46 folios are in Montesquieu's hand

    IV. (N.A. Fr. 12.835); 354 folios comprising Books XVI–XXI, of which 16 folios are in Montesquieu's hand

    V. (N.A. Fr. 12.836); 357 folios comprising Books XXII–XXV, XXVII, one chapter of Book XXVIII, and three chapters of Book XXIX, of which 18 folios are in Montesquieu's hand

---

*This Appendix is based on Professor Robert Shackleton's painstaking research as presented in his "Les secrétaires de Montesquieu," in Nagel, II, pp. xxxv–xliii, and his "Le manuscrit de la Bibliothèque Nationale," in Nagel, III, pp. 567–77. Readers may also wish to consult his "La genèse de 'L'Esprit des lois,'[n] in *Revue d'Histoire littéraire de la France*, LII (1952), 425–38.

**G. I, p. xxxvi.

Of the nineteen different secretarial hands identified by Professor Shackleton within the extant Montesquieu manuscripts (see his "Les secrétaires de Montesquieu," Nagel, II, pp. xxxv–xliii), eight* are present in the MS. copy of *The Spirit of Laws:*

e	(1733–1738)	j	(1742–1744)
g	(1739–1741)	l	(1743–1746)
h	(1740–1743)	n	(1746)
i	(1741–1743)	o	(1746–1747)

CHRONOLOGY OF COMPOSITION

The earliest drafted segments of the MS. are two chapters in hand e (XI, 6,** and XVII, 6) and twenty-four chapters, as well as twenty chapter titles and one Book title (Book III), in hand g. The major portion, that is, 228 of 416 chapters, is in hands h, i, and j.*** A third group of chapters consists of a revision begun in the year 1743 in hands l and M, and a fourth group is a revision complete by December, 1746 in hands l, n, o, and M.

As Professor Shackleton has suggested, the presence in the MS. of 218 chapters in secretarial hands e, g, h, and i reveals that a significant portion of *The Spirit of Laws* was complete by 1743. Most important as well, in terms of the chronology of composition of the work, are the twenty chapter titles in hand g (1739–1741), revealing the existence of at least a rough plan of the work berween 1739 and 1741.

Noticeably absent from the MS. are all of Books XXVI, XXX, and XXXI, all but one chapter of Book XXVIII, and all but three chapters of Book XXIX. All told, a total of 183 chapters printed in the first edition of 1748 are not present in the MS. Equally interesting are

---

*Not including M (Montesquieu) and a few passages in hands p and s inserted after publication of the work.

**Corrected by g, h, i, and l.

***Ten chapters are in hand j (VIII, 1, 2, 4, 5, 7–11, 13), and hands h and i account for approximately 168 and 50 chapters respectively. Hand h is visible throughout the MS., whereas hand i appears only in the first eleven Books.

portions of the MS. that were not carried over into the first or subsequent editions of *The Spirit of Laws*. A convenient printing of these deleted passages is available in Nagel, III, pp. 579–598.

METHODS OF COMPOSITION

Whatever the flaws of organization evident in *The Spirit of Laws*, the MS. now owned by the Bibliothèque Nationale reveals that Montesquieu struggled to give shape to his masterpiece as best he could. He experimented with the basic structure of the work by changing the sequence of various chapters, deleting and adding passages, and occasionally splitting chapters in two. And he labored long to give his work the stylistic polish he desired. Corrections are introduced in the margins, between the lines, and on inserted sheets of paper.

Montesquieu instructed his secretaries to leave a wide left-hand margin as well as considerable space between the lines to enable him to make corrections and to allow for the addition of footnotes. Most of these notes are placed in the left-hand margin, sometimes cross-referenced to the text by number, but more frequently with a simple cross (+), or with more elaborate symbols such as ✢, ∓, or ≠. Very infrequently, a tiny patch of paper bearing a footnote is glued to the relevant page.

CHRONOLOGICAL TABLE OF CHAPTERS IN THE MANUSCRIPT COPY OF THE SPIRIT OF LAWS*

Column A: Chapters that entered the MS. prior to 1741. [e and g]
Column B: Chapters that entered the MS. between 1741 and 1743. [h and i]
Column C: Chapters revised after 1743. [l and M]
Column D: Chapters revised prior to 1746. [l, n, o, and M]

*This table was drawn up by Professor Shackleton and included in his "Le Manuscrit de la Bibliothèque Nationale," in Nagel, III, pp. 576–577.

Column E: Chapters not present in MS. but added for the first edition
of 1748

Column F: Chapters added to editions subsequent to that of 1748

BOOK	A	B	C	D	E	F
I		1–3				
II		1–5				
III	2,6–8	1,3–5, 9–11				
IV		1–8				
V	3	1,2,4–11, 14–18	12	13,19		
VI		1–5,8,9, 12,13,15–21	11	6,7,10,14		
VII		1–4,6,7, 9,13–17	5,8,10–12			
VIII	19,21	1–11,13, 14,17,18	20	12,15,16		
IX	1,6	2,4,5			3,7–10	
X		2–4,6,12, 14–16	1,5,17	7–11	13	
XI	6–8	2,5,11		1,3,4,9, 10,12–19	20	
XII		4–6,10, 13,15,17, 18,21,23–25,28	26,27	1–3,7–9, 11,12,14, 16,19,20, 22,29,30		

BOOK	A	B	C	D	E	F
XIII		2,10,15, 17	12,16,18	1,3–9,11, 13,14,19	20	
XIV	2,10	1,3–8,11, 12,15			9,13,14	
XV	1,2,7	3–6,8,10, 13,19		11,12,16– 18	14,15	9
XVI		1,3–11, 13–15		2,12,16		
XVII	6	1–3,5,7		4		8
XVIII		1,2,4,6, 9,10,12, 14,15,18	5,8,20	3,7,11, 13,19	16,17,21– 27,29–31	28
XIX		2–4,6– 10,12–19, 21,24,27	5,22	1,11,20, 23,26	25	
XX	14	4,5,8,10, 12,13,15, 18,22,23	2,3,9	1,7,11, 19,20	16,21	6,17
XXI	21	3,22	4,5,20	1,2,6–11, 13–17,19, 23	18	12
XXII		5,9	2,3,7,8	1,4,6,10, 14,18	11–13,15– 17,19–22	
XXIII		1,2,4,7, 10–13,15– 18,21,28, 29		3,5,6,8,9, 14,19,20, 22–27		

BOOK	A	B	C	D	E	F
XXIV	4,6–8, 10,22	1–3,9,11, 12,14–17, 23,25,26	5	18–21,24	13	
XXV		3–5,7,8, 13,15		1,2,6,9– 12,14		
XXVI					1–25	
XXVII		1				
XXVIII			44		1–43,45	
XXIX			2,14	18	1,3–13, 15–17,19	
XXX					1–25	
XXXI					1–21,23– 34	22

APPENDIX IV:

The following "Explanatory Note" was added to the edition of 1757 in light of criticisms of Montesquieu's definition of virtue as the principle of democratic government. See also Book III, chapter 5, and Editor's Notes, pp. 383–385, note 2*.

For the better understanding of the first books of this work, it is to be observed that what I distinguish by the name of virtue, in a republic, is the love of one's country, that is, the love of equality. It is not a moral, nor a Christian, but a political virtue; and it is the spring which sets the republican government in motion, as honor is the spring which gives motion to monarchy. Hence it is that I have distinguished the love of one's country, and of equality, by the appellation of political virtue. My ideas are new, and therefore I have been obliged to find new words, or to give new acceptations to old terms, in order to convey my meaning. They, who are unacquainted with this particular, have made me say most strange absurdities, such as would be shocking in any part of the world, because in all countries and governments morality is requisite.

The reader is also to notice that there is a vast difference between saying that a certain quality, modification of the mind, or virtue, is not the spring by which government is actuated, and affirming that it is not to be found in that government. Were I to say such a wheel or such a pinion is not the spring which sets the watch going, can you infer thence that it is not to be found in the watch? So far is it from being true that the moral and Christian virtues are excluded from monarchy, that even political virtue is not excluded. In a word, honor is found in a republic, though its spring be political virtue; and political virtue is found in a monarchical government, though it be actuated by honor.

To conclude, the honest man of whom we treat in the third book, chapter five, is not the Christian, but the political honest man, who is possessed of the political virtue there mentioned. He is the man who loves the laws of his country, and who is actuated by the love of those laws. I have set these matters in a clearer light in the present edition by giving a more precise meaning to my expression: and in most places where I have made use of the word virtue I have taken care to add the term political.